VICTOR W. MARSHALL

AGING
IN
CANADA

Social
Perspectives

Fitzhenry & Whiteside

For Joanne Gard Marshall

© Fitzhenry & Whiteside Limited 1980

Fitzhenry & Whiteside
150 Lesmill Road
Don Mills, Ontario M3B 2T5

Canadian Cataloguing in Publication Data

Main entry under title:
Aging in Canada
Bibliography: p.287
ISBN 0-88902-118-X bd.   ISBN 0-88902-119-8 pa.
1. Aging — Social aspects — Canada.   2. Aged —
Canada.   I. Marshall, Victor W.
HQ1064.C3A35   305.2′6   C80-094193-4

Printed and bound in Canada

Preface

The aging of individuals is a biological process; however, it is possible that the most important things about aging are social rather than biological or psychological. Both survival and the quality of life in the later years are influenced by social relations, economic history, family connections, and other social factors. Psychological aging may be a universal process, but the individual's experience of aging depends in large measure on social context.

In Canada, the experience of aging occurs within a society which is itself aging. More people are surviving childbirth and childhood to live into the later years, and life expectancy at the later ages is also lengthening. The average age of our population is rising, and an ever larger proportion of our population are old. The implications for our society of this population aging demand close and immediate scrutiny. Changes, planned or not, are likely to be profound and complex, and if we are to cope adequately with changes of such magnitude, we must begin to set our course now. This book therefore considers the aging of individuals within the aging of their society, and it concentrates on the social aspects rather than on other important aspects of aging.

The book is aimed at a diverse audience of social and health science students, social service and health care personnel, policy makers and research-oriented scholars, advocates of and activists for the aged. As a result, the articles selected or commissioned for the book represent diverse interests, but are united by a common concern with social aspects of aging.

I thank the authors who have prepared articles especially for the book, or who have allowed their work to be reprinted. I wish also to thank them for their interest in seeing the book appear. They have been remarkably cooperative in this venture, making my editorial task easier and, in fact, very enjoyable.

Particular thanks are owed Neena Chappell, Frank Denton, Betty Havens, and Byron Spencer for their advice in the organization of the book and for help in selecting authors or articles. Dennis Bockus approached me to do this book a few years ago and continued to nurture the idea until it appeared to be a feasible project. He has brought a meticulousness and craftsmanship to the book which complements some of my own weaknesses and has been invaluable through all stages in the book's production.

My own activity in editing has been supported at various times over the past few years by the Department of Behavioural Science, University of Toronto; the Department of Sociology, McMaster University; and the Département d'Administration de la Santé, Université de Montréal. I am, in addition, grateful for support as a National Health Scientist from Health and Welfare Canada.

My daughter Emily has been bemused by this activity and has been patient with her dad. I am fortunate in having support, encouragement, critical judgment and tolerance from Joanne Gard Marshall. I would like to dedicate this book to her. May we grow old together.

Contents

1

INTRODUCTION
Social Perspectives on Aging

Victor W. Marshall

We are born, grow up, grow old, and die. Others preceded us and will follow us. Society will go on. Societies, like humans, grow older in a way: they accumulate experience, develop a character, partake of history. The interweaving of biography and social history is the stuff of individual life and the manner in which societies endure. There is a "micro" and a "macro" side to aging, a personal and a social side, an inside and an outside view. If we have policy concerns about the aging of the society, these are not abstract issues, for they touch our loved ones and will touch us. The kind of life older people in our society can live is the kind of life we will live. For this reason alone, aging ought to be of concern to us all.

There are other reasons. Our society is itself aging in a different way than merely in the accumulation of experience. The average age of the population is rising, and the numbers and proportions of older people are increasing dramatically. The implications of the changing age structure for the lives of both old people and younger people have only recently begun to be examined in a systematic way, but the need to address these implications is widely recognized. If health care is to be provided to those in need, and the growing numbers and proportions of older people are to receive adequate, and better than adequate, health care, the costs to the young will increase. Similarly, if we are to ensure that increasing numbers of older people can escape poverty and lead economically secure lives, free to enjoy their later years, the economic costs to the young will be high.

Health and income security for an aging population have become major policy concerns for people of all ages, but they are by no means the only policy concerns. The aging of the population, and the way in which this affects males and females differently, has profound implications for family life, use of leisure time, the organization of work, planning of housing, and communities. For example, if we ghettoize the old in institutions, highrise apartments for the elderly, and the like, we necessarily ghettoize the young elsewhere. If we continue to use seniority as a basis for provision of job protection, by implication we privilege the old over the young.

We need to know about the aging of the society: what are the patterns, what is the present like, and what kind of future can we envision? We also need to know what kind of present and future we *want* to have, because nothing is inexorable. If the future is not completely within our power to shape, it is at least partially so.

1

The Scope of the Book

The study of aging in all its aspects is referred to as "gerontology". This book, therefore, brings together material in only one sub-area of gerontology — social gerontology. This field of inquiry intersects with several academic disciplines: economics, demography, political science, political economy, epidemiology, and sociology. Several applied disciplines are represented, especially in the latter part of the book. These include nursing, medicine, social work, health administration, and health planning. The sociological emphasis in the book reflects not only my own editorial bent, but the fact that many of the sociologists represented have worked, alone or in research with others, within these more applied areas.

Gerontology is one of the least "ivory-tower" of the academic areas. As argued above, its subject matter is of both long-range and immediate relevance, and few gerontologists have the patience to remove themselves too far from either direct fields of application or the policy domain.

The psychological aspects of aging enter into the work collected here only peripherally, and biological aspects not at all. This represents a deliberate choice on my part and is only partially accounted for by a shortage of space. The greatest need in Canada, I feel, is to bring together and stimulate new research in the social aspects of aging, precisely because knowledge of the social aspects of aging is not universal. It might fairly be assumed that the fundamental biological and psychological processes of aging, about which not a great deal is known, are universal. What is discovered about these processes through research done in other countries can be "imported" with reasonable assurance that the same processes are operative within Canada. While it is scandalous that we have to import much of this knowledge (despite the important contributions of a small number of eminent Canadian gerontologists in psychology, geriatrics, and biology), it is possible to do so. We cannot, however, rely for basic data about the social aspects of aging on research conducted in other societies, because by definition, the social aspects of aging are context-specific. This context is social and historical, and Canada is not demonstrably similar enough to any other society (even that of the United States) to allow direct translation of research findings from other countries into the Canadian context.

Most of the articles in this book have been prepared originally for it. Only six have appeared previously in print. In some cases I selected for publication a paper presented at an academic meeting. In others I asked the authors to cover specific material and to write explicitly with a teaching goal directed at upper-level social science or health science students. My goals, as editor, have been multiple and varied, undoubtedly leading to some of the rough edges of the book. I wanted to: (1) bring together a number of basic *facts* about age and aging in Canada; (2) illustrate the major and most important *theoretical approaches* which characterize social gerontological research in Canada; (3) provide examples of principle *sources of data* which could be used in studying age and aging, such as survey data, material from archives, ethnographies, participant observation, vital statistics, and content analysis; (4) provide examples of different *research designs,* including evaluation research; and (5) represent a *critical stance* toward social research, theory, methodology, and policy in the field of aging. As Estes and Freeman (1976) have indicated,

> ...in the long run, the professionals who research, legislate, plan or implement interventions for the elderly, influence how different individuals *experience* the aging process. Social researchers, planners, and practitioners involved in intervention programs are not neutrals. Rather, they are actively engaged in modifying and structuring social reality for the aged (emphasis in original).

The five principles enunciated above recognize and accept this position and, while I cannot claim that all or even most of the authors whose work appears in the book agree with my editorial stance in its entirety, I do believe that the general thrust of social gerontology in Canada is socially committed, self-critical, and policy-oriented and that this thrust is fairly represented in the book.

Canadian Social Gerontology: directions and limitations

The major theoretical approaches to understanding age and aging found in this book do not closely coincide with the array of such approaches found in other textbooks in the field. This is the first Canadian text in the social aspects of aging, and theory in this country is, thankfully, taking something of a different tack than has been dominant in the major bastion of social gerontology, the United States. The little discussion in this book about such theoretical issues as the debate between "activity theory" and "disengagement theory", or the "role-less role of the aged" is, on the whole, critical of such theory. Perhaps because of the recency with which social gerontology has developed in Canada, we seem to be able to avoid having to re-fight all the skirmishes of the past intellectual history of the United States. In general, theory about aging in Canada is more structural, collectivist, and historically grounded than the predominantly attitudinal, individualistic, and consensually oriented theorizing south of the border (see Marshall and Tindale, 1978-79). This does not mean that we have been insular in formulating our theoretical approaches, for we have drawn heavily on Marxist and Weberian strains in social economic theory, and on the European phenomenologists and American symbolic interactionists for our social psychology. In these respects, Canadians interested in age and aging have followed the orientations of Canadian social scientists in general.

Therefore, although I considered including in this introductory chapter a systematic review of the sociological theories of gerontology, I have not done so. Such reviews are readily available elsewhere (for example, Bengtson, 1973; Hendricks and Hendricks, 1977). Most of the predominant theoretical approaches are, none the less, at least touched on in the papers in the book. These include symbolic interactionist approaches (Chapters 6,8,9,15,16), age stratification theory (Chapter 5), minority-group theory (Chapter 7), disengagement and continuity theory (Chapter 12), environmental theory (Chapter 26), and role and socialization theory (Chapters 6 and 11). Much of the book is critical of existing theory and could itself perhaps be called "critical theory", except that the term has many different meanings. In general, Canadian social gerontology may be learning to walk without having to pass through the awkward crawling stage.

The sources of data available to date to Canadians interested in social aspects of aging have been somewhat limited, and great reliance has been placed on official statistics. These have often been difficult for academics and practitioners to access. They are scattered in many provincial and federal departments and ministries and often take the form of in-house reports used, perhaps, by governments but not released to the general public. One value of this book, I hope, is that it makes more accessible some of this scattered information from government.

Except for government-conducted work and opinion polls by agencies such as the Canadian Gallup Organization, there have been no national interview or even questionnaire studies of high quality in Canada to gather experiential and attitudinal data from individuals (see Environics Research Group, 1972). It is therefore difficult to know how the demographic features of the aged, and changes in these features associated with aging, are *experienced* by individuals, or what these features mean to them.

While the relative absence of large-scale survey data distinguishes Canadian social gerontology from that conducted elsewhere, the relative absence of historical material on the aged is common throughout the world. The humanities are only recently being recognized again as having something worthwhile to say about aging. I say again because, until the rise of social science, it was precisely to the humanities that we turned for understanding about old age and aging. Few social scientists can match Margaret Laurence (her novel, *The Stone Angel*) in conveying an understanding of aging.

The historical understanding in Canadian social gerontology comes largely from sociologists, many of whom take a historical perspective; and their work is well represented in this book in chapters by Chappell, D'Arcy, Myles, Synge, and Tindale.

Anthropologists in Canada have rarely dealt explicitly with gerontological questions (for one example, see Counts, 1977), and Guemple's chapter in this book is a rare anthropological treatment of aging in one Canadian ethnic community. This lack of attention means that we have very little knowledge of ethnic differences in aging within Canada's "vertical mosaic" (Zay, 1978).

One of the greatest lacks in Canadian research on aging is in the general area of political science. With the exception of some research in political economy (e.g., Bryden, 1974), no political scientists have directed research efforts toward such issues as age patterns in political support or ideology, or age differentiation in power or the allocation of goods. The importance of the political domain is evident in the following assertion of the conditions under which Canada's elderly might in fact eventually reach a level of income adequacy comparable to national averages:

> That will depend upon the interaction of complex factors — particularly work incentives, roles assigned to different age groups in the population, the productivity of the entire economy, and the values by which the total economic output is distributed. The process by which these factors interact and work themselves out will in turn naturally occur in the political arena (Schulz and Associates, 1974: 185-86).

Coping with the political, social, economic, and indeed the ethical implications of the aging Canadian society is a matter of some urgency in Canada, and for this reason many of the authors represented in this book are at pains to at least raise the policy implications of their research. As I argue in the introduction to Section III, however, research coverage is spotty in relation to the need for accurate knowledge in the formation of public policy, and smooth relationships between governmental agencies and the academic community have not as yet been established. Canada has, for example, no centralized agency for support of gerontological research in the health or social fields, like the National Institute on Aging and Administration on Aging in the United States. Canadian social scientists have not been systematically trained in gerontology, although the first interdisciplinary gerontology institutes or programs are now being established.

The Recent Growth of Canadian Gerontology

The past decade has seen major development of gerontology in Canada. Canadians have an image of their nation as young and vigorous and, indeed, throughout the nation's history, Canada has been a demographically "young" nation, made so by reasonably large birthrates, declining rates of infant and child mortality, and the infusion of young immigrants. More recently, as the absolute numbers of old people and their proportion in the society increased with declines in birth rate and immigration, the age structure has become older. With forecasts suggesting that the next half-century will see a doubling in the proportion, and a tripling in the absolute numbers over the age of 65, policy-makers and social scientists have become concerned that a lack of knowledge about the processes of aging and the nature of a society with a different age structure might hinder our ability as a nation to provide for this growing segment of the population. After years of effort, the Canadian Association on Gerontology was established in 1971. That this Association exemplifies the tremendous upsurge of interest in age and aging is shown by the fact that its membership has increased from 84 to over 800 in eight years.

Yet the state of our knowledge of age and aging is still low. There simply have not been enough researchers working long enough to develop a very sound knowledge base. In many respects the authors collected in this volume are pioneers — young pioneers, for the most part. Many of them have worked, of necessity, virtually alone, without the benefit of colleagues who share their research interest in gerontology. A minority have been more fortunate, in colleagues and in funding support, and their research is often the first significant research effort in their particular area.

As gerontologists, we are aware of the flow of generations, of the need to pass on what is known to our successors, and more important, of the need to have successors. My hope is that this book will nourish a new generation of students and stimulate them to try to fill the many gaps in our knowledge of the social aspects of aging in Canada. Thus, while the book reflects the growth of social gerontology in Canada, I hope it will contribute to its eventual maturity.

I

Thinking Systematically About Aging

The five chapters of this first section lay the groundwork for the entire book, and I expect they will be consulted from time to time as context or foundation for the other articles in the book. Denton and Spencer provide basic data on the aging of the population in the past and projected to the future (Chapter 2) and Shulman describes its geographical distribution (Chapter 3). It is important to recognize how *many* older people there are in Canada, but also how *few*. More important, it is essential to have an understanding of the entire age structure of the population, and to avoid simply dichotomizing the population into all those above or below the age of 65 or some other arbitrary age. The changing demographic situation is the stimulus for great concern about the evolving age structure of the Canadian population. Chappell's paper (Chapter 4) reminds us that, in a sense, this has always been so, and it provides a sketch of the historical background to the contemporary social and health-service provisions for the aged and to the present debates in these areas.

Denton and Spencer, in Chapter 2, also provide a detailed explanation for how population projections are made. Of course, the specific assumptions which might appear in any given population projection — assumptions about anticipated birth, death, and migration rates, for example — might vary from projection to projection, and this should be kept in mind in any attempts to assess projections of the future which often appear in gerontological discussions.

In a sense, the paper by Denton and Spencer sets a major theme for this book, since these authors look both to the future and to the past. A further application of their work appears as Chapter 22, as they project health-care costs under different assumptions concerning the changing population structure.

Norman Shulman's paper on the aging of urban Canada also touches, of course, on the aging of rural Canada. His major theme is that population aging will not be uniformly distributed throughout Canada, but will vary regionally and by degree of urbanization. It seems likely that the overall balance between the rural and urban populations in Canada will roughly stabilize, as has been the case in several other western countries, at around three-quarters urban. (For U.S. data on this issue see Beale, 1976; De Jong and Sell, 1977; Tucker, 1976; Vining and Strauss, 1977; and Wardwell, 1977).

The nature of rural life will, however, become more urbanized, and even now it is not, strictly speaking, possible to isolate rural and urban living patterns as fully distinct types. The integration of rural areas into metropolitan and regionally dominated entities is increasingly great, based on communications and economic linkages and erosion of major differences between rural and urban populations on educational levels and other lifestyle features. None the less, it must be admitted that research on Canada's rural aged is almost completely non-existent, and we can only speculate about the important differences which might persist on the basis of rural-urban variability.

It has often been said that a nation can be judged by the treatment it gives to its elderly. The greatest scandal in our own society is that about half of our older people live under conditions of real poverty (definitions vary, but data which support this assertion appear in Chapter 19). Chappell, in Chapter 4, helps us to understand our societal failure by examining social policy toward the elderly as it developed historically. She writes that the social policy situation is highly unstable, and this is evident as this book goes to press in the political controversy over the failure of some provincial jurisdictions to maintain fully universal health coverage for the Canadian population.

Chapter 5, by Tindale and Marshall, delineates a theoretical perspective which might be of some use when addressing questions of aging from several social science areas, including not only sociology, but economics, political science, and history. The chapter also briefly and critically reviews age-stratification theory, which is a major but relatively new theoretical approach I believe to be most useful. It also critiques the major social-psychological approach now in use, referred to as the "normative approach", which is found in developmental social psychologies and in role-theoretical approaches, and also as the social psychological component of age-stratification theory. Taken together, chapters 5 and 6 therefore both critique the most important theoretical approaches in social gerontology and outline alternatives which appear to be more fruitful and which in fact characterize much of the Canadian research effort, as can be seen from several other papers in this book.

Chapter 6 is also included because of its substantive discussion of the sociology of aging and dying. A number of Canadian gerontologists (Cape, 1978; Chappell, 1975; Marshall, 1975a,b,c, forthcoming; Moore and Newton, 1977; Posner, 1976) have focused on the implications for older people of their closeness to death. Gerontology and thanatology overlap only partially, because much of the research in the latter has little to do with aging *per se*; but some attention should be paid to this very important aspect of the experience of aging: that the aging are also dying. The material on aging and dying in this chapter can be compared to the Inuit case described by Guemple in Chapter 10.

While the chapters of this first section are presented to provide some conceptual and methodological tools of use in confronting the remaining chapters of the book, additional theoretical and methodological exercises are found as appropriate in various chapters. There is no overriding theoretical approach for understanding the social aspects of aging. Attempts to produce one (e.g., disengagement theory) have not been highly successful. We should not expect to find an integrated theory of aging, because aging is part of life. Therefore, the most appropriate theoretical approaches will be taken from the best existing theory in the social sciences and will not be distinctively gerontological. Similarly, the methodological principles most appropriate for gaining an understanding of aging are the best principles of social science in general. There are different matters of emphasis of course, such as the great importance of longitudinal research design, and the need in many cases to measure health status as a variable important in relation to social variables. In general, however, a search for any specific gerontological methodology would be fruitless.

2

CANADA'S POPULATION AND LABOUR FORCE
Past, Present, and Future

Frank T. Denton and Byron G. Spencer
Department of Economics
McMaster University

The long-term development of a nation, in all its social and economic aspects, is inextricably linked with changes in population. With the passage of time, those who are born today become the school children, the young adults, the workers, and eventually the retired of the future. As they live their lives, their actions and decisions not only affect themselves and their contemporaries, but affect also the conditions under which future generations will live.

The "baby boom" which followed the Second World War, and the subsequent "baby bust", provide good illustration. The Canadian birth rate rose sharply in the 1940s and remained at a high level until the end of the 1950s. In consequence, a large bulge was created in the age structure of the population and, throughout the whole of their lives, those born during this period will be affected by the fact that they are part of this bulge. Much of their schooling took place under relatively crowded conditions, and as they have entered the labour force they have felt the influence of large numbers of their contemporaries competing for jobs at the same time. When they reach retirement age, the demands for support which they make on the economy, and hence on the working generations which follow them, will be relatively great, by virtue of their numbers. In contrast, those born in the latter part of the 1960s and the early part of the 1970s, when the birth rate was low, will experience quite different circumstances. They can expect less crowded classrooms as schoolchildren, less competition for jobs as workers, and smaller costs, in total, for their support in old age.

The wide variation of the birth rate in recent decades has been accompanied by marked fluctuations in the annual rate of immigration to Canada and by a continued decline in death rates. All of these changes have left their mark on the size and composition of the population and have had a major bearing on the characteristics of our society and our economy. One of the most important facts to recognize in connection with demographic changes is that even though some of their effects are felt immediately, it takes many generations for all of the effects to be fully realized.

It is not the purpose of this chapter to discuss the social and economic consequences of population change. That is the topic of other chapters, and one which has been treated elsewhere (e.g., Denton and Spencer, 1975; United Nations, 1973). Instead, we limit ourselves to a review of the record of population and labour-force growth in Canada, and some projections into the future. The material presented here may be of interest in its own right, but it is intended also to provide background for subsequent chapters.

The Growth of the Population and the Labour Force

In 1867, at the time of Confederation, the population of what is now Canada totalled about 3.5 million. By the time of the 1901 census it had reached 5.4 million, and by the 1976 census it was 23 million. In roughly eleven decades, the population has thus increased almost sevenfold.

Some of the major features of population and labour-force growth in this century are indicated in Table 1. The numbers of males and females in the population are recorded for each of three broad age-groups, in each of the years in which a national census was taken, from 1901 to 1976. Estimates of the total labour force and of the female labour force are provided also.

As is evident from Table 1, the total population has grown from one census to the next, without exception. There were very large proportionate increases in the early part of the century, especially in the years prior to the First World War, when the Canadian West was being settled rapidly and immigrants were pouring into the country. There was rapid increase again in the decade and a half following the Second World War, when large-scale inflows of immigrants coincided with the sustained high rates of fertility associated with the "baby boom". In the decade ending with the 1961 census, the population increased by more than 30 percent. While increases have continued, the rates of increase have been falling in recent periods as a result of declines in both the birth rate and the rate of immigration. In the decade ending in 1976, the increase was only fifteen percent.

Systematic attention is given to the *components* of population change in Figures 1 and 2. Figure 1 is concerned with the elements of "natural increase". Natural increase is calculated as the number of births less the number of deaths. It is convenient to express births, deaths, and natural increase relative to population size, and this is what is done in Figure 1. Birth, death, and natural increase rates per 1,000 population are plotted for the period from the 1870s to the 1970s.

There was an extended decline in the birth rate from the last quarter of the nineteenth century to the latter part of the 1930s. Observers of the day expected that this decline would continue, or at least that the birth rate would remain at a low level. However, that was not to be. Instead, there was a sharp increase in the 1940s, followed by a period in which the rate remained at a consistently high level, year after year. This period lasted until the very end of the 1950s. The rate then decreased just as sharply as it had

TABLE 1:
THE POPULATION, BY AGE AND SEX, AND THE LABOUR FORCE, BY SEX, CANADA, CENSUS YEARS 1901 TO 1976

Sex and Age		1901	1911	1921	1931	1941	1951	1956	1961	1966	1971	1976
							– Thousands –					
Population												
Males:	0-19	1,219	1,557	1,930	2,185	2,184	2,700	3,251	3,895	4,302	4,338	4,216
	20-64	1,394	2,095	2,385	2,895	3,326	3,839	4,281	4,650	5,036	5,676	6,358
	65+	139	171	215	295	391	551	623	674	717	782	875
Females:	0-19	1,186	1,506	1,898	2,136	2,135	2,609	3,138	3,729	4,128	4,157	4,025
	20-64	1,302	1,715	2,155	2,583	3,096	3,777	4,170	4,573	5,009	5,653	6,391
	65+	133	165	206	281	377	535	622	717	823	962	1,127
Total		5,371	7,207	8,788	10,377	11,507	14,009	16,081	18,238	20,015	21,568	22,993
Labour Force:												
Total		1,855	2,744	3,236	3,955	4,545	5,232	5,794	6,510	7,450	8,649	10,308
Female		284	423	568	760	948	1,200	1,408	1,825	2,326	2,968	3,859
							– Percent of Total –					
Population												
Males:	0-19	22.7	21.6	22.0	21.1	19.0	19.3	20.2	21.4	21.5	20.1	18.3
	20-64	26.0	29.1	27.1	27.9	28.9	27.4	26.6	25.5	25.2	26.3	27.7
	65+	2.6	2.4	2.4	2.8	3.4	3.9	3.9	3.7	3.6	3.6	3.8
Females:	0-19	22.1	20.9	21.6	20.6	18.6	18.6	19.5	20.4	20.6	19.3	17.5
	20-64	24.2	23.8	24.5	25.0	26.9	27.0	25.9	25.1	25.0	26.2	27.8
	65+	2.5	2.3	2.3	2.7	3.3	3.8	3.9	3.9	4.1	4.5	4.9
Total		100.0	100.0	100.0	100.0	100.0	100.0	100.0	100.0	100.0	100.0	100.0
Labour Force:												
Female/Total		15.3	15.4	17.5	19.2	20.9	22.9	24.3	28.0	31.2	34.3	37.4

NOTE: All figures prior to 1951 exclude Newfoundland. The population figures relate to June 1 of each census year, while the labour force figures are annual averages. The labour force figures from 1951 to 1976 are based on estimates from the Statistics Canada Labour Force Survey. All labour force figures prior to 1951 are based on estimates from Denton and Ostry (1967). All labour force estimates prior to 1976 have been adjusted by the authors to make them consistent with new definitions introduced into the Labour Force Survey in the latter year.

FIGURE 1:

ANNUAL BIRTH, DEATH, AND NATURAL INCREASE RATES, CANADA, 1876-1976

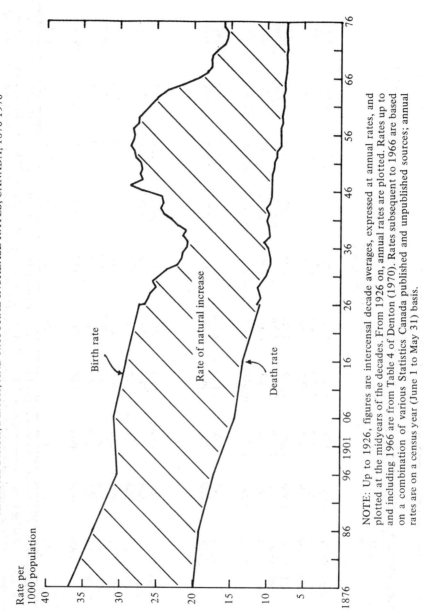

NOTE: Up to 1926, figures are intercensal decade averages, expressed at annual rates, and plotted at the midyears of the decades. From 1926 on, annual rates are plotted. Rates up to and including 1966 are from Table 4 of Denton (1970). Rates subsequent to 1966 are based on a combination of various Statistics Canada published and unpublished sources; annual rates are on a census year (June 1 to May 31) basis.

FIGURE 2:
ANNUAL IMMIGRATION, EMIGRATION, AND NET IMMIGRATION RATES, CANADA, 1876-1976

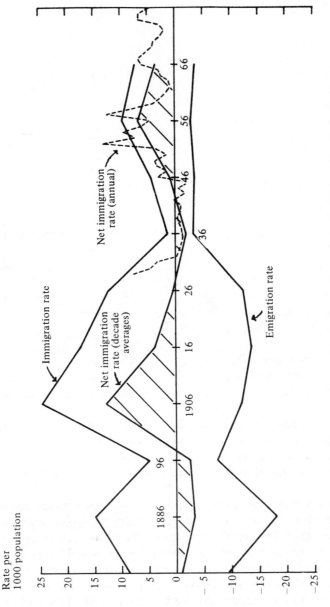

NOTE: Immigration and emigration figures are intercensal decade averages, expressed at annual rates and plotted at the mid-years of the decades. The decade averages are based on Denton (1970: Table 9) and Statistics Canada (1976: Table 3). Annual net immigration rates up to 1971 are from Statistics Canada (1976: Table 4); for subsequent years, they are based on unpublished data provided by the Canada Employment and Immigration department.

increased earlier, falling to the lowest levels ever recorded in Canadian demographic history by the late 1960s and continuing to fall in the early 1970s. Throughout the whole of the period from 1947 to 1959, the annual birth rate never fell below 27 per 1,000 population; in sharp contrast, the 1977 rate was only 15.5.

The story of the death rate is quite different. There have been no substantial fluctuations, but instead a rather steady and gradual decrease in the overall rate. The declines in infant mortality have been especially dramatic, but all groups have shared in the decrease, and average life expectancies have risen markedly over the decades. Based on 1931 mortality conditions, a newborn male would have been expected to live to an age of 60 years, on average, and a newborn female to an age of 62; based on 1971 conditions, their life expectancies would have been 69 and 76.

The net immigration component of population change represents the difference between the numbers of immigrants and the numbers of emigrants. Again, it is convenient to express migration relative to population size, and this is done in Figure 2. The rates are plotted for intercensal decades from 1871-81 to 1961-71, and the net immigration rates are plotted annually as well, from the end of the 1920s.

Taking the last hundred years as a whole, the gross immigration rate is characterized by generally high levels over long periods, and by substantial volatility over shorter ones. Prior to the Second World War, periods of high immigration coincided with periods of high emigration, as the figure indicates: many who came to Canada stayed for only short periods before moving on again, typically to the United States. Nevertheless, net immigration has been positive in most decades, and quite substantial in many. In the present century, the depressed decade of the 1930s represents the only extended period in which the numbers of people leaving Canada exceeded the numbers arriving.

The short-run variation of immigration is evident in the series of annual net rates plotted in Figure 2 for the period since the late 1920s. As the series indicates, year-to-year fluctuations have been pronounced: immigration is much more volatile than an inspection of decade averages alone would suggest.

Changes in the size of a population and changes in its age composition go hand in hand: the factors that are responsible for the one are responsible also for the other. The distributions among the broad age groups 0-19, 20-64, and 65-and-over are recorded in Table 1, for males and females in each of the national census years since 1901. For these groups, there are only two instances in which the population failed to increase from one census to another: the 0-19 age groups declined in size between 1931 and 1941 and, more recently, between 1971 and 1976. The earlier decreases were so small as to represent virtually no change; they were a consequence of the low birth rates of the 1930s and, to some extent, of the excess of emigration over immigration in that period. The more recent decreases were quite substantial, reflecting primarily the very sharp drop in the numbers of births in the early 1970s.

With these exceptions, the historical pattern has been one of growth in each age group from census to census. Over the 75-year period as a whole, the number of people under the age of 20 — males and females combined — increased more than threefold, the number in the range 20-64 increased almost fivefold, and the number 65 and over increased about sevenfold.

In some very general respects, the composition of the population today is not greatly different from what it was twenty, fifty, or seventy-five years ago. Roughly half the population is in the 20-64 age range, and the overall numbers of males and females are about equal, as in times past. However, changes have taken place, and they are important ones. The proportion of young people has declined quite sharply in recent years, an inevitable consequence of the declining numbers of births. In 1966, people under 20 represented 42.1 percent of the total population; in 1976, they represented only 35.8 percent. At the older end of the age spectrum, the proportion aged 65-and-over has risen, over the long term. In 1901, when the Canadian population was a younger one on average, people 65-and-over represented 5.1 percent of the total; in 1976, they represented 8.7 percent. There have been changes in the sex composition of the population, too. It is a curious fact that males exceed females at birth. However, women tend to live longer than men, and the gap in life expectancies has widened. Largely for this reason, there were 1,127,000 women 65-and-over in 1976, compared with only 875,000 men.

The size of the labour force — the total number of persons with jobs or looking for jobs — is obviously related to the size of the population. But it is related also to the age composition of the population and to the labour-force participation rates in individual male and female age groups — that is, to the proportions of people in these groups who wish to be employed. Labour-force growth in Canada has been closely linked with population growth, and hence with all of those factors that are responsible for population growth. In addition, though, there have been major changes in the patterns of participation. Men now retire much earlier, on average, than they did in previous decades. The average age of school-leaving has risen too, so that the male working life has been shortened at both ends. At the same time, female participation rates have risen markedly, in response to changing social and economic circumstances.

The long-run pattern of growth of the labour force is indicated in Table 1. In 1901, the Canadian labour force numbered some 1.9 million people; in 1976, it numbered about 10.3 million. In 1901, women represented a little over 15 percent of the total; in 1976, they represented a little over 37 percent. In round numbers, almost two out of every five members of the working population today are women. The growth of the female labour force has been especially rapid since the Second World War, and the growth continues at a rapid pace.

The age structure of the population has important implications for the economic burden that a society must bear in supporting its dependent members. Those who are economically "productive" are typically those in the conventional working-age range who provide the labour required to produce the national output and the national income. Others — the young and the old — are, in a basic sense, dependent on this group, and as the age structure of the population changes, the burden of dependency may change also.

Various measures of dependency can be calculated and a number are provided in Table 2. The upper part of the table provides measures based on the sizes of young and old age groups relative to the group aged 20 to 64, the latter taken as a rough approximation to the working-age population. The first measure is the "youth" dependency ratio — the ratio of the population aged 0-19 to the population 20-64. In 1901, the youth ratio was 0.89 — that is, there were 89 people under the age of 20 for every 100 people aged 20-64. In 1976, the ratio was 0.65, the lowest recorded over the entire three-quarters of a century. However, the transition from the high 1901 level to the low 1976 one was not steady. Consistent with the general decline in the birth rate, the youth ratio fell in most of the decades before 1941; it then rose, as a result of the "baby boom", until 1966, since which time it has declined sharply.

The second row of Table 2 provides values of the "elderly" dependency ratio — the ratio of those 65 and over to those 20-64. In 1901, this ratio was 0.10. The ratio has increased considerably since then, and by 1976 it had risen to 0.16.

The sums of the foregoing two dependency ratios, which we may take as rough measures of the total dependency burden, are provided in the third row. The figures in this row are somewhat less than one. They vary over the period, ranging from 0.99 in 1901 and again in 1966, to 0.79 in 1941. The 1976 ratio was 0.81, only slightly higher than the lowest level recorded in the table. By this criterion, then, the population of today is characterized by a relatively low dependency burden.

It will be evident that the dependency measures just considered are far from precise, especially when compared over long periods of time. For one thing, while the age group 20-64 may be adequate as a rough approximation to the working-age population today, its adequacy for the earlier decades of the century is questionable. The average age of entrance of men into the labour force was considerably younger in earlier periods, and the average age of retirement was considerably older. Moreover, the population-based

TABLE 2:
SELECTED DEPENDENCY RATIOS, CANADA, CENSUS YEARS 1901 TO 1976

Type of Ratio	1901	1911	1921	1931	1941	1951	1956	1961	1966	1971	1976
Ratio to Population 20-64											
Population: 0-19	0.89	0.80	0.84	0.79	0.67	0.70	0.76	0.83	0.84	0.75	0.65
65+	0.10	0.09	0.09	0.11	0.12	0.14	0.15	0.15	0.15	0.15	0.16
0-19 and 65+	0.99	0.89	0.83	0.90	0.79	0.84	0.91	0.98	0.99	0.90	0.81
Total Population	1.99	1.89	1.83	1.90	1.79	1.84	1.91	1.98	1.99	1.90	1.81
Ratio to Labour Force											
Population: 0-19	1.30	1.12	1.18	1.09	0.95	1.01	1.10	1.17	1.13	0.98	0.80
65+	0.15	0.12	0.13	0.15	0.17	0.21	0.21	0.21	0.21	0.20	0.19
0-19 and 65+	1.44	1.24	1.31	1.24	1.12	1.22	1.31	1.38	1.34	1.18	0.99
Non-Labour Force	1.63	1.63	1.72	1.62	1.53	1.68	1.78	1.80	1.69	1.49	1.23
Total Population	2.63	2.63	2.72	2.62	2.53	2.68	2.78	2.80	2.69	2.49	2.23

NOTE: Ratios are based on figures in Table 1.

ratios ignore the dependency implications of increases in the labour-force participation of women. It is appropriate, therefore, to consider dependency measures which take account directly of the size of the labour force, rather than inferring it from the population deemed to be of working age. A few such measures are provided in the lower half of Table 2.

The picture is altered in detail when ratios of population to labour force are considered, but in broad terms it remains substantially the same. The levels of the ratios are higher than the ones in the top half of the table, but the patterns of change through time are generally similar, and it is these patterns that are of principal interest. Relative to earlier levels, the 1976 ratios are now seen to be even lower than before. The overall ratio of persons not in the labour force to persons in the labour force was 1.23 in 1976, and this is by far the lowest level of that ratio recorded in the table. As before, we conclude that the current dependency burden is a relatively light one, by historical standards.[1]

The Future Population

The "baby boom" of the 1940s and the 1950s has accounted for much of the very rapid expansion of the labour force in the late 1960s and throughout the 1970s. Those who were born during the baby-boom period can be expected to remain in the labour force for several decades, of course, but eventually they will reach retirement age and become part of the dependent population. The children of the 1960s and the 1970s, and those born later, will become responsible, in the second and third decades of the next century, for the national income base which will support the baby-boom generation in its old age. The prospect of a large increase in the fraction of the population in the elderly dependent category has been a source of concern for many.[2] It is useful, therefore, to attempt to attach some numbers to the future size and age distribution of the population.

The population at the end of any period is equal to the population at the beginning of the period, plus births and immigration, minus deaths and emigration. We have made projections of fertility rates for females of different ages in the child-bearing range[3] and of mortality rates for males and females of different ages. These projections, together with assumptions about the numbers and age-sex distributions of immigrants and emigrants, allow us to make projections of the population, both in total and for particular age-sex categories. The population is moved ahead one year at a time for as many years as there are in the projection period. Each year, the existing population is aged by one year, mortality rates are applied to calculate the numbers of deaths, and fertility rates to calculate the number of births. Immigrants are added at each age, and emigrants are subtracted.

We report here a projection of the population based on a particular set of assumptions concerning the future course of fertility, mortality, and rates

TABLE 3:
A PROJECTION OF THE POPULATION OF CANADA, BY SEX AND AGE, 1976 TO 2051

Sex and Age	1976	1981	1986	1991	1996	2001	2011	2021	2031	2041	2051
						– Thousands –					
Males: 0-19	4,216	4,087	4,137	4,389	4,639	4,701	4,683	4,986	5,135	5,270	5,498
20-64	6,358	7,126	7,836	8,290	8,657	9,151	10,204	10,490	10,614	11,245	11,515
65-69	339	380	395	453	466	470	608	837	925	752	963
70-74	241	274	308	320	367	378	399	612	764	645	695
75-79	150	176	201	226	237	271	282	366	502	552	450
80+	145	154	178	207	238	260	314	338	474	620	596
Females: 0-19	4,026	3,891	3,928	4,160	4,393	4,450	4,430	4,715	4,856	4,984	5,200
20-64	6390	7,146	7,827	8,249	8,609	9,102	10,154	10,386	10,454	11,083	11,353
65-69	382	445	487	568	564	568	744	1,045	1,122	907	1,159
70-74	292	349	409	450	528	526	564	875	1,073	903	966
75-79	212	249	301	357	397	466	474	624	875	938	759
80+	240	284	345	430	530	624	806	888	1,220	1,611	1,603
Total	22,993	24,561	26,351	28,099	29,626	30,966	33,662	36,162	38,014	39,510	40,758
						– Percent of Total –					
Males: 0-19	18.3	16.6	15.7	15.6	15.7	15.2	13.9	13.8	13.5	13.3	13.5
20-64	27.7	29.0	29.7	29.5	29.2	29.6	30.3	29.0	27.9	28.5	28.3
65-69	1.5	1.5	1.5	1.6	1.6	1.5	1.8	2.3	2.4	1.9	2.4
70-74	1.0	1.1	1.2	1.1	1.2	1.2	1.2	1.7	2.0	1.6	1.7
75-79	0.7	0.7	0.8	0.8	0.8	0.9	0.8	1.0	1.3	1.4	1.1
80+	0.6	0.6	0.7	0.7	0.8	0.8	0.9	0.9	1.2	1.6	1.5
Females: 0-19	17.5	15.8	14.9	14.8	14.8	14.3	13.2	13.0	12.8	12.6	12.8
20-64	27.8	29.1	29.7	29.4	29.1	29.4	30.2	28.7	27.5	28.1	27.9
65-69	1.7	1.8	1.8	2.0	1.9	1.8	2.2	2.9	3.0	2.3	2.8
70-74	1.3	1.4	1.6	1.6	1.8	1.7	1.7	2.4	2.8	2.3	2.4
75-79	0.9	1.0	1.1	1.3	1.3	1.5	1.4	1.7	2.3	2.4	1.9
80+	1.0	1.2	1.3	1.5	1.8	2.0	2.4	2.5	3.2	4.1	3.9
Total	100.0	100.0	100.0	100.0	100.0	100.0	100.0	100.0	100.0	100.0	100.0

of migration.[4] The total fertility rate (the sum of the fertility rates for individual ages) is assumed to increase, in equal annual increments, from its 1974 level of about 1.9 births per woman, to a level of 2.1 births per woman by 1984, and to remain at that level thereafter, to the end of the projection period.[5] (A rate of 2.1 is roughly equal to the natural replacement rate — the rate required, in the long run, if the population is to be able to reproduce itself). The fertility rate for women of each age is assumed to be a constant proportion of the total rate throughout the projection period. The mortality rates for particular ages and sexes are assumed to decline over the period 1971-91 by the same percentages as they did in the period 1951-71. A common view is that the pace of decline must diminish in the longer run, and it is assumed therefore that the percentage decreases will only be half as great in the period 1991-2011, and that there will be no further decreases after 2011. Annual immigration of 120,000 and emigration of 40,000 are assumed throughout the projection period, implying net immigration of 80,000 per year. The latter may be regarded as a "medium" level of net immigration: by historical standards, it is neither very high nor very low.

The above assumptions, in conjunction with the population reported in the 1976 census, allow us to calculate the size and age distributions of the population in future years. The results are summarized in Table 3. The total population and its distribution among twelve age-sex groups are shown in the table at five-year intervals for the period from 1976 to 2001, and at ten-year intervals thereafter, to the year 2051. The focus of attention is the older population, and greater age detail is therefore reported for this group than for the younger ones.

The total population is projected to grow throughout the entire period of 75 years, increasing by about a third between 1976 and 2001 and by a third again between 2001 and 2051. The older population, however, increases much more rapidly, under the assumptions made here (and indeed, under a much wider range of assumptions). The population 65-and-over is projected to increase by more than three-quarters by the end of this century, and then to double in the fifty years following. In relation to the overall population, the population 65-and-over is projected to increase from about 8.7 percent of the total in 1976 to 11.5 percent in 2001 and to 17.6 percent in 2051. If the assumptions underlying our projections prove to be even roughly in accord with future developments, we can expect a very substantial relative increase in the older population in the decades ahead.

It is of interest to observe that the projected increases in the numbers of older women greatly exceed the projected increases in the numbers of older men. The reason is that mortality rates have fallen more sharply for women than for men in recent decades, and our projections assume that the trends will continue. Under the assumptions made, men 65-and-over will constitute 6.6 percent of the population in 2051 (compared with 3.8 in 1976), while women 65-and-over will constitute 11.0 percent (compared with 4.9 in 1976). Such prospective developments clearly have implications for future social policies.

The Future Labour Force

The labour force is, of course, drawn from the population. It is possible, therefore, to project the labour force once we have projected the population, provided only that we make assumptions concerning the labour force participation rates for each age-sex group.

We have made a set of assumptions about future participation rates. These assumptions involve an extrapolation of historical trends in the rates for each of nine age groups, separately for each sex. Roughly speaking, we have assumed further declines in the participation rates of young men, and a continuation of the tendency towards earlier retirement among men over 55. In the case of women, we have assumed a continuation of the trend towards lower participation rates among those under 20 and over 65. For women in the age groups between 20 and 65, though, we have assumed a continuation for some years to come of the recent strong increases in participation rates. For all ages and both sexes, the rates are assumed not to change after the year 1991.

The results of these assumptions, in terms of the size and age-sex distribution of the labour force, are reported in Table 4. The overall labour force is projected to grow by some 45 percent by 2001, and by a further 23 percent by 2051. In the earlier period, the female labour force is projected to grow by about 59 percent, the male labour force by about 37 percent; in the later period, the proportionate increases are 21 percent for females and 24 percent for males. The labour force 65-and-over is projected to decrease for some years, in spite of the projected increases in the numbers of older people, a consequence of the declining male participation rates in this age group. By the 1990s, the participation rates cease to decline and the older component of the labour force starts to grow.

Dependency Implications of the Projections

The population and labour-force projections have implications for the economic burden of dependency in future decades. To draw out these implications, we present some calculated dependency ratios in Table 5.

Much the same message is contained in both the ratios based on population and those based on the labour force. In general, the youth-dependency ratio declines between 1976 and 2011 and then remains roughly constant thereafter. The elderly-dependency ratio, however, rises sharply, more than doubling between 1976 and 2031, with most of the increase taking place after the year 2001. The net result of the fall in the youth ratio and the rise in the elderly one is a somewhat lower overall dependency ratio for the

TABLE 4:
A PROJECTION OF THE LABOUR FORCE OF CANADA, BY SEX AND AGE, 1976 TO 2051

Sex and Age	1976	1981	1986	1991	1996	2001	2011	2021	2031	2041	2051
						— Thousands —					
Males: 15-24	1,558	1,656	1,533	1,339	1,349	1,558	1,685	1,591	1,771	1,792	1,828
25-44	3,017	3,500	4,098	4,514	4,564	4,447	4,381	4,851	4,868	5,020	5,273
45-64	1,835	1,889	1,952	2,107	2,449	2,841	3,583	3,419	3,484	3,811	3,791
65+	133	130	118	109	116	120	146	197	234	213	240
Females: 15-24	1,258	1,366	1,293	1,156	1,160	1,338	1,447	1,365	1,519	1,537	1,567
25-44	1,658	2,153	2,707	3,192	3,211	3,103	3,039	3,361	3,372	3,475	3,652
45-64	909	986	1,060	1,194	1,403	1,643	2,038	1,903	1,952	2,124	2,108
65+	44	43	43	44	47	49	60	82	96	90	100
Total	10,411	11,723	12,803	13,655	14,299	15,099	16,380	16,769	17,296	18,062	18,559
						— Percent of Total —					
Males: 15-24	15.0	14.1	12.0	9.8	9.4	10.3	10.3	9.5	10.2	9.9	9.9
25-44	29.0	29.9	32.0	33.1	31.9	29.5	26.7	28.9	28.1	27.8	28.4
45-64	17.6	16.1	15.2	15.4	17.1	18.8	21.9	20.4	20.1	21.1	20.4
65+	1.3	1.1	0.9	0.8	0.8	0.8	0.9	1.2	1.4	1.2	1.3
Females: 15-24	12.1	11.7	10.1	8.5	8.1	8.9	8.8	8.1	8.8	8.5	8.4
25-44	15.9	18.4	21.1	23.4	22.5	20.6	18.6	20.0	19.5	19.2	19.7
45-64	8.7	8.4	8.3	8.7	9.8	10.9	12.4	11.3	11.3	11.8	11.4
65+	0.4	0.4	0.3	0.3	0.3	0.3	0.4	0.5	0.6	0.5	0.5
Total	100.0	100.0	100.0	100.0	100.0	100.0	100.0	100.0	100.0	100.0	100.0

TABLE 5:
A PROJECTION OF SELECTED DEPENDENCY RATIOS, CANADA, 1976 TO 2051

Type of Ratio	1976	1981	1986	1991	1996	2001	2011	2021	2031	2041	2051
Ratio to Population 20-64											
Population: 0-19	0.65	0.56	0.51	0.52	0.52	0.50	0.45	0.46	0.47	0.46	0.47
65+	0.16	0.16	0.17	0.18	0.19	0.20	0.21	0.27	0.33	0.31	0.31
0-19 and 65+	0.80	0.72	0.68	0.70	0.72	0.70	0.65	0.73	0.80	0.77	0.78
Ratio to Labour Force											
Population: 0-19	0.79	0.68	0.63	0.63	0.63	0.61	0.56	0.58	0.58	0.57	0.58
65+	0.19	0.20	0.20	0.22	0.23	0.24	0.26	0.33	0.40	0.38	0.39
0-19 and 65+	0.98	0.88	0.83	0.85	0.86	0.84	0.81	0.91	0.98	0.95	0.96
Non-Labour Force	1.21	1.10	1.06	1.06	1.07	1.05	1.06	1.16	1.20	1.19	1.20
Total Population	2.21	2.10	2.06	2.06	2.07	2.05	2.06	2.16	2.20	2.19	2.20

NOTE: Ratios are based on figures in Tables 3 and 4.

remainder of this century and through the first decade of the next, as compared with 1976, and then a pronounced increase in the following two decades or so. In spite of the increase, by 2031 the overall dependency ratio is no higher than it was in 1976, whichever form of the ratio one looks at. While measures such as the ones we are looking at should be viewed merely as rough indicators of dependency, it appears that future increases in the older population of the order indicated in our projections would certainly not impose an unmanageable burden on the economy or on the population of working age.

Concluding Remarks

We have reviewed the growth of the population and the labour force over periods of many decades and have provided projections of their future development to the middle of the next century. The past seventy-five years have witnessed substantial increases in the relative size of the older population, and in the years ahead we can expect further increases. These increases will be especially pronounced in the first few decades of the next century if, as we have assumed in our projection, fertility rates do not again rise to high levels.

The impact on society and the economy of changes in the age distribution of the Canadian population are not investigated here. However, we note that, under the assumptions we have made, a projected decrease in the relative size of the youth population coincides with the projected increase in the relative size of the elderly component. Furthermore, the fraction in the middle years is projected to be slightly larger in the future than it has been in the past. These prospective changes, taken together, would seem to suggest that overall there will be no "crisis" associated with the expected general aging of the population, as some have suggested. None the less, there are important implications in terms of educational, health-care, pension, and other requirements which should be anticipated as a basis for informed social planning and policy formulation.

Notes

1. It should be noted that even the more refined dependency ratios based on the labour force are not ideal. They neglect such considerations as differences in productivity among members of the labour force, the distinction between full-time and part-time workers, the size and composition of the nation's capital stock, changes in technology and productivity through time, and the omission of housework and volunteer work in the measurement of the labour force and the gross national product. Nevertheless, the ratios do serve a useful purpose when interpreted with appropriate caution.

2. There have, for example, been expressions of concern about the ability of pension funds, both public and private, to meet their future obligations, and concern also about the size of future health-care bills as the population grows older and increasing numbers of individuals reach ages which typically have high health-care requirements.

3. Fertility rates are the average numbers of births per woman of a given age. The childbearing range is taken to be from 15 to 50 years of age.

4. This set of assumptions is one of many on which a projection might be based. For experimental projections of the population based on other assumptions, see Denton and Spencer (1979).

5. The total fertility rate may be regarded as the average number of children that would be born to a woman by the end of her child-bearing years, assuming that she does not die before the end of those years.

3

THE AGING OF URBAN CANADA*

Norman Shulman
Ministry of State for Urban Affairs
Ottawa

This paper examines the aging of Canada's population, focusing on the current and forecast distribution of the elderly among the provinces and specific cities. The demographic characteristics of a society have a major impact on the needs and demands of the population. The rate of growth and the spatial-distribution, age-distribution, and population flows all affect the level and types of services that are required. Perhaps the best known recent example of demographic impact is the "baby boom": the increased fertility rate in the immediate postwar years led to increased demands for elementary, high school, and then university facilities and shelter. The important downstream effects of such demographic shifts are compelling reasons for paying attention to these patterns.

While the salient demographic feature of the 1940s was the baby boom, it was overshadowed in the 1950s by the urbanization of the country and in the 1960s by the metropolitanization of the population. Since the mid—1970s, the key demographic feature has been the aging of Canada's population. This transition, which is described elsewhere in this book (see Chapter 2), has seen the proportion of elderly increase as the proportion of young people has dropped. This trend is expected to continue its gradual but steady course at least into the 2030s.

In viewing the elderly, it is important that we distinguish between what has been called the "young-old" (under 75) and the "old-old" (over 75). The former have different lifestyles, life expectancies, and needs than the latter and it is therefore useful to distinguish between the two. The percentage of elderly who are "old-old" is expected to increase from 37 percent in 1976 to over 44 percent (approximately 1.5 million) by 2001, and to over 50 percent by 2041 (Stone and Fletcher, 1978: 24).

A second important factor is the sex difference in life expectancy. Females continue to enjoy greater longevity than males and will continue to form a higher proportion of the elderly population.

This national picture of aging trends provides a rather reliable view on which to base estimates of future needs for facilities and services for the

---

*Several people, particularly Leroy Stone, provided valuable background data. The assistance of Michael Nelson is acknowledged. The views expressed are the personal views of the author and not necessarily those of the Ministry of State for Urban Affairs.

TABLE 1:
RURAL-URBAN PROPORTIONS FOR (A) THE TOTAL POPULATION AND (B) THE POPULATION 65 AND OVER FOR CANADA AND THE PROVINCES (1971) (in thousands)

	Canada	Newfoundland	P.E.I.	Nova Scotia	New Brunswick	Quebec	Ontario	Manitoba	Saskatchewan	Alberta	B.C.
(A) Total Population											
Rural	5,157	223	69	342	273	1,167	1,359	302	435	432	530
	23.9	42.7	61.7	43.3	43.1	19.4	17.6	30.6	47.0	26.5	24.3
Urban	16,411	299	43	447	361	4,861	6,344	686	491	1,196	1,654
	76.1	57.3	38.3	56.7	56.9	80.6	82.4	69.4	53.0	73.5	75.7
Total	21,568	522	112	789	634	6,028	7,703	988	926	1,628	2,184
(B) Over 65											
Rural	436	16	9	36	23	84	120	26	40	34	38
	24.8	48.4	69.2	49.3	42.6	20.2	18.6	27.6	42.6	28.3	22.7
Urban	1,319	17	4	37	31	330	524	68	54	86	167
	75.2	51.6	30.8	50.7	57.4	79.9	81.4	72.4	57.4	71.7	77.3
Total	1,755	33	13	73	54	414	644	94	94	120	205
% Aged	8.1	6.3	11.6	9.2	8.5	6.9	8.4	9.5	10.2	7.4	9.4

SOURCE: Statistics Canada, Cat. No. 92-715.

elderly. There are, however, important variations within the national scene from province to province, city to city, and by size of city, which may hold important implications for demands that can be expected and the types of policies and programs required. While this kind of fine-tuning is important, it must be prefaced by the caveat that as we focus in on more specific areas, data become thinner and the risk of unexpected change becomes greater. With this in mind, we turn to an examination of the distribution of elderly in the country.

Rural-Urban Differences

The proportion of people living in urban centres has increased over the years to a current level of approximately 75 percent. When the elderly are compared with the rest of the population, we find that they are about as likely as the rest of the population to reside in urban centres. Using a definition of "urban" as a place with a population of 1,000 or more, we find in Table 1 that 23.9 percent of all Canadians lived in rural places in 1971, as compared to 24.8 percent of people over 65.

Provincial Differences

Since the provinces have jurisdiction over the delivery of several services which are very relevant to older people (e.g., health care), variations in provincial concentration of elderly is a matter of some importance. As Table 2 shows, two provinces, P.E.I. and Saskatchewan, have higher proportions of elderly than the others and they "aged" more than others in the last census decade. A second group of provinces — Manitoba, British

TABLE 2:
PROVINCIAL AGE INDICES: 1961 AND 1971

Province	55 to 64 age group		65+ age group		Amount of Change
	1961	1971	1961	1971	
B.C.	107	110	134	116	−15
Alberta	93	90	92	90	− 5
Saskatchewan	104	115	121	126	+16
Manitoba	107	113	118	120	+ 8
Ontario	107	101	107	104	− 9
Quebec	92	95	76	85	+12
Nova Scotia	97	109	113	114	+13
New Brunswick	92	100	103	106	+11
P.E.I.	106	108	99	137	+40
Nfld.	76	84	78	75	+ 5
Canada	100	100	100	100	
Percent of Total Population	7.1%	8.0%	7.6%	8.1%	

SOURCE: Bairstow, 1973.

Columbia, and Nova Scotia — have somewhat lower proportions of elderly but are still above the national average of 8.1 percent.

It is important to note that the absolute number of elderly can be as important as the proportion they represent. For example, while Ontario, at 8.4 percent, is only slightly over the national average of 8.1 percent in the percentage of its population which is over 65, its percentage (36 percent) of all elderly in Canada, and the absolute number of elderly who reside in Ontario, are high. The total percentage of elderly in Ontario is expected to rise to 40 percent by 2021 and to triple in absolute numbers to over two million in that period.

A second key province is British Columbia which housed 12 percent of the nation's elderly in 1976. While the growth of its over-65 population was less than the provincial average growth rate, the increase in the 55-64 group was over 54 percent. As a result, the proportion over 65 is expected to continue to increase to 17 percent by 2021 and the absolute number of elderly in British Columbia is expected to grow fourfold to about one million.

In contrast, Quebec may decrease from the 24 percent of all elderly in Canada that it held in 1976 to about 22 percent in 2021.

City Size

Most of Canada's elderly (77 percent) lived in urban centres (1,000 or more) in 1976. Over 50 percent lived in centres of 100,000 or more while only 23 percent resided in rural areas. This distribution is very similar to that of the general population.

There is some evidence that elderly people are slightly over-represented in small towns (Auerbach and Gerber, 1976; Norland, 1974). According to Yeates (1978) in 1971, the elderly population of small centres, usually defined as centres with a population between 1,000 and 10,000, was 17.4 percent as compared to 15.1 percent of the general population. Statistics Canada (1977f: 43) reports the figures 11.5 percent and 13.1 percent, which represent the same trend at a slightly lower scale than reported by Yeates.

In 1976, about 53 percent of Canada's two million elderly lived in metropolitan centres and forecasts are that this will rise to about 59 percent by 2021. The approximately 29 percent who live in the three largest cities (Toronto, Montreal, and Vancouver) is expected to increase only slightly by the turn of the century (Stone and Fletcher, 1978) but the absolute number of elderly in these cities is expected to triple to about 1.6 million in that period.

One significant aspect of these kinds of concentrations is the variation in services available to elderly people in centres of different size. At present, most large cities have a broader array of social services than do small towns. At the same time, the demand for certain services such as specialized health care may be very high in large cities because of the concentration of elderly people.

Specific Cities

It follows from the preceeding comments that the large metropolitan centres usually house large numbers of elderly people. A number of metropolitan centres have a higher than average proportion of elderly. Victoria tops the list with over 15 percent of its population over 65, followed by Vancouver (10.5 percent) and Winnipeg (10.2 percent). In contrast, cities like Edmonton (6.5 percent) and Sudbury (5.3 percent) are below average.

City-specific concentrations can also be seen for a larger set of urban places with populations of 25,000 or more in 1971 (see Table 3). The index

TABLE 3:

DISTRIBUTION OF THREE AGE GROUPS OF OLDER PEOPLE AMONG CENSUS AGGLOMERATIONS AND CENSUS METROPOLITAN AREAS IN CANADA, 1971

Urban Area	55-64		65-74		75 and over	
	Rank	Index	Rank	Index	Rank	Index
Kelowna, B.C.	3	1.25	1	1.69	4	1.69
Victoria, B.C.	1	1.29	2	1.58	1	2.41
Vancouver, B.C.	7	1.15	3	1.44	5	1.45
Medicine Hat, Alta.	2	1.28	4	1.36	3	1.73
Chilliwack, B.C.	14	1.10	5	1.31	6	1.39
Charlottetown, P.E.I.	11	1.12	6	1.24	2	1.93
St. Hyacinthe, Que.	8	1.15	7	1.23	10	1.34
Windsor, Ont.	27	.98	8	1.20	17	1.13
Barrie, Ont.	15	1.08	9	1.20	13	1.21
Brantford, Ont.	4	1.18	10	1.20	8	1.35
Thunder Bay, Ont.	13	1.11	11	1.16	21	1.07
Timmins, Ont.	18	1.06	12	1.15	41	.77
Nanaimo, B.C.	5	1.18	13	1.14	16	1.17
Saint John, N.B.	12	1.11	14	1.11	12	1.29
Winnipeg, Man.	10	1.12	15	1.10	11	1.32
.			.			
.			.			
.			.			
Halifax, N.S.	40	.92	46	.78	36	.82
Thetford Mines, Que.	34	.96	47	.78	49	.67
Trenton, Ont.	52	.82	48	.77	26	1.00
Sault Ste. Marie, Ont.	50	.87	49	.75	47	.71
Sorel, Que.	36	.94	50	.75	50	.67
Calgary, Alta.	56	.78	51	.73	32	.88
Edmonton, Alta.	53	.81	52	.73	40	.77
Rouyn, Que.	41	.92	53	.71	56	.44
Rimouski, Que.	54	.80	54	.66	51	.66
Kamloops, B.C.	55	.80	55	.64	46	.71
Port Alberni, B.C.	45	.90	56	.61	55	.57
Chicoutimi-Jonquière	58	.73	57	.60	57	.39
Sudbury, Ont.	57	.78	58	.57	58	.39
Prince George, B.C.	59	.52	59	.33	59	.33
Baie-Comeau, Que.	60	.48	60	.25	60	.10

SOURCE: Yeates, 1976.

provides a measure of the proportion of the population of a given age range in a city relative to the proportion in that age group across the country, i.e., the percentage 65 and over in a city is divided by the percentage 65 and over in the nation. For example, as shown in Table 3, Victoria with about 7.2 percent of the country's over-75 population has 2.4 times the national average of 3 percent and has by far the largest concentration of "old-old". It is noteworthy that five centres fall in the top category and an equal number in the bottom grouping, indicating the variation that exists among cities. As the number and proportion of elderly in the population increases, these variations among cities are likely to become more pronounced. As a result, some cities and provinces will require substantial increases in the kinds of services and resources that elderly people require.

We do not as yet have adequate information on which specific cities are currently attracting retired people, but there is some evidence that cities with mild climates are among the preferred places. Victoria is perhaps the clearest example of this preference. A study of elderly in that city (Capital Region Planning Board, 1969) showed that in their sample of 801 retired people, 640 had been employed prior to age 65 and only 46 percent of these had worked in Victoria. The study indicates that 25 percent had come from the Prairies, 12 percent from other parts of B.C., 10 percent from Ontario and Quebec, and so provides evidence of the attraction of mild climate for older people.

This difference in the attractiveness of cities may be an important factor in future concentration patterns. Unfortunately, the migration data required to examine these patterns are not currently available. At present, only some preliminary migration data, aggregated to the provincial level, are available.

Migration Patterns of the Elderly

A recent study of the interprovincial migration of the elderly (Rowe and Pong, 1978) based on Old Age Security and census data leads to two general conclusions. First, it appears that the *patterns* of migration among the elderly are quite similar to those of the general population. Second, the *rate* of migration by the elderly tends to be low in comparison to the general population (5.3 per 1,000 as compared with 18.1 per 1,000 in the general population), but there is something of a peak around retirement age and the peak approaches the migration rate of the general population.

The small discrepancies between the migration patterns of the elderly and of the general population that do exist suggest that there is a degree of return migration around age 65. This could be accounted for by newly retired people returning to their "home towns". If this is a pattern which continues, it may have important impact on the future concentration of elderly in Canada.

Only Saskatchewan and Quebec appear to show a migration loss greater than their gains. Ontario and Quebec had the lowest out-migration rates (2.9 per 1,000 and 4.8 per 1,000, respectively). The highest in-migration rates were in British Columbia (11.4 per 1,000) and Alberta (11.0 per 1,000), while Quebec (1.7 per 1,000) followed by Ontario (4.2 per 1,000) had the lowest rates. The greatest effects of movement by the elderly were in British Columbia and Alberta. In Table 4, the migration rates by sex for each province show that British Columbia receives the most elderly, while Alberta has the next highest in-migration followed by Ontario.

These data serve as a possible harbinger of the future distribution of elderly in Canada. They suggest that some provinces are likely to receive a significant influx of older people and therefore will be far above the national

TABLE 4:

NET MIGRATION RATES

Province	Age	Male	Female
Newfoundland	55-59	−2.79	0.77
	60-64	1.63	2.89
	65+	−1.49	−0.26
Prince Edward Island	55-59	3.05	4.52
	60-64	6.89	4.62
	65+	0.23	1.58
Nova Scotia	55-59	1.66	2.07
	60-64	2.44	3.82
	65+	0.61	1.78
New Brunswick	55-59	1.62	1.77
	60-64	4.77	3.52
	65+	−0.07	0.14
Quebec	55-59	−0.22	0.32
	60-64	−0.10	1.36
	65+	−0.90	−0.49
Ontario	55-59	1.72	2.04
	60-64	2.84	4.53
	65+	2.05	2.09
Manitoba	55-59	0.07	−1.06
	60-64	0.08	2.73
	65+	−0.02	0.61
Saskatchewan	55-59	−3.17	−3.12
	60-64	−2.01	−1.64
	65+	−3.84	−3.09
Alberta	55-59	−0.67	1.27
	60-64	1.94	2.49
	65+	0.70	3.42
British Columbia	55-59	7.23	9.16
	60-64	9.57	10.46
	65+	4.53	4.62

SOURCE: Rowe and Pong, 1978.

average in the proportion of elderly. For these provinces — and some specific cities within them — preparation to meet the changing needs of the population will have to occur quite soon.

Conclusion

The data provided here document a number of important trends. First, the population of the country is aging steadily, with those over 65 continuing to represent a growing proportion of the population. While this proportion will increase to more than 12 percent by the turn of the century, this will still fall within the range found in many other western industrial nations.

Within these national parameters, there are likely to be some important variations in the growth of the elderly population, with some provinces and cities experiencing this growth sooner and to a greater extent than others. For example, British Columbia, which already houses a relatively high proportion of elderly, can be expected to continue to attract large numbers of elderly, with the result being a very large number and proportion of elderly in that province. Within the province, some cities, such as Victoria, can also expect to see the influx of older people continue. As a result, these places will be in the vanguard of those experiencing the important shifts in the kinds of housing, cultural facilities, and social services required by the increasingly vocal and powerful elderly.

Within the limitations of currently available data, there appears to be little basis for alarm. Adequate time is available for planning and preparing for the changing needs in services that will accompany the expected population changes. But in some parts of the country and particularly in some cities, those preparations must be put in motion now if the needs and demands of the elderly are to be met.

4

SOCIAL POLICY AND THE ELDERLY*

Neena L. Chappell
Department of Social and Preventive Medicine
University of Manitoba

The current situation of Canada's elderly is closely linked with federal social policy. This is evident from their economic situation: 55 percent were receiving all or part of the guaranteed income supplement in 1976. In other words, over half have such minimal income, even after receiving the universal old age security payment, that additional public funds are necessary for their survival. Furthermore, all federal assistance programs together with provincial supplements total an amount less than the poverty line set by the Economic Council of Canada (Dulude, 1978:41-45; Collins, 1978:102).

For a better understanding of why a majority of our elderly live in poverty, this chapter examines the historical development of social policy from the beginning of Confederation to the present. This history is restricted to a discussion of legislation relating to the elderly and the working assumptions reflected in this legislation. Many other issues, such as voluntary agencies, housing policy, familial support systems, etc., which are also relevant for the societal position of the elderly are not discussed.

The First Century of Social Policy

In 1867 neither income security nor social service programs were an issue in the formation of Confederation. The British North America Act made no mention of welfare measures and the government's minimal contribution was limited to poor-relief administered at the local level. Those in need were left to rely mainly on private charities or religious organizations. This, of course, reflected the working assumption of the time: individuals are responsible for their own resources, for obtaining and retaining employment, and for providing for the contingencies of life including old age services, health services, and others. However, the BNA Act did assign responsibility for quarantine centres and marine hospitals as well as for "special" groups (such as the Armed Forces and veterans) to the federal government and responsibility for other hospitals, asylums, charities, and charitable institutions to the provinces (Bryden, 1974:20-22; Government of Canada, 1970:16-20). The particular significance of this allocation lay in the fact that any jurisdiction not specifically assigned federal responsibility necessarily falls within the provincial domain. Since health and welfare were not specifically mentioned,

---

*Prepared for this volume. The research for this paper was supported by a National Health Research Scholar award (No. 6607-1137-48) to the author.

they would therefore be considered provincial areas when they arose as issues later.[1]

The market ethos, which left each individual family to care for itself, prevailed into the 1920s. The few exceptions which did exist were either limited or implemented for reasons other than social welfare. For example, the Annuities Act of 1908 had little effect, as few people took advantage of it. Workmen's compensation was instituted less as a social security measure than as a means to end lawsuits against employers by injured workmen. Custodial care for the mentally ill was used primarily to remove the "insane" from the community (Government of Canada, 1970:34). The twenties, however, did see the federal government's first major intervention in old age income security with the passing of the Old Age Pensions Act in 1927. Despite lobbies against such a program by private insurance companies (Bryden, 1974:58-59), it established a national, non-contributory, means-tested plan, providing for twenty dollars a month at age seventy (Barber, 1972:11; National Health and Welfare, 1974:9). It was also a cost-shared, federal-provincial partnership incorporating federal power to make grants to the provinces while maintaining provincial power to legislate and administer.

In the economic depression of the 1930s, with heavy unemployment and agricultural distress, the financial resources of the municipalities became unable to provide relief. This, together with at least partial recognition that the causes of unemployment and declining income were national and international, led the federal government to greater involvement in national income provisions. Assistance came as special grants in aid, made on an *ad hoc*, year-to-year basis. Although Ottawa funded at least half the costs, it continued to insist that unemployment and other relief expenditures were primarily the responsibility of the provinces (Barber, 1972:11; Government of Canada, 1970:36).

The thirties also brought a change in the working assumption of policy-makers. It was recognized that individuals could become destitute through the exigencies of life and through no fault of their own. The values of independence and self-sufficiency, however, were still dominant, reflected in the belief that, while it was a public responsibility to provide for those who could not work (such as the aged, the blind, the disabled), such provision should not discourage the incentive to work and to save for one's own retirement (National Health and Welfare, 1973:4-6,17,20). It was after the Depression and two world wars, in a climate of postwar prosperity, that this new assumption was implemented and the so-called welfare state introduced.

The many policies enacted in the period 1940-70 were aided by the efforts of various interest groups (such as trade unions, welfare associations, and the aged and their children), all of whom helped to make income and social security a political issue. The recognition of these issues was reflected in the establishment of the federal Department of National Health and

Welfare in 1945 (Bryden, 1974:183-88). Furthermore, the legislation which evolved was primarily directed towards universal rather than group-specific benefits, although some legislation was aimed explicitly toward the aged.

In 1940 an amendment to the BNA Act added unemployment insurance to the list of exclusive federal powers. In 1948 concern with insufficient hospitals for the sick led to the establishment of the National Health Grant Program through which the federal government agreed to share the cost of hospital construction with the provinces. An amendment to the BNA Act in 1951 conferred non-exclusive authority on Parliament to make laws in relation to non-contributory, universal, old age pensions resulting in Old Age Security payments to all persons 70 and over (later lowered to age 65) and a means-tested payment to those 60-65 years of age. The Unemployment Assistance Act was passed in 1956. The Hospital Insurance and Diagnostic Services Act of 1957 insured hospital care for the entire population, through a fiscal policy in which the federal government agreed to share the cost of running hospitals (excluding tuberculosis hospitals and sanatoria, institutions for the mentally ill, and care institutions, such as nursing homes and homes for the aged). In 1960 the guaranteed income supplement program gave additional funds to old-age pensioners whose income was less than $1,620 a year. In 1964, the 1951 amendment to old age pensions was extended to an income-tested supplement, including survivors' disability benefits irrespective of age. In 1965/66 the Medical Care Act was passed (although not implemented until 1968) providing a national insurance scheme for physician services, and the 1966 Canada Assistance Plan provided social assistance to anyone in need whatever their age or reason for lack of income. The Canada Assistance Plan filled gaps, paying for health-care services not covered by hospital insurance and medicare (eg., homes for the aged and nursing homes). Based on income, it replaced the 1956 Unemployment Assistance Act, old age assistance, and blind and disabled persons allowances. It was also in 1966 that the Canada/Quebec Pension Plan became effective (and after a ten-year transition period became fully effective in 1976 [Bryden, 1974:8,104,125; Health and Welfare, 1970:8,94; Lee, 1975; LeClair, 1975; Collins, 1978:112,117]).[2]

By the end of the first century, then, Canada had evolved what Collins (1978:61) calls "six layers" of provision for the elderly: old-age security payments, guaranteed-income supplements, Canada/Quebec Pension Plan, and different forms of provincial supplements (including decreased property taxes and health premiums, decreased transportation costs, etc.), as well as private pension plans and private savings. In addition, hospital and physician services were insured and the Canada Assistance Plan provided for services not included in these two. In 1967-68 income and social security programs totalled some 10.4 percent of the GNP (Government of Canada, 1970:52). However, despite this growth in public programs, the seventies brought with it increasing dissatisfaction on the part of the elderly, of welfare organizations, of both provincial and federal governments, and of others.

The Seventies

Although the three decades prior to 1970 brought a proliferation of policies (enacted, amended, and/or replaced), the average yearly income for all elderly males was just over $4,000 and for elderly women just over $2,000 in 1971 (Penning, 1978:99-101). The low level of benefits from public programs, on which most elderly depended, accounts for this situation. Few have income from private sources. Private pension plans are available only to those who work in the paid labour force, excluding most women, especially among those who are elderly today. For those who are employed, private pensions are scaled to earnings (C/QPP operates in the same way). Many do not provide spouses' benefits and those which do often provide minimal levels that are terminated on the death of the husband. In addition, few Canadians can afford to save. Dulude estimates only the top 20 percent of income groups between the ages of 45 and 64 have sufficient income to save, after meeting basic needs (Dulude, 1978; Collins, 1978). In other words, despite the existence of many programs, the benefits are insufficient to keep most elderly out of poverty. This has led to a general questioning of the country's social security programs.

The low level of benefits, of course, reflects the belief that payments which are too high will discourage younger persons from saving for their own retirement and older persons from accepting paid employment. While this can be viewed as consistent with the market ethos, it ignores the fact that few Canadians earn sufficient money to save during their younger years and, once they reach 65 there is compulsory retirement in all provinces except Manitoba (private sector only) and New Brunswick (Dulude, 1978:59) and a general discrimination against hiring older persons across the country. The changing market conditions have not helped the elderly's dilemma. In 1921, fully 59.6 percent of men 65 or over and 6.6 percent of women were employed in paid labour but these figures dropped to 20.0 percent and 5.1 percent respectively in 1971 (Long Range Planning, 1973:D-6). Most of the employed men in 1921 were working on farms, an employment area which has shrunk considerably over the years to be replaced by employment in business where there is more likely to be compulsory retirement. These figures demonstrate the ability and willingness of the elderly to work in paid employment, when the opportunity is provided. Said another way, the working assumptions behind current legislation have not changed significantly since the Depression. They still maintain the values of self-sufficiency but in a society which does not provide the opportunity for such independence (Dulude, 1978; Collins, 1978).

The concession to the market ethos has also resulted in the maintenance of the gap between the haves and the have-nots, leaving almost unchanged the income inequalities among Canadians (Canadian Council on Social Development, 1973:94; Taylor, 1978). While income redistribution resulting from transfer payments does involve *intergenerational* distribution, Bryden (1974:206-10), Collins (1978), and Pesando and Rea (1977:75,97-99,113-117) all come to the conclusion that *class* redistribution is minimal. The public pension system is progressive (i.e., the amount of wealth transferred decreases as permanent income increases) at the bottom of the income scale but regressive (i.e., the amount of wealth transferred increases with permanent income) in the upper ranges so that the main burden is on those in the lower-middle income range and below to assume a disproportionate share of income maintenance for those who have been reduced by age to the bottom of the income scale. Women, of course, are the dominant fraction of poorly paid workers who subsidize both the state and private pension systems. Although old age security payment, guaranteed income supplement, and provincial supplements alter the regressivity of C/QPP somewhat, the total package is progressive only at the lower levels. And the old age tax exemptions are even less progressive since they provide more saving for those with more money.

While the income being transferred to the elderly remains minimal, the cost of both these payments and of health care continues to rise. From 1970 to 1975 the growing population of elderly people, cost-of-living increases, and improvements in benefits all contributed to a substantial increase in expenditures for old age security, guaranteed income supplement, and spouses' allowance, an increase in excess of 100 percent (Health and Welfare Canada, 1976a:5). Health costs were increasing annually by 12 to 16 percent and costing 7.1 percent of the GNP in 1971. An increased awareness of cost escalation resulted in a federal/provincial review in the early seventies.

As well as providing a discussion of increasing costs, this review also served as a forum for the provinces' growing dissatisfaction with federal interference in provincial jurisdictions. The provinces still formally maintained responsibility for the health area and administered the programs, but the federal government had taken the initiative in income maintenance during the expansion years. Ottawa's responsibility for statistics permitted it to develop uniform standards for benefits, thereby influencing planning and development. In addition, Ottawa's power to finance allowed it to specify the requirements to be met for the provinces to receive health-care funds. Ottawa, for example, defined the institutions and services for which cost would be shared in the hospital insurance program, as well as the formula for sharing. The provinces did have an "opting out" arrangement (agreed to in 1964), but the financial advantages generally meant that they in fact "opted in".

The federal government's power to influence program development is evidenced in the hospital construction grants. While initially designed to provide a needed service, these grants were totalling over $60 million by the mid-sixties. From their inception in 1948 to 1970, Ottawa had approved the cost for over 130,000 beds and 15,000 bassinets in newborn nurseries. The result was what some perceived as an oversupply of acute-care beds and escalating costs which led to the phasing out of the grants beginning in 1967 and ending in 1972.

Finally, the national health insurance plans which were cost-shared at the federal level had resulted in an expansion of the traditional, "medical" view of health and health care. More than ever, the personal health-care system was oriented to treating existing illness, rather than developing alternative forms such as preventive, custodial, and home care (Lalonde, 1974:12,25). The coverage provided by both hospital and medical insurance resulted in this development; the former provides for care in hospitals, outpatient clinics, and medical and nursing schools. Services by non-medical personnel are covered only if the facility is listed as a hospital. The latter provides the services by or under the supervision of a physician. Andreopoulos (1975) and LeClair (1975) have demonstrated the profound effect this public policy has had on "medicalizing" our health-and-welfare system. Because hospital insurance began first, every town and city was encouraged to build hospitals, and physicians were given an incentive to hospitalize their patients. Then medicare committed funds to "sick" care (without the decrease in the number of physicians predicted by some).

While both the federal and provincial governments espouse support for the position that a patient should not be hospitalized unless absolutely necessary, cost-sharing with other facilities such as nursing homes (unless the patient is on welfare) or health professionals who are not working with physicians has not been established. Direct expenditures on health are mostly physician-centred, including medical care, hospital care, laboratory tests, and prescription drugs. Adding dental care and the services of those such as optometrists and chiropractors, the personal health-care system can be seen as mainly oriented to curing what in many cases could have been prevented. (It has been estimated that for each physician the system incurs about $50,000 in expenses for his or her services and about $100,000 for hospital care, laboratory testing, special nursing care, etc. (see Andreopoulos, 1975:5).

The lack of non-medical services is particularly relevant for the elderly. As Havens (1977) pointed out after her study of Manitoba in 1971, available residential resources are best able to meet the needs of the elderly at the extremes (either very sick or very well) but less able to meet the needs of those in the intermediate range (see also Neysmith, this volume). Non-residential resources show a low ability to meet need. Similarly, Dulude (1978:92) notes that 45 percent of the over 100,000 elderly in nursing homes in 1975 were in "self-sufficient" or "level 1" care and therefore probably able to live in the community if support services were available. Although the Department of National Health and Welfare established a committee for developing pilot home-care programs as early as 1957, there were only 26 programs operating in six provinces by 1967 (National Health and Welfare, 1970). While today (in 1978) most communities provide VON, Canadian Arthritic and Rheumatism Society, Canadian Red Cross Society, and visiting homemaker services, Manitoba is the only province to provide a universal home-care program. In some provinces medical authorization is still required (Shapiro, 1978).

To summarize, the seventies have seen a critical review of existing income security and social welfare programs which affect the elderly. The income security payments are too minimal to provide an adequate standard of living; they maintain income differences between the haves and the have-nots; and they suggest a stagnation of the working assumption behind such programs since the 1930s rather than a recognition of societal changes which have decreased the elderly's opportunities for self-maintenance. The cost of both income security and social welfare programs to the federal and the provincial governments has been increasing at an alarming rate; and the provinces have become increasingly dissatisfied with federal interference within areas of provincial responsibility. Finally, public policy, instituted primarily at the federal level, has expanded a medicalization of the health-care system to the neglect of non-medical aspects.

With a growing awareness of these problems, it seems reasonable to ask what is being done, if anything. Unfortunately, the answer does not indicate substantial change, at least in the near future. Turning first to income payments, it seems clear that cost considerations will prevent any significant improvement from the public purse. A recent address by the federal minister of Health and Welfare (Begin, 1978) supports this conclusion. A policy of economic independence for the elderly was praised but it was also noted that since government pensions are not sufficient to maintain the elderly in our society, private pensions should be more accessible and equitable. It would appear that the public sector has done what it is going to do in this area, a situation which leaves two-thirds of Canada's older population living below the poverty line.

Although not promising, there is nevertheless a mechanism now established for a health-care system which includes non-medical services for the elderly. As a result of the review undertaken in the early 1970s and the expressed provincial dissatisfaction, a "block-funding" approach was adopted in 1977 for health services. Ottawa agreed to provide the provinces with a lump-sum payment for such services, freeing them from having to shape their health care to federal cost-sharing criteria and indeed even from spending the money on health care. At the same time it gives them some financial security. The Social Services Financing Act of 1978 provided the same block-funding arrangement for social services. (This new bill replaces welfare services provided under the Canada Assistance Plan but not direct social assistance to individuals.) Block-funding will, of course, permit the flexibility for the provinces to develop non-medical-care facilities and community support services to help maintain the elderly in the community. Whether the provinces will utilize this opportunity for these purposes, especially in a period of economic restraint, remains to be seen.[3]

While others have suggested several alternatives for improving the present system, the purpose of this chapter has not been directed towards such a goal. Rather, the aim has been to acquaint the reader with the historical development of public policy which relates to the elderly, for a better understanding of their current situation.

Notes

1. In 1928 a Committee of the House of Commons investigated several social security measures, including insurance. During 1935 it placed the Employment and Social Insurance Act on the statute books, which would have allowed the federal government to directly administer a health and welfare program financed by premium payments. The legislation, however, was found to be unconstitutional in the courts. The result was that provincial responsibility for health care was reconfirmed (National Health and Welfare, 1974:3).

2. The legislation mentioned here is intended only as an overview and is not meant to be comprehensive. The interested reader should pursue additional readings. Similarly, neither the role played by various interest groups nor provincial differences have been detailed (see, for example, Andreopoulos, 1975, for a discussion of the Canadian Medical Association's involvement in the national health insurance program). However, the major acts which have relevance for Canada's elderly have been highlighted. Later legislation has introduced minor change, but left the situation largely similar to that at the end of the 60s. (For example, spouse's allowance was introduced under old age security and cost-of-living increases were added to various programs in the 1970s.)

3. The provinces, during the winter of 1979, decided to reject the offer of block funding from Ottawa. Such a decision reflects a continued priority on traditional medical services and education, rather than on personal social services.

5

A GENERATIONAL-CONFLICT PERSPECTIVE FOR GERONTOLOGY

Joseph A. Tindale
Department of Sociology
York University

and

Victor W. Marshall
Department of Behavioural Science
University of Toronto

Most gerontology has focused on the adjustment of individuals to an ongoing social system, failing to recognize that life in society is characterized by conflict, negotiation, and compromise over politico-economic and other interests (Collins, 1975:20-21; Marshall and Tindale, 1978-79). In this chapter, we would like to bring together some of the material on age stratification with some theorizing about social class which remains rare in gerontology. Our intent is to present the outline of a theoretical approach which we feel is needed to comprehend some basic dimensions of aging today and in the future.

From Concensus Theory to Stratification Theory to Class Theory

As we have already argued (Marshall and Tindale, 1978-79), gerontology is an individualistic discipline, a tinkering trade where individuals are asked to adjust to systemic demands. The major theoretical strands of social gerontology and the social psychology of aging (and most of the former is, in fact, the latter) all utilize a notion of equilibrium and downplay conflict. We argued (1978-79) that disengagement theory postulates a moving equilibrium as society and the individual smoothly sever their ties; activity theory argues that the equilibrium usually and ideally continues with the individual linked firmly to the society. In addition, developmental theory argues that the life course is a series of movements from equilibrated plateau to equilibrated plateau (see, for example, Brim, 1976; Levinson *et al.*, 1978). The general thrust of gerontological scholarship has been to view any lack of fit between individual and society as requiring changes in the former rather than the latter.

Hendricks and Hendricks (1977:119-26) treat age-stratification theory as one of the "emerging theories" and indeed refer to it as the most promising development in social gerontology. The theoretical model (for it is not a tightly organized theory) has been developed by Matilda White Riley in association, principally, with Marilyn Johnson and Anne Foner (Foner, 1974, 1975, 1978a; Foner and Kertzer, 1978; Riley, 1971, 1976; Riley, Johnson, and Foner, 1972). The perspective views age strata as cross-cutting class strata, playing their part in social differentiation through the ordering of people and roles. "Thus each age stratum is composed of people similar in age or life stage, who tend to share capacities, abilities, and motivations related to age. Age is also a criterion for entering or leaving roles, and for the different rewards and obligations associated with these roles. In short, age is a basis of 'structured social inequality'" (Foner, 1974).

A generational-conflict theory of aging can build upon the advances of age-stratification theory, but a shift in emphasis is required. As Hendricks and Hendricks (1977:124) indicate, age-stratification theory does not deal explicitly with factors exogenous to age structures, such as profound historical events, even though the importance of these is recognized. It rests on a concept of cohort, paying only lip-service to generation (Foner [1974] would be an exception). Moreover, the intentional participation in social process tends, Hendricks and Hendricks argue, to be downplayed or ignored in age-stratification formulations. Yet consciousness of stratum position is one of the defining characteristics of class and is a precursor and necessary precondition for class-like action. Finally, and most importantly, it must be stressed that age-stratification theory is not primarily a theory of stratification in relation to economic conditions. Rather, it is a perspective stressing the allocation of people in a division of labour; and of socialization of individuals to an acceptance of that allocation.

Rather than focusing on differences in class, status, and power of various age groups, age-stratification theory emphasizes the behavioural and attitudinal implications of individual aging interacting with cohort flow. Individual aging includes psychological and physiological change or development and age-related role changes; while cohort flow refers to the fact that as one cohort follows another, members of all undergo their aging in different historical periods (Foner, 1974; Riley, 1976). While individuals within cohorts, and cohort groups, may vary in rankings of rewards, power, and prestige, in age-stratification theory these differences tend to be viewed as continuous, rather than qualitative; and no dynamic relations between different strata (or classes) are postulated.

The above difference in emphasis recapitulates the disagreement between European sociologists who follow, in various ways, the Marxist tradition and American sociologists who tend to focus on social stratification. The latter see differences of degree rather than those based on fundamental conflicts of interest (the position taken by Marxist scholars). The distinction is nicely articulated by Ossowski (1963).

None the less, the foundation for developing a class analysis is readily available in age-stratification theory. To build on this foundation, it is necessary to clearly articulate the following concepts: generation, cohort, class, conflict, interest, and consciousness.

For sociological purposes, generation will be the predominant unit of analysis rather than cohort. A *cohort* consists of individuals born at approximately the same time and who move through the life cycle together. The definition of the boundaries of cohorts is arbitrary, and based primarily on practical rather than theoretical considerations (Maddox and Wiley, 1976, p.16). A *generation* is a cohort, large proportions of whose members have experienced significant socio-historical changes. As Foote (1960, cited in Cain, 1964:302) has noted, "the turning points between generations are more sociological than chronological.... What distinguishes one generation from another is not a sequence of small gradations but rather marked qualitative divergencies, occurring rather suddenly." The important historical changes which have probably contributed to the development of different generations among the series of aging cohorts in Canada would include all wars in which Canadians have fought, the Depression, and the introduction of the birth-control pill.

Some generational marker experiences are more dramatic than others: they affect more people more severely or strongly. Others have a target impact on one segment of the population cross-cut by age, but spin-off or relational effects on others. For example, it might be argued that "the pill" had a dramatic direct effect on young women of "child-bearing age" for the first time following its introduction in the early 1950s; but spin-off effects on men of the same age, on parents, and others cannot be denied.

Our understanding of *class* is one composed of conflicting interest groups who, because of their relation to property, possession of status, and consciousness of their relative position, exercise power in a historical and dialectical fashion to impose their interests on each other.[1] Differences of *interest* are inevitable, because the gain of one party is often at the expense of the other. These are created by the division of labour and by the development of private ownership of property. As long as surplus value is extracted from the worker who produced it and given to another who did not, there will exist exploitation and the basis for different interests.[2]

Generations can also possess different interests which at times reside within class boundaries and in other instances cross class lines. While class interests are constructed in history, so too are the relationships between cohorts of people. Any particular cohort develops a cohort biography as the life of the group is carried forward. Within any particular cohort there will be individual experiential differences, but our focus rests on the cohort itself. When large proportions of the membership of a cohort share typical biographies in relation to significant historical events and come to constitute a "generation", we have the basis for different generational interests.

The movement from cohort to generation implies the possibility of a qualitative development of *consciousness*; that is, shared historical experiences of cohort members may lead to significant changes in consciousness (just as, in Marxist terms, shared class experiences may lead to the development of class consciousness). At this point, generational conflict becomes a possibility.[3]

For conflict analysis, it is not necessary to argue that generational consciousness is "true consciousness" or correct recognition of generational interests (nor is a parallel assumption necessary for class analysis). What is necessary, however, is to delineate how perceived generational differences of interest result. Such delineation is part and parcel of the research process which would bring theory together with empirical data. Research with this perspective must establish generations by isolating the shared historical experiences of cohort members and identify conceptions of generational interest and patterns of generational conflict. Moreover, it is our belief that the coincidence of class and generational interests is a phenomenon little recognized, yet important, and likely to be of growing importance in the future.

Class-based Generational Conflict

Class-based generational conflict has several dimensions which roughly follow along the lines of differential interests already established. On-going bases for class conflict founded on inequality of income and alienation from labour provide sources for generational conflict between cohorts.

The fact that greater than fifty percent of Canada's aged fall below government poverty lines is an established feature of life for our aged (Collins, 1978:43).[4] There are demographic and social changes afoot which, based on the low incomes of working-class aged, point to considerable tension ahead. Leroy Stone (1977) argues that by modestly increasing the labour-force participation rates of the aged much of the projected financial burden, as the "baby boom" ages, could be alleviated. He envisages that a substantial portion of today's young workers will "raise an irresistable clamour" to be allowed to continue as paid members of the labour force beyond some arbitrary retirement age.

This scenario is problematic. To this point employment opportunities for the aged have not opened up (Statistics Canada, 1977c). A general problem of increasing unemployment makes it exceedingly difficult for the aged to increase their participation rates. Therefore, if Stone's proposal for easing the financial burden is to occur, the likelihood of generational conflict ensuing is high. The young, especially those under 25 who traditionally have higher rates of unemployment than those 25-64, may expect the aged to move over and pass on their jobs. Even where companies offer early retirement at full or near full pension as an incentive to get rid of highly paid senior people, some of these older employees will resist (Foner and Kertzer, 1978).[5]

While early retirement at full pension theoretically alleviates the poverty of some aged, it does not take into account the large numbers of people who are not entitled to private pensions (Powell and Martin, this volume) nor does this fit with Stone's proposal, which depends on some of the aged continuing to be producers after age 65. While early retirement can be offered to some, others will demand the right to continue working for reasons of money but also because they argue they have a right to continue being useful both to society and to themselves.

Lofland (1968) suggested that generational conflict would soon come to take on an importance roughly equivalent to existing concerns like capitalist/worker tensions. The relevance of age does not rest simply with the proportionately growing number of aged (Neugarten, 1973). The bases for conflict lie with the tensions and deprivations of economic and cultural life which in cases of relative scarcity sometimes pit various cohorts of people against each other in generational conflict. This structural base for conflict undercuts Neugarten's somewhat casual generalization (1973) that: "Under fortunate circumstances, an equilibrium is created whereby all age groups receive an appropriate share of the goods of the society and an appropriate place for their different values and world views." The potential conflict is always there: equilibrium is never achieved.

Foner (1974) is closer to the mark when she asks, "Why do sharp political struggles between young and old erupt only sporadically?" She argues that membership in non-age-graded associations provides opportunities for cross-socialization to opposing political views and that age, in being both inevitable and universal, results in mobility or cohort flow which continuously moves younger persons to see where their future interests lie while allowing the aged to tolerantly sympathize with the frustrations of the young. These two conflict-reducing mechanisms, she argues (1974; also Foner and Kertzer, 1978), are most effective where the issues are material and least so in cases of ideal or ideational disputes.

In her view, material disputes across generation boundaries unite workers of all ages in a fight to protect class interests. Ideal disputes on the other hand, such as the "radicalism" of the late 1960s, are seen as challenges to the system as a whole and thus to the status middle-aged and older persons have earned for themselves. The result is generational, as opposed to class, conflict; and these issues are of intermittent importance simply because such generalized upheavals of principles are themselves sporadic (Foner, 1974).

Generational conflict is, however, not limited to the intermittent emergence of ideational issues. Thomas (1976), in his study of generational conflict in sixteenth- and seventeenth-century England, reveals how older manual labourers were gradually given less and less hard labour to do by younger workers until they were eventually pushed out of a job entirely, and this before their physical condition demanded they do less work. Class tensions brought about by low demand for labour put pressure on all workers so that when the shop owners initiated a process of gradual exclusion (Mathiesen, 1974) against their older workers, they had the support of younger workers. And although there were undoubtedly some generation-based tensions, exclusion operated as an individual cooling out process, thereby minimizing conflict. A modern-day parallel exists whenever senior workers are encouraged to take early retirement.

Some Promising Areas of Research

Streib (1976) points to an irony in the study of age and social class. While gerontologists have concentrated on the association between aging and systemic poverty, it is also the case that the very rich are disproportionately aged, with the median age of 66 centi-millionaires, according to *Fortune Magazine*, being 65 years of age. Streib argues that this leads to some important research questions dealing with the relationship of age to the accumulation of fortunes, the transmission of wealth, and the consciousness of class among the very wealthy; and he stresses the importance of "the tax structure of a capitalist society" in this regard. Furthermore Streib argues that the absence of age solidarity and the maintenance of class solidarity is evidenced by the failure of the aged wealthy to take steps to ameliorate the plight of the poor in their age class.

Rose (1965) argues that one indicator of potential development of aging class consciousness is the age segregation implied in developments such as retirement communities. However, as these communities tend to attract the wealthier segments of the aging population, upper-class or middle-class consciousness may well prevail over age consciousness which would link to the deprived aged who are the concern of Rose. In general, we would contend that a major unrecognized debate within the literature of social gerontology is to assess the relative merits of the "young-old" thesis (Neugarten, 1974) and the "aging minority group" thesis (Rose, 1965; Streib, 1965). The former rests on a concensus view of society, while the latter rests on a view similar to that which we advocate. An adequate test of these contradictory models for the future can be easily formulated from a generational conflict perspective.

We are intrigued by the possibility of unrecognized generational conflict stemming from political policies aimed at securing the support of a large "baby boom" cohort. One such policy is rent control, which helps relatively young people secure inexpensive housing. However, a large proportion of small landlords, who are adversely affected by rent control, is aged.

Much more detailed research on the historical bases of age differentiation needs to be done. Keith Thomas argues that age was not a highly important basis of social differentiation in England until the period between the sixteenth to mid-eighteenth centuries (Thomas, 1976). In the sixteenth century a person asked his or her age might well reply with a round number or an even digit. Fischer (1977:82) claims this was common in America in the seventeenth century. Literacy and the development of parish registers contributed to the use of exact ages, as did the development of bureaucracies and the administration of civil rights and duties. Thomas and Fischer show that age gained over this period in social relevance, being increasingly tied to the regulation and administration of everyday life.

In early modern England, "the preference for age and seniority was shared by all those corporate institutions which set a value on hierarchy, stability, and continuity" (Thomas, 1976:208). To be more precise, "Essentially, it was men in their forties and fifties who ruled" (1976:211). Thomas also shows that class intersected with age, in that the normal rules of seniority could be bent by the inheritance and utilization of wealth. Almost every election produced a group of well-connected Members of Parliament under the age of 21; teenagers of fine families were knighted, and given commissions in the army and navy.

Thomas demonstrates that in the sixteenth and seventeenth centuries, there was "a sustained drive to subordinate persons in their teens and early twenties and to delay their equal participation in the adult world" (Thomas, 1976:214). Apprenticeship and formal education grew, as well as other means of prolonging infancy or childhood, such as restrictions against early marriage and strict prohibitions against alternative forms of sexual activity (Thomas, 1976; also Laslett, 1977). The relevancy of this analysis to contemporary concerns is readily apparent and is symbolized by the term "youth dependency ratio" which refers to children and others who are presumed to be still in school rather than in the work force.

There is great concern with the growth of the supposedly non-productive segments of the population at both ends of the life cycle, and the economic burden this may place on people in the middle of the age structure. Conflict because of this is anticipated by Neugarten (1973) who states,

> ...anger toward the old may also be on the rise. In some instances, because a growing proportion of power positions in the judiciary, legislative, business and professional arenas are occupied by older people, and because of seniority privileges among workers, the young and middle-aged become resentful. In other instances, as the number of retired increases, the economic burden is perceived as falling more and more upon the middle-aged taxpayer.

Conclusion

We have not, of course, set out a theory; rather, we have presented the rudimentary outlines of a generational-conflict perspective. Further research will lead to the articulation and testing of theory within this framework. There are undoubtedly many areas in social gerontology which are tangential to our concerns and for which this approach is not highly suitable, however we believe that many of the important questions in the field can benefit from the application of this approach.

Notes

1. Hochschild (1975:565, fn. 25) is instructive when she states:
We can distinguish between the bourgeoisie (those who own the mode of production on a large or small scale), the new middle class (professionals who sell their labour for wages but have authority over other workers), the working class (those who sell their labour for wages but have little or no authority over other workers), the lower classes and the chronically unemployed.

2. The important points are the control of the labour process by the employer and the relation of the employee's labour to property. As Marx (1890:180) argues:
The labour-process, turned into the process by which the capitalist consumes labour-power, exhibits two characteristic phenomena. First, the labourer works under the control of the capitalist to whom labour belongs....Secondly, the product is the property of the capitalist and not that of the labourer, its immediate producer.

3. We here ignore two other common uses of the cohort concept, which focus on demographic characteristics of people born at a given point in time and on lineage or familial uses of the term "generation" (Bengtson and Cutler, 1976).

4. Leo Johnson (1977) examined changes in purchasing power for selected occupations, in the period 1946-71. Of doctors, dentists, lawyers, and pensioners, only pensioners experienced a decline.

5. The Ontario Secondary School Teachers' Federation has suggested just such a policy (*Toronto Star*, May 6, 1978:c2) whereby early retirement at full pension would be offered as a means of protecting jobs. The money saved by not having to pay salaries to the newly retired individuals would in part be used to pay the pension, but the remainder of the money and the vacated spaces would be utilized to forestall a large number of anticipated future terminations of young teachers. If a large number of eligible senior teachers fail to take advantage of the scheme, the potential for conflict between these teachers and the younger ones eager to keep their jobs would be increased.

6

NO EXIT
An Interpretive Perspective
on Aging*

Victor W. Marshall
Department of Behavioural Science
University of Toronto

In this chapter I characterize the contrast between a *normative* and *interpretive* approach to aging, demonstrate the normative bias in current approaches to socialization in the gerontological literature, and indicate some ways in which the career and status passage concepts are particularly fruitful.

The Normative Bias of Socialization Theory

Most sociology, including that utilized in gerontology, reflects a normative bias. This point is made by Allan Dawe (1970), who sees the predominant theoretical tradition of sociology as stemming from a conservative reaction to the French Revolution. This sociology stresses the problem of order, the question of why there is not a "war of each against all". The solution to the Hobbesian problem places the link between the individual and society as near perfect. Through socialization processes conceived as highly efficient, the individual internalizes roles. Roles, the expectations for behaviour or complexes of norms appropriate for the incumbent of a given status or position, provide the mediating links between the individual and the society; for society is made up of role-behaviour. Internalization of roles thus implies that social norms become *constitutive*, rather than merely regulative, of the self. Conformity, then, is seen as normal and as not needing explanation. Only deviance needs to be explained, and the explanation rests on a notion of incomplete or warped socialization. A major contemporary exponent of this view is, of course, Talcott Parsons (1951), and the same description of normative sociology is given in Wrong's paper, "The Oversocialized Conception of Man in Modern Sociology" (1961). When Matilda Riley, *et al.* (1969) draw their approach to socialization in old age, "mainly from the

---

*This chapter is a condensed and slightly modified version of a paper entitled "No Exit: A Symbolic Interactionist Perspective on Aging", which appeared in *International Journal of Aging and Human Development*, Vol. 9, no. 4 (1978-79):345-58. The title change reflects a movement to a somewhat more general formulation of the perspective. Copyright 1979, by Baywood Publishing Company, Inc..

work of Parsons" they adopt this sociology of order conception. The approach is incorporated into age-stratification theory (see Tindale and Marshall, this volume). Another major exponent is Neugarten (Neugarten and Datan, 1973; Neugarten, Moore and Lowe, 1965).

Though taking issue with Neugarten and Riley on a number of points, Irving Rosow also takes a sociology-of-order conception of socialization:

Adult socialization is the process of inculcating new values and behavior appropriate to adult positions and group memberships. These changes are normally internalized in the course of induction or training procedures, whether formal or informal. They result in new images, expectations, skills, and norms as the person defines himself and as others view him (Rosow, 1974:3).

Rosow argues that "the transition to old age in America represents a special problem in adult socialization" because this transition differs from "normal status passages" in marking a movement

(1) to a *devalued position* (2) with *ambiguous* norms, (3) *role discontinuity*, and (4) *status loss* (5) that mobilizes *low motivation* or resistance to possible socialization (6) whose processes would be set in *informal contexts*. Thereby, on each factor, aging reverses the optimal conditions of socialization...(Rosow, 1974: 117—18).

According to Rosow there cannot be adequate socialization for old age because clear expectations for conduct in old age do not exist, and because aging individuals have neither the opportunity nor the incentive to internalize those expectations that do exist. This may well be the case, but it might also be that these considerations represent a rather restricted issue; for it is only within a normative sociology that internalization of *shared* expectations is seen as important.

An Interpretive Approach to Socialization

The second, less dominant sociological tradition outlined by Dawe encompasses the symbolic interactionist approach to sociology and other *interpretive*[1] theoretical approaches. This tradition, rooted in the Enlightenment impulse toward liberation, focuses on the ways in which individuals seek to gain control or mastery over their situations, relationships, and institutions. As with the *philosophes* the concern is with "how humans could regain *control* over essentially man-made institutions and historical situations". The extent to which norms are shared is not pre-judged. Rather than seeing order as obtaining in society because of semi-perfect internalization of the society by individuals, through socialization, this second sociology sees any departure from a Hobbesian state of chaos or anarchy in terms of two concepts: a concept of *central meaning* and a concept of *control*.

First, central meanings held by the individual (as contrasted to values shared by the members of a collectivity) are employed to link a biography together. Identity thus becomes an important concept. Let us call identity a sense of sameness or continuity of the organization of selves over time (after Erikson, 1957). Following Goffman (1963), the meaning attributed by an individual to his or her biography may be termed the individual or *felt* indentity; that view of the self (or selves) displayed for others may be termed the personal or *presented* identity; the meanings which others attribute to the self (or selves) may be termed the *social* identity. Individuals attempt to negotiate, in terms of felt identity, in a world where others cast social identities on them. One strategy actors use is through presentation of self (presented identity). The dimension of action is intrinsically related to meaning, for the self arises in social interaction, and situations which bring selves together are controlled by the imposition of meaning.

Second, "to control a situation is to impose one's definition upon the actors in that situation. The concept of control refers essentially to social relationships whose properties cannot be reduced to the individual definitions and courses of action from which they emerge" (Dawe, 1970). *Individuals negotiate with one another to work out some sense and semblance of order* (Strauss, *et al.*, 1963; Goffman, 1969), and that sense of order is always changing and subject to re-negotiation, as individuals bring together their biographically meaningful lines of action and attempt to exercise some control or power. Norms are not something "out there" to be learned, and internalized, and which thence determine behaviour; rather, norms are viewed as claims involved in, and outcomes of, continuous negotiation processes. As Blumer tells us, this is not so only for novel forms of interaction but for habitual or familiar interaction:

> We have to recognize that even in the case of pre-established and repetitive joint action each instance of such joint action has to be formed anew....Repetitive and stable joint action is just as much a result of an interpretative process as is a new form of joint action that is being developed for the first time....A gratuitous acceptance of the concepts of norms, values, social rules, and the like should not blind the social scientist to the fact that any one of them is subtended by a process of social interaction....*It is the social process in group life that creates and upholds the rules, not the rules that create and uphold group life* (Blumer, 1969:18-19. Italics mine).

In this perspective, norms are *invoked* in social interaction. We use conceptions of appropriate behaviour in our attempts to negotiate with others. We *sometimes* do as others say. But our conformity to the expectations of others (and their conformity to ours) is less massive than the normative, or social-order, perspective would suggest. For example, Neugarten (1970) suggests that:

> every society has a system of social expectations regarding age-appro-priate behavior. The individual passes through a socially-regulated

cycle from birth to death...a succession of socially-delineated age-statuses, each with its recognized rights, duties, and obligations....This normative pattern is adhered to, more or less consistently, by most persons....

Rosow (1974: 10-11, 52, 54-79) argues that normative expectations for the aged are *not* clear, and he bemoans this fact, but Neugarten argues that behaviour in the aged is under the strong influence of norms (1970):

For any social group it can be demonstrated that norms and age expectations act as a system of social controls, as prods and brakes upon behavior, in some instances hastening an event, in others, delaying it.

For Neugarten, normatively regulated old age exists as the general pattern and is *normal*; for Rosow it does not exist, but is none the less viewed as *normal*.

This position stands in marked contrast to that of the symbolic interactionists and interpretive sociologists. As Turner suggests (1962):

The actor is not the occupant of a position for which there is a neat set of rules — a culture or set of norms — but a person who must act in the perspective supplied in part by his relationship to others whose actions reflect roles that he must identify...testing inferences about the role of alter is a continuing element in interaction. Hence the tentative character of the individual's own role definition and performance is never wholly suspended.

The human capacity for socially *constructing* reality is emphasized by the interpretive sociologist, whose imagery of the actor portrays an individual searching for meaning, constructing identity, and seeking to direct interactions with others in ways compatible with that sense of identity. As Dawe argues, the key notion of this "second sociology"

is that of autonomous man, able to realize his full potential and to create a truly human social order only when freed from external restraint. Society is thus the creation of its members; the product of their construction of meaning, and of the action and relationships through which they attempt to impose that meaning on their historical situations (Dawe, 1970).

Aging as a Career or Status Passage

As Dawe notes, the capacity of an individual to control the situations of life varies (1974):

It depends partly on the nature and scope of situational definitions; partly on the relationship, in terms of projected outcomes, between the consequent courses of action; and partially on differential access to facilities and subjection to limiting conditions...the extent to which control depends upon normative, calculative and/or coercive mechanisms become empirical questions [*sic*].

The notions of career and status passage are useful in directing us to some appropriate empirical questions within this perspective. To speak of aging as a status passage is to point to a person negotiating a passage from one age-linked status to another, and then to others, finally coming to the end of the passage through life, at death. The older notion of "career" is closely related to that of "status passage". Both concepts correspond in the temporal domain to the negotiated-order concept discussed earlier:

> Just as an orientation toward the solution of everyday problems and the ongong negotiation of social order link people and their activities in a "horizontal" way, the activities of individuals themselves are linked "vertically" over time. The concept of "career" captures the nature of this vertical linkage (Hewitt, 1976: 177).

A career or a status passage may be thought of either from the perspective of the individual or from an objective perspective. Everett Hughes, who developed the present meaning of the career concept, makes the distinction:

> However one's ambitions and accomplishments turn, they involve some sequence of relations to organized life. In a highly and rigidly structured society, a career consists, *objectively*, of a series of status [*sic*] and clearly defined offices. In a freer one, the individual has more latitude for creating his own position or choosing from a number of existing ones...but unless complete disorder reigns, there will be typical sequences of position, achievement, responsibility, and even of adventure. The social order will set limits upon the individual's orientation of his life, both as to direction of effort and as to interpretation of its meaning. *Subjectively*, a career is the moving perspective in which the person sees his life as whole and interprets the meaning of his various attributes, actions, and the things which happen to him (Hughes, 1971: 137. Italics mine).

A number of dimensions of status passages, or careers, are outlined in the works of Becker, Glaser and Strauss, and Hughes.[2] *Objectively*, any status passage can be defined in terms of physical and social time and space. The duration may be long or short, and given meaning as such by others. The passage may be treated as preparatory, initiatory, educative, selective, or ritualistic. The passage may involve physical movement, or horizontal or lateral movement in social status. It may be viewed by others as desirable or undesirable, inevitable or optional, voluntary or involuntary, reversible or irreversible, repeatable or unique. The passage may occur collectively, aggregatively, or solo. It may be guided or controlled by others, or self, or collectively guided or controlled. If undergone with others, the degree to which co-passagees may communicate with others at the same stage of the passage, or ahead of them, might vary. The passage may vary in moral authority or societal legitimation.

Subjectively, people may be aware, in different degree, that they are actually undergoing a passage. Awareness of any of the aforementioned objective properties of the passage may vary. One may or may not decide, for example, to voluntarily accept an inevitable passage (e.g., to accept one's dying). One may attempt to seize, or may surrender, control over the passage. The passage, or subpassages may be viewed as of crucial or trivial importance.

This listing of objective and subjective properties of status passages (careers) is not exhaustive. What does this list have to do with socialization theory? Socialization theory in the normative tradition postulates that the lives of aging individuals will be shaped by the extent to which shared norms exist to define acceptable behaviour, and the extent to which these norms are internalized.

Status-passage theory postulates that the lives of aging individuals will be shaped by themselves, in the context of others, as they manipulate these properties and properties like them. Viewing later life as a status passage or career removes the artificial boundary which normative theorists have established between the individual and society. "Socialization," in the normative tradition, is a concept which provides an important link between the abstraction "individual" and the abstractions "society" or "group"; but these abstractions, I argue, mislead us. If life is viewed as a sequence of meaningful negotiations with others, we do not need the abstract concept "society", and thence no longer need the concept "socialization" *as an abstract concept*, except when discussing its use in previous work. There remains, however, one useful way to employ the term "socialization". The term may be used to refer to concrete attempts by some agents to shape the careers or status passages of others.

I will now suggest the fruitfulness of this approach to understanding later life. The degree of control over the passage becomes of central importance to aging persons.

No Exit: aging as a terminal status passage

People can exit from the marital-status passage at virtually any time (through desertion, separation, or divorce); they can skip school, have an abortion, quit their jobs. But aging, as noted by Glaser and Strauss, and as is evident to us all, is an *inevitable* status passage (1971: 15). There is an exit at the end, in death, but there is no way to escape having to go through the passage. This fact, as writers such as Heidegger have told us so well, places a special accent on the passage. Aging is a status passage unlike any other.

This point may become clearer by turning to research on medical students. Some studies, notably *The Student Physician* (Merton, Reader, and Kendall, 1957) stress the future-orientation of the students. As they pass through the status passage of the school, the students think of themselves as nascent professionals. The *Boys in White* study found the students pre-occupied with their present status (Becker, Geer, Hughes, and Strauss, 1961). They were too busy learning to be students to be concerned with learning to be doctors. They focused, not on the outcome of the passage, but on the passage itself. Their concerns, so evident in the *Boys in White* monograph, were to gain as much *control* over their status passage as possible.

The theoretical point I wish to stress is that individuals may be preoccupied in different measure either with "getting out" of the passage or with the passage itself. Although control over the passage is but one of many dimensions, it is particularly important in the case of aging, for there is no exit from the passage (except through death). With aging comes recognition that time is running out. Life, which has so often been viewed as a preparation for *something to come*, becomes preparation for dying and for death itself. Only the passage and its termination become relevant. Elsewhere I have argued that preparation for death involves the endeavour to make sense of death itself and to make sense of one's biography. This theme appears in disengagement theory, developmental ego-psychology, and in Butler's conception of the life-review process (Marshall, 1975b). The status passage of aging becomes expanded backward to encompass the entire biography of the person. Neugarten makes a similar argument in developmental terms (1966, 1970).

We human beings are fundamentally motivated to endow our experience in this world with meaning. Control over our biographies is sought through the creative re-construction of the past through reminiscence. I argue elsewhere that this process is most successful when it is conducted socially (Marshall, forthcoming).

Glaser and Strauss (1971: 15) argue that inevitable or non-reversible status passages require "that there be institutions and organizations to manage, direct and control them". But, as Rosow has shown, there is little institutional or organizational control over the inevitable and irreversible status passage of aging. Sub-passages which intersect in later life do, of course, come under institutional and organizational control: illness and chronicity as well as death and dying, come under the control of the health-care institution. Poverty, which is often age-related, brings the passage under organizational control within the social service/welfare institution. But significant areas of aging peoples' lives come under no one's control. This point is made most strongly by Rosow. While Rosow sees this as a "failure of socialization", we see it rather differently when we look at it from the interpretive perspective.

Absence of "socializing agents" may be cause for alarm or rejoicing, as is evident if we contrast the perspectives held by adolescents and by parents concerning the chaperoning of a party. When adults are not around to chaperone adolescents, their activity does not break down into a "war of each against all". Rather, they mutually regulate their behaviour, negotiating among themselves for some measure of individual and collective control over their situations (which, in this instance, frequently involves much competition if not conflict). Perhaps as adults enter the status passage of late life, something similar happens when they find themselves without chaperones, or "socializing agents". Perhaps they are able to work things out for themselves.

Institutionalization severely threatens the aged's ability to maintain status-passage control, for so much is structured for them, and compliance with institutional routines is deemed necessary to keep things "running smoothly" (Goffman, 1961; Marshall, 1975a, c; Posner, 1974). Only contrast the typical resident of a nursing home with the "bag lady" described by Sharon Curtin (1972: 91): "Tough, mean, ignorant. Formed by her society. But she was still quite a lady, quite a woman. She survived. She managed." The "bag lady" described by Curtin managed to maintain high degrees of status-passage control by cultivating great skills in managing the urban environment, and also by frightening other people away from her by real or presented craziness. Isolation was the price she paid for control.

Older people may be fortunate that there are few norms to guide their behaviour in later life, and few socializing agents or agencies. This situation leaves the aging at least relatively free from normative constraints (if often not free from objective constraints such as poverty, isolation, declining health). It is hoped that in this relative freedom they can seek, with others, to construct a passage through their last years which maximizes personal control.

It is a fundamental postulate of an interpretive social psychology that reality is socially constructed and sustained. This implies that *any and all aspects of status passage control can be viewed as socially constructed.* Hochschild (1973) gives us a portrayal of a group of older people who are given the opportunity to construct a way of life which gives them relatively high equanimity in the last years. She also points out (1973: 139) that Merril Court, the apartment-building community she studied, "was an unexpected community, an exception." Hochschild emphasizes that people gain some measure of control over their lives *interactionally*. Community facilitates the gaining of status passage control, whereas isolation prevents it (1973: 139; also Marshall, 1975a,c).

Not all who are isolated feel lonely and not all who feel lonely are isolated. But even for the confirmed urban hermit, isolation may be involuntary. Or rather, the choices of whom to see and talk with are made within an increasingly narrow band of alternatives.

The objective and subjective aspects of career or status passage must thus be brought together in any analysis. A study focused at the level of the individual's subjective status passage must of necessity shed light on objective properties of the passage. As Hughes (1937) puts it, "a study of careers...may be expected to reveal the nature and 'working constitution' of a society....In the course of a career the person finds his place within these forms, carries on his active life with reference to other people, and interprets the meaning of the one life he has to live." The degree of freedom to manipulate objective conditions (physical or social) is undoubtedly less than the degree of freedom to give a subjectively acceptable accent to these conditions. None of these illustrations make reference to the internalization of shared norms concerning appropriate age-related behaviour; yet they all refer to older people making their way through the later years.

Conclusion

I have suggested that socialization theory in gerontology (including the work of such exemplars as Neugarten, Riley, and Rosow) has focused on issues stemming from a normative perspective in which socialization is viewed as a process through which individuals come to internalize expectations for age-related conduct. While not denying the utility of this approach, I have argued that at the very least it ignores many important aspects of aging, and that its emphasis on shared expectations presents a distorted image of the processes of aging. Drawing on a distinct tradition in sociology which emphasizes the human capacity to construct and share meanings, and the human tendency to attempt to control, through symbolic interaction, situations in keeping with biographically meaningful intentions, I suggested the utility of the "status passage" and "career" concepts. These concepts, which have considerable currency within the symbolic-interactionist tradition, and are more generally congruent with interpretive sociology, lead to an enumeration of various properties of objective and subjective careers. The status passage of aging was described as a distinct career because there is "no exit" from it. Aging is one of the very few inevitable and irreversible status passages; and it of course encompasses sub-passages, such as childhood and dying, which are also inevitable and irreversible. But aging in later life is additionally distinctive in that the passage leads nowhere but to death. Because it is not preparatory for other statuses, as are many other status passages, passagees come to focus on issues of controlling the passage. Issues of status-passage control were illustrated in terms of the subjective-objective distinction. Subjective status-passage control centres on the construction and maintenance of identity in later life, and the relationship of identity to preparation for death. Status-passage control was then explored in relation to the situation of the aged in relation to others. One set of others might be deemed "agents of socialization", and includes those who socialize the aged into homes for the aged and hospitals. These reduce the amount of individual control which people may exert, whether they traverse the passage solo or in aggregate or collective fashion. Others can, however, assist in maintaining or creating status-passage control, for reality is constructed *socially*. The isolation of many aged constitutes an objective fact which forces them, in a sense, to live in a reality constructed by others, rather than controlling their passages through old age in a community of others.

One final point must be made. Our world is a world of meanings. Moreover, people do not always agree on meanings. Divergences in meanings point to the importance of active interpretation processes, and in turn suggest the importance of the "control" or "power" aspects of this perspective. Older people do not possess complete freedom to contruct a world of their choice. To say that our world is a world of meanings is not to say it is a world of ideas alone. The interpretive perspective, with its emphasis on the *processes* of negotiation, emphasizes this. The perspective, therefore, has much to offer gerontology not only as a social psychology, but in relation to structural approaches which emphasize power and control.

Notes

1. Dawe calls the "first" sociology a "sociology of order", and the "second" a "sociology of control". I will use the terms "normative" and "interpretive", respectively. The latter encompasses *selected* strands of symbolic interactionism, phenomenology, and neo-Marxist and ethno-methodological sociologies.

2. The careers/status passage notion is central to much of Hughes' work (1937; 1971), and influenced Becker and Strauss during their time at the University of Chicago (1956). The properties of status passage outlined here draw on Becker, Hughes, and particularly Glaser and Strauss (1971).

II

The Meaning of Age and Aging

Contemporary post-industrial societies provide few situations or occasions which bring the generations together. Except for familial contacts, which frequently bear ritual overtones when these involve the old or very old, most people spend much of their entire life, and especially their free time, with others who do not differ in age from them by more than five, ten, or fifteen years (Blau, 1973: 68-69; Rosow, 1967: 27). As a result, it is often difficult for the young to get a "feeling" for what it is like to be old. The articles in this section have been selected because they put flesh on the statistical skeleton of population data presented in some of the preceding selections. Many fictional accounts, and a few films, also admirably evoke a sense of the *meaning* of age and aging. These articles, however, offer something more: some conceptual tools which show the power of social science concepts in enhancing our understanding of later life.

Abu-Laban and Abu-Laban, in Chapter 7, systematically review the literature which suggests that the aged might be considered a minority group, comparing that possibility with the argument that women are also a minority group. The juxtaposition of the aged and women in their analysis is more than just pedagogically convenient, because the aged, and especially the older aged, are disproportionately women. Whether the aged are, or may come to be, a minority group in sociological terms depends in large measure on the economic status of both women and the aged. Readers may wish to compare this argument with that concerning the possibility of generational conflict presented in Chapter 5. Elsewhere (Marshall, 1979), I have contrasted this perspective with the more optimistic view of Bernice Neugarten (1974; 1979) that age will be less important as a differentiator of status in the future than it is now.

Judith Posner, in Chapter 8, argues that older women are doubly stigmatized in a way which might lead to creation of a true minority. However, she also sees this stigmatization as linked to a tendency for women to deny their age. While I personally do not share Posner's contention that the stigma of aging is linked with a stigma of dying (a point she makes in more detail elsewhere [Posner, 1976] and which has been made by others), this article is theoretically challenging and also a lot more interesting to read than much of the literature on attitudes toward the aged. It is, in fact, generally found in such research that people tend to devalue and negatively stereotype the old, and to retain their stereotypes as they themselves become older. To cope with the unhappy fact of growing into their own stereotypes, there is a distinct tendency for older people to exempt themselves from the status "old" and to view themselves as young for their age (Rosow, 1967: 30-33).

Joseph Tindale's paper is something of a rarity in gerontology because it focuses on a major, but neglected, subgrouping: poor, old men. Much gerontological research has focused on "captive populations" who are easy to get at because they live in nursing homes, hospitals, and the like. The old, poor men studied by Tindale are, by contrast, difficult to research. Theoretically, this article shows the importance of historical and generational factors and can be read in the light of the paper on generational conflict theory, by Tindale and Marshall, which appears as Chapter 5 of this book. In fact, several of the authors of papers in this book take a historical approach, and, as I noted in Chapter 1, this represents something of a contrast between Canadian and American social gerontology.

The participant-observation methodology used by Tindale is not only suitable for this particular study population, which would be impossible to study through traditional survey research methods, but is generally well suited to gathering data about the *experience* of aging and the meaning of age-related phenomena to participants. Tindale has made this argument systematically elsewhere (Marshall and Tindale, 1978-79). The notion of aging as a career or status passage parallels that presented elsewhere in the book, and again represents something of a Canadian perspective in the social psychology of aging. See also the papers by Marshall (Chapter 6) and Matthews (Chapter 15).

Lee Guemple describes a Canadian society, the Inuit, where the aged are not stigmatized, but on the contrary are held in high regard. Among the Inuit of the Canadian North, old age was not suddenly encountered on reaching 65, but was experienced with secession of active economic activities, and with decline in health. Both household and community provide support systems for the elderly, in a manner suggestive of the rural families early in this century described by Jane Synge in Chapter 14. As with that style of life, the situation of the Inuit is, Guemple argues, rapidly changing, and the cosmology whose meanings allow them to so well integrate life and death is disappearing with conversion to Christianity and other modern ways.

While each of the papers in this section has its own message, when taken together I hope they will encourage sensitivity to the differences among Canada's aged. To speak of the aged of Canada, one must attend to male and female, rich and poor, the various ethnic groups and the ways they differentiate the experience of aging (about which virtually nothing is known, see Zay, 1978), age differences within the old age category, and functional differences of health status, economic, and familial roles. While our interest in the social aspects of aging leads to a search for patterns, we will expect diversity in the ways in which age and aging are experienced.

7

WOMEN AND THE AGED AS MINORITY GROUPS A Critique*

Sharon McIrvin Abu-Laban and Baha Abu-Laban
Department of Sociology
University of Alberta

Almost forty years ago, a parallel was drawn between the Negroes' and women's subordinate positions in American society (Myrdal, 1944: appendix 5). About a decade later an examination was made of the minority-group characteristics of the aged (Barron, 1953). More recently increasing numbers of researchers have begun to label women and the aged as minorities and to further expand the minority concept to include such groups as youth, students, the handicapped, communards, the poor, and homosexuals (see, for example, Newman, 1973; Sagarin, 1971; Kinloch, 1974).

Traditionally, the minority concept has been applied only to analyses of racial and ethnic groups. Moves to broaden the applicability of the minority-group concept have been met on the one hand by some opposition to viewing such "new categories" as minority groups and on the other by attempts to redefine the concept of minority group in order to accommodate new perspectives. The definition most commonly cited by both proponents and opponents of the extension of the minority-group concept is that developed by Louis Wirth. He defines a minority as "a group of people who, because of their physical or cultural characteristics, are singled out from others in the society in which they live for differential and unequal treatment and who therefore regard themselves as objects of collective discrimination" (1945: 347).[1] Arguments regarding the extension of the minority-group label beyond its traditional referents to other disadvantaged segments of the population have tended to centre around elements contained in this definition. However, in spite of attempted empirical clarifications and some attempts at reconceptualization, the controversies continue.

This chapter proposes to critically examine major arguments concerning the propriety of applying the minority label to women and the aged, two subgroups which currently are on the periphery of the traditional minority perspective. Of all the new categories to which the concept of minority group has recently been applied, those based on sex and age merit special attention, for these criteria have universal applicability for the assignment

*An earlier version of this essay appeared under the same title in the *Canadian Review of Sociology and Anthropology*, Vol. 14, no. 1 (1977): 103-16.

of roles and statuses in society. Moreover, most of the aged are women. To the extent that these two overlapping sets are minority groups, there is the implication of a double jeopardy. Further, these two groups have been among the first beneficiaries of the expansion of the minority concept, with the result that the literature carries several arguments both for and against their inclusion. We will first examine the literature with regard to the applicability of the minority concept to women and the aged and then discuss factors related to disagreements between researchers. A better understanding of these particular controversies should provide insights into the advantages and disadvantages of a still further expansion of the minority-group concept.

Women and Minority Status

Gunnar Myrdal's (1944: appendix 5) analogy between the social situation of women and that of Negroes is often cited as the first reference to women as a minority group (Streib, 1965:36n; Barron, 1953:477). However, although Myrdal indeed comments at some length on women's disadvantaged position in American society and forcefully draws the parallel between that and the Negroes' subordinate position, he states elsewhere in his discussion (67n) that women do *not* constitute a minority group. He apparently reserves the use of the minority concept for "colour castes" (e.g., Japanese, Chinese, and Mexicans) and immigrant groups (e.g., Czechs, Italians, and Poles) (Myrdal, 1944:1237). In recent years, Myrdal's analogy between women and Negroes has acquired a high degree of popularity among social critics and sociologists alike. In particular, supporters of women's liberation have frequently drawn analogies between racism and sexism and at times have been accused of "cashing in" on the black movement and diverting its purposes.[2]

Helen Hacker (1951) applies the minority-group perspective to the analysis of women's disadvantaged position in society.[3] Although frequently cited to support the assertion that women constitute a minority group, Hacker in fact concludes that the minority-group concept cannot be applied to women for two main reasons: first, many women are not aware of being discriminated against as a group; second, many women do not regard differential treatment based on sex as objectionable. Hacker suggests that the thorough sex-role socialization of most women precludes the application of the minority-group label.

Hacker recognizes, however, the utility of studying women as possessors of "minority-group *status*". To support the attribution of this status to women (and as a partial listing of the characteristics of a minority group) Hacker suggests the existence of the following characteristics of the female experience: (1) a distinctive subculture; (2) group self-hatred; (3) job and wage discrimination; (4) legal discrimination; (5) discrimination relating to social conduct; and (6) discriminatory socialization practices within the family.

Barron (1953) similarly describes women as constituting a partial or quasi-minority group. He acknowledges that women occupy a subordinate position and are debarred from full and equal participation in society. However, he argues that women are encompassed within the families of the supposed majority and are thus, in his view, unable to function as a separate subgroup in society. For this reason, Barron sees women as appropriately qualifying for quasi-minority status.

The belief that women do not constitute a minority group is supported by Streib (1965), who bases his position on Simone de Beauvoir's (1953) early belief that women are not bound together by a distinctive subculture since they have no group past or history, no religion of their own, and no collective consciousness. Further, women are dispersed in society and, in Streib's view, are more inclined to identify with their social-class position than with their sex.

Newman (1973) also argues against the propriety of the minority label for women. His position is based upon his definition of minority groups, which represents one of the most recent attempts to redefine the concept of minority group and broaden the range of collectivities that may be subsumed under it. Based on Schermerhorn's (1970) insights, Newman defines minority groups as those that "vary from the social norms or archetypes in some manner, are subordinate with regard to the distribution of social power and rarely constitute more that one-half of the population of the society in which they are found".

Although Newman sees women in general as having a subordinate status in society, in his view this is not equivalent to minority status. In Newman's terms, women do not qualify as a minority group, because they constitute more than one-half of the population and, more importantly, because they do not vary from the social norms and archetypes. Interestingly, although Newman rejects minority status for women, he regards women who support and identify with the "Women's Liberation Movement" as a minority group because they possess a distinctive ideological trait which separates them from the social norm and have group consciousness (175-76). Newman argues that this "minority movement" has been on the scene for over a century.[4]

Table 1 summarizes the arguments discussed above and distinguishes between characteristics invoked as qualifying women for status as a minority group and others which are cited as eliminating women from eligibility for minority status. The table reveals two broad patterns: the existence of substantive discrepancies regarding the characteristics of women and the existence of disagreements concerning the essential defining characteristics of a minority group per se.

For example, there is disagreement concerning the existence of a female subculture. Whereas Hacker (1951) sees a tendency toward a separate female subculture, Streib (1965) and Newman (1973) deny the existence of

TABLE 1:
WOMEN: ARGUMENTS FOR AND AGAINST MINORITY STATUS

For	*Against*
Physical characteristics	
None	None
Sociocultural characteristics	
1. Subordinate social status (Barron; Newman)	1. Dispersed; encompassed within the family system; not functioning as an independent subgroup (Barron; Streib)
2. Tendency toward separate subculture (Hacker)	2. Lack of distinctive subculture (Streib)
	3. Lack of distinctive belief system; behaviour does not vary from social norms or archetypes (Newman)
	4. Constitute more than one-half of the population (Newman)
Differential treatment	
1. Objects of prejudice and stereotyping (Hacker)	1. Lack of awareness of being discriminated against on a group basis (Hacker)
2. Discriminatory socialization practices (Hacker)	2. Acceptance of the propriety of differential treatment (Hacker)
3. Restrictions on behaviour and full participation in society (Barron; Hacker)	
4. Discriminatory treatment in employment practices, education, and the legal system (Hacker)	
Group consciousness/awareness	
1. Group self-hatred (Hacker)	1. Lack of group identification (Hacker; Newman; Streib); stronger identification with social class position than with sex (Streib)

one. In part, this disagreement revolves around the definition of a subculture. Hacker argues that although group identification among women is missing, there are language differences and distinctive subgroup interests which define the "women's world" (e.g., interest in people, family, and what may be generally summarized as the expressive domain). On the other hand, Streib supports his negative position by emphasizing women's lack of group past or history and their lack of collective consciousness or a distinct religion. Similarly, Newman argues that women lack a distinctive belief system and, in addition, that their behaviour does not vary from social norms or archetypes because there are roles for women that are considered "very desirable".

Barron and Streib emphasize that because women are dispersed among the families of the supposed majority, they do not (and cannot) function as an independent subgroup in society. The implication here is that a major distinguishing feature of a minority group is that it should constitute a relatively closed system and not be merely a status category (Francis, 1951:229). Although not explicitly stated by Wirth (1945), this distinctive element of minority status is probably implicit in much of his discussion, as evidenced by his illustrations and typology of minority groups.

None of the writers examined questions the subordinate social status of women in society or the existence of discriminatory treatment, but several writers seem to assign little or no import to differential treatment.

It is interesting to note that none of these authors singles out the distinguishing physical characteristics of women as significant aspects of possible minority status. Sex, along with age, is one of the most basic classifications made in human societies. Yet secondary sexual characteristics are not singled out for consideration.

The Aged and Minority Status

Barron (1953) is generally acknowledged as one of the first to study the aged from the minority-group perspective. He concludes that the aged possess the following minority-group characteristics: (1) they are viewed by some as a menace and a group to fear; (2) they experience prejudice and stereotyping in employment; (3) they possess feelings of self-consciousness and defensiveness; and (4) they increasingly benefit from antidiscrimination legislation paralleling that for ethnic minorities. In Barron's view, these characteristics qualify the aged for status as a *quasi*-minority group. Barron's position is that neither the aged nor women constitute genuine minority groups and for the same reason: both are found within the families of the supposed majority and hence are not unique subgroups functioning independently in society.

In opposition to Barron's above-noted conclusions, Breen (1960:157) argues that "in many parts of our society [the aged] constitute a functioning subgroup". In addition, Breen sees the following characteristics as contributing to the development of minority status among the aged: their relatively high visibility and negative self-concept, and the fact that they are treated as stereotypes, discriminated against in the labour market, and segregated in institutions and special housing. In combination, these characteristics underline the minority status which, in Breen's view, the aged are progressively acquiring.

Taking a somewhat more definitive position, Palmore (1969) contends that the aged *are* a minority group. They qualify, he maintains, because they are the objects of negative stereotyping and discrimination and, in addition, they manifest self-hatred and increasing group consciousness. Palmore raises the issue of degree of characteristics in arguing the legitimacy of the concept as applied to the aged. He maintains that while some may feel "the aged are no more like minority groups than are women [and] children", there is an important difference. In Palmore's view, "while these other groups may have some minority group characteristics, we believe that there is more prejudice, segregation, and discrimination directed toward the aged than toward women and children" (57).

In a similar vein, Jarvis (1972) also views the aged as a minority group. To support this contention, he cites the physical visibility of the aged, the exclusion of those over sixty-five from many occupations, lower pay for those over sixty-five, social and physical isolation of the elderly, the expectation that older people will "pursue passive, acquiescent roles", negative self-definitions among older persons, and the increasing numbers of groups concerned with the interests of the aged.

Newman (1973) also regards the aged as a minority group, primarily on the basis of their physical distinctiveness and subordinate power position in society. In contrast to his elaborate examination of the minority status of women (which, as noted in the previous section, he rejects), his examination of the status-role of the aged is much less searching. This appears to be the case because in his judgment the aged qualify as a physical minority group, whereas women do not.

Gubrium (1973), distinguishing between a minority group and an interest group, maintains that the aged constitute the former because of their age awareness (negative self-image). If and when this develops into group consciousness, the aged may be viewed as an interest group. In sharp contrast to previous authors, Gubrium argues that it is not necessary that a collectivity have group consciousness or be an active interest group to qualify for minority group status. "It is only when the delineation of a particular collection of persons is devalued that it is acted toward, and itself acts like a minority group" (157). The aged are a minority group, Gubrium maintains, because they meet these conditions.

Streib (1965), in a widely quoted article, takes the position that the aged are not a minority group. He argues that because the aged do not have distinctive cultural traits and do not have "consciousness of kind", they are more of an aggregate or social category than a distinct group. Streib outlines what he regards to be important elements of minority-group status according to his understanding of Wirth's definition. He concludes that the aged do not qualify as a minority group for the following reasons. First, the status-role expectations associated with age are variable throughout the lifecycle. Thus the characteristic of "agedness" occupies only a fraction of a person's life span. Second, self-image evidence indicates that many chronologically "old" people do not regard themselves as old but rather as middle-aged. This renders the criterion of "old age" problematic. Third, stereotypes regarding the aged are refuted in two important areas: work performance and appropriate activities. Research indicates that younger people not only favourably evaluate older people's work performance but also regard as appropriate for older people many activities which are even more vigorous than those which older people regard as appropriate for themselves. Fourth, there is a lack of readiness on the part of the aged to organize as an identifiable pressure group. Fifth, older people do not face restricted access to power, privilege, and civil rights. On the contrary, older people are disproportionately represented in elite and superordinate positions in society. Finally, the deprivation of the aged in several areas may be questioned. For example, although a large proportion of the aged may be classified as underprivileged, many of them, in Streib's view, were also underprivileged prior to retirement. In addition, unequal access to work is a characteristic not solely of the aged but also of the middle-aged. Streib further notes that the amount of involuntary residential segregation of the aged is minimal and finally questions the extent of social isolation of the aged, suggesting that it may be related to social class. Regardless, Streib asserts, "a deprived group is not synonymous with a 'minority group'" (1965:43).

Atchley (1972) also argues against the applicability of the minority concept to the aged. To begin with, he agrees that age discrimination is similar to racial discrimination in that it is dependent on the "visibility" of the stigmatizing characteristic(s). (According to him, "Old people who 'do not look their age' escape the effects of age discrimination."[5]) He also agrees that many older people, like members of racial minorities, have an inadequate income, feelings of self-hatred, a low status, and inequality of opportunity. The major reason Atchley gives for the inappropriateness of the minority-group concept for older people is that there is variability in discriminatory treatment. Older people, for example, do not face discrimination in the holding of political office. Like Streib, Atchley observes that the aged are disproportionately represented in this area.

Table 2 summarizes the arguments for and against minority-group status for the aged. Like Table 1, it reveals definitional as well as substantive disagreements. For example, while Atchley (1972), Breen (1960), Jarvis

TABLE 2:
THE AGED: ARGUMENTS FOR AND AGAINST MINORITY STATUS

For	Against
Physical characteristics	
1. Visibility (Atchley; Breen; Jarvis; Newman)	1. Not constant through life cycle (Streib)
	2. No agreement on parameters of agedness (Streib)
Sociocultural characteristics	
1. Subordinate social status (Atchley; Barron; Gubrium; Jarvis; Newman)	1. Overrepresented in some power positions (Atchley; Streib)
2. Functioning subgroup in many parts of society (Breen)	2. Dispersed; encompassed within the family system; not functioning as an independent subgroup (Barron; Streib)
	3. Lack of distinctive cultural traits (Streib)
Differential treatment	
1. Objects of prejudice and stereotyping (Breen; Palmore)	1. Refutation of stereotyping in the vital areas of 'work performance' and 'appropriate activities' (Streib)
2. Economic deprivation (Atchley; Jarvis); discriminatory treatment in general (Palmore); discriminatory treatment in employment practices (Barron; Breen; Jarvis); restrictions on full participation in society (Barron); social and/or physical segregation (Breen; Jarvis)	2. Deprivation (poverty, unemployment) does not characterize only the old; no restricted access to power, privilege, and rights; minimal involuntary residential segregation; social isolation may be class-related (Streib)
3. Antidiscrimination legislation paralleling that for ethnic groups; arouse fear, seen as a threat (Barron)	3. Discrimination is situational (Atchley)
Group consciousness/awareness	
1. Negative self-concept (Atchley; Breen; Gubrium; Jarvis; Palmore)	1. Variability in self-definition of agedness (Streib)
2. Group identification, increasing group consciousness, increasingly likely to organize (Breen; Jarvis; Palmore)	2. Lack of group identification, no consciousness of kind, lack of readiness to organize (Streib)
3. Group consciousness not necessary, organization not a requirement (Gubrium)	

(1972), and Newman (1973) point to the visibility of the aged as an aspect of minority status, Streib (1965) questions this, noting that there is no agreement among observers on the parameters of agedness.

Although several writers agree that there is a general pattern of disadvantage, Streib questions whether this is sufficient for the attribution of minority-group status. Some writers argue that the old have subordinate social status and power positions, whereas others (Streib and Atchley) argue that older people are overrepresented in some power positions (basically political). There is disagreement concerning whether the aged constitute a subgroup. Writers disagree on the issue of older people's readiness to organize. As in the case of women, the group consciousness of the aged is also questioned, with Gubrium taking the uncommon position that group consciousness is, in fact, not even necessary for minority status.

Discussion

Proponents and opponents of the extension of the minority label to women and the aged share some common understandings. For example, it is agreed that women and the aged tend to occupy subordinate positions in society and that both groups are subjected to discriminatory treatment in many institutional areas. However, the disagreements between the two sides in the controversy overshadow the agreements. In the remainder of this paper we will discuss certain factors related to these disagreements.

Ideological Utility of the Minority-Group Concept

Ideological considerations appear to have played an important part in encouraging the extension of the minority-group concept or perspective to the study of women, the aged, and other subordinate groups. The central focus of these considerations has been on discrimination and its personal and social consequences. Hence, to label a subgroup as a minority serves to announce some humanitarian inclinations regarding that group. It implies recognition of differential treatment which is at odds with the society's or the researcher's manifest value system. The increased outspokenness of disadvantaged people is a related factor prompting the wider use of the minority concept and the continued emphasis on discriminatory treatment.

Some of the disagreements seem to reflect an element of territoriality regarding the minority concept. To the extent that one moves to broaden the concept to include more and more disadvantaged categories of human-kind, one runs the risk of muting the humanitarian message regarding the racial groups to whom the concept was first applied. The minority concept, as an ideological weapon, may be Janus-faced: while it may sensitize different categories of people to commonalities of disadvantage, it may at the same time divert attention from the "original" minority groups. Part of the disagreement regarding the potential broadening of the concept may reflect an awareness of this. Additionally, the minority concept, when used as a form of ideological shorthand to communicate concern regarding women or the aged (see Blau, 1973; Davis, 1969; Hochschild, 1973a; Kirkpatrick, 1955:158; Blalock, 1967:100), may cloud some important structural considerations. In fact, for those wishing to translate humanitarian inclinations into social action, the structural uniqueness of women and the aged in contrast to "traditional" minorities may have important implications both for the nature of the experiential component and also for the potential militancy of these groups.

Experiential versus Structural Components

The analytical utility of identifying experiential commonalities among groups which are differentially articulated into the social structure has been demonstrated by Myrdal's (1944:appendix 5) aforementioned analogy between the social situation of women and that of Negroes and, more recently, by Blauner (1969) in his use of the colonial analogy for the analysis of racial conflict in America. Blauner's argument rests on a simple, but necessary, distinction between colonialism as a socioeconomic and political system and colonization as a process. Though Afro-American and colonized peoples are part of different social systems, Blauner successfully argues that they commonly share the *experience* of colonization. Likewise, in the process of subordination, women and the aged, among others, may have experiences similar to those of racial and cultural minorities as well as colonized peoples. As a consequence, the experience of minority status may be characteristic of many people who are in some way stigmatized. This experiential component is particularly worthy of note in social-psychological studies that take into consideration the attributes of relationships between those with a surfeit of power and those with power deficiencies. However, the component of experiential commonality has been emphasized by some writers (Hacker, 1974; Breen, 1960) at the expense of delineating structural differences. And, inevitably, to be black is not the same as to be old or to be female.[6] Nevertheless, other writers have called attention to structural differences. Barron (1953) and Streib (1965) were among the first to argue that women and the aged do not qualify for minority status, because both groups are encompassed within the family system of the "majority" and hence do not function independently in society. But both of these writers stopped short of detailing the implications of family membership and of considering still other structural differences.

Since the family tends to be regarded as a unit of equivalent evaluation with respect to social-class position, being part of the family system may have some of the following consequences for both women and the aged: (1) it may conceal their oppression, both from themselves and from the "majority"; (2) identification with the family may limit their subgroup identification, hence dampening their militancy potential; (3) they have access to vicarious achievement/mobility opportunities, for example the pleasure of "having" a "successful" adult child or a "successful" husband to compensate for lower personal status. Researchers attempting to understand the tepid consciousness of women or the aged might do well to look at the family as a desensitizing agent.

An additional aspect concerning the role of the family relates to traditional sex-role socialization. In the traditional family system members of the "majority" (fathers) socialize a portion of their offspring (daughters) to "minority" status (or at least acquiesce while others do). A situation in which members of the so-called majority group replenish the ranks of the minority group with some of their own offspring underlines a unique aspect of women's subordinate status in society.

The roles of women and the aged in institutional structures and their patterned relationships with their respective superordinate counterparts are qualitatively and quantitatively different from those roles and relationships characterizing ethnic or racial minorities. In a society stratified along ethnic, sex, and age lines, as Lieberson (1970:173) notes, "ethnic groups are the only strata that have the inherent potential to carve their own autonomous and permanent society from the existing nation without, in effect, re-creating its earlier form of stratification all over again." Neither disadvantaged age groups nor disadvantaged sex groups possess a similar potential for the creation of an autonomous, viable society. The only practical course of action available to these groups is to direct their efforts to changing the existing system (Lieberson, 1970:173-74). One important implication of the aforementioned structural differences is that Wirth's (1945) well-known typology of minority groups, involving the policy alternatives of assimilation, pluralism, militancy, and secessionism, is not altogether realistic in relation to women and the aged.

Conceptual Ambiguities

Even allowing for variations in the quality of researchers' interpretive insights or methodological techniques, Tables 1 and 2 reveal differences in the characteristics attributed to women and the aged, as well as differences in the characteristics attributed to minority status, suggesting major conceptual difficulties at both the nominal and the operational levels. The differences tend to cluster around two issues: those regarding subculture and subsystems and those regarding group consciousness. Not unexpectedly, these are the qualities in most definitions of minority group which are probably the most difficult to measure.

1. *Subculture and/or subsystem*   With reference to both women and the aged, some writers claim the existence of a distinctive subculture while

others deny its existence. Some writers view the aged as possessors of an incipient subculture (Rose, 1962) or as a "functioning subgroup" aware of their identity and of restrictions on their full and equal participation in society; others sharply disagree. The qualities invoked to substantiate or disavow the existence of a subculture differ. For example, while some maintain that there is no women's subculture because women lack a distinct religion or history, others argue that there is a distinct subculture because of a characteristic language style and unique interest patterns. While one may be tempted to suggest that androcentric bias has contributed to the inability to perceive a female subculture, an even stronger case may be made for definitional ambiguities.[7] Such debates regarding the presence or absence of subcultures are familiar (as illustrated, for example, by the long-running adolescent subculture exchanges of a few years past).

A related disagreement concerns the ability of a particular group to function as a subsystem or as a separate subgroup in society. Assuming that the condition of "functioning as a subsystem" is an important characteristic of a minority group, two observations become important. First, the literature reflects little, if any, concern with an empirical operationalization of this element or with changes in a group's position over time, either away from or in the direction of separate group existence (minority status). Second, since the openness or closure of a "subsystem" is a matter of degree, the question concerning the point at which a collectivity is transformed into a "subsystem" becomes important to answer.

Apart from substantive disagreements concerning whether or not women and the aged function as separate groups in society, there is no agreement on the minimum degree of "separateness" necessary for minority status, nor is there agreement on the importance of this characteristic relative to other characteristics. The previously noted arguments by Barron (1953) and Streib (1965) on the one hand and Breen (1960) on the other are a case in point.

2. *Group consciousness*   The extent and nature of group consciousness has also occupied those debating the minority-group characteristics of women and the aged. The importance placed on this aspect is exemplified by Hacker. In 1951 she did not regard women as a minority group, mainly because in her judgment they lacked group consciousness (but none of the other defining characteristics of a minority group). In 1951 Hacker viewed women not as a minority group, but as possessors of "minority-group *status*". Twenty-three years later, Hacker (1974) has asserted that women are now a minority group because, in her estimation, a sufficient degree of group consciousness has developed among them. Regardless of whether Hacker's 1951 and 1974 conclusions were accurate or inaccurate, they were not based on methodologically reproducible procedures. The criterion of reproducibility is particularly important in view of the fact that some other writers (e.g.,

Eichler, 1973:44) continue to assert that the element of group consciousness is missing among women.

Another variation on the complexities of measuring group consciousness or group identification is found with the aged. To the extent that it is agreed that older people must age-identify to qualify as a minority group, there are problems involved in measuring agedness. These raise the classic issue of objective, as opposed to subjective, definitions of personal characteristics. With reference to the objective determination of agedness, researchers have found, for example, that gross categories such as "over-fifty" or "pre-retirement" *versus* "post-retirement" are insensitive to many important subtleties (Cumming and Henry, 1961; Thompson and Streib, 1958). Also problematic is the use of inconsistent age categories, for example utilizing data derived from the "over-forty" age-group to support assertions about the aged (see Breen, 1960). Self-image also presents problems. Researchers have found that when people are asked to indicate how old they regard themselves, there is a consistent tendency to view themselves as younger (Tuckman and Lavell, 1957; Zola, 1962). For example, Streib and Schneider (1971) found that about one-third of their respondents saw themselves as middle-aged at seventy. Other research indicates that personal attribution of agedness is related to social status (Rosow, 1967), sex (Leake, 1962), and ethnicity (Crouch, 1972). For older people, as Streib (1965) pointed out, agedness is not constant through the lifecycle. There is a *process* whereby one moves or is pushed to a realization of advanced age and its societal implications. The aging individual must come to terms with changing personal conditions, a gradual "minoritization" unlike that any other subordinate group may experience. These observations suggest that the problems in measuring the group identification of the aged are of a different type than those found with women.

As an example, it is easier for one to reject the attribution of "old age" than it is for women to reject the gender label. Perhaps because of this women have thus far been more vocal and active than the aged. In addition to this, however, the group mobilization of women has attracted and will probably continue to attract more out-group hostility than the mobilization of the aged. A unique factor contributing to the difference between the situation of women and that of the aged is that all people will acquire the status of old age with sufficient longevity. For this reason, it is probably easier for non-aged males (the "majority") to identify with the aged and tolerate their mobilization than to identify with women and readily accept their mobilization.[8]

To the extent that group consciousness is agreed upon as a crucial defining element of minority-group status (but remembering that Gubrium, for one, claims it is unnecessary), there needs to be allowance made for its relativity. Towards this end: (1) process needs to be acknowledged and reintegrated into the minority group perspective; (2) there should be agreement concerning what is to constitute a sufficient degree of consciousness; (3) it should be noted that the extent of group awareness and identification varies even within the "traditional" minorities. In the absence of a clear and precise conceptual apparatus, and given the condition of ongoing change in society, substantive disagreements, such as we have examined, would seem inevitable.

Attempts at Redefinition

Existing conceptual deficiencies have led several writers to redefine the field of majority-minority relations (see, for example, Gordon, 1964; Shibutani and Kwan, 1965; van den Berghe, 1967; Schermerhorn, 1970; Sagarin, 1971; Newman, 1973; Kinloch, 1974). Most pertinent to the present discussion are the works of Sagarin, Newman, and Kinloch, which have considerably expanded the range of collectivities under the minority-group concept. However, the attempts to reconceptualize the field to encompass such subordinate groups as women and the aged, among others, have not been satisfactory. The new definitions and classifications of minority groups have masked important differences in the institutional roles of traditional and "new" minority groups and have also failed to address standing issues in the current controversy.

For example, Sagarin (1971) has taken Goffman's concept of stigma as the unifying thread for the analysis of minority groups, including deviant people and other disadvantaged groups traditionally excluded from the field. Kinlock (1974:50) has redefined a minority group as "any group that views itself and/or is defined by a dominant power elite as unique on the basis of perceived physical (race, sex, age), cultural (religion, ethnicity), economic (social class), and/or behavioural (deviation) characteristics and is treated accordingly in a negative manner".

Newman's (1973) reconceptualization of the field readily admits the aged, along with several other "new" collectivities, into the arena of majority-minority relations. But it has serious drawbacks. According to Newman, minority groups are distinguished on the basis of difference from social norms or archetypes. These differences may be physical (blacks, the aged, the handicapped), cognitive (Jews, religious sects, social communes), or behavioural (homosexuals). As noted earlier, Newman's conceptual scheme does not recognize women as a minority group, with the exception of those who support and identify with the Women's Liberation Movement. To quote Newman: "There are highly desirable normative social roles for both men and women in society...[and] being female is not a form of variance from society's sexual norms" (Newman, 1973:176).

It should be noted that Newman's definition of minority groups refers to social norms and archetypes, whereas his discussion of women as a minority group refers to *sexual* norms. That this is problematic can be shown by substituting racial norms for sexual norms and arguing that there are desirable roles for Negroes (e.g., being subserviant, hard-working, appreciative of paternalism, etc.) and that being black is not at variance with society's racial norms. The "highly desirable normative social roles" for women do not, in fact, compare favourably with those for men. Studies indicate that both men and women evaluate the male role and traits more favourably than the female (Fernberger, 1948; McKee and Sherriffs, 1956). A study by Broverman, *et al.* (1972) indicates that stereotyped female traits which mental health therapists regard as healthy for women are not regarded as healthy for males or "people". Newman's (1973) suggestion, then, that there may be dual archetypes in society, would only seem valid if in the area of role allocation these archetypes were regarded as equally desirable for males or females. Also, to regard certain women but not others as members of a minority group is as problematic as regarding some blacks as members of a minority group and others as members of the majority group.

There is no agreement on the necessary and sufficient conditions which define minority status. At the same time there has been a tendency to treat minority status as an all-or-none attribute, rather than as a variable capable of assuming different magnitudes. Thus the minority label has been applied equally to all traditional minority groups even though they may differentially possess the elements that define minority status. To be sure, writers have compared minority groups on certain variables, such as discriminatory treatment, but on the whole there has been no concern about viewing minority groups as higher or lower on an overall index of minority status. This tendency has been carried over into the debate concerning the minority status of women and the aged. The nearest that writers have come to regarding minority status as a variable has been to view women and the aged as quasi-minority groups. But this may be judged as a phase in the process of finding a yes or no answer to the question. The tendency to view minority status as an attribute rather than a variable has been an important factor in concealing important structural differences among minority groups, both "new" and traditional, and thus has contributed to disagreements in the field of study.

To alleviate some of the conceptual problems noted above, researchers need to agree upon the necessary and sufficient conditions of minority status and also to determine the importance of these conditions relative to each other, as well as to different types of subordinate groups. Also, there is a need to explore the implications of the multidimensional nature of the minority concept and to explicate different elements both in terms of the requisite levels minimally necessary for minority status and in terms of more generally acceptable measurement techniques and procedures.[9] Unless some degree of consensus on criteria and measurement techniques is established, different researchers will continue to arrive at different conclusions concerning the same group.

Conclusion

The current debate over broadening the minority-group concept to include the aged and women, among others, is in part attributable to the confounding of experiential commonalities and social-structural elements. The formulation of a strategy that would distinguish between these elements has probably been hindered by their fusion in most definitions of a minority group and, as well, by the ideological utility of the minority-group concept. When attempting to study disadvantaged groups, the researcher may find that assessments of the analytical utility of the minority concept are overshadowed by the concept's ideological lure. Although the minority concept may have ideological benefits, our examination indicates that it suffers from definitional ambiguities at both the nominal and the operational levels. We would suggest that minority status be treated as a variable rather than an attribute and that recognition be given to the multidimensional character of the concept. Further, it would seem crucial to consider both the experiential and structural components of specific subordinate statuses and to carefully explore the implications of both similarities and differences between groups. To parsimoniously lump all the disadvantaged under the minority-group label may be ideologically useful, but it is analytically premature.

Notes

1. This definition, focusing on both social structural and social-psychological attributes, encompasses at least four important elements. The first and perhaps most basic element in the definition is that minority status may be a product of racial (or physical) and/or cultural traits (e.g., language, religion, or national origin). The second important element in the definition is its intra-societal focus, thereby emphasizing the relativity of minority status. The third major element in Wirth's definition is its emphasis on discriminatory and unequal treatment of minority groups thus focusing attention on majority-minority *relationships*. Finally, the definition contains the element of group consciousness as a major defining characteristic of minority status.

2. A historical parallel can be drawn here with the abolitionist movement of the 1800s (see Myrdal, 1944).

3. As an interesting sign of our times, Hacker (1974) recently noted that when her article was first written it was rejected on the grounds that it was too journalistic; some twenty years later it was critically described as impersonal and professorial.

4. One is faced with questions here regarding the various subgroupings under the umbrella of women's liberation. Does each subgroup constitute a separate minority group? At what point in time is any organized group or movement large (or mature) enough to warrant being labelled as a minority group? Does any social or political movement qualify for the minority group label?

5. It should be noted, however, that even if one does not "look" her/his age, there are many situations in western society (e.g., completing employment application forms) which require age information and in which only direct misrepresentation will protect the individual from age discrimination. "Acceptable" appearance is not enough. Chronological age is a barrier to full participation in Canadian society (see Baum, 1974).

6. Note, for example, various studies of those who experience a so-called double negative, e.g., old women, black women. The double burden faced by aged women is also suggested cross-culturally by Simmon's (1945) study of the aged in preliterate societies. Simmons (81) concludes that "wherever aged women have been respected, old men have rarely been without honor; but prestige for aged men has offered no assurance of the same status for women. If either sex has lost respect in old age, it has been more likely to be the women than the men." For a collection of recent articles examining the problems of being old and female, see Institute of Gerontology (1974; 1975).

7. One is also tempted to ask: Whose *subculture*? If population numbers are considered a pivotal consideration, then perhaps it is misleading to refer to a female *subculture*.

8. This is not to deny that women researchers have been more active in research on the aged than in many other areas (see Hochschild, 1973b:144). For several reasons, women may identify with and/or be interested in the aged. However, if males were forced to choose between the two, the "cause" of the aged might seem more reasonable than the "cause" of women.

9. The degree to which the different elements of this multidimensional concept must coexist has not been made clear. As a recent example of this, Stoll (1974:44-45) singles out *one* component of Wirth's definition (i.e., "different and unequal treatment") to conclude that, using this definition, men, because "they are singled out as being inappropriate for child rearing and housekeeping", may also be viewed as a minority group. Similarly, Unger, *et al.* (1974) use not only unidimensional but also unusual indicators of women's minority-group status.

8

OLD AND FEMALE
The Double Whammy

Judith Posner
Department of Sociology
Atkinson College

A few years ago a television ad appeared on the scene which was relevant to aging women and suggested to them that "You're not getting older, you're getting better". These ads depicted beautiful, middle-aged women with slightly greying hair, before and after it was coloured. This was a significant advertising campaign because it brought into relief a particular set of norms regarding aging and women. What it really says is, "Contrary to popular belief, ladies, aging doesn't have to be a drag". It raises issues with more traditional advertising slogans such as "Hate that grey, wash it away".

What are the subtle sociological implications which underlie such thinking? The latter ad clearly suggests a form of age denial. It says, if you don't like the stigma of being old, fake it! The former actually suggests the same thing, but in a far more subtle and sophisticated fashion. It pretends to destigmatize aging, yet urges women to eradicate the unaesthetic physical changes associated with this process, i.e., grey hair. This paper is going to address itself to two interrelated issues — the status of women and the status of the aged. Finally, we will deal with the double whammy — the status of the aging female. Borrowing Cynthia Epstein's terminology from *Black and Female*, some of the implications of the aged women's dual minority status in our society will be considered.

The Concept of Stigma

First of all, it is necessary to delineate a theoretical perspective for looking at these issues. Such a perspective necessarily focuses on the concept of deviance or stigma in our society. We draw on the work of Erving Goffman who delineates the concept of the stigmaless person — the ideal North American member —

> For example, in an important sense there is only one complete unblushing male in America: a young, married, white, urban, northern, heterosexual Protestant father of college education, fully employed, of good complexion, weight, and height, and a recent record in sports. Every American male tends to look out upon the world from this perspective, this constituting one sense in which one can speak of a common value

*Reprinted from *Essence*, Vol. II, no. 1 (1977): 41-48, with permission.

system in America. Any male who fails to qualify in any of these ways is likely to view himself — during moments at least — as unworthy, incomplete, and inferior; at times he is likely to pass and at times he is likely to find himself being apologetic or aggressive concerning known - about aspects of himself he knows are probably seen as undesirable (Goffman, 1963:128).

Careful scrutiny of the above passage reveals all persons in our society are stigmatized in one way or another, however small. This broad framework for looking at deviancy makes a good starting point for a discussion of the aged and women. Both of these groups are deviations from the mean. Both of these groups are, in the term of Simone de Beauvoir, the *other* (de Beauvoir, 1961:15).

> The category of other is as primordial as consciousness itself. In the most primitive society, in the most ancient mythologies, one finds the expression of a duality...Otherness is a fundamental category of human thought.

In her two major works dealing with women and the aged respectively, Simone de Beauvoir elaborates on the concept of other.

> A man never begins by presenting himself as an individual of a certain sex; it goes without saying that he is a man. The terms *masculine* and *feminine* are used symmetrically only as a matter of form, as on legal papers. In actuality the relation of the two sexes is not quite like that of two electrical poles, for man represents both the positive and the neutral, as is indicated by the common use of man to designate human beings in general; whereas woman represents only the negative, defined by limiting criteria, without reciprocity...A man is in the right in being a man, it is the woman who is in the wrong (1961:15).

> Among primitive peoples the aged man is truly the Other, with the ambivalence that the word implies. In masculine myths the woman, the Other, appears as an idol and as a sex object at the same time. Similarly, for other reasons and in another manner the old man in those societies is both a sub-man and he is also the intercessor, the magician, the priest, below or beyond the human state, and often both together (1972:85).

> Goffman defines stigma in the traditional Greek meaning of the term (1963:1): "...bodily signs designed to expose something unusual and bad about the moral status of the signifier." This definition alludes to the fact that members expect to find some correlation between the external presentation of self, what Goffman calls the "personal front", and the internal moral self. Reminiscent of the maxim "You can tell a book by its cover" this notion of stigma has particular relevance for the analysis of the aging females' social position in our society. As will be shown, because women are cherished for their personal fronts, the visible signs of aging pose a particular dilemma for them.

The Status of Women

Research on the role of women in recent years has emphasized two major interrelated themes. One is that women's position in society is based on *derived status* (Hacker, 1951). This refers to the fact that her societal role rests in large part on the position of the man to whom she is attached. A daughter is attached to her father's identity, a wife to her husband's, and so on. Secondly, women are associated with *being* while men are more oriented towards *doing* (Chodorow, 1971). This being and doing distinction revolves around the fact, as de Beauvoir herself points out, that man is subject and woman is object. In fact, this is the actual basis of the well-worn cliché referring to women as sex objects. The object-like role of woman is based on her external beauty, and the fact that such beauty is the possession of a legitimate member of society, namely a male. Women, we are told, are the fragile, weaker sex. They are other. They are not known for their intellectual or occupational pursuits in the external community. Rather, they are known for their personal fronts — for just being. Their main hope is that they are well-endowed. If not, they must learn to fake it by becoming adept at personal-front management and all that it entails, e.g., the use of cosmetics, plastic surgery, etc. In short, they must learn to hide their stigmas.

Goffman refers to the paraphenalia for altering and managing the personal front as "body props" and "identity kits". My own observations of social interaction and recreational activities in a home for the aged reflect the importance of personal-front facilities for women in particular. Women at the home participated in a wide range of personal-front rituals, including beauty salon appointments, physical fitness programs, and weight reducers' clubs. Men, on the other hand, seemed to be less interested in these activities and more involved with performance pastimes such as bowling and card playing. Similarly, staff tended to manage male and female residents in different ways. They did not seem to be as concerned about clean clothes and mussed hair with respect to male residents. But female residents, even those labelled senile, were carefully clothed and fussed over. They were regularly treated to hair brushings and bows. In short there seems to be some mutual consensus among staff and inmates alike that the personal front is more relevant for women than for men.

How many times have we heard it said that it doesn't matter if a *male* is good looking? Where does this strange duality between men and women and their physical identities come from? But we are also aware of the fact that these deep-rooted stereotypes are presently in rapid upheaval. Men are also becoming sex objects as epitomized by the appearance of a nude Bert Reynolds in the centrefold of *Playgirl* magazine. Similarly, more and more men are indulging in cosmetics and the sort of camouflage techniques traditionally associated with women. However, one important fact must be kept in mind when considering the implications of such changes. The association of female status with good looks is not changing, it is merely becoming partially extended to men as well.

Another important feature of the status of women everywhere is their designation as a mysterious, enigmatic even contaminating creature. As symbolized by her otherness, her objectness, or as de Beauvoir suggests her genital concaveness, her moral character is also hidden and less vulnerable than her male counterpart. Woman is therefore feared. In addition, her peculiar life processes, including menstruation and pregnancy, depict her as a bizarre biological organism, as threatening as she is awesome. As Karen Horney writes—

> I think I have shown that men's disparagement of women is based upon a definite psychic trend towards disparaging them — a tendency rooted in the man's psychic reactions to certain biological facts...(Horney, 1972).

In *The Dangerous Sex* anthropologist Hays (1966) also documents historical and cross-cultural evidence of this same point. In sum, though woman is object, she is in some sense a feared object due to her contaminating association with blood and the miraculous act of childbirth.

The Status of Aging and the Stigma of Dying

Simone de Beauvoir states the almost universal position of the aged quite adamantly: "It is the tendency of every society to live, and to go on living: it extols the strength and the fecundity that are so closely linked with youth and it dreads the worn out sterility, the decrepitude of age" (1972:40). Although she and numerous anthropologists have documented exceptions to this rule and to the fact that some societies revere the aged, her perspective emphasizes an essential feature of aging everywhere. De Beauvoir contends that all societies are bound to stigmatize the aged, at least in part, due to the biological repulsiveness of the aging process. She also notes that although the status of the aged in societies above subsistence level is somewhat random, societies in poor ecological niches with poor technology tend to have low regard for the elderly. In other societies, however, old men may have an important role to play in the magico-religious system of the society. In advanced agrarian cultures, old men frequently function as the primary link between the living and the dead, the latter of whom may be responsible for many important aspects of everyday life, including subsistence success. However, even in these societies, de Beauvoir carefully indicates that the old occupy an ambiguous, if not paradoxical, position. They are necessary to religious ritual, and yet they are feared and avoided for their association with the dead. This fact brings us to the most important aspect of the position of the aged. The aged are also contaminated because of their nearness to death.

From the perspective delineated here, the older person's personal front is reminiscent of this taboo. The particular physical characteristics associated with old age, e.g., grey hair, wrinkled skin and weight loss are reminiscent of the skeleton or corpse and helps to explain our avoidance and denial of aging. These signs or stigmas connote internal deterioration and moral decay. The relevance of aging/dying persons to death however, raises a more primary question: Why the fear of death? Do all cultures fear death to the same extent as we do? Is there some correlation between a culture's attitude towards death and the position of the aged in that society?

Very briefly, we do know that many societies deal with death more openly than we do. We also know that the binary opposition of life and death, and concommitantly good and evil, so characteristic of our culture may not hold true for Eastern cultures which frequently emphasize the unity of life and death, yin and yang, or self and other. In our society however, the aged are especially separate from the non-aged, just as our concepts of life and death are distinctly antithetical. This strict boundary between life and death is also reflected in our medical model which tends to keep patients alive at all costs without regard for the equality of life.

In a youth-oriented society such as ours, the stigma of aging hardly needs further documentation. Numerous quantitative studies focusing on the perception of old people by young people and other older people support the notion that the aged are deviant, second-class citizens in our society, and many other more subjective, or qualitative features of everyday life point in the same direction. A startling passage from David Sudnow's study of management of dying in hospitals points to the contaminative character of aging:

Two persons in "similar" physical condition may be differentially designated dead or not. For example, a young child was brought into the ER with no registering heartbeat, respirations, or pulse — the standard "signs of death" — and was, through a rather dramatic stimulation procedure involving the coordinated work of a large team of doctors and nurses, revived for a period of eleven hours. On the same evening, shortly after the child's arrival, an elderly person who presented the same physical signs, with what a doctor later stated in conversation, to be no discernible differences from the child in skin colour, warmth, etc., "arrived" dead, with no attempts at stimulation instituted. A nurse remarked, later in the evening: "They [the doctors] would never have done that to the old lady [i.e., attempt heart stimulation] even though I've seen it work on them too." During the period when emergency resuscitation equipment was being prepared for the child, an intern instituted mouth-to-mouth resuscitation. This same intern was shortly relieved by oxygen machinery and when the woman "arrived" he was the one who pronounced her dead. He reported shortly afterwards that he could never bring himself to put his mouth to "an old lady's like that" (Sudnow, 1967:101).

The above quote exemplifies the fact that death, dying, and aging represent a neat symbolic package. It is difficult to think of one without the other. More importantly it is impossible to analyse the status of the aged in our society without referring to their physical characteristics and moral implications.

The Status of Aging Women

The status of women and the status of the aged have been briefly summarized. We now turn to two rather interesting cross-cultural facts which support the thesis that aging females are doubly stigmatized in many cultures.

First of all, in many societies aging females are less threatening and more expendable than aging males. The classic example of the Inuit woman who is left on the ice to die is a case in point. Like infanticide patterns in many cultures, the female is usually the first to go. Interestingly enough, however, at the same time that aging females are frequently the least important members in many societies, they are concommitantly impotent and non-threatening. While younger women are dangerous and taboo due to menstruation, such mystical powers are not attributed to older women, and they therefore become harmless. Whereas older men in the same society may retain their fearsome but awesome paradoxical status, an aging woman may practically become a non-entity.

Secondly, cross-cultural studies of incest reveal that in most societies incest between mother and son (older female and younger male) is regarded as the most heinous incest. The older woman who has intercourse with her son is considered more gross than the older man who does the same with his daughter. It is somehow less appropriate for a woman to be "old and/or sexy"! By the time she is 25 or at most 30, she is completely passé and at 40 a veritable hag (Spencer and Gillen, 1966).

In fact, if we extend the above rules of incest to our culture's implicit norms of conduct regarding the appropriate ages for betrothed couples we discover a similar theme. Women are not supposed to be older than men. Although ideally men shouldn't be too much older than women either, consider the different societal reactions to John (38) married Jane (20) vs. Jane (38) married John (20). "Robbing the cradle" is not nearly so extreme an affront to society as "being old enough to be his mother". The existence of this norm reflects two themes. One is the superiority of the male over the female. The other is the importance of youth and beauty for women. It is as though being female is somehow synonymous with youth and beauty and antithetical to aging and ugliness. We now turn to the sociology of everyday life, specifically the portrayal of women in advertising, for documentation of the double whammy.

In an article called "The Double Standard of Aging" Susan Sontag points to the non-reciprocal aging process for men and women.

In a man's face lines are taken to be signs of "character". They indicate emotional strength, maturity — qualities far more esteemed in men than in women. (They show he has "lived".) Even scars are often not felt to be unattractive; they too can add "character" to a man's face. But lines of aging, any scar, even a small birthmark on a woman's face, are always regarded as unfortunate blemishes. In effect, people take character in men to be different from what constitutes character in women. A woman's character is thought to be innate, static — not the product of her experience, her years, her actions. A woman's face is prized so far as it remains unchanged by (or conceals the traces of) her emotions, her physical risk-taking. Ideally, it is supposed to be a mask — immutable, unmarked (Sontag, 1972).

Recent research into how men and women feel about their bodies indicates similar results (*Psychology Today*, 1973). Men become more satisfied with their bodies as they age. Women become more anxious. Furthermore, research indicates that many men who married beautiful women feel betrayed as aging begins. Advertising in particular exploits this socio-psychological fact by gearing a lot of products to aging anxiety, and such advertising is largely geared toward women in particular.

Scott Francher states that contemporary advertising alienates the aged person from society (1973). This is because most ads are youth oriented and do not even depict aged persons. Unfortunately, the ones that do employ them only in relationship to negative stereotypes about the aged. Furthermore, it should be noted that few age-oriented products are actually directed towards men. This includes everything from hair colouring, false teeth, laxatives, complexion creams, etc. The thrust of most of these ads is the denial of the aging process. The method is the hard sell, i.e., the war on wrinkles. The victims are usually women.

Much of the advertising associated with the female body and aging in particular is reminiscent of Salvation Army rhetoric. The style of expression is aggressive and military. Women are told that their bodies are their battlegrounds. For example, one ad for multiple vitamins which suggests "Fight Fat" is reminiscent of the old cliché about the battle of the bulge. Another ad for skin cleanser states: "The Battleground: Where you need all the help you can get." It goes on to "map out" the specific "enemies" of your complexion as though on a military map (dirt, oil, bacteria, etc.). Another ad reminds us that since no product can cure acne we have to "fight everyday to keep the battle from spreading". Swedish formula tells us there is "no need to let your complexion become the victim of this condition." Another ad for a complexion states "Don't let your mirror become your enemy". And how can we avoid this? Denial or deceit is the answer.

So one skin cream states, "Let Oil of Olay help you lie about your age beautifully." Another famous ad for the Playtex bra illustrates this same theme. A beautiful, middle-aged woman, in a knit dress which exposes her girlish figure, bends over a birthday cake. Just as she is about the blow out the candles she scans the cake with her hand and pulls a few of them out. The narration: "Playtex bra will help *support* her story." Another ad for the same product depicts a beautiful, full-breasted middle-aged woman posing in her bra. The caption: "*Support* when you need it most." And it is noted that playtex bra "lifts" and "separates". This phrase is reminiscent of the "face lift", the archetypal personal-front management strategy for aging women in our society. In fact, it is tempting here to draw even further interpretations of this ad. For example, one wonders if the word support has deeper meaning, e.g., economic support, socioemotional support, etc. A third Playtex ad calls its product "the-no-visible-means-of-support-bra", clearly alluding to the woman's dependent economic position. In short, the imagery in this particular series of ads, and numerous others as well, depicts the aging woman as being "dragged down" as epitomized by sagging aged breasts. The advertising ploy for such female ads, then, usually revolves around providing perk-me-up products for dragged out dames.

Conclusion

Aging and dying are not sexless. In many ways the aging process reflects and exaggerates various issues related to male-female socialization or sex-role stereotyping. It is no coincidence that a great deal of gerontological literature focusing on *men* deals with retirement and that an increasing amount of literature focusing on *women* deals with widowhood. Traditionally, in our society, men gain their identity through work and occupational roles and women gain their identity through the men to whom they are attached. Thus the aging process reflects these discrepant bases of identity. Another area in which men and women differ greatly is in attitudes towards the body. Physical aging seems to be far more traumatic for the woman in our society than for the man, and it certainly starts a lot earlier. This paper has attempted to outline one possible perspective for examining the position of aging women in our society — the perspective of the body.

9

IDENTITY MAINTENANCE PROCESSES OF OLD POOR MEN*

Joseph A. Tindale
Department of Sociology
York University

Most urban centres of North America include within their populations a group of old men who are considered to be inferior. They are the aged of skid row, and bear a multi-dimensional stigma. As well as being poor and old, they are labelled as derelicts and winos. The men invoke protective mechanisms to safeguard their self-esteem as much as possible. These include the labelling of their fellows who deviate from their norms, exchange relationships with officialdom, and the control of information whenever possible. In this paper I draw on extensive ethnographic material (Tindale, 1974) to portray the everyday lives and processes of identity maintenance employed by such a population in a Canadian city.

Methodology

The data were collected throughout 1973 and the first part of 1974. A participant observation approach was undertaken. I initially made contact by working once a week in the hostel soup kitchen and in the friendly visiting group it sponsored. After four months I used these contacts to gain entry to a downtown park and meet more men. Simultaneously, I was spending time with them in their rooms, in bus terminals, and in a few bars.

When the study was initiated I intended to research both men and women. As the data collection process got underway, however, I rapidly found that meeting and gaining information from women was going to be exceedingly difficult. In the rooming houses I found very few women, and no women came to the hostel for meals, or lived there. In the parks, the few old women I talked to either rebuffed me or, at best, were indifferent to my approach. Neither could I draw on my male contacts for help. The men, while they knew these women, had little or no contact with them. As a result of these difficulties I eventually dropped women from active investigation.

Neither were the men easily accessible. A history of unemployment, poverty, and abrasive relationships with authority makes men exceedingly wary of communication with anyone who can be perceived as an outsider. They talk freely only to those who offer unrestricted companionship.

*I would like to acknowledge the considerable contribution made by Victor W. Marshall both as an editor and for his critical comments on earlier drafts of this paper.

For the first while in the park I did not try to extract much information from new contacts. I was willing to allow them to guide the conversation. Once the men knew me, I began to explore each of them at their own pace (Dean, 1967), discovering the various informational potentials slowly.

These sessions in the park and other locales generated several hundred pages of verbatim field notes which were kept in chronological order with attached criticisms. A simple index system devised by Whyte (1943) was utilized. This was later supplemented by the construction of a biography for each man. When analysis commenced, I organized the data by subject headings such as housing, food costs, rents, friends, family, drinking, etc. In this way I could check names in one direction against subjects in the other, and quickly assemble a clear composite picture.

The impression I gained of these men and their experiences can be more easily understood by examining some short selections of life history material on three of them.

Some Typical Careers

Roy Lancet is from Nova Scotia, and at age 65 has been in Ontario at least since the depression in the 1930s. It has been so long since he has had contact with any of his family that he is not sure of his parents' names, and has no idea where two step-siblings are. He was a freight-train hobo during the depression and spent a few years in a "Royal Twenty Centre" (a government work camp paying 20 cents a day). Twelve years ago he lost a leg in an auto accident and was on a disability pension until late 1973 when he was able to transfer to the more lucrative Old Age Security. Like the others, Roy is single and rents a small room. He and a man named Wallace share food, each spending approximately $7.00 per week to eat.

Don Sawchuk came to Canada from Poland around 1920 and worked a farm in Saskatchewan until 1927 when the crops failed. For part of the depression he worked laying track for the CPR, though he soon came east to Sudbury where a daughter lived. He is 77 and has been in the city aproximately 35 years. Don has only the Old Age Security for financial support. He rents a single room and has numerous physical complaints. He sees his daughter every year or two and rarely sees any of his old friends. One old friend, Stanley Berry, died in the spring of 1973. Confined by arthritis, Don rarely goes more than a block away from his room.

Jim Sanderson is a 78-year-old man who, though once married, lives alone in a rented room. Originally from Sarnia, his early adult life took place in Detroit where he went to work for Ford after serving part of World War I in the American armed forces. Until about 1930 Jim worked the winters at Ford as a drill press operator and in the summers boarded Great Lake freighters as a sailor and, at his peak, as a mate.

When lake work disappeared during the depression, Jim spent most of the summers between 1930-1940 working as a fruit picker just east of the city. He returned to the boats after the "dirty thirties" for about another ten years, but for the most part since 1950 he has been a skid row resident who worked irregularly as a dock labourer until the early 1960s.

The biographies make evident that these work and family careers are best understood by reference to significant historical events. This concept of career draws on the work of Everett Hughes (1971) and Erving Goffman's notion of moral career (1961). Hughes' definition (1971:137) distinguishes the objective from subjective contexts of career:

> However one's ambitions and accomplishments turn, they involve some sequence of relations to organized life. In a highly and rigidly structured society, a career consists, objectively, of a series of status (sic) and clearly defined offices. In a freer one, the individual has more latitude for creating his own position or choosing from a number of existing ones...but unless complete disorder reigns, there will be typical sequences of position, achievement, responsibility, and even of adventure. The social order will set limits upon the individual's orientation of his life, both as to direction of effort and as to interpretation of its meaning. Subjectively, a career is the moving perspective in which the person sees his life as a whole and interprets the meaning of his various attributes, actions, and the things which happen to him.

While it cannot be said that complete disorder reigns, the careers of these old men are not typical in the manner suggested by Hughes. This does not prevent, however, a subjective interpretation of career by the men as part of the process of defining their identity and maintaining it. Jim Sanderson will always retain some impression of himself as a respectable member of the company of men who sail the Great Lakes. Nevertheless, this is not a straightforward process as Goffman (1961:127) points out:

> One value of the concept of career is its two-sidedness. One side is linked to internal matters held dearly and closely, such as image of self and felt identity; the other side concerns official position, jural relations, and style of life, and is part of a publicly accessible institutional complex. The concept of career, then, allows one to move back and forth between the self and its significant society, without having to rely overly for data upon what the person says he thinks he imagines himself to be.

Because the careers of these old men vary from the dominant normative patterns in our society, they are engaged in a moral career which is tainted with stigma (Goffman, 1963:3). Significantly, though, the relationship between the individual and his others is not passive.

Career development in a particular profession was never firmly established with most of these men. For those who did work in one particular area, events like the depression have disrupted smooth development. In the social arena, many of the men have never clearly embarked on the project of starting a family. The auxiliary features of health and material surroundings have consistently been less than secure.

The Impact of the Depression[1]

Readings in economic and political history,[2] coupled with the realization that a man 65 today was 16 in 1930, lead me to feel the Canadian depression was a strongly determinative period in the lives of these men. A suggestion of the difficulties encountered is revealed in the statement Roy Lancet made when I asked him about work during the depression.

> No there wasn't any work! I used to ride the trains back and forth from Toronto to Ottawa. Six months each way, and there'd be a year gone. And boy, it was cold sleeping in those boxcars in winter. Some priests were pretty good. There was one in Lindsay and he'd give you an hour's work and a meal...I was able to work a little. I picked tobacco sometimes, for a dollar a day plus room and board then. For awhile I was working for the railroad at 25 cents per hour.

Roy's comment is typical of the experiences of many men in my sample. Yet, given those hard years, none of these men identify the depression as the significant feature of their lives, when careers and family hopes were dashed. Only persons like Leonard Barstik, who lost a sizable real estate investment and his job, now see the depression as a catastrophic period which eliminated most of their life chances. The indigent aged, except in a few isolated cases, are not the people who lost fortunes during those hard years. They were poor before the depression, poorer still during it, and only a little less poor after it. This is not to say the depression did not have an impact on these men's lives. It did, and they remember the hard times. The point, though, is that the thirties are not easily separable from the seventies. The men are still vulnerable, and they are still made to feel like "bums" on relief, when relief is all they have.

The old skid rowers are vulnerable in the sense they are at least as poor now, relatively speaking, as they were in the thirties. Roy suggested that inflation has raised the cost of living until he is less certain of eating now than he was during the depression.

These aged indigents continue to be made to feel like bums because they are still on relief. Bryden (1974:1), in discussing the evolution of federally supported pensions for the elderly, makes a strong argument regarding the dominance of "market ethos" thinking amongst Canada's legislators. This ethos argues that property is sacred, men are self-sufficient producers, and those who are dependent at any age after adolescence are "considered to be more in need of moral exhortation and uplift than material sustenance" (Bryden, 1974:20). This ethos, while it has been rationalized somewhat over the ensuing years, continues to affix a stigma to all those receiving transfer payments, whether they be welfare or old age pensions. It is consistent with this that the missions who provide food handouts to the skid rowers feel this entitles them to pass moral judgment and in some cases, exhort the indigents to follow middle class and Christian values to a new life.

The careers of these men, while not fully determined, were partially molded during the depression. The character of their labours through these ten years to a large degree set the pattern which maintained itself throughout the rest of their lives. Their jobs, subsequent to the depression, as the earlier life-history material suggests, were of low to moderate skill, and of short to moderate duration. Any problems that had arisen in the course of the depression with respect to drinking, family, or health continued for at least several years, and, in most cases, will follow them to their graves.

Soon after the depression my respondents became permanent residents of the city. There was some work to be had, and, in having a residence, they became eligible for some pension benefits which became generally available (see Chappell, this volume). Even with their residential stability established in the late 1940s, the work careers of these men did not change significantly. The only noticeable alteration was that they were no longer so mobile. Trips were infrequent and short. One of only two excursions made by Jim Sanderson in 1973 was to a small town a few miles outside the city when he went to visit the people for whom he had picked fruit during the depression.

> Yes, it was really nice to go and see those people; they're real good people. There are three families who live next to each other up there.... They're real down to earth people, not "high hat" at all, happy to see a sort of hobo like me.

This last line of Jim's is instructive. It reveals an acknowledgment of his stigmatized condition as a hobo. Only really good people who are not "high hat" will associate happily with one stigmatized as he is. At the same time, these men do not consider their work careers to be failures; they have some regrets but are not ashamed of their past.

Stigma Management

Amongst their fellows, these men are respectable and do not feel threatened. It is when talking to people like me or officialdom that stigma management comes into play. As Goffman states (1963:51):

> The area of stigma management, then, might be seen as something that pertains mainly to public life, to contact between strangers, or mere acquaintances, to one end of a continuum whose other pole is intimacy.

> One form this management takes is the control of the distribution of information within the limits their public identity will allow (Goffman,

1963:61). The men are slow to reveal aspects of their past or personal elements in their present life except when they want to do so. The subject of family relations is the most prominent area where information is controlled. Unlike traditional understandings of the family as presented in the geronto-logical literature (Rosow, 1967; Shanas *et al.*, 1968; Rosenberg, 1970; Tunstall, 1966), the familial relations of my respondents are akin to those found in skid row populations generally (Wallace, 1965; Spradley, 1970) and more particularly to the findings of Bahr and Caplow (1974) and Garrett and Bahr (1976). Broken marriages and infrequent or non-existent visits from children are seen by the men as forms of failure which carry a stigma with them. They do not discuss family very often or in great detail.

The stigma derived from work careers, drinking, or physical appearance is acknowledged and manipulated. It is used on the one hand to cover (Goffman, 1963:102) for the hard-to-bear familial stigma, and in this sense is a feature of control of information. On the other hand, these stigmas are accepted superficially in exchange for something desired from officialdom. When dealing with mission staff for example, there is an implicit notion that the men are inferior and that they should improve the moral tenor of their lives. The men sometimes feign reformation, but are able to laugh behind their humble smiles, i.e., they go to church only if a meal is served in return.

Another illustration of this is revealed in the relationship the men have with a local hostel which was new in 1973, and was designed to accommodate 24 skid row men as permanent residents. The staff has encountered considerable difficulty in trying to fill the residence. Skid rowers attach a stigmatized label of their own to any of their generation who are perceived to have fully accepted the self definition which mission staff try to impose. Such a man is labelled a "mission stiff". To avoid this label, manage the mission staff, and serve their own needs, men move into the hostel but not permanently (Wiseman, 1970:210). As Jim Sanderson says:

> "Not many of them go there to live permanently. They stay three maybe four months, and when they've fattened themselves up, they leave to go on a big drunk, living off the fat they've put on in the hostel." "None of them are there with the idea of staying, eh Jim?" "Well, maybe a few have good intentions, but not many."

Conclusion

This participant-observation ethnography of the old poor men in a Canadian city makes clear the relationship between career and identity maintenance. In the sense employed by Hughes, their objective careers are atypical, disjointed movements from job to job, which do not involve an adventuresome procession through progressive stages of increased responsibility. Notwith-standing this, subjectively, the men strive to make sense of their careers in a manner which allows them to attach meaning to at least some portion of their working lives in a way which contributes to the ongoing struggle for identity maintenance they are now engaged in.

As old men on skid row they no longer work at all, their families have disintegrated in any number of ways, and their identities are challenged by a public which defines them as derelicts. As a means of defence, they invoke stigma management through control of information and the imposition of a norm of reciprocity in their dealings with officialdom. Amongst themselves, the men have their own definitions of respectable behaviour and stigmatize as "mission stiffs" those who are seen to be selling out to the identity presented to them by the larger public.

These old poor men are both the product and producers of their history. They have had careers marked with false starts and disjunctures, making a sustainable sense of identity difficult in the world of the dominant reality. Nevertheless, these men are survivors and they have learned to cope.

Notes

1. The material in this section draws heavily on an earlier article entitled "Management of Self Among Old Men on Skid Row," *Essence* Vol. 2 No. 1.

2. See: Granatstein and Stevens (1972), Horn (1972), Grayson and Bliss (1971), and Piven and Cloward (1971).

10
GROWING OLD IN INUIT SOCIETY

Lee Guemple
Department of Anthropology
University of Western Ontario

The treatment the Inuit (Eskimo) traditionally accorded their old people during the precontact period has been a source of some consternation to members of the Euro-North American cultural tradition because of a seeming paradox. We know that Inuit lavished care and concern on their old people and invested considerable interest in them. But we also know that they sometimes abandoned them on the trail (Freuchen, 1961: 194-203) and that they stood ready at times even to help them to dispose of themselves by drowning or strangulation (Rasmussen, 1908: 127). Our own notion of what people are like makes it difficult for us to see how they could be so affectionate in one context and cold-hearted in another, when the chips were down.

The aim of this essay is to try to resolve the paradox; to show how the attitude of love and affection is not incompatible with the idea of killing one's own parents or helping them to kill themselves. To do so we must make a brief foray into the cognitive universe of the Inuit — into their own notion of how the world (of people and things) works. Only then can we fathom how they manage to mix sentiment with seeming cruelty without a sense of contradiction.

First, however, it will be useful to offer some background material on aging in Inuit society. Inuit have no generic term for "senior citizens". Instead, they use one term for an old man, *ituq*, and another for an old woman, *ningiuq*. These terms are used mainly while speaking about the old people, seldom when speaking to them.

It is difficult to establish the age in years at which people are consigned to old age. Like us, Inuit associate adulthood with work status, and old age constitutes a kind of "retirement" from full participation in community affairs. But Inuit do not keep vital statistics like we do. We cannot reckon an age of retirement for them. Besides, everyone is encouraged to continue working for as long as possible so that retirement comes not by convention, but by the gradual process of biological aging. While doing research in the Belcher Islands Inuit community, I was able to calculate the mean age at which men acquire the label of *ituq* at about fifty years of age (Guemple 1969). Women seem to maintain the status of adult somewhat longer, but will ordinarily pass over into being classed as *ningiuq* at age sixty or so.

Men become old when they can no longer hunt on a year-round basis but pass on the task of routine hunting to younger members of the household — generally a mature son or son-in-law. Hunting in winter is very demanding and because of its importance to the maintenance of life it is the crucial determinate of male status. At somewhere around fifty years a man can no longer sustain the strength and stamina to perform this task on a regular basis and will "retire". His withdrawal can be gradual but is often dramatic.

Women's allocated tasks are both more varied and less strenuous with the result that advancing age does not limit their effectiveness nearly as much as it does men's. Women routinely share work among themselves and the heavy work is often passed along to mature girls even in early adulthood while the older women tend to younger children and infants. Loss of strength and agility will not quickly be noticed in a woman. She will simply spend more time at home, performing other routine tasks such as cooking or sewing. The transition to old age is thus more gradual and comes later in the lifecycle than it does for men.

The onset of old age is hastened by debilitating diseases and may be slowed by what I have elsewhere called "renewal" (Guemple, 1969). The major forms of physical impairment that affect premature entry into old age are arthritis and blindness. The cold, damp character of the traditional igloo and tent tend to promote arthritis; and the incidence of blindness due to trachoma and glaucoma is relatively high. Men also suffer a relatively high incidence of corneal abrasion and snow blindness which can often lead to partial impairments of sight. In the recent past tuberculosis has also taken a considerable toll, particularly in those people who have been sent out to hospital to have portions of lungs or bones removed to rid them of infection.

Old age can also be delayed in some instances. Men often accomplish this by extraordinary effort in hunting during the spring and summer seasons when the demands of production are not so great; and they sometimes undergo symbolic renewal by taking younger women as wives in their maturity. Women cannot aspire to marry younger men in their later years; but they can and frequently do assert they are still able to perform their primary functions by seeking to adopt children. It is said that adopting a child makes an old woman feel young again; and while the primary aim of adoption is not stated to be renewal, it is the only reason given that makes very much sense.[1]

Old people are well cared for in Inuit society because they can draw upon two interlocking social institutions as sources of support: the household and the community at large. Members of a household share equitably; so long as there are younger workers in the household to work on behalf of their elders their interests are seen to with great care and devotion (Gubser, 1965:122; Hawkes, 1916:117). The rules of residence stipulate that young hunters stay home until they marry, and so an aging elder can expect to have his son do much of his hunting for him. When the daughters marry their husbands will come to live in the household, and they are answerable to their fathers-in-law, at least until after the first child is born. They may also remain in the household of an in-law if there is need and relations between the son-in-law and other household members are cordial.

Old people can expect some support from the community at large so long as they are able to contribute to the fund of resources from which others draw. Inuit rules of sharing enjoin that successful hunters share a portion of their catch with those who were less successful; and mature hunters are generally only too happy to be able to offer support to other community members, since it is the single source of prestige in the local hunting community. In return, the old people offer the produce of the hunting of their sons or sons-in-law or, as circumstances permit, they offer the help in sewing and gathering wood by their daughters, and they themselves will pitch in to help in any way they can to the general good. Men often offer work in repair jobs, executing technically difficult parts of various pieces of technology where knowledge and patience are particularly needed. They go for short hunting trips around camp, and often school young hunters on how to set snares, stalk land animals, etc. Women contribute their domestic labour for sewing, cooking, cleaning, baby tending, and so on. In the evenings, the old people, as keepers of the sacred and secular lore of this non-literate society, maintain a sense of tradition by telling stories and offering advice which experience shows to be particularly applicable to some predicament.

This system seems to work well so long as old people have someone to rely on to make their contribution to the community pool; and the institutional structure appears to break down only when the old people are left stranded by the departure of their children from the household and the community for one reason or another for an extended period of time. In that context, members of the community at large gradually come to view the old couple as parasitic and begin to complain about their dependency. So far as I am aware, community members would not flatly refuse to feed old people in such a situation; but they often receive a lesser share or the least desirable portion. And they may from time to time suffer the indignity of being gossiped about or verbally abused for their failure to contribute adequately.

As the couple grows into old age, one or the other will die leaving the survivor to move in with a son or daughter or with some more distant relative. The children generally accept the added burden gracefully; though more distant relatives may find it a bit inconvenient to be saddled with a sibling or cousin in old age. The Inuit of the Canadian North never collected material possessions as a form of wealth. The need to be continually on the move prevented the accummulation of luxuries. But men with ambition often collected people as a kind of "wealth"; and old men or women who were not too feeble were generally welcome in the household of an influential hunter if they had no children to care for them. Seldom were old people to be found in utterly desperate straits unless the entire community was impoverished.

If old people were well treated and cared for by their fellows in the traditional culture, they appear also to have been the objects of startling cruelties. Inuit are known to have abandoned their old people on the trail from time to time with very little ceremony; and there are even cases where the children stood ready to help them end their lives if asked to do so. Such behaviour strikes us as terribly inconsistent and begs for an explanation.

The well-documented facts are that Inuit sometimes abandon their old people. This was generally done either by leaving them behind while on the trail or by allowing them to go off on their own to make an end to themselves. When old people were abandoned, it was most often done out of necessity, seldom out of indifference to the old (Burch, 1975:148-50; Gubser, 1965:122; Jenness, 1922:236; Low, 1906:165; Spencer, 1959:252), though cases of apparently cruel treatment are known (Stefánsson, 1914:130).

Freuchen (1961:200-03) describes a typical case with his usual dramatic flair: a couple is travelling from one community to another accompanied by their immature children and an old woman, the wife's mother. Sometime during the night, the old lady, having faced an arduous day on the trail, decides the burden of living is too heavy for her to carry any longer, that she should now end the struggle to survive, that she has become a millstone to her children and grandchildren. She tells the two adults that she can go on no longer. They try to dissuade her, but she persists. Finally they agree, and in the morning they pack their gear and depart with only a word or two of farewell, leaving the old lady behind in the igloo, alone with her thoughts and her few meagre possessions.

Other examples appear to be even more unfathomable. An old man, perhaps nettled over some incident which has led to a quarrel or an insult to his sense of dignity, calls his two sons to him and tells them that he is old and useless, the butt of community jokes. Because of this, he has decided that, with their help, he will do away with himself. The sons encourage him to think positively, to remember the joys of playing with his grandchildren, and so on, but he insists that he has seen enough of life and wishes to be rid of it. Eventually, they leave off pleading, and under his direction, fetch a seal skin line and, wrapping the middle around his neck a couple of turns, take the ends and strangle him.

The conventional explanation of these situations is that the old are stoic about death and embrace the notion of their dying fearlessly and with resignation, when they feel they are no longer useful. So the sons or daughters accept the old person's decision with but very little coaxing.

There are a number of problems with this formulation of their reaction to the possibility of death. For one thing, it assumes that life in the Arctic is a continuous struggle for survival which people perceive and respond to by a sort of stoic resignation. While this notion is one of *our* favourite themes, it is certainly not part of the Inuit repertoire. They do not see their lives as endangered by their marginal situation. They know its hazards well and have what are to them adequate means for coping with them. It is strangeness that creates a sense of threat, not familiarity; so their situation strikes us as threatening. The Inuit do not perceive it to be so.

How then are we to explain their casual acceptance of the death of loved ones, particularly the old? The answer is that old people do not, in Inuit cosmology, really die. In order to understand this statement, it will be necessary to set aside momentarily our consideration of old age as such and examine briefly the Inuit conception of the underlying character of people, whether old or young. That inquiry will provide us with the basis for solving the riddle of their indifference to death.

Inuit believe that the essential ingredient of a human being is its name. The name embodies a mystical substance which includes the personality, special skills, and basic character which the individual will exhibit in life. Without that substance he will die; and should he exchange his name substance for another through a ritualized renaming process, he will become a different person.

The name substance is derived from other humans, but is not thought of as biological in character; and it bears little resemblance to units of heredity such as genes or of some more metaphorical analogue of biological inheritance such as "blood". The name substance is induced into the body within three or four days after birth; and the process of naming a child is viewed by Inuit as one in which a ritual specialist divines what particular name substance has entered its body. Often the name is that of some recently deceased community member, frequently a relative of the child. But it is never the substance of a parent or sibling of the child and the most frequent "choices" of names are those belonging to members of the grandparental generation. The names of children who are sickly are sometimes changed shortly after birth, and shamans and a few others change their names in adulthood and thus become different persons; but most people keep their given names throughout their lifetimes. At death, the name separates from the body but remains in the vicinity of the body or of the place of death for three or four days during which time it is thought to be dangerous to living humans. After that time, it is thought to return to the underworld to wait till it can enter the body of a newborn child. Names thus cycle as do the social identities which are attached to them.

Names are never exclusively held by individuals in Inuit society. Three or sometimes four individuals may bear the same name and thus be the same person in principle. We might express this idea in a different way and say that from the standpoint of the Inuit community at large, the society consists of a limited number of names each having its own social identity — personal history, personality, work skills, attributes, and attitudes, etc. — attached to it. The identities are shared out in the community among its members on roughly a one-for-four basis, and cycle. At birth, individuals step into one of these well-established identities and bear them in latent form until they come to full expression in adulthood. During their lifetimes, they may contribute to their shape; and at death, they pass their part of the identities on to the next generation fully formed. These identities are indestructible; they neither die nor dissipate, but instead go on endlessly cycling through one generation after another.

Since the name substance is not inherited from the parents and not' passed on to one's own biological posterity, parents contribute little to the children's identities except body substance which, to Inuit, is of little significance. And, since the social identity comes to the individual fully formed, it is not something the individual or the community were believed to be able to change in any major way, though in special cases it was possible to actually change identities.

We are now in a position to see why Inuit are relatively casual about the death of old people even if they are bound tightly to them in life. Children permit their parents to do away with themselves because they are not attached to them as we are to our parents. Every individual shares a community of spirit with others, but in Inuit society, that community is with those who bear the same name, not those who share the same blood or some metaphorical analogue. Sentiments link parents and children together, but these can never be binding because parents and children share nothing more vital than those sentiments.

A more compelling reason for the seeming indifference to the death of the parents is related to their understandings about the fate of the person concerned. In our cosmology, the death of an individual means at best his departure to another place, at worst the end of all being, the end of all subjective experience of self. In either case, it is a mystery that makes life precious, that makes us rather bear those ills we have than fly to others. In Inuit cosmology, the persona is the one enduring, immutable substance. Whatever else may happen, Inuit know that their persona live on, not in consciousness, but certainly as fully formed social entities. It is this fact of their existence, and not a resigned stoicism, that makes them indifferent to death when the body becomes infirm and the will to live weakens.

The treatment of the old we have described here and the cosmological order we have explored to explain what give them confidence and courage in facing old age and death is part of a tradition that is now on the verge of extinction across the Arctic as conversion to Christianity and the transition to modern living conditions gradually replace the aboriginal customs and beliefs. Modern-day old people of the North live in pre-fab homes, draw old age and disability pensions, take their sustenance from the shelf at the store, and receive their medical care from the local nursing station or hospital. These benefits have done much to make old age comfortable materially; and old men and women alike are quick to express their gratitude for these amenities. That the cosmological explanations we offer serve them as well in death as the material comforts we lavish on them in life is a little more difficult to assert with confidence.

Notes

1. The principal reason given for adoption by older women is that the adoption will provide someone to take care of the adopter "when they are old". But this same reason is given when the prospective adopter is in her sixties and the child is but one or two years of age. Further, the same reason is given by older women who have numerous children of their own, in some cases children already grown to maturity, and ready to care for the parent.

III

Work, Leisure, and Retirement

Age by itself means nothing other than that it indexes the passing of time. Our interest in aging is in the *changes* which occur with the passing of time, and major changes of interest to gerontology are in the allocation of time to leisure and to work. Within the years we now normally think of as the working years (remember that retirement at about age 65 is a social invention of this century), age is still highly relevant. For example, age discrimination has been found in some American industries as early as about age 35 or 40, and has been found to be significant after about age 45 (Sheppard, 1970). This occurs despite the fact that, in general, skill at industrial work increases with age, especially as regards accuracy (Koyl, 1977).

In a rare research report which can be classified as "industrial gerontology", Mervin Chen (Chapter 11) describes age-related changes in supervisory style among industrial foremen in Hamilton, Ontario. His paper is useful in suggesting a number of possible interpretations for age-related differences. Socialization processes occur over time and probably influence the supervisors, but structural and technological factors which vary by career stage also have their influences. In particular, the precariousness of older workers because of changes in the technology of the work place is relevant, and the important finding that qualification for full pension benefits frees supervisors somewhat from the constraints of superiors has important implications for social policy.

In general, it must be said that the implications of aging in different industrial and nonindustrial work settings is a major unresearched area in Canada. Much well-informed but largely anecdotal information can, however, be gleaned from various submissions to the Senate Commission on Retirement Age Policies.

Chapter 12, by Barry McPherson and Carol Kozlik, brings together the existing Canadian survey data on leisure participation and presents some heretofore unpublished analyses. These data are highly relevant to questions about retirement and the kinds of future people envision for themselves. They also have implications for the health status of older Canadians, who are likely to remain basically sedentary observers rather than physically active participants in recreational activity. The material raises some questions about the relative importance of social psychological causes of behavior as contrasted with structural factors such as ageism. To answer these questions, McPherson and Kozlik argue, calls for longitudinal data, that which is so necessary and yet so scarce. Despite the limitations imposed by the necessity

103

of using a number of cross-sectional surveys, this article provides a good example of how useful knowledge can be gained at relatively small cost from secondary analysis of existing data sets.

There is little Canadian research on the experience of retirement, but the two papers in this section have implications for our understanding of retirement and call for some remarks. The experience of retirement and a decision to retire at a given age (for those given the opportunity for choice in this area) is affected by work experiences and orientation and by the perspective taken toward leisure and the use of free time. It appears likely that compulsory retirement will be eliminated in Canada in the very near future, leaving more room for individual choice as to whether to work or retire. Chen's paper, however, is a reminder that social pressure can be quite strong regardless of legal regulation.

Mandatory retirement is, perhaps, the major social aspect of aging to receive widespread media attention in Canada during the past few years. This is partly because of recent changes in US legislation which raised the age of compulsory retirement to 70. The Senate Commission on Retirement Age Policies, through its continuing hearings across Canada in 1978 and 1979, has kept media attention alive for a protracted period. It has been argued, however, that the great concern for mandatory retirement deflects our attention away from the truly important aspects of retirement: our failure to provide a minimally decent level of economic security to all older Canadians (Orbach, 1978). As Powell and Martin show in a later chapter, the greatest proportion of the Canadian work force have no job-related pensions, and there are also important class and sex differences in economic security in the retirement years.

Although people have often been asked their opinion regarding issues such as appropriate retirement age or compulsory retirement, little can be stated with any certainty. Orbach (1978) has noted the biasing effects of question wording. For example, a poll conducted by the Harris Company for the National Council on Aging (1975) in the United States, used the wording: "Should a person be forced to retire because of age if he wants to continue working and is still able to do a good job?" It is surprising that 14% of the respondents answered yes to such a question. The fact that most respondents said such persons should not be compelled to retire was taken as a strong indication of opposition to mandatory retirement. On the other hand, a Canadian survey (Ciffin and Martin, 1977, discussed in Orbach, 1978) asked about compulsory retirement with a less-biasing question, "Do you agree that a compulsory retirement age is a good idea?" On a five-point agree-disagree scale, strong agreement was found from 39% of retired men and 30% of retired women. Persons active in the work force and aged 55 and over were even more strongly in favour of a compulsory retirement age, with 46% of men and 37% of women strongly agreeing.

Victor W. Marshall   105

Henretta, Campbell and Gardocki (1977) have pointed to the difficulty of conducting research which serves two purposes: the accumulation of basic scientific knowledge and the gathering of information for advocacy. Advocates for any given position might well be tempted to word questions, or to design sampling strategies, in a manner so as to produce results in keeping with positions they wish to advocate. For instance, Leonard Cain has examined a survey which showed little need for medicare during the United States Medicare debate. Funded with AMA funds, the survey stacked the deck by sampling and wording questions so as to produce such results (Cain, 1967). Less insidiously, there is a temptation by advocates and policy makers to ignore data which does not reinforce their positions, or to employ variably rigorous methodological standards depending on the nature of the study results.

Clearly, some people wish to retire early, and others late; while some people, strangely, wish to be compelled to retire. Whether work is seen as intrinsically rewarding or not, and whether the individual forsees the retirement years as carrying the possibility of enjoying leisure while remaining economically secure, ought to affect one's perspective on retirement and retirement age.

11

AGE AND CLOSENESS OF SUPERVISION
A Transitional Model*

Mervin Y.T. Chen
Department of Sociology
Acadia University

While many researchers in industrial and organizational sociology have sought to establish the consequences of different supervisory styles (e.g., Kahn and Katz, 1953; Likert, 1961; Nealy and Blood, 1966; Fleishman, Harris, and Burtt, 1955), some were also interested in their causes. Among these studies, personality (Poe and Berg, 1952; Fiedler, 1967), technology (Woodward, 1965; Meissner, 1969; Dubin, 1965), and the nature of the organization (Etzioni, 1961; Crozier, 1971) are isolated as factors accountable for differences in supervisory style. Strangely, a standard sociological variable — age — has been neglected. As an attempt to fill this gap, this chapter focuses on the interactional effect of age and some organizational factors on some dimensions of supervisory style. Discussion will be concentrated on the relationship between only one dimension of supervisory style — closeness — and the environmental variables. A more detailed analysis is found elsewhere (Chen, 1974).

A supervisor-worker relationship is viewed as a goal-oriented role system. To accomplish the goals, the behaviour of the people involved in the role system is governed by certain norms. In the work situation, a foremost norm is that a supervisor has the authority to supervise. To enforce compliance, various means may be used, including explicit checking of the actions of workers. As with all role performances, variations may be expected, and it was expected that supervisors would vary in the extent, or closeness, with which they check the actions of the workers.

Closeness of Supervision

Closeness of supervision is operationally defined as "the degree to which the supervisor checks up on his employees frequently, gives them detailed and frequent instructions, and in general limits the employees' freedom to do their work in their own way" (Katz, *et al.*, 1950).

Factors Affecting Closeness of Supervision

The choice among the variety of ways for a supervisor to play his or her role is often conditioned by some environmental variables: background charac-

*I am indebted to Drs. Frank E. Jones, Robert E. Drass, Harish C. Jain, and Victor W. Marshall for their counsel.

teristics of the supervisor, organizational structure, and technology. The influence of these variables on the closeness of supervision is discussed below.

Background variables Research has shown that these variables have influence upon organizational behaviour. Traditionally, age and the length of service have been factors underlying status orders. The literature on guilds and early craft unions has shown clearly the importance of age in the acquisition of skills and status (Pirenne, 1932). However, in contemporary modernized societies, the rate of accumulated experience of a technically trained person is far less rapid than the rate of innovations produced by aggregate experts (Moore, 1966: 23-41; Miller and Form, 1964: 516-17). Thus, while age and seniority may bring status in industry or in other organizational settings (e.g., Strauss, 1968), they may also make skills and knowledge obsolete, and may even induce insecurity in the technically incompetent. This may bring the worker more under the influence of his or her superior. It is also possible that, when authority of competence is not strong, increased reliance will be put on authority of position (see Hall, 1977: 197-235, for a discussion of typologies of authority). Thus, supervision may tend to be more strict.

Another factor of extreme sociological importance is the web of intricate interpersonal relationships that exist in industries. As Roethlisberger and Dickson have observed, these relationships are subtle, finely shaded, and sometimes become complicated (1939: 554-55). Since authority is unequally distributed in organizations, occupants of higher offices are vested with authority of sanctions. However, in most cases, evaluation is not entirely objective. Superiors have plenty of room for personal discretion. Thus, to achieve assigned goals is important, but to achieve them in one's superior's way is likely more important. A newly appointed young supervisor could hardly know the subtlety of this nature. He or she might learn "the ropes" only after unpleasant, possibly painful, experiences. It seems reasonable to hypothesize that the older supervisors' style of supervision may be more susceptible to the influence of the superior; whereas younger ones may be more responsive to the "formal" requirement of their job.

Structural variables Group size is simply defined as the number of workers under a supervisor's supervision. The perceived superior's supervisory style refers to the supervisor's perception about how he or she is supervised by the immediate superior.

Technological variables Task complexity indicates the level of knowledge that is required by the task (technical complexity) and the number of different interdependent operations and activities that are involved in carrying out the task (functional complexity). Worker autonomy refers to the degree that workers can control the pace or rhythm of their work and the extent to which workers can make decisions about what tools and material are to be used.

It is hypothesized that the structural and technological variables are inversely related to the closeness of supervision.

Methods and Findings

Data were gathered by questionnaires administered in seven manufacturing industries in Hamilton, Ontario. The sample, randomly drawn, was composed of 114 first-line supervisors (foremen). Supplementary material was provided by informal observations and interviews.

The degree of closeness of supervision was measured by seeking agreement or disagreement on a five-point range to three questions in Likert-type format. Respondents were asked: (1) In general, to get the work done, is it necessary to give detailed and frequent instructions to your subordinates? (2) In general, to get the work done properly, is it necessary to keep a close eye on your subordinates? (3) Should a foreman insist that the standard method of doing the job be followed under all circumstances? A complete score is obtained by adding the individual score of each question and high scores indicate a close supervisory style.

Multiple regression was used to assess the aggregate effect of the independent variables, with age controlled, on the responses to the three questions. The distribution of mean scores of closeness is shown in Table 1. It can be seen that closeness of supervision declines slightly as a supervisory style, with increasing age. However, the point of interest in this essay is the age differences in correlates of supervisory style.

TABLE 1:
DISTRIBUTION OF MEAN SCORES OF CLOSENESS, BY AGE GROUPS

Young Group (39 or younger)	Middle Group (40-49)	Old Group (50 or older)
N = 32	N = 42	N = 40
Mean = 9.43	Mean = 8.57	Mean = 6.70
s.d. = 2.32	s.d. = 2.31	s.d. = 2.32

The following patterns, evident in Table 2, are saliant with respect to correlates of supervisory style:

1. Supervisors of the middle age group are different from the young and old groups. While their supervisory styles are more susceptible to the effect of the length-of-service variables (YAF and YWFC), the styles of the "young" and the "old" supervisors are more likely to be influenced by some of the structural and technological variables (SOG, COMP, and PSSS). The length-of-service variables are all positively correlated with the degree of closeness of the middle age group. They indicate that the longer a supervisor works for a company, the more likely he/she would supervise closely.

2. Difference also exists between the young and the old age groups. While the degree of closeness to which the young and the old supervisors supervise their workers is affected by the same kinds of variables, perceived

TABLE 2:

MULTIPLE CORRELATIONS BETWEEN THE INDEPENDENT VARIABLES AND
CLOSENESS, BY AGE GROUPS

	Multiple R	DF	F	Independent Variables			
Young Group	.69*	$\frac{6}{25}$	4.0	COMP⁺	SOG⁻	YWFC⁺	SSE⁻
Middle Group	.52*	$\frac{4}{37}$	3.5	YAF⁺	YWFC⁺	SEE⁻	
Old Group	.62*	$\frac{5}{34}$	4.0	PSSS⁻	SOG⁺	COMP⁺	SSE⁻

NOTES:

1. The Independent Variables listed here are only those which entered into the multiple regression equation have an F value which is significant at .05 level or better.
2. The '+' and '−' signs attached to the Independent Variables indicate the directions of the relationships.
3. *$p < 0.05$.
4. COMP = task complexity; SOG = size of group; YWFC = years worked for the company; SSE = secondary school education; YAF = years as foreman; PSSS = perceived superior's supervisory style.

superior's style (PSSS) is the one variable that differentiated the old from the young. It is, in fact, the strongest variable accounting for the variance of closeness of the old supervisors' style. Although the other variables, i.e., group size (SOG), task complexity (COMP), and secondary school education (SSE), also have some influence, it is considerably smaller. The beta weight of PSSS is -0.601, which is much larger than those of the other three variables (SOG, 0.390; COMP, 0.311; SSE, -0.208). Thus, it seems clear that the older supervisors are susceptible to their subjective view of their superiors' style. (The negative correlation indicates that if they think that they themselves are closely supervised — high PSSS score, they are most likely to control their workers less closely — low closeness score.) The closeness of the young group's supervision, in turn, appears to be a result of the complexity of the tasks the group is assigned to do and the number of workers under supervision.

To sum up, it appears that a pattern has emerged from the analysis. Each age group seems to respond to different variables in developing its supervisory style. Based on the findings, the following model, tentatively labelled as the "transitional model", is formulated:

Young Age ----------- Middle Age ------------- Old Age
     ↓   ↓   ↓

Initial period -------- Transitional period ------- Mature period
     ↓   ↓   ↓

| More subject to the effect of task complexity, group size, skill level of group, and worker autonomy | More subject to the effect of length of service | More subject to the effect of perceived superior's supervisory style |

Discussion

The differences between the age groups may be viewed as a socialization process of supervisors. Transmittal of supervisory styles has been observed and reported in many previous studies (Katz, *et al.*, 1950 and 1951; Fleishman, Harris, and Burtt, 1955; Leavitt, 1964). Leavitt sharply pointed out that to a greater and lesser extent, any assigned job becomes two jobs: one job is to carry out the assignment and the other is to please the superior. All these studies indicated that low-ranking managers tend to imitate the supervisory style of their superiors. But none of them has paid attention to the role age plays in this phenomenon.

In the "transitional model", the three age groups may be considered as a historical continuum in terms of one supervisor. The way authority is exercised changes through the years in respect to responses to some of the influencing factors in the environment. The first few years in the career of a supervisor can be called the "initial" period. (We should not consider the age groups as operationally defined in this study too rigidly.) In this period, the supervisor is not far from training and is less aware of the "politics" of the industrial world, and thus, tends to be more responsive to the "formal" requirements. In other words, he or she does what the work requires. As time goes by, the supervisor accumulates more experience and enters into a "transitional" period. In this period, as reflected by the data, the length-of-service variables have more effect than the technological factors on the selection of supervisory styles. The longer one works for the company and/or the longer one is a supervisor, the stronger the tendency to control one's workers closely. And finally, the supervisor reaches a point which may be called the "mature" period. By this time he or she has learned the web of intricate relations in the environment, and "knows the score". Technological variables of course still exert influence on supervisory style. However, the perceived superior's style carries more weight in influencing the choice of his own supervisory style. In other words, to achieve the production goals is important; but to achieve these in the superior's way seems to be even more important.

In brief, the supervisory style a supervisor adopts has been viewed as the end product of the interaction of personal background characteristics and the structural and technological variables in the working environment. Some factors have more effect than others on a supervisor's selection of supervisory style at different career stages. Remarks made by some of the supervisors who participated in the present study are illustrative of our discussion above. One young supervisor, a college graduate, in Company A, said:

> I know that I am not as experienced as the old guys. But I know the technical aspect of the job well enough to be in my position. And I have great potential. When Doug [the plant manager] asked me the other

day about my aspiration in this company, I told him plainly that I'd like to sit on his chair some day.

What an older and outspoken supervisor in Company F told me about one of his colleagues, who was also a young, community college graduate, is most illustrative of our discussion about the old group:

> Roger is a typical book worm. He has been trying hard to apply the stuff he learned in school. But it doesn't work. Theory is one thing; reality is another. It is what the bosses say that counts in this place, not what the books say. Sooner or later he'll learn his lessons.

In addition to maturational and socialization processes, a complementary explanation for the transition is related to the perceived basis of job security. While most of the industries stress experience of their staff, they need competent young people with potential for organizational development. The better-trained young supervisors, such as the one mentioned above, feel they have the potential the company needs. They, therefore, tend to be more sensitive to the technical aspect rather than the social aspect of the job.

The older supervisors are in a precarious position. Their situation is precarious not merely because of age, but also because their technical knowledge is usually obsolete and they may feel they have little potential to adjust to the new. In many cases, almost the only factor that gives an old supervisor authority is seniority. It seems to be only natural for the older supervisors to act in a more acquiescent manner in relation to their superiors. The interpretation is given some support by the fact that, in the sample studied, only those who had already qualified for full pension benefits were less sensitive to superior's style. One supervisor in the study described the degree to which he is influenced by his immediate superior this way: "Jim [his boss] is kind of authoritarian; I don't pay much attention to him. I can walk out of this plant any time with full pension." Based on the above discussion, it is hypothesized that the perceived basis of job security changes, with age, from technical competence to the length of service, to acquiescence to superior, the latter stage reflecting a recognition of the precarious position of the older supervisors.

As for the middle-aged supervisors, while their technical knowledge may not be up to date as their young colleagues, they have accumulated seniority and experience. They feel secure about their jobs because of the fact that an organization cannot afford to lose its experienced personnel.

Summary

Our effort has been directed toward an analysis of the relationship between the closeness of supervision and some background and organizational variables. Findings suggest that age is the strongest differentiating variable.

A "transitional model" that involves three periods in correspondence to three age groups was developed. In each period, the supervisor responds to different influencing factors in the environment so that the way authority is exercised changes. "Maturation" and "job security" are considered as explanatory factors of the phenomenon. Although we believe the "transitional model" is a reasonable one, it still has to be considered tentative, because the design of this study is cross-sectional rather than longitudinal.

12

CANADIAN LEISURE PATTERNS BY AGE Disengagement, Continuity or Ageism?

Barry D. McPherson and Carol A. Kozlik
Department of Kinesiology and Sociology
University of Waterloo

Relatively few studies have examined the leisure patterns of adults at various stages in the life cycle, particularly in Canada, but most of what has been done indicates that as people age they participate in fewer and less demanding leisure activities. On the other hand, there are a few studies which contradict this pattern (eg., Atchley, 1971). This raises the question of whether people disengage (cf., Cumming and Henry, 1961) from social participation, including leisure activities, as they age; whether individuals continue to adhere throughout adulthood to the pattern which results from their socialization experiences prior to late adolescence or early adulthood; or whether adults are directly or indirectly forced by the presence of age-related factors to give up participation in specific leisure activities as they grow older. Unfortunately, studies have been unable to explain the existing patterns due to a reliance on cross-sectional, rather than longitudinal, data. Nevertheless, the basic descriptive information that is presented in these studies does provide some baseline data concerning the social participation patterns of particular age cohorts in the leisure domain. Moreover, when other demographic factors are introduced as controls (eg., gender, ethnicity, education, and income) a more definitive picture of the adult leisure scene emerges.

The purpose of this paper, then, is to briefly review two earlier Canadian studies which have examined the leisure pursuits of adults, to provide a secondary analysis of the most recent national survey on the use of leisure time by Canadian adults, and to raise some methodological and theoretical problems inherent in research on leisure patterns over the life cycle. First, some methodological caveats are introduced.

Classification and Measurement of Leisure Activities

Many descriptive typologies of leisure activities have been generated. Some of the more common polarities include: instrumental-expressive, active-passive, individual-group, family-non-family, intellectual-manual, and expensive-inexpensive. Most recently, Milton (1975) trichotomized leisure activities into: (1) inside-the-home/low-interaction activities (eg., television viewing, listening to records or radio, reading for leisure); (2) outside-the-home/low-interaction activities (eg., attendance at the theatre; visiting a museum, art gallery, or sport event; jogging; cycling; hobbies and crafts); and (3) outside-the-home/high-interaction activities (eg., participation in sport or in educational courses). Unfortunately for conceptual neatness, arguments can be generated to support or refute placing a given leisure activity into almost any category. For example, whereas reading can be considered a passive activity in the physical sense, it can be considered an active form of leisure in the cognitive domain. Therefore, because of varying classification systems found in different studies, it is difficult to compare the results of one study with another. Hence, little cumulative knowledge is derived.

Similar conceptual problems arise when the frequency or intensity of involvement in leisure activities is reported. In some studies, individuals merely report whether they engage in the activity or not, without reference to frequency. In other studies, a wide range of frequency intervals are employed, ranging from daily to weekly to yearly. Furthermore, some of the studies utilize or recode the reported frequencies to qualitative categories, such as "never", "sometimes", "regularly", or "as often as possible". This diversity in scaling creates interpretation problems when one wishes to compare studies. With these caveats in mind, let us turn to an examination of two earlier studies of adult leisure patterns in Canada.

Recent Studies of Adult Leisure Patterns in Canada

Hobart (1975) analyzed data, collected in Alberta between 1967 and 1969, concerning involvement in individual and group athletics. He sought to determine the degree of active participation for men and women in three age groupings[1]: under 35 years, 35-55 years, and over 55 years. He found, not surprisingly, that for all three age categories, men participate more than women[2] and that there is a sharp decline in active sport participation from one age category to the next, for both males and females. In an attempt to account for this pattern, regression analyses were run for each of the three age categories. Although very little of the variance was accounted for, a higher level of educational attainment was the most powerful predictor for the young and middle-aged men and for the middle-aged women. Unmarried status was the most powerful predictor for the young women, while, for the older men, amount of income was the most important predictor.

Finally, when compared to a national sample (Milton, 1975), Alberta reported a greater amount of sport participation in the three age categories. Although no explanation was offered for this differential rate of participation, it clearly suggests regional differences in life-style, perhaps due to opportunity set, environmental conditions, and early socialization experiences.

Based on a secondary analysis of data collected in an appendix to the March 1972 Canadian Labour Force Survey, Milton (1975) analyzed the responses of approximately 50,000 adults to determine the degree and type of participation in a variety of leisure activities. Utilizing the three qualitative types of leisure pursuits noted in the previous section, he examined the differential leisure patterns of various social sub-groups within Canada and found that the patterns vary by social status. More specifically, he sought to determine the influence on leisure pursuits of age, sex, marital status, level of education, relation to head of the household, and attendance at community events. In view of the concerns of the present study, only the findings pertaining to age as an independent variable are reported here.

For home-centred leisure activities, age was positively related to involvement with television, radio, and reading, but inversely related to record listening. For outside-the-home/low-interaction activities, age was inversely related to attendance at paid and free events, to physical activity, and to hobbies, although the patterns varied somewhat for those with higher levels of educational attainment. For example, males over the age of 65 with higher levels of educational attainment reported greater involvement in physical activity than the less-educated, younger groups. This finding stresses the importance of introducing controls into the analysis of leisure behaviour across age groups. That is, even within the same age cohort, life-chances and life-styles vary because of differences in social status. Finally, for outside-the-home/high-interaction leisure activities, age, as expected, was inversely related to active sport involvement and to involvement in adult education. Interestingly, only a few Canadians reported involvement in sport for an average of one hour or more per week (18 percent) or in adult education (7 percent). However, the degree of sport involvement may reflect a seasonal anomaly in that respondents were asked to report on their degree of involvement in the winter months of January and February.

Purpose and Methodology of the Present Study

In October 1976, Statistics Canada conducted a survey of the participation rates in fitness activities, physical recreation, and sport by over 50,000 Canadian adults. Also included in this supplementary questionnaire to the monthly Labour Force Survey were questions pertaining to other leisure pursuits. The purpose of this secondary analysis was to present and discuss adult leisure patterns by age distribution for two types of leisure activities: (1) sport activities, as a participant or as a spectator, and (2) popular culture activities such as watching television, listening to records, going to movies, reading books or magazines, and engaging in crafts or hobbies. For both types of activities, controls for gender, education, and income were introduced to the age distributions. Finally, the data patterns for the observation of spectator sports and for the popular culture activities were presented for those who indicated low or high commitment to an activity, as represented by the reported frequency of participation.

Results[3]

Active Sport Participation Patterns by Age

Table 1 indicates the percentage of participants who engaged in sport at least once in the previous 12 months or in an exercise program at least once in the previous month. Clearly, participation rates decline with age, with dramatic decreases appearing after 19 years and after age 64 — two points in the life cycle which respectively often mark the beginning and end of participation in the labour force. The table also illustrates how the same pattern holds for specific sport (eg., golf, swimming) or exercise (eg., exercise programs, jogging) activities. The one encouraging statistic is that 37 percent of the adults over 65 engage in some type of exercise.

TABLE 1:
PERCENTAGE PARTICIPATION IN SPORT AND EXERCISE PROGRAMS BY AGE*

Age	Sport[+]	Exercise[‡]	Jogging[‡]	Golf[+]	Swimming[+]
15-16	82.0	86.9	53.4	16.9	60.5
17-19	73.3	75.4	34.6	15.3	53.3
20-24	66.3	63.4	19.9	15.0	44.7
25-34	61.3	62.3	12.2	12.9	38.4
35-44	51.2	53.3	9.2	11.1	30.7
45-54	37.2	50.1	5.3	8.9	20.4
55-64	24.5	45.7	2.4	6.7	11.7
65 and over	9.7	37.0	4.0	2.5	3.6

*SOURCE: Adapted from *Culture Statistics, Recreational Activities, 1976*. Statistics Canada, Catalogue 87-501.
[+]Participated at least once in the past year.
[‡]Participated at least once in the past month.

When controls were introduced, it was found that men (54 percent) participated in sport to a greater degree than women (46 percent), but that the sex difference was less marked for exercise activities (60 percent of the men and 58 percent of the women were involved). Generally, participation rates increased with level of education and with income. For example, only 40 percent of those with incomes between $4,000 and $6,999 were involved in sport compared to 71 percent of those earning over $20,000. This linear pattern is different than the inverted-U pattern which emerges for the popular culture activities which are analyzed later.

Sport Participation as a Spectator

The inverse pattern of involvement by age holds, with the decrease quite pronounced after age 19 among those who had been highly involved. This may reflect a lack of opportunity to attend sport events after the high school years. When controls are introduced, we find that males consume sport more at all ages. At both low and high commitment levels for all age groups, except over 65 years of age, those with a high school education are the most involved, followed in order by those with some post-secondary education, those with an elementary school level, and those with a university degree. For the over-65-years-of-age group, those with an elementary school level of attainment watch sports more or as much as those with a high school diploma.

TABLE 2:

PERCENTAGE OF SPORT PARTICIPATION AS A SPECTATOR BY AGE

		Commitment	
Age	*Participants*	*Low (1/month)*	*High (5 or more times/month)*
14-19	40.5	9.9	9.2
20-24	26.0	9.4	3.4
25-34	21.5	8.1	3.0
35-44	21.4	6.8	4.3
45-54	15.1	5.8	2.2
55-64	9.7	4.2	1.0
65 and over	4.9	1.9	0.5

With respect to income, those earning between $10,000 and $19,999 tend to watch more sport at all age groups between 20 and 64, at both low and high degrees of involvement. For those under 20 and over 65, those earning less than $9,999 consume more. Those with no income or an income more than $20,000 consume less in all age groups.

Popular Culture Leisure Activities

Table 3 indicates very clearly that leisure patterns tend to be activity-specific in terms of degree of involvement. For example, a high percentage of adults consume television at all ages, while only between 30 percent and 40 percent are involved in crafts and hobbies. Nevertheless, the pattern of declining involvement by age holds for all activities except reading newspapers and magazines. One interesting anomaly that appears is the slight increase in the percentage of those over 65 who are highly committed to television viewing. This percentage is similar to those between 14 and 19 years of age, in that both groups have a higher percentage of free time than other age cohorts. What is not known is whether this relatively high percent-

TABLE 3:
POPULAR CULTURE LEISURE ACTIVITIES BY AGE

Age	Television			Record Listening			Movies		
	Percentage Who Participate	Commitment Low[a]	High[b]	Percentage Who Participate	Commitment Low[a]	High[b]	Percentage Who Participate	Commitment Low[c]	High[d]
14-19	91.6	14.5	11.8	88.7	28.8	5.1	58.1	19.1	6.0
20-24	92.3	14.2	9.9	73.3	30.0	3.1	54.0	21.8	3.6
25-34	92.9	13.8	8.8	63.0	32.7	1.3	44.5	19.1	1.3
35-44	90.4	18.9	6.7	51.9	30.8	0.7	23.2	14.1	0.7
45-54	88.9	18.7	7.0	40.4	25.3	0.6	17.2	10.9	0.5
55-64	86.4	18.2	9.3	31.0	20.0	0.4	10.7	6.7	0.4
65 and over	83.5	14.8	11.6	18.5	11.2	0.3	7.4	4.2	0.3

Age	Books			Newspapers, Magazines			Craft, Hobby		
	Percentage Who Participate	Commitment Low[e]	High[f]	Percentage Who Participate	Commitment Low[e]	High[f]	Percentage Who Participate	Commitment Low[a]	High[b]
14-19	58.5	25.2	1.4	66.3	42.5	0.6	36.7	16.1	1.2
20-24	58.3	23.6	1.7	74.6	43.8	0.5	40.5	14.8	1.4
25-34	59.8	24.0	1.3	77.2	41.5	0.7	43.1	15.1	1.2
35-44	52.7	21.4	1.1	76.0	37.9	0.7	36.9	13.4	1.4
45-54	48.9	19.1	1.0	74.4	34.6	0.8	35.4	12.3	1.6
55-64	48.2	19.2	1.6	71.8	31.1	1.2	34.5	11.8	1.7
65 and over	45.0	16.0	1.7	65.9	27.3	0.9	29.3	8.5	2.1

[a] Less than 3 hours per week.
[b] 30 hours or more per week.
[c] Once per month.
[d] Five or more times per month.
[e] Less than 3 hours in past month.
[f] 30 hours or more in past month.

age of committed viewers represents a real interest in what is consumed, or whether television merely provides an inexpensive and convenient way of filling free time.

The relatively stable pattern at all ages for the consumption of newspapers and magazines in all likelihood is accounted for by the daily reading of at least one newspaper. The slight decline after age 65 could be accounted for by such factors as failing eyesight,[4] disengagement, or a declining income which provides less money for purchasing discretionary items. Definitive explanations cannot be offered, however, because questions pertaining to the motivations of respondents for consuming specific leisure activities were not included in the original questionnaire. This is one major limitation of secondary analysis: *post hoc* explanations tend to be speculative rather than empirically or theoretically grounded in the data set. Nevertheless, the patterns do raise questions for future study and thus are worthy of mention.

In terms of sex differences by age for popular culture activities, some variation exists. For television and movies there are few sex differences except for those over 65 where females tend to consume more television and movies than males, both in absolute numbers and in percent. For record listening, men tend to listen more until 34 years of age while women listen more in the middle and later years. This pattern is especially pronounced at the higher levels of commitment. For reading books and for crafts and hobbies, women are more involved at all ages, especially at the higher levels of involvement. For crafts and hobbies, the differential involvement by sex increases with age. To illustrate, of those who spend less than 3 hours per week on a hobby, from 20 to 24 years of age 56.8 percent of those involved are females, whereas in the over-65 age group 71.3 percent of those involved are females. Finally, concerning the reading of newspapers and magazines, there are few sex differences except at the high level of commitment where males are more involved. However, this greater involvement by males at the high level of commitment does not hold for those under 19 and those over 65 years of age. What this may suggest is that the higher commitment between the ages of 20 and 64 by males may be accounted for by the reading of trade or professional periodicals related to their occupations.

In general, the influence of education and income follow a similar inverted — U pattern (see Figure 1). At all age levels over 19 years, those with a high school education and those earning less than $10,000 tend to be more involved, followed by those with some post-secondary education and those earning between $10,000 and $20,000. People at the extremes, those with an elementary school or university level education and those with no income or an income over $20,000, tend to be less involved. The major anomaly in this pattern is the not-too-surprising finding that those with a university degree are more involved in reading books at all ages, and at both levels of commitment, than they are in the other forms of leisure analyzed in this study.

FIGURE 1:

INVERTED - U PATTERN OF INVOLVEMENT IN LEISURE BY CANADIAN ADULTS, CONTROLLING FOR INCOME AND EDUCATION

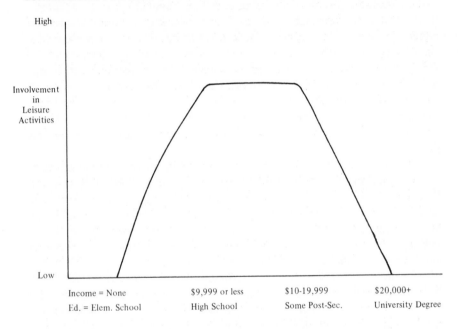

Discussion

This recent survey of the leisure patterns of Canadian adults clearly suggests that involvement declines by age and that different age cohorts are involved in specific activities to varying degrees. What is not clear is why this pattern of declining involvement occurs. On the one hand it may be argued that individual and/or institutionalized disengagement occurs (Atchley, 1977:25-26) and hence aging leads to decreased social participation. Unfortunately, only large-scale, longitudinal surveys or, at the least, retrospective questions of a particular age cohort concerning their earlier involvement at specific times[5] could begin to determine the impact of disengagement on leisure patterns by age distributions.

Another alternative explanation is that each age cohort has undergone unique socialization experiences and almost develops a sub-culture of its own within the broader social structure. For any given age cohort, the values, opportunity set, and childhood experiences concerning sport and leisure may be different from those of other cohorts; for example, for those who are 65 years of age and over in 1979, their early socialization featured an average work week of approximately 50 hours, a high value on work, few vacations, little education beyond elementary school, and few opportunities to engage in any form of leisure in their late adolescent or early adult years. In view of the support for the "continuity" approach to aging,[6] it might be argued that this cohort would never acquire a high value for or experience with leisure. So when those aged 65 and over report little involvement compared to a 25-34-year-old cohort, it is feasible that this specific cohort would have reported low involvement in leisure at all ages had they been asked. Projecting ahead, it might be argued that except where declining physical condition inhibits involvement in an activity such as sport, the 25-34-year-old cohort of today will be considerably more involved when they reach age 65 than are those in today's over-65 cohort. Again, only longitudinal studies with the same subjects can provide definitive support for this projection.

A third alternative explanation for the pattern of declining involvement by age is derived from the theory of age stratification (Riley, Johnson, and Foner, 1972). This approach suggests that age strata exist wherein individuals acquire normative beliefs as to how one should behave while a member of a particular age stratum. The presence of this stratification system is perpetuated by age grading wherein opportunities, interactions, and role responsibilities are related to chronological age. Thus, age discrimination, or ageism, may operate to restrict the opportunity set and to define the normative standards in the leisure domain. More specifically, relatively few opportunities are provided for adults to participate in sport once they leave the educational setting. Similarly, the record and movie industries quite clearly direct the content of their product and their marketing approach toward specific age groups. Thus, there is little social reinforcement in the adult world for the individual who thinks and acts young. In short, this explanation argues that as one gets older specific activities are dropped, or not learned in the first place, because of a lack of opportunity and because of restrictive behavioural norms based on societal perceptions of age-appropriate behaviour. That is, age discrimination may operate in the leisure domain as it does in other areas of social participation.

In summary, while patterns of leisure involvement at different stages in the life cycle have been presented, patterns over the life cycle for individuals born at the same point in time have *not* been described. Moreover, a definitive explanation for the inverse relationship between age and leisure involvement is not yet available because of theoretical and methodological limitations in the studies completed to date. Ideally, a Statistics Canada survey on a regular basis with the same subjects would greatly assist in providing some answers to the questions raised in this descriptive study.

Notes

1.This is yet another methodological inconsistency which creates interpretation problems across studies; that is, a variety of quantitative and qualitative age groupings are utilized. Moreover, many studies include only one category for those "65 years and over." Quite clearly the 65-year-old represents a different birth cohort than the 80-year-old in terms of life-style.

2. This pattern should change since the young women of to-day are more likely to be socialized into sport earlier in life, with the result that as adults sport will be a more integral part of their life-style. This should be reflected in more active female age cohorts in the future.

3. Appreciation is expressed to Terry Stewart, Leisure Studies Data Bank, Department of Recreation, University of Waterloo for generating the cross-tabulations for the popular culture activities analyzed in this study.

4. This explanation is introduced because the category "65 and over" includes those in their 70's and 80's. Again this is a limitation to the analysis of leisure patterns in the later years in that such a large age grouping may hide cohort or health differences in social participation patterns.

5. On the other hand this type of design has the inherent weakness of the accuracy of recall by the respondents concerning earlier periods in their life cycle.

6. This approach argues that as individuals grow older they are predisposed toward maintaining continuity in habits, associations, and preferences established in the earlier years. That is, early experiences and life-styles are maintained as much as possible (cf. Atchley, 1977).

IV

Aging and the Changing Family Context

As increasing proportions of people live into the later years, the very nature of the family changes. While we are accustomed to think of "the family" as a nuclear family of a married couple and a few children, sociologists and gerontologists now see that even a three-generational concept of the family is inadequate. Many families today, and more in the future, consist of four and even five generations of living persons. Of these, two generations may be in the retirement years. One gerontologist, Bernice Neugarten (1979), has argued that "parent-caring" has emerged as the important issue in the family. Another central familial issue lies with the increasing proportion of widowed persons, especially females, in the later years. Women who marry may, on the average, anticipate living several years as widows, and for them it is possible to think of widowhood as a new stage in the family life cycle, with its own characteristics and needs.

The first chapter in this section, by Sharon Abu-Laban, briefly reviews the changing theoretical attempts to characterize the family life of older people, and the evidence relevant to theory. Other important critical reviews of this literature are those of Sussman (1968) and Troll (1971), which are general reviews, and Marcus (1978), who, like Abu-Laban, interprets knowledge about aging and the family in the Canadian context.

Abu-Laban correctly points to the mythology of happy and supportive three-generational family units, cites Laslett's research which shows that this myth does not accurately characterize the family life in many European societies, and speculates that immigration patterns as well as norms favoring independence in North American society probably make supportive three-generational families in Canada historically rare as well. This is one case in which we are fortunate to have at least some research. In Chapter 14, Jane Synge draws on material from people in the Hamilton, Ontario region to suggest there were quite distinct familial patterns affecting the situation of the aged in rural and urban environments. She contrasts a value of cooperation in the rural areas with a valuing of independence among the urban middle and working classes. However, the factors affecting relations of urban old people with their children are numerous and complex; they include the health and financial status of the older generation, the marital status and financial situation of the children, and whether both members of the couple survive.

123

It is always important to consider the historical perspective in which contemporary social patterns have developed. This is especially so in the study of aging, where individual lives and relations between the generations have been shaped through history. It would be a mistake to assume that the patterns found by Synge apply in other parts of Canada, such as the prairie west (see, for example, Kohl, 1976) with its more recent flows of immigration; the Atlantic provinces, with their different economic bases and rural-urban patterns; or Quebec, with its greatly different culture and history. Jane Synge's paper may, however, be taken as exemplary of the kinds of research needed to help us understand the historical context, and also of the types of data which are useful in researching the phenomena of aging. Too much gerontological research has relied on the sample survey. Historical material, both primary and secondary sources, and life-history or "oral history" interview techniques have an important but generally neglected place in such research.

Abu-Laban describes the precarious situation of the widowed in contemporary society, and Synge shows that such precariousness is not new. In Chapter 15, Anne Martin Matthews brings together the demographic data which show the dramatic increase in the proportion of women who are living as widows and describes not only their low income levels but the implications of widowhood for identity. As Matthews points out, when considering the needs of older widows, it is crucial to view widowhood as a process rather than a state, for these needs, and the kinds of support available to the older widows, change over the months and years following bereavement. Readers may wish to speculate why so little is known about the experience of widowhood in males or females anywhere, with very little Canadian research in this area. As it comes to be recognized that widowhood is a *typical* phase of family life, perhaps we will be motivated to systematically try to find out more about it.

While reading the selections which deal specifically with aging and changing family contexts, readers should remember that several other selections in the book present data on the importance of family type and family experiences. Thus, Lee Guemple in Chapter 10 describes the strong bonds between the generations among Canada's Inuit, while Joseph Tindale, in Chapter 9, shows how the family relationships of old poor men were fractured during the depression years. The labeling of some old people as senile, described by D'Arcy in Chapter 16, begins as a family affair, and family status is important in affecting marginality, institutionalization, and the economic security of older people, the topics of several other chapters.

13

THE FAMILY LIFE OF OLDER CANADIANS*

Sharon McIrvin Abu-Laban
Department of Sociology
University of Alberta

Family relationships traditionally provide the major sources of interpersonal support, warmth, and commitment for most people of all ages. However, the nature of family relationships changes over the life course and among the most dramatic changes are those that tend to accompany the later years of adult life.

The significance of changes in family relationships in later adulthood will become increasingly salient, for more and more Canadians are experiencing the time period loosely referred to as "old age" and usually defined chronologically as age 65 and over. The 1971 census indicated some 1,744,410 Canadians were 65 and over, 8.1% of the total population. Projections are that by the year 2001, one out of ten Canadians will be 65 and over (Statistics Canada, 1974b). However, researchers are just beginning to be aware of the significance of this phase of the life course to a fuller understanding of the family.

This paper examines some of the characteristic features of family life in later adulthood. However, before beginning a discussion of the specifics, an important cautionary observation must be made. Much of the exisiting data use age 65 as the turning point marking old age; thus people above this age are arbitrarily assumed to be both "old" and analytically similar. It is misleading to categorize all people over the age of 65 as the same. There are important differences within this age group which have implications for probable family relationships. First, there are two generations of people over the age of 65. It is estimated that one out of ten people age 65 and over has a child who is also over the age of 65; hence some "senior citizens" have children or (as the case may be) parents who are also senior citizens (Atchley, 1977:300). Second, at the least, there should be recognition of differences between those in the 65 to 74 age category and those age 75 and over. Typically, these two age groups differ, both in terms of health and in probable availability of family support ties. In combination, however, the later years of adult life have some important characteristics which distinguish them from other points in the family life cycle. The following discussion will examine some of these distinctive characteristics.

Marriage in the Later Years

A happy marriage is a boon in all phases of the life course, particularly so in old age. Given current patterns in the timing of marriage and childbirth and increases in life expectancy, the average couple today can anticipate many years of marriage together after their last child leaves home. What are the chances for a marriage in the latter years, particularly after retirement, to be a happy one?

It appears from self-reports that older people have a good chance of having a happy marital relationship. Research on marital satisfaction, at various stages of the family cycle, suggests that marital satisfaction, for both husband and wife, is at its peak in beginning, pre-child, "honeymoon" stage marriages and in post-retirement marriages (Rollins and Feldman, 1970). While these data may initially appear to suggest that with tenacity in the maintenance of a marital relationship, problems stand a good chance of being satisfactorily resolved, we, in fact, do not know. The seemingly positive data on marital satisfaction in the later years are based almost entirely on cross-sectional research studies which compare different age groups at the same point in historical time. Longitudinal studies, following the same cohort of people throughout the duration of their particular marriages and into old age, would give us more useful information indicative of changes over time, but these studies do not exist. Further, it should be noted that the older people, interviewed after some forty years of marriage, are possibly marriage survivors; presumably the less successful marriages were the ones more likely to have ended along the way and one might expect the originally more rewarding marriages to be those still in existence. It is further possible that older people may feel more social desirability pressure to indicate that theirs is a happy marriage than do people at other phases of the life course.

However, the evidence which suggests the two high peaks of marital satisfaction to be at the beginning and at the end of marriage promotes consideration of the similarities between these two periods. Aging and the retirement experience may contribute to the creation of parallels between the early years of dyadic attachment of young people and of older people. There are some common features: (1) among both there is usually a child-free, adult-centred life style; (2) research on both the happily married post-retired couples (Clark and Anderson, 1967) and the newly married (Blood and Wolfe, 1960) indicates that there is task performance which cuts across traditional sex role boundaries; (3) both groups tend to have (or make) time to do things together; (4) both groups, similarly, must usually function on a reduced income, in contrast to those in other stages of the marital cycle; (5) both groups may, also, have a heightened appreciation for their relationship, the younger group because the union is newly formed and its endurance not tested, and the older group because of an awareness that their union continues in the face of the uncertainty of life and the reality of death.

Retirement provides the older couple with great amounts of discretionary time and the greater possibility of joint participation in activities which they can structure. However, the idealized vision of retirement as a time to freely roam the far corners of the globe, must, in fact, be reconciled with changed finances (income drops about one half at the time of retirement), and with the possibility of decreased physical vigor on the part of one or both partners. In a recent, large-scale Alberta study, comparisons between pre- and post-retirees found that people tended to overestimate the importance of travel and underestimate the impact of poor health on their post-retirement activities (Third Career Research Society, 1976).

The difficulties created by a disabling physical condition or a low, fixed income in a time of inflation are more common to the later years of retirement than to new retirees. In fact, the current generations of older people, having shared the historical experience of the depression years of the 1930s, have often learned to do with less; future generations of senior citizens, coming from eras of affluence, may be less equipped to deal with diminished income; they may also be less committed to the work ethic. As it currently stands, however, retirement appears to be associated with a redirection, on the part of a work-oriented generation of husbands, toward an increased emphasis on socio-emotional and expressive activities. This may be a contributing factor in the reported high rates of marital satisfaction among post-retired couples.

Among such couples there also appears to develop an interdependence which provides mutual support in coping with physical problems common to later years. About three out of four people who are 65 and over have a chronic health condition. Couples not only tend to help one another in time of illness, but marriage appears to act as a deterrent to institutionalization. The serious illness of one partner can put a tremendous strain on the

TABLE 1:

MARITAL STATUS OF THE OLDER POPULATION, BY AGE AND SEX, CANADA 1971 (Percentage Distribution)

	Males		Females		Total	
Marital Status	65-69 years	70 years and over	65-69 years	70 years and over	65-69 years	70 years and over
Single	10.7	10.4	10.8	10.7	10.7	10.6
Married	80.4	66.6	55.2	31.0	67.2	46.5
Widowed	7.5	22.0	33.0	57.8	21.0	42.3
Divorced	1.4	1.0	1.0	0.5	1.1	0.6
Total	100.0	100.0	100.0	100.0	100.0	100.0
Persons	296,050	485,810	323,910	638,640	619,955	1,124,445

SOURCE: Compiled from *The Canada Yearbook, 1973* (Ottawa: Information Canada, 1973), Table 5.15, p. 213.

healthier spouse, but important support tends to be provided within the marital relationship.

Thus, the available evidence argues well for the benefits of marriage relationships in older age. As well, our society has stressed the husband and wife roles as important components of adult life. Yet, marital relationships are differentially available in older age. Table 1, indicating the marital status of the older population in Canada, reveals both age and sex differences in the likelihood of being married in later years. Among people in the 65-69 year age group, 80% of men are married, in contrast to a little over half (55%) of the women. In a society which places high value on marriage and at an age where marriage appears to hold particular rewards, we see many who are outside a couple relationship. This dramatic shift is revealed even more clearly in the seventy years and over age category. At this stage, most men are still married (67%) but only 31% of women are married. Hence we see that women in particular are likely to find themselves living outside the marriage relationship in old age.

Widowhood

While much public and research attention has been given to issues relating to divorce and its disruptiveness for the individual, the family and society, the most common form of broken marriage is caused by the death of one of the partners. Nowhere is this truer than in older age. Further, given the fact that women tend to marry men older than themselves and that there is now a seven-year differential in life expectancy at birth which favors females, the chances of being the surviving spouse are far greater for women than for men, as Table 1 illustrates. At ages 65-69, only 7% of men are widowed; in contrast 33% of women are widowed at this age. At age seventy and over, 22% of men are widowed, in contrast to 58% of women.

There have been debates in the literature about whether coping with the death of a spouse is more difficult for a woman or for a man. The loss experienced in widowhood is that of the unique companion of probably much of one's lifetime; both widowers and widows must go through the difficulties of bereavement and work through the grief process, which is likely to involve not only sorrow, intense longing and somatic difficulties but also guilt, anger and temporary disorientation in time and place. In addition, however, the surviving partner has lost a socially important role, that of spouse. Canadian society emphasizes the normalcy of the married role and this has been internalized by older Canadians. The difficulties which arise when coping with the loss of this important role are in some ways different for women than for men.

For the current generation of older women (in possible contrast to future generations), the role of wife has provided much of their status in the community and through this role they may have become increasingly dependent, over time, on their husband's instrumental skills, e.g., occupational, financial, mechanical, and so on (Bernard, 1972). The new widow may find she has to learn or relearn many competencies or else transfer her dependencies to someone else. During this time, the older widow stands a good chance of finding a community of other widows who can help to provide support and social integration (Blau, 1961). In making this reintegrative move toward support from other women, the widow must adjust to what she may define as a drop in status; moving out of the couple relationship and into the company of women only (Lopata, 1970:52).

Older males, on the other hand, may be dependent on their wives' homemaking skills (Berardo, 1967) and, as well, on their wives' interpersonal skills. Older husbands appear to be more likely than older wives to regard their spouse as their single closest confidant (Lowenthal and Haven, 1976), and, further, they may be dependent on their wives' skills as, in essence, the socio-emotional representatives of the family. Men who lose a spouse are more likely to find themselves isolated from kin and neighbors (Berardo, 1967). The difficulties are further compounded for men without an occupational role. In contrast to older women, who may be able to turn to other widowed women for companionship, the widowed man is likely to find himself in a minority compared to other men (most of whom are still married). In addition, he may feel less skilled at maintaining socio-emotional ties with his, probably now long grown, children. Widowed people, generally, are a high risk group in terms of morbidity and mortality rates (Holmes and Rahe, 1967); this is particularly true for the widower (Bock, 1972). The widower, however, does have a distinct advantage in that his chances for remarriage are very favorable.

Remarriage

Remarriage, as an option to the widowed older person, is also differentially available. The probability of remarriage is greater for males than for females in later years. A major contributing factor is the sex differential in life expectancy: in 1971, the life expectancy for males, at birth, was 69.2 years, compared to 76.1 years for females (Science Council of Canada, 1976:14). The sex differential in life expectancy lends to the shortage of potential husbands in the older age categories. Table 2 illustrates this by showing the sex ratio (the number of males per hundred females) for selected age groups in Canada in 1971.

It is currently common social practice for men to marry women somewhat younger than themselves. In 1921, grooms were, on the average, 4.4 years older than brides; in 1971 there was a 2.3 year difference favoring males (Kalbach and McVey, 1976:95). A study in the United States found that 20% of grooms over age 65 had brides who were under 45; in contrast, only 3% of brides over 65 had grooms under age 45 (Treas, 1975:104). This means that

Table 2 shows that for the age group 0-44 the sex ratio is 103 males per 100 females; for the 65-74 age group the sex ratio is 87 males per 100 females; for those 75-84 it is 74 males per 100 females; and for the age group 85 and over it is 66 males per 100 females. The steady decline in the sex ratio at later ages has implications for remarriage.

TABLE 2:

SEX RATIO BY SELECTED AGE GROUPS, CANADA 1971

Age Group	Sex Ratio (Males Per 100 Females)
All ages combined	100.2
0-44	103.2
45-64	97.5
65-74	87.1
75-84	74.2
85-89	68.4
90 and over	59.4

SOURCES: Based on *Census of Canada, 1971,* Catalogue 92-715, Vol. 1, Part 2, Bulletin 1, 2-3, p. 7-1, 7-2. The sex ratios for the age groups "85-89" and "90 and over" are based on *Perspective Canada* (Ottawa: Statistics Canada, 1974), Table 1.12, p. 11.

older males have a theoretically wide age range for selecting potential mates, whereas older women's choices are often limited to age categories where there is a shortage of potential husbands.

The limited research, thus far, on remarriages among older widowed people suggests that such marriages tend to be successful. Yet remarriages sometimes must occur in the face of social convention. McKain's (1972) study of post-retirement marriages in which both partners had been widowed previously, indicated that about one-fourth of the couples almost didn't marry because of social pressure. Older people who successfully remarry after the death of a mate, often marry someone similar to their first spouse and, as well, someone previously well known to them, perhaps during the first marriage itself. Certainly the predicted increase in remarriages in the later adult years provides research challenges yet to be explored. For example, what is the impact on adult children when the long familiar parental dyad not only breaks, through death, but is then reconstituted? What is the impact on an older male or an older female of moving into the role of step-parent to middle-aged children or of attempting to meet the perhaps conflicting expectations of two sets of adult children and two sets of grand-children? Researchers have tended to emphasize the complexities of inheritance decisions in such marriages (McKain, 1972; Sussman, 1976), however, the emotional ramifications on the conjugal unit and beyond would appear to offer intriguing research possibilities.

Given the discrepancy in life expectancy between sexes and social custom favouring age differentials between mates, remarriage is not a likely possibility for most older women. Writers who urge remarriage and/or sexual expression for the older population often overlook two important considerations: (1) the differential availability of males and females in the later years make monogamous, heterosexual relations an unlikely option for many older women; and (2) importantly, the current generations of people age 65 and over have had historically different socialization experiences with regard to sexuality and sexual expression and this may well be reflected in terms of *their* definitions of their sexual needs and the ways appropriate for them to express these needs.

The differential likelihood of remarriage has household implications which are reflected in Table 3. The information in this table groups those 65 and over into one common category which, as emphasized earlier, is problematic, but the table suggests some of the magnitude of change in family life involved for people age 65 and over, particularly for women. In contrast to the 15-64 age group where some 95% of both men and women are living in a family setting, 18% of the men and 36% of the women age 65 and over are living alone, apart from any family relationships. Thus women are far more likely to be alone in old age than are men. These statistics also suggest the meaning behind the responses in a 1973 study consisting of 616

TABLE 3:

PERSONS AGED 15-64 AND 65 AND OVER RESIDING WITH A FAMILY, LIVING ALONE, OR LIVING IN COLLECTIVE HOUSING, BY SEX, 1971[1]
(Percentage Distribution)

	Males		Females		Total	
	15-64 years	65 years and over	15-64 years	65 years and over	15-64 years	65 years and over
Living in a family[2]:						
Own family	88.6	74.1	89.3	53.5	88.8	62.8
Other family or group[3]	5.9	8.1	5.4	12.7	5.7	10.7
Total family	94.5	82.2	94.7	66.2	94.5	73.5
Living alone[4]	3.6	11.1	3.9	24.6	3.8	18.4
Living in collective housing[5]	1.9	6.7	1.4	9.2	1.7	8.1
	100.0	100.0	100.0	100.0	100.0	100.0
Total persons	6,673,875	774,405	6,647,030	950,775	13,320,905	1,725,180

SOURCE: *Perspective Canada II* (Ottawa: Minister of Supply and Services, 1977), Table 3.10, p. 45.

1. Excludes approximately 141,000 persons for whom the relationship to head of household could not be determined.

2. The family in this case is an economic family which is defined as a group of two or more persons living together and related to each other by blood, adoption or marriage.

3. Includes persons living with economic families of which they are not a member and persons sharing households with other non-family persons.

4. Does not include persons living alone in collective housing.

5. Includes persons living in hotels, motels, nursing homes, staff residences, military and work camps, jails and penitentiaries, rooming and lodging houses and other institutions.

interviews with a probability sample of senior citizens in Toronto. When asked to indicate the single most serious problem faced by senior citizens, the most common response, given by 34% of the respondents, was loneliness (Canadian Radio and Television Commission, 1974).

Relations with Adult Children and Other Kin

Older people are often actively involved in giving and receiving emotional support through a broad network of kin. Researchers differ on the importance of siblings in old age; however, the extent of contact between parents and adult children has been widely examined. Between the aging parent and the adult child there is often a two-way flow of assistance and emotional support. While there are social class variations in the type of help given, older parents are far from being the passive recipients of their adult children's bounty. Reciprocal help is given in the form of home services, monetary assistance, assistance in time of illness and other crisis situations and, in addition, older parents often provide child care services (Shanas, 1967; Adams, 1968a). Various studies have found that older parents are in frequent contact with at least one of their adult children. While we have measures of the frequency of contact between adult parents and one of their adult children, we do not have adequate information on the number and type of adult children who infrequently contact their adult parent. The widely lauded accessibility of one adult child does not inform us about the total family picture of the particular older person, or the number of other adult children who may be in infrequent contact and the implications of this, if any, for parents and for the adult children themselves. Further, while we have studies measuring the frequency of contact between parents and one of their adult children, we do not have adequate information on the *quality* of that contact, both from the perspectives of the parent and of the child.

Current studies suggest that contact between generations is heavily maintained by women; they write letters, phone, visit, maintain the integrative rituals of family holidays, and provide care in time of illness. One may speculate on the significance of this fact in light of increased participation in the labour force by women and the necessarily decreased amount of time they will have to devote to such intergenerational family maintenance and support.

Given current trends in the timing of marriage and child bearing, the role of grandparent to very young children is actually not common for people age 65 and over. For people in this age category and beyond, grandchildren may be more typically teenagers and older. While some relationships between grandparent and grandchild are quite rewarding, a United States study found that about one-third of the grandparents studied reported discomfort with the grandparent role (Neugarten and Weinstein, 1964). We have little information on the great-grandparent role, but clearly the stereotype of grandparenthood as an all encompassing role in older age is problematic. Meaningful grandparenting appears to be associated with preferences for particular grandchildren. In contrast to the parent role, in grandparenthood there is greater freedom to express preferences and the expression of preference for favourite grandchildren was related, in one study, to enjoying the role itself. Those who expressed no preference were likely to be less attached to grandparenting in general (Lopata, 1973a). Various studies have attempted to look at the functions of the grandparent role. Kalish (1975), however, makes a suggestion which would seem to hold interesting research possibilities, in addition to serving as a possible warning: perhaps grandparents' relationships with their adult children provide training for the observant grandchild which may be reflected in how these children eventually relate to their aging parents.

We often find an implicit equation of real caring on the part of adult children with participation in multigenerational living arrangements, as supposedly occurred in the "good old days". In actual fact, social historians and historical demographers now question whether three-generation households were ever very common (Laslett, 1971). Not many people lived to advanced old age and, given the history of immigration to Canada and the fact that young people are the ones likely to move, multigenerational family units were probably historically uncommon in this country. Moreover, a norm of independence tends to operate in North American society, stressing the independence of both older parents and their adult children. Older people themselves give verbal assent to this norm. They do not express a wish to live with their adult children but, rather, see such a move as fraught with hazards for all concerned.

However, for some older people who face the wrenching trauma of widowhood, broader family supports in the form of joint living arrangements appear to be available. Previously unpublished data from the 1971 census for the population of Alberta (Government of Alberta, 1977) indicate that among widowed older people, 27% of the men, in both the 65-74 and the 75 and over age groups, share housing with children or other relatives (this category includes both single and married children and other kin). Of widowed women in the same age groups, 30% share housing with children and/or other relatives. Widowed men appear to be about as likely as widowed women to share housing with single children alone (9% of both men and women in the 65-74 age group and from 6% to 7% of men and women in the 75 and over age group share housing with single children).

There are filial norms operating which tend to obligate adult children to meet the needs of dependent parents, particularly the very old. Older parents themselves tend to give verbal assent to norms of autonomy and independence from adult children, yet running through the gerontological literature are speculations concerning the accuracy of these reports (e.g.,

Kalish, 1975:78-79; and Sussman, 1976:228). For those older people whose lives are going relatively smoothly, it is presumably easier to profess commitment to such norms. Yet advancing age does have its real problems and in times of crisis, people of all ages, young and old, tend to turn for help in the direction of what is regarded as one of life's constants, the bond of kinship.

Conclusion

This brief discussion has focused on typical shifts in family relationships in later years. It has not considered the family life of single older people (11% of the population age 65 and over have never been married), or that of older people who are divorced (less than 1% of the population 65 and over), or of those who married but remained childless. Among the current generations of older people, most are or have been married; most of these marriages will be or have been broken, not by divorce, but by death; most of these marriages have produced children.

In a society which values marriage relationships, there is evidence that the marriages of older people are rewarding but ephemeral. The likelihood of being the surviving spouse is far greater for women than for men. In a society which stresses independence of parent from adult child and vice versa, the older parent (in particular over the age of 75) may verbalize the norms of autonomy, yet find it increasingly difficult to live within the norms in the face of widowhood, increasing physical disabilities, dwindling income and shrinking social contacts.

Yet the later years of family life often provide older people, particularly men, with the time to reassess the quality and importance of interpersonal ties and, as well, give a time perspective in which to view the meaning of family and kinship. There are difficulties common to family life in the later years and these are not widely known. This suggests the need to make valid information available to the general public and, as well, perhaps provide transition counselling to enable people to work through some of the family changes associated with advanced age. This paper has raised some research questions needing further study. That there are not only problems but many *unknowns* about family life during the later years of adulthood suggests the need for social scientists to attend to the analytical significance of what is becoming an increasingly prevalent stage in the family cycle.

14

WORK AND FAMILY SUPPORT PATTERNS OF THE AGED IN THE EARLY TWENTIETH CENTURY*

Jane Synge
Department of Sociology
McMaster University

The first part of this paper outlines the changes in the proportions of aged who work and the rise of pension schemes over the past half century. The second part uses life-history interviews with people born before 1908 to examine the family and institutional strategies of support in old age in the era before the introduction of pension schemes. I will argue that in the early twentieth century old age was for many not a period of ease or retirement. Uncertainties about means of family and economic support were greatest among the urban working classes who were not bound by property or inheritance considerations or by firm traditions relating to family responsibility for the aged.

The Historical Context

To give context to this argument, it should be remembered that in 1901 the proportion of the population aged 65-and-over stood at 5 per cent, in 1921 at 4.8 per cent, and in 1971 at 8 per cent. The introduction of universal pensions is a feature of the last few decades (Chappell, this volume). Prior to that time elderly people lived from their own work, from their savings, from support given to them by their families, from private charity, and from public aid. Anderson has described the changes in Britain (Anderson, 1977). Bryden (1974:25-28), in his history of policy making and old age pensions in Canada, points out that the fall in the proportion of people employed in small businesses and on farms in the late nineteenth and early twentieth centuries hit the elderly very hard. The new urban industrial conditions made it harder to adjust their work level to their health and strength. In the city, residential space and food, the basic needs, had to be bought with cash wages. Within the urban working-class family, ties and obligations were no longer reinforced through the existence of family property that could be handed from generation to generation.

*The research on which this paper is based was supported by the Canada Council and by a grant from McMaster University. An extensive report of the full study is in preparation, and some additional material is found in Synge (1977; 1978; 1979).

In nineteenth century Ontario some municipalities had offered outdoor relief, but they were not required to do so. Counties could establish houses of refuge and industry. Private charities supplemented this provision. By 1906 all counties were required to establish homes (Splane, 1965). Throughout the first quarter of the century, there had been intermittent discussion of possible pension schemes, part of the discussion fueled by home concerns, part by new legislation and developments in Europe. It was often argued that state-supplied pensions would encourage people to be spendthrift and irresponsible. The shiftless would be rewarded at the expense of the hardworking. Children might learn to neglect their parents. While state pensions might be necessary in European countries, with their lower standard of living and higher population densities, private saving and family responsibility were held by many to be adequate (Fischer 1977:160). While government pension plans were being introduced from the 1920s on, it was only in 1951 that universal pensions for those over 70 and means-test pensions for those aged 65-70 were introduced.

TABLE 1:
LABOUR FORCE PARTICIPATION RATES BY AGE GROUP AND SEX, 1911-1971

	Males							
	14-19	*20-24*	*25-34*	*35-44*	*45-54*	*55-64*	*65+*	*Total*
1971	46.6*	86.5	92.6	92.8	90.3	80.1	23.6	76.4
1961	41.4*	87.2	94.1	94.3	91.9	81.9	28.4	78.1
1951	48.8	92.3	96.4		93.2		38.6	82.2
1941	55.4	91.5	97.9		95.2		58.9	85.9
1931	57.3	92.6	97.7		95.8		69.0	87.4
1921	65.4	92.3	96.2		94.3		71.0	88.3

	Females							
	14-19	*20-24*	*25-34*	*35-44*	*45-54*	*55-64*	*65+*	*Total*
1971	37.0*	62.8	44.5	43.9	44.4	34.4	8.3	39.9
1961	34.2*	49.5	29.6	31.1	33.4	24.4	6.7	29.7
1951	31.4	46.8	24.2		19.6		5.1	23.6
1941	30.1	46.5	27.5		15.2		19.9	24.5
1931	29.1	47.0	21.7		13.5		22.8	23.6
1921	29.5	38.3	19.9		11.8		19.0	20.5

*For the age group 15-19 rather than 14-19.
SOURCE: Urqhart, M.C. and K. H. A. Buckley (eds) 1965. *Historical Statistics of Canada.* p. 62 Toronto: Macmillan Company of Canada; Statistics Canada, 1971 *Census of Canada* Vol. 3, Part 1. "Labour Force and Individual Income." 2-1, 2-2.

Trends in the Employment of the Aged

Table 1 shows that in the early twentieth century the proportion of the Canadian population aged 65-and-over who were working was high. In the 1920s and 1930s over 60 percent of men aged 65-and-over were working. By 1971 this figure had dropped to less than one quarter. In the early decades of the twentieth century, married women did not usually work. However, the labour force participation rate for women aged 65-and-over was relatively high. In the 1920s and 1930s, about one elderly woman in five worked. This suggests that elderly widows were being forced into the labour market. Just as was the case for men, their rate of participation has dropped sharply in recent decades. Nowadays, fewer than one of ten women aged 65-and-over is in paid employment.

Strategies of Coping

Over the years 1974-1976, I collected structured, tape-recorded life history interviews with a quota sample of men and women, all born before 1908 and drawn so that respondents' fathers were representative of the different socioeconomic groups in the textile-producing and metal-working city of Hamilton, Ontario, in the early twentieth century, and interviews with men and women who grew up on farms in the rural hinterland. Respondents were mostly of Protestant Canadian or British immigrant origin. The structured interview schedule followed the respondents' lives from childhood, through schooldays, adolescence and young adulthood, up to about 1930, by which time most respondents were in their thirties. One section of the interview was devoted to relationships with parents after the respondent left home and the support and care of parents in old age.

In this analysis I do not deal with the subsample of recent continental European immigrants. Their family traditions were rather different from those of the Anglo-Canadians, and while the Anglo-Candadian working classes generally lived in modest comfort, the continental European immigrants had the least well-paid jobs and the poorest living conditions (Synge, 1976). The discussion is based on analysis of 35 interviews with people raised on farms, 33 interviews with working-class people, and 30 interviews with middle-class people.[1]

When considering strategies for coping with old age in the past, one must make oneself aware of the kinds of family cycles that were typical. Since detailed, historical demographic analysis is not yet available for Canada, we draw on analyses of life cycles in the United States. Historical demographers have shown that for women who were born in the 1880s, there was commonly no "empty nest" stage (Wells, 1973). The first spouse to die often died at about the time of the marriage of the last child. Children's feelings of responsibility to the surviving parent were probably greater then than nowadays when children can expect that their parents will live together for part of the "empty nest" stage. Shanas (1967) has described how the flow of help between generations varies, depending on such factors as the social class of parent, social class of child, numbers of children, and distance between residences.

Discussions of the family's responsibility for the aged in the early twentieth century usually ignore the fact that a substantial number of people either did not marry or did not have children. Research on the population of Massachusetts shows that, of the cohort of women born in 1890 who reached adulthood, about one quarter did not marry, and about one fifth of all women who married could expect to be childless (Uhlenberg, 1969:407-420). Only half of the women who married could expect to follow the pattern of having children and having their spouses survive until the children reached adulthood. Because the last century has seen such dramatic shifts in the timing of life-cycle stages and in the extent to which people experienced marriage, childlessness, and early deaths of children, spouses, and parents, one must be careful to interpret historical material on the care of the aged in the context of demographic features of the late ninteenth and early twentieth century.

Not one of my respondents mentioned having had parents who spent periods in houses of refuge or homes for the elderly. One suspects that this was partly because such institutions would be more likely to be filled by the childless than those who had children to whom they could look for support. In addition, respondents might have been embarrassed to mention that they had allowed a parent to become dependent on public welfare or charity.

The Rural Pattern

Farm people were asked about their parents' later years. They were asked where their parents lived, with whom, whether they had savings or pensions, and to what extent sons and daughters cared for them. They were also asked about the arrangements for holding and passing on of property.

There was one clear pattern among these farm people, most of whom were owners: parents remained on or near the home after the marriage of the inheriting child. Among the Anglo-Canadians in the Ontario countryside it was not usual, as had often been the case in rural Ireland (Arensberg, 1940), for sons to delay marriage until middle age, when parents became too feeble to run the farm. Rather, it was expected that some sort of compromise be worked out. The younger or older couple might move to a new house built on the property or nearby. "Yes, they (my parents-in-law) stayed on in the house till they built a place out back for them" (WPO5, farm woman, born 1883).[2] Farmers' wills often have contained provisions regarding the amount of house space, meat, and produce the surviving wife is to receive as she lives in the farmhouse with the inheriting children.

On the farm, house space and food were not as limited as they were in the city. The working-class city home rarely had more than three bedrooms and in the city food cost money. On the farm provision of the personal services so often required by the old was burdensome, especially in the summer when wives and daughters might be needed for outdoor work. One farm woman said: "My father was gone [dead]...My mother and my two aunts were there and it was quite a burden" (WPO7, farm woman, born 1892). No urban working-class family could have taken in three elderly people.

Lack of help on the farm could be a major problem for the old. In the early twentieth century industrial wages were relatively high but several respondents talked of staying on the farm out of a sense of responsibility to their parents. Old farmers without children to help them found it hard to carry on:

> He (father) died of a heart attack. He dropped dead on the kitchen floor. But I think that probably a lot of this was brought on by his overwork. Because after his brothers died or moved away, he was the only one on a hundred acres. And while we had help, help, even in those days, was never anything to write home about. (MP10, farm man, born 1900).

The childless elderly on the farms might seek hired help, though this was hard to come by. One man who came as an immigrant from Britain in the 1910s and spent time as a farm labourer talked of the abominable food and foul living conditions on a farm run by a childless couple who were simply too old to carry on. To assure their comfort in old age, farmers needed children. Children from Dr. Barnardos' Homes in England went mainly to farms. The children's classic, *Anne of Green Gables* (1908), set in Prince Edward Island, starts with the discussion of how an elderly brother and sister needed to adopt a boy to help outdoors. A girl, Anne, was sent by mistake.

Social and economic life in the countryside had strong elements of cooperation, and social control was strong. Neighbours were dependent on one another for day-to-day services as well as help in emergencies. J.K. Galbraith (1964:47) discussed the importance of "being a good neighbour" in his account of the Ontario Scottish community in which he grew up during the First World War:

> A man was also excluded from society if he was unneighbourly...Every farm was subject to sudden emergencies...A man was obliged to put his neighbour's needs ahead of his own and everyone did. Occasionally there were complaints that a man called for help too readily. But no one ever declined. Again, the social penalty would have been too severe.

In a tightly knit community, any neglect of obligations to elderly parents would be noticed.

The Urban Pattern

We now outline the various strategies for coping with old age among urban working-class and middle-class people. Respondents were asked about any experiences of poverty in childhood. All respondents emphasized the value of family independence, and those who had received charity found this experience most degrading. We must point out that working-class people rarely had any savings and that the only period of real family prosperity was when the children were working but not yet married (Copp, 1974). City people were also asked about their parents' old age. They were asked about their parents' means of support, work, saving, and pensions. They were asked about the extent of the responsibilities felt by sons and daughters. They were asked about where and how their parents lived in their later years.

One suspects that respondents overestimated the help they gave. For example, they might not have mentioned cases of parents being sent to houses of refuge and industry. Nor would one expect many respondents to talk of any fears of being deserted in old age that their own parents may well have had, as one man did:

> When he [father] worked in the parks—Macassa Lodge was down at the foot of John Street—the old people would come out and talk to him about how their children had put them in the home. And he [father] had a fear of it. (MB12, man, born 1901 in England, arrived in Canada in 1908).

Several respondents did talk of aunts who had terrible fears of being left destitute or institutionalized in their later years and who were continually saving and economizing. As already noted, it is probable that the inmates of homes were drawn disproportionately from among those with no children.

The urban working-class fathers of our respondents had no conception of retirement. Working-class men worked as long as they were able. As age crept up on them, they might seek less physically demanding jobs. Some lodges gave small pensions to infirm members. Men generally died before their wives. While both husband and wife were alive, they were expected to maintain an independent residence. As soon as one died, it was expected that children consider taking in the surviving parent. Responsibility fell on the unmarried before it fell on the married. "We all signed off the house to my sister Dora who was single [and looking after mother]. All the kids signed off the house and gave it to her" (MCWO3, man, born 1904). Goode (1963; also, Abu-Laban, this volume) has commented on the extended family of western nostalgia. I would suggest that this conception may have come about in part because of the tendency to think of older people as living in families. However, the expectation was that the available unmarried son or daughter (in those times more numerous) live with aging parents. Married children with their own children generally lived in independent households and would take in their aging parents only when this became necessary through the dissolution of the parents' household through death or financial hardship, and when there were no unmarried children available to help.

We have a considerable amount of material on financial dealings in working-class families. The great majority of working-class respondents who worked for pay in their teens gave their earnings directly to their mothers. The expectation was that children living at home would contribute the bulk of their earnings to their parents. Once the child left home or married, parents could not expect contributions. The first commitment of the married man was to his wife and family. The same pattern existed in New England cities and in England (Hareven, 1977:198; Stearns, 1972). "I always had to give everything. I'd go home with my pay envelope without opening it and then I'd get 25 cents or 50 cents" (MCW07, man, born 1902). "Every cent I earned my mother got" (MB10, man, born 1901 in England, arrived in Canada in 1902).

There was, of course, in some working-class families, a shift in the balance of power within the family in the children's late teens or early twenties. Teenage sons in industrial work would earn nearly as much as their fathers. A son and a daughter together could earn as much as their father. In 1911 one third of all family income was earned by co-resident children (Dominion Bureau of Statistics, Census of 1911, unpublished data for the city of Hamilton). Since parents valued the income, they tried to make home attractive to grown children. Boys, often making near men's wages, might leave if displeased with the treatment they received at home. One young rivet-maker had, in fact, been on poor terms with an older brother, and he overheard his parents talking about the situation.

I hear my mother talking to my father..."You know...if he [respondent] keeps bugging his brother like that he [the brother] is going to leave home..." So I went in and I says, "There is a possibility I could leave home too!" That really startled her. You see the impudence.

"I don't know, Mag" said father. "There's a lot of truth in what he says. He could leave home."

(MB01, man, born in Britain in 1900, arrived in Canada in 1907)

There was no set pattern among these Anglo-Canadians, like some other societies, whereby one particular child was designated as responsible for his or her parents. A variety of patterns existed, and support was often shared. Daughters could not be completely relied upon because their husbands might oppose the giving of support. While farm parents had generally known their children's spouses for years, urban working-class youth married people their parents did not know. They met at work or at dances. Working-class parents had a special interest in developing respect

and friendship with their sons-in-law. The following accounts show some of
the variety in working class strategies.

> We took over his house and he [father] lived with us. He couldn't save
> anything because he earned so little...When we took over the house, he
> had it right in the agreement that he should have the back bedroom as
> long as he lived (MB12, man, born 1901 in England, arrived in Canada
> in 1908).

Widows might move from household to household.

> My father died in 1934. For the next 25 years my mother lived with me
> or others of her children. We, the family, supported her (MB10, man,
> born 1901 in England, arrived in Canada in 1902).

For working-class women left alone in old age, one strategy for survival
was the keeping of boarders. Modell and Hareven (1973) have shown that in
Boston in the 1890s, the keeping of boarders was associated with the "empty
nest" stage in the life cycle and with widowhood. A number of our respondents talked of how their parents saved for a house when the children were in
their teens and contributing their wages to the household. "And we all
chipped in. We started to work very early. So that's how we got it [the house]
(MB09, man, born 1907 in England, arrived in Canada in 1912).

A house provided some security. In several families the house was
made over to the child who undertook the support of parents in old age. A
widow could sell a house and pay a lump sum to the child who took her in.
Parents who become dependent have always wanted to have something to
offer. For example, the receipt of even small pensions has raised the status of
the aged in their families. Grandparents are enabled to buy small presents
for their grandchildren, and those who live with relatives can make some
financial contributions to the household.

Among urban, middle-class families, where the aged usually had their
own financial support, daughters, especially unmarried daughters, were
expected to provide emotional support and companionship to aged parents.
Sons and sons-in-law were not needed for financial support. The unmarried,
middle-class daughter, whose earnings were not needed, was expected to
care for and provide companionship to her parents, even before they
reached old age. The daughter of a modest businessman described her
reaction to the idea that she stay at home after leaving school:

> In those days, there were a lot of girls stayed home, I mean in the class I
> was, helping mother. If there was more than one, one nearly always
> stayed home. That was one of the things I was afraid of. I'd never have
> much money though I'd be taken care of. My parents would get old, and
> I'd be afraid to leave them.

We saw that happen so often when I was young, where the unmarried daughter was sort of left in a bad spot. But it seemed to be sort of taken for granted. There seemed to be in every family an unmarried aunt who was available to come and that kind of thing (WCM11, woman, born 1892).

Another middle-class woman described what happened after her widowed mother's heart attack:

I was going on to be a teacher. The doctor called up my oldest brother and laid down the law. Was there any reason why I had to go and work? And I didn't have any financial reason why I had to. And could we carry on the house and look after our mother? Had father left provision in such a way that we could carry on in the same house we kids had grown up in? That was possible; and Dr. _____, his word was law with us...So I stayed at home, and the house was run the same as ever (WCM01, woman, born 1892).

We suggest that the emphasis in childrearing on respect for and obedience to parents buttressed traditional expectations of family obligations and family support for the aged who could no longer work. When asked about parents' values in childrearing, the most common response was that parents emphasized respect and obedience. Few respondents mentioned being expected to show consideration or affection. "We had to respect our parents. You wouldn't dare talk back to them" (WCW12, woman, born 1907).

Religion was also a powerful force. Many respondents talked spontaneously of religion as a source of values in childrearing.

I was an Anglican, and you learn the ten commandments. This is what my life was made up of. I was expected to do unto others and respect my father and mother, and not to steal, and not to lie. That came naturally (WBO5, woman, born 1902 in Britain, arrived in Canada in 1907).

[We were expected to be] good citizens, to go to church. Supposed to act right to people (WCWO7, woman, born 1900).

This was an era of traditional values, and independence and self development were not yet seen as goals in childrearing (Lynd & Lynd, 1956:143-145).

Conclusion

This paper has provided some limited data on strategies for survival among the aged prior to the introduction of universal pension schemes. It has been argued that the nineteenth century conception of the life cycle was one without marked changes, such as retirement, in the later years. There was simply a gradual slowing down. However, with the twentieth century came mandatory retirement for men in industrial work and increasingly, for women, a period of "domestic retirement" as children began to marry and leave home several years before the mother's death, thus creating an "empty nest" stage. We have shown that while there were clear expectations in solid farm families that the aged remain on or near to their farms, there was no such clear-cut expectation among the urban working class, among whom the degree of support in old age would depend on the vagaries of health, the quality of relationships with children, fluctuations in the employment market, and the local institutional provisions. Nor in the city was there the same degree of social control as in the countryside, where neglect of needy kin would be noted.

In the absence of research, we can only speculate as to the extent to which these data from one Canadian region may be taken as paradigmatic of broad-based changes in the status of the aged which accompany industrialization or modernization.

Notes

1. Respondents who grew up on farms were all drawn from people still living in the countryside, outside Hamilton. They are probably from the more successful farm families, and well disposed to farm life. Professionals, managers, and owners of business that employed more than one or two non-family members were taken as being middle class.

2. Figures in parentheses represent case identifiers. The same code is used in other publications from this project.

15
WOMEN AND WIDOWHOOD

Anne Martin Matthews
Department of Family Studies
University of Guelph

There are over one million widowed people in Canada. Eighty-two percent of them are women, and the proportion is increasing (Statistics Canada, 1978b). Among Canadians over age 65, the proportion of men who are widowers has declined from 20.4 percent in 1961 to 16.7 percent in 1971; the proportion of women over the age of 65 who are widows has increased from 48.4 percent to 49.4 percent (Statistics Canada, 1977d). The sex-selective nature of widowhood is even more obvious when one considers the differences in absolute numbers of widows and widowers. Among the over-age-65 cohort, the number of widowers actually declined between 1961 and 1971, while the number of widows increased by 37.1 percent (Table 1). For all ages, widows outnumbered widowers by nearly four to one in Canada in 1971; by 1976, the proportion had increased to nearly five to one (Statistics Canada, 1977d, 1978b).

TABLE 1:

PREVALENCE OF WIDOWS AND WIDOWERS, 65 YEARS AND OVER, CANADA, 1961 AND 1971

	1961	1971	Percentage Change 1961-71
Widowers	137,277	130,235	−9.5
Widows	346,903	475,635	+37.1

SOURCE: 1971 Census of Canada, Cat. No. 99-725, Table 26.

This profile of the prevalence of widowhood in Canada indicates why discussions of widowhood tend to focus on women. The reasons for this are fairly obvious, and include such factors as the differential life expectancy of males and females;[1] the consequences of the mating gradient, whereby husbands are generally two to three years older than their wives; and the differential in rates of remarriage for widows and widowers.[2] Not only will most married women in Canada be widowed in later life, but also, most will remain widowed for the rest of their lives. Consequently, this discussion of widowhood in Canada focuses on the situation of widows rather than widowers.

Another dominant characteristic of widowhood in Canada is its age-relatedness (Figure 1). The age at which widowhood begins has steadily

FIGURE 1:
PERCENTAGE OF MEN AND WOMEN WIDOWED BY AGE, CANADA, 1976

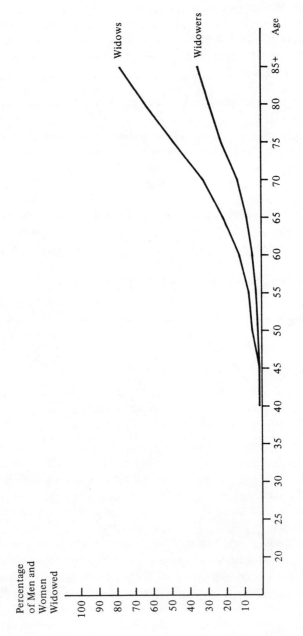

SOURCE: 1976 Census of Canada. Unpublished tabulation, Statistics Canada.

increased in recent decades, with the result that widowhood is now associated not only with women, but also with the aged. A century ago the onset of widowhood was generally coincident with the marriage of the last child, while today many more couples jointly survive the "empty nest" phase (Foner, 1978b). Nevertheless, the proportions of the widowed in each age cohort increases dramatically from age 50 onward (Table 2).

TABLE 2:

WIDOWED POPULATION 15 YEARS AND OVER, BY SEX AND AGE COHORTS, CANADA 1971

	Widowers		Widows	
	N	Percentage of Age Cohort*	N	Percentage of Age Cohort*
Total, 15+ years	191,125	2.5	752,895	9.8
15-19	1,365	0.1	1,540	0.1
20-24	1,340	0.1	2,405	0.1
25-29	1,615	0.2	3,970	0.5
30-34	1,800	0.2	5,480	0.8
35-39	2,640	0.4	9,670	1.5
40-44	4,350	0.6	16,935	2.7
45-49	6,990	1.1	31,065	4.9
50-54	9,290	1.7	46,900	8.7
55-59	13,730	2.9	69,955	14.5
60-64	17,780	4.6	89,355	22.6
65-69	22,710	7.6	106,945	33.0
70-74	26,860	13.0	116,055	46.0
75-79	28,580	20.4	107,335	57.8
80-84	26,785	31.3	81,495	68.7
85-89	17,660	43.4	45,215	76.1
90-94	6,200	54.6	14,995	79.6
95+	1,400	55.7	3,595	77.8

SOURCE: 1971 Census of Canada, Cat. No. 92-730, Table 1.
*Percentages are my own calculation.

With the increase in the age at widowhood, the years that a widow can expect to live have also increased. Half of those widowed at age 65 can expect fifteen more years of life, and one-third can expect twenty more years (Riley and Foner, 1968:159). During that time their lives as widows will become quite different from what they knew as married women.

In attempting to profile the widowed in the Canadian population, one must note the ways in which they differ from the rest of the Canadian population. For one, the widowed are more urban than most Canadians. While just over three-quarters of the Canadian population lived in urban regions in 1976, 81.1 percent of the widowed population did. The largest single disparity occurred in cities with populations of 500,000 or more, where 37 percent of all Canadians, but 39 percent of the widowed, resided (Statistics Canada, 1978b). There is some evidence that widows often relocate to large urban areas, motivated by such factors as proximity to children, the greater availability of community and social services, and housing suitable for those living alone (Hoffman, 1970).

Elderly women in Canada are far more likely than the rest of the population to be poor (Ross, 1975:22-23), and this is particularly true of older widows (Dulude, 1978:38). As Table 3 demonstrates, widowed older women struggle to survive on incomes considerably lower than those of others in their age group. A report of the Advisory Council on the Status of Women highlights the finding that the main cause of the widow's economic woes is "the extreme financial vulnerability of most elderly married women".

TABLE 3:

PERCENTAGE OF MEN AND WOMEN AGED 65 AND OVER, IN VARIOUS INCOME GROUPS, BY MARITAL STATUS, CANADA 1970

	% of 65+ Population	0	$0-999	$1,000-1,999	$2,000-2,999	$3,000-4,999	$5,000-9,999	$10,000 & Over
		%	%	%	%	%	%	%
Women								
Single	5.9	1.3	5.7	49.4	12.7	15.1	12.6	3.2
*Married	21.6	4.5	28.2	50.9	7.2	5.3	3.1	0.8
Widowed	27.3	1.6	7.2	59.9	12.8	10.8	5.9	1.8
**Divorced	0.4	–	–	–	–	–	–	–
	55.2%							
Men								
Single	4.7	1.1	6.7	52.7	13.2	12.9	10.1	3.3
*Married	32.2	0.6	4.7	32.3	15.5	19.3	20.0	7.6
Widowed	7.5	0.9	5.1	51.5	14.1	13.8	10.8	3.8
**Divorced	0.4	–	–	–	–	–	–	–
	44.8%							

*Includes separated
**Not available

SOURCE: 1971 Census of Canada, Cat. No. 94-760, and Cat. No. 92-730. Adapted from Dulude (1978: 39).

A third have no personal income other than Old Age Security, and over half of Canadian married women aged 55 to 64 have no income at all. "When their husbands die, it appears that most of them will inherit nothing but poverty" (Dulude, 1978:40).

Throughout the widowhood literature, accounts of the devastating effects of financial insecurity on bereaved women abound (Caine, 1974; Love, 1974; Wylie, 1977). Worries about basic economic survival can become so pervasive in widowhood that some researchers have found them to be the cause of long-term lack of affiliation and low morale among the widowed. Harvey and Bahr conclude that, "The widowed have appeared to have more negative attitudes than the married because they are much poorer than the married, and they have appeared less affiliated for the same reason" (1974).

Atchley corroborates this finding in an older working-class group of widows in which inadequate income also led to decreased social participation and increased loneliness and anxiety (1975).

In addition to a drop in socioecomonic status, widows experience profound changes in other spheres of their lives. Unfortunately, we lack any Canadian data on the lives and adjustment of our widowed population.[3] In considering the changes in self-identity and support systems that accompany widowhood, therefore, we must look to the findings of research conducted outside Canada.

Self-Identity

Most of the research done in the area of widowhood conceptualizes this life event as a role loss, or as a form of role exit (Blau, 1973). The research analyses widowhood in terms of change from the role of wife to the role of widow. A more recent development in the field, however, is the recognition that widowhood for many women is far more than a loss of role. It undermines the basis of the widow's identity. The personal accounts of a number of widows highlight this identity crisis.

I was conscious of my hands dangling uselessly by my sides. I was a person with no job to do, no place to fill, no function in life (Evans, 1971:139).

Many widows feel that they are less than "complete" individuals. At the heart of their identity problems is the fact that those around them view them as widows, not as wives, which is how many still think of themselves (Lopata, 1973b). Another difficulty in losing the role of wife is that most widows lack another major role upon which to now focus a new identity (Lopata, 1973a). For many widows, their late husbands served as a link between themselves and society, and the wives' worlds revolved very much around their spouses (Lopata, 1973b).

Widows cope with this identity crisis in a number of ways. Some women re-orient their occupational roles by taking a job or increasing their emotional commitment to the job they already have. Other widows focus on personal contacts and may become more involved with friends and family.[4] The extent of the readjustment depends, of course, on the extent to which the role of wife was central to their identity. One factor influencing this pattern of identification with the role of wife is social class.

For many women, especially working-class women, the role of mother tends to supercede the role of wife. They may thus experience less personal loss than middle-class wives who have balanced their roles of wife and companion and mother. A strong traditional sex-role orientation within the family often prevents working-class women from doing this. As a consequence, their identities seem less affected by marriage than is the case for middle-class women who think of their relationship with their husbands as more of a "we" than an "I" relationship (Lopata, 1973d). Middle-class women are also more likely to encounter critical disorganization in their lives upon the death of their spouses, and to suffer very personal forms of loneliness for them as unique individuals. At the same time, however, they are also better equipped than working-class women with the social, educational, and economic resources to restructure their lives and identities in time. Working-class women have fewer friends, fewer organizational memberships, less money, and fewer personal resources. Overall they are plagued more by loneliness and isolation than are middle-class widows (Troll, Miller and Atchley, 1979:75).

Whatever the varying degrees in the extent of identity crises in widowhood, the loss of the spouse does affect the self-concept of a wife. Widows are more likely than married elderly to think of themselves as old. They are generally more unhappy, more inclined to worry, and more likely to anticipate death in the near future than those who have not lost their spouses (Riley and Foner, 1968:353).

Other more positive changes are associated with widowhood as well. In an American study, over half the widows interviewed reported that they had changed since their bereavement, but only 20 percent defined the change as a negative one. Many (42 percent) stated that they were now more independent and free than prior to widowhood. A further 33 percent believed that "This time of my life is easier than any other time" (Lopata, 1973a:88). The kind of relationship maintained with the spouse, educational level, and ease of adjustment to widowhood are critical factors influencing the widow's perception of this change. Significantly, a change in self-concept is a healthy sign for the widow. Lopata found that widows who reported no change in self-concept since bereavement were more lonely and isolated than those who reported change (1973a:89).

Support Systems

An individual's support system may be defined as that set of personal contacts through which the individual maintains her social identity and style of life. The support system can be economic, service, social, or emotional (Lopata, 1978). This network may contain a wide variety of contacts but the concern here is with such relatives as children, siblings, and in-laws, as well as friends.

Widowhood affects not only the identity and self-concept of women, but also their social roles and relations with family and friends. Patterns of interaction with adult children usually increase for a time after bereavement, but do not remain so for long. We know that for all types of contact, daughters interact more with a widowed parent than when both parents are living. While middle-class sons and daughters are almost equally likely to help their widowed mother in some way, daughters are more apt to be engaged in mutual aid with the widow, receiving as well as giving patterned help (Adams, 1968b). However, both sexes are more likely to say that "obligation is important, and less likely to say that enjoyment is important, in relations with a widow than when both parents are living" (Adams, 1968b). In widowhood, women's relationships with their children generally become no closer, and change toward fewer rather than more contacts where they change at all (Adams, 1968b; Lopata, 1973a).

The fact remains, however, that many widows do not desire deep involvement in the role of mother after the role of wife is over. They prefer "intimacy at a distance" from their adult children (Lopata, 1973a:146). Indeed, recent research has found that although the majority of older women have regular contact with their children, the frequency of this contact has little impact on the widow's feelings of loneliness and life satisfaction (Arling, 1976).

However much obligation colours the relationships between widows and their children, new evidence from Lopata (1978; 1979) indicates that children are by far the most viable members of the widow's support system. Siblings, in-laws, and other relatives were not actively involved in any of the support systems of the widows studied by Lopata. In a major critique of the theory of modified extended kinship relations, Lopata found that where widows were involved at all in their support systems, they were dependent on their children in all areas of support except the economic one (1978).

Some Canadian research suggests that perhaps this lack of support from the extended family, while a disadvantage in the initial period of bereavement, may in fact facilitate the reorganization of social roles later in widowhood. Walker, MacBride, and Vachon suggest that "a closely knit network made up predominantly of relatives could become a disadvantage [to the widow] if she seeks to make new friends, find a job, or develop a new life style" (1977). They maintain that while such networks are appropriate for maintaining a static social identity, in widowhood a woman's identity "is anything but static" (1977).[5]

The impact of widowhood on friendship very much depends upon the proportion of the widow's friends who are also widows. The findings of Lopata (1973a; 1977) corroborate Blau's theory that change in marital status, not the fact of being unattached, reduces the social participation of widowed women. Widowhood has an adverse effect on social participation only when it places the widow in a situation different from that of her age and sex peers (Blau, 1973:80). Younger widows, with most of their friends still married and involved in couple-companionate relationships, experience a decrease in social participation. Older women, with many already widowed friends, do not suffer such a decline in their activity levels.

Problems of Widowhood

As important as friendships, both old and new, and continuing family relationships are in the lives of widows, they are not enough to dispel the single major problem for bereaved women: loneliness. They do not compensate for the loss of the husband. "Friends and activities made loneliness easier to manage, but did not end it or appreciably diminish it" (Weiss, 1973).

While most widows live apart from their families, this is by no means synonymous with loneliness and social isolation. Many widows who live with relatives and non-relatives report extreme loneliness; some widows living alone report only mild incidences of loneliness. Nevertheless, loneliness in some degree is a problem for most widows. Almost half the widows in a study by Lopata listed loneliness as their most serious difficulty, and a third cited it as their second major problem (1973c). A number of studies duplicate Lopata's findings, and indicate that the more recently widowed feel more lonely than those who have been widowed some years (Shanas, et al., 1968:271-72). This suggests that the loneliness which widows experience is related much more to relative "loss" than enduring "isolation".

One of the most pervasive of all sentiments expressed by widows is the feeling that their new status is a drop in rank from the marital state. Many widows hate the word "widow". It "is a harsh and hurtful word. It comes from the Sanskrit, and it means 'empty'" (Caine, 1974:221). Many widows feel that they are "second-class citizens", and this is often reinforced by friends and relatives who convey to the widow just how awkward her loss makes them feel (Aitken, 1975; Caine, 1974:81). The widow is a woman in a male-dominated society — without a mate in a social network of couples. This latter lack in particular contributes to the feeling of status loss in widowhood.

Preventive Intervention

While many researchers have studied the problems of the widowed, far fewer have attempted to develop programs of intervention. The programs which have been developed have varied in approach, from intervention at the time of bereavement, to intervention by professionals after widowhood, to such self-help programs as the widow-to-widow model initiated by Silverman (1968). A Canadian equivalent to Silverman's program is presently being carried out through the Clarke Institute of Psychiatry in Toronto, in conjunction with their two-year study of bereaved women (Vachon, 1976). Perhaps this research will help identify factors associated with satisfactory adjustment in widowhood.

Conclusions

While the focus of this paper on widowhood in Canada has been restricted to widows, it is not meant to underplay the stressful impact of widowhood on the lives of men. Some new research, in fact, suggests that loss of the spouse is more oppressive to men than to women (Barrett, 1978; Berardo, 1971). While we have progressed significantly in our understanding of the problems that bereavement presents for women, a discussion of widowhood in Canada will not be complete until we acquire more information on sex differences in the experience of loss of spouse.

It is also regrettable that this analysis has had to rely so heavily on data gathered outside Canada. Some research on the immediate effects of bereavement is being conducted by the Clarke Institute of Psychiatry.[6] This is indeed a positive step in providing information on adjustments and stress reactions in the first two years after bereavement. Nevertheless, we must recognize that widowhood is a continuing process rather than a status (Troll, Miller, and Atchley, 1979:79). Consequently, both short-term and long-term effects of widowhood in Canada need to be identified. Most widowed have been, or will be, so for a considerable portion of their lives. The transition from married to widowed is one that calls for many long-term changes in identity, and reorganization of social roles.

Notes

1. From 1961 to 1971, the life expectancy of men increased by one year (from 68.4 to 69.4 years); in the same period the life expectancy of women increased by 2.3 years (from 74.2 years to 76.5 years). Readers will note that I sometimes present data up to 1971, and at other times up to 1976. Unfortunately, complete data on widowhood for years beyond 1971 are not readily available. I am grateful to Darlene Flett, of Health and Welfare Canada, for furnishing the data presented in Figure 1.

2. From 1961 to 1971, the rate of remarriage per 1,000 widowers in Canada increased from 29.2 to 35.9 per year. In this same time interval, the remarriage rates for widows declined from 11.2 to 10.5 per year.

3. Current Canadian material includes a personal account of widowhood (Wylie, 1977) several in-progress reports of a preventive intervention study (Vachon, 1976; Walker, MacBride, and Vachon, 1977), and surveys of the social science literature on specific aspects of widowhood and bereavement (Aitken, 1975; Martin Matthews, 1975; Haas-Hawkings, 1978).

4. Research by Lopata (1977) has found, however, that those widows who did not have friends outside the family prior to the death of their husbands generally did not develop any new friends after widowhood.

5. This appears to be yet one more example of the "strength of weak ties" (Granovetter, 1973).

6. The sample for this study consisted of 175 widows under the age of 69, able to speak English, and living in Toronto (Vachon, 1976; Walker, MacBride, and Vachon, 1977).

V

Health Status and Health Care

The health of most older Canadians is good, and they enjoy a system of health care delivery which has been much praised. In general, neither the health of older Canadians nor the ways in which they obtain health care differ qualitatively from the situation of younger people. Most people, contrary to widely held stereotypes, maintain quite high levels of health throughout life or until very old age, and they consider themselves to be in reasonably good health despite an increase in the likelihood of some degree of activity limitation as they get older. Health care in Canada is obtained, by people of all ages, largely through the same fee-for-service, private-practitioner, physician-controlled, highly technological, and hospital-centered system (for descriptions of this system see Andreopolous, 1975; Coburn *et al*, 1980, Taylor, 1978). A difference between the old and the young is that the old are exempted from the requirement to pay premiums for their health insurance, and they often receive financial assistance (varying from province to province) for institutional care, drugs, and prosthetics.

There is no question but that Canadian older people in general receive high quality *medical* care compared to almost any other nation's elderly. Questions abound, however, concerning the extent to which the *health* of older Canadians is optimized through the predominately *medical* system as it now exists. It is generally agreed, for example, that we are too dependent on doctors, hospitals, and institutions in our care for the aged (see Chapter 23 in this book; Lalonde, 1975; and Ontario Council of Health, 1978) and that Canada has done too little to create conditions which will allow older Canadians freedom from dependency on the medical care system.

Although most older people are in quite good health, aging does generally lead to greater health deficits and limitations in the ability to freely move about, in perception, and in the ability to fully care for oneself. Aging is associated with a growth of chronic health-care problems and with an increase in the effects of acute health problems (such as the number of days it takes to recover from simple ailments). Older people are also more likely to have compounded or multiple health problems than are younger people (Bayne, 1978). The Canadian government considers people over the age of 60 to be at risk for "heart and circulatory diseases, cancer, arthritis, rheumatism, diabetes and other chronic diseases connected to the aging process" (Lalonde, 1975:59), and heart and cerebrovascular diseases are the major causes of hospitalization of the aged in Canada.

Maximizing freedom from disability is the official goal of the Canadian Government (Lalonde, 1975:37). The papers by Gutman and by Flett, Last, and Lynch in this section, as well as those of Havens and of Tilquin *et al* in the next section, present data specifically on this point. There is age-related disability serious enough to warrant programmatic attention, but disability is not so severe as to confirm common stereotypes which seem to suggest that the later years are associated with inexorable debility and decline.

As other papers in this book suggest (see chapters 2, 19, and 22), health care for the aged is of great importance for the polity and the economy, because older people are great consumers of health services. Although older people are less than one-tenth of the population, they account for almost two-fifths of patient days in acute care and allied specialty hospitals (Clark and Collishaw, 1975). Recent Ontario data, probably representative for Canada, show that in the fiscal year ending March 31, 1977, people over age 65 accounted for 36 percent of the services of therapeutic radiologists, 33 percent of psychiatric services, 28 percent of urologists, 25 percent of osthenopathic and opthalmological services, 23 percent of general surgeon and internist services, and 17 percent of general practitioner services (Ontario Council of Health, 1978). Most of the people delivering these services have had little or no specific educational preparation for servicing an older population. The utilization of such services will increase, barring changes in the overall pattern of health care delivery, due to demographic changes alone which will yield more older and, especially, more *very* old people in the future.

Some of the policy dilemmas in this area centre on the extent to which old age, like many other aspects of the life cycle, has become unduly "medicalized". The Canadian *health-care* system is primarily a *medical* system, dominated by physicians and focused on high-technology, hospital-based care. Chapter 17, by Flett, Last and Lynch, describes an experiment to provide better nursing care on-site in high-rise apartment buildings for the elderly, in an attempt to reduce their dependency on physician visits and hospitalization (the average Canadian woman over age 65 spends more than eight days per year in hospital). Their research shows that appropriate nursing surveillance can lead to fewer physician visits and less hospitalization; but the authors also stress the need to ascertain the extent to which less highly trained or qualified health workers could positively intervene in maintaining good health among the aged.

The paper by Gutman, like that of Flett, Last and Lynch, and also that of Tilquin and associates in the next section, shows the importance of non-medical factors in maintaining independent living among the elderly. Important non-medical factors are the presence of a confidante, ability to obtain help with shopping and other domestic chores, availability of transportation and proximity to services. Carl D'Arcy's paper (Chapter 16) in a sense makes the same argument. The mental health status of Saskatchewan's older population changed dramatically in response to changes in the service system, suggesting, of course, that there is more to mental illness than one might at first think.

Sociologists distinguish between *disease*, which is a physiological state, *illness*, a subjective state in which the individual recognizes that something is physiologically wrong, and *sickness*, a social state in which illness is recognized by others and expectations for the behavior of the sick person are mobilized by others in the milieu. There is some evidence that older people are less likely than younger people to recognize disease or physiological assaults, and a majority are likely to perceive themselves as "healthy for my age". It is difficult to say how much of the variability by age can be attributed to aging per se and how much to cohort effects. The dynamics of self-definition and social definition as ill or sick, as outlined by D'Arcy and drawn from the interactionist perspective on deviance, are easily translatable to the case of physical illness.

Some sociologists (Gerson and Skipper, 1972; Parsons, 1951) speak of the "sick role", a set of expectations for the rights and obligations of the sick. As formulated by Parsons, the sick role applies, if at all, to acute illness episodes, for in chronic sickness the person is not expected, as Parsons argues is the case for the sick, to try to get better. Rather, the chronically sick must learn to live with the limitations of their chronic conditions. Some limitations in activity might not be, or be recognized as, health limitations. Here a sensitivity to the fit between person and environment is called for (see Chapter 26). In the future, technological changes will greatly lessen the impact of many limitations on physical mobility. For example, two-way television and telecommunications will allow older people greater ease in maintaining daily contact with others. Highly sophisticated yet easily used self-monitoring systems for chronic conditions such as cardiovascular and hypertensive problems are being introduced and can greatly enhance the feelings of security which an older person might have (Tobin, 1975).

The papers in this section have many important methodological features. D'Arcy's paper shows the usefulness of analyzing existing vital statistics data from a novel theoretical perspective and also points to the value of a historical approach.

Gutman makes a point which is also found in some of the papers in Section VII on institutionalization and alternatives: it is necessary to take a fine-grained approach to the characterization of living environments, be these institutional or not. Just as all nursing homes or hospitals should not be lumped together if we want to understand their effects on the experiences of people inhabiting them, we should recognize the differences between different types of private housing stock, homes, apartments, and retirement housing facilities.

Methodologically, Gutman's findings that older people living in retirement housing are different in a number of respects from those living freely in the community has implications for the accumulation of knowledge about aging and the aged. It is not possible, as is so often done, to draw general conclusions about the total non-institutionalized aged population from studies which can be conveniently conducted in senior citizens' high-rise buildings and similar age-segregated living environments. The great majority of older people live in their own homes, and have to be studied there, if they are to be studied at all.

A noteworthy feature of the paper by Flett, Last and Lynch is its use of a quasi-experimental design. A great deal of research is needed to evaluate social and health delivery programs for the aged, and this paper is exemplary in describing the accommodation of scientific ideals to real-world realities. Fully-experimental designs can seldom be utilized in real-world research, because individuals can seldom be ethically allocated to experimental and control groups on a fully random basis, and complete control over the lives of people in both groups cannot be realized. Use of a matched case-control sample is one good alternative research design strategy in such instances. Similarly, while it would have been preferable to have data from before the nursing intervention started, in real situations this is often not possible, and accommodations have to be made.

For some reason, both social gerontology and social research in health care are very underdeveloped fields of scholarship in Canada. There are, for example, very few medical sociologists in Canada, and less than a handful who systematically conduct age-related research. Therefore, the knowledge base in social aspects of aging and health care is somewhat limited when compared with countries such as the United States. Most people interested in gerontology, however, cannot ignore health as an important variable.

The fact that health is not isolated from many of the other concerns of the aged is shown by the fact that it is discussed in several papers in the next two sections of the book. I would argue that just as no social scientist would ignore a variable as fundamentally important as age, sex, or social class, no social scientist interested in aging and the aged could afford to ignore their health status. This, incidently, makes it imperative to develop a better conceptual understanding of disease, illness, and sickness, and better measures to overcome the problems of the functional status measures in common use today.

Finally, and this applies beyond this section alone, our knowledge in the field of aging and the social sciences is likely to increase from the accumulation of many studies that do not fully meet the ideal criteria found in methodology textbooks although recognition of the necessary departures from these conditions makes for good scholarship.

16

THE MANUFACTURE AND OBSOLESCENCE OF MADNESS
Age, Social Policy and Psychiatric Morbidity in a Prairie Province*

Carl D'Arcy
Psychiatric Research
University Hospital, Saskatoon

"When a belief in witchcraft was accepted in a disordered society looking for scapegoats who could be blamed for its terrors, senile women were burnt or hanged as witches. In the nineteenth century, if they were indigent they were relegated to the almshouse or the workhouse infirmary. Society had changed, not the women. Thus the key to prevention, control and therapy of mental pathology lies not alone in the impaired individual, but also more significantly in understanding the perceptual and social environment in which he exists."

George Rosen (1968)

This paper is concerned with the psychiatric morbidity patterns of the older age group, 70 years of age and over, in the Province of Saskatchewan during the period 1946-1970 and the extent to which these morbidity patterns are responsive to social policy and organizational changes, with regard to the delivery of psychiatric care specifically and health and welfare services more generally.

While the problem of the aged and the delivery of psychiatric services has often been noted and is certainly not unique to the province, the level of responsiveness of the psychiatric morbidity patterns of the aged probably is. This responsiveness results from some unique social and institutional aspects of the province.

It is important to stress here that in order to understand fully the impact of these changes in the delivery of health and welfare services, it is necessary to understand the social and institutional context in which they occurred. More specifically, certain peculiarities of the demographic structure of the

*An earlier version of this paper was read at the Scientific Sessions of the Research Committee on the Sociology of Medicine of the International Sociological Association, Toronto, 21 August 1974. It was subsequently published in *Social Science and Medicine* 10 (1976) 5-13. Reprinted with the permission of Pergamon Press.

province, and the lack of facilities for the care of the aged are due both to the recency of the settlement of the province and the changes in distribution of the provincial population.

Besides being of intrinsic interest in and of itself, it is felt that the material reported here has significant theoretical import.

The data reported dramatically demonstrate, in a real way, the negotiated character—in a social-structural and organizational sense—of deviance categories in general and the phenomena of "mental illness" in particular.

The Theoretical Perspective

The conceptual framework which is used here to help understand the phenomena of the changing morbidity patterns is in essence an explicated version of "societal reaction" or "labelling" theory of mental illness.

With respect to the application of societal reaction theory to the phenomenon of mental illness, Scheff (1966) has developed the most systematic and explicit statement of this theoretical orientation. Partial aspects of this theory can be found in the works of Erikson (1957; 1964; 1966), Goffman (1961), Laing and Esterson (1964), Lemert (1951; 1967), Szasz (1961; 1970), Freidson (1970), and Rosenhan (1973). These writings are of a speculative-intuitive nature and have generated numerous, but not logically connected, research suggestions.

From a "societal reaction" or "labelling" perspective, "mental illness" is not seen as the universal result of specific sets of behavioral acts but rather it is seen as a result of the meaning attributed by others to behavioral acts. This attribution of meaning is seen as a social system product which is generated out of a complex nexus of events involving the social response of a historically rooted cultural and structural context, with its vested interests and moral entrepreneurs, to individual everyday actions which are adjustments, bargainings, and random or trial acts. It is these cultural, structural, and interpersonal contexts of action that form the "contingencies"—the contingent factors that determine the meaning attributed to behavioral acts, and whether or not a person is labelled a saint, deviant, or mentally ill. From this perspective to use Goffman's phrase "...in the degree that the 'mentally ill' outside hospitals numerically approach or surpass those inside hospitals, one could say that mental patients distinctively suffer not from mental illness, but from contingencies" (Goffman, 1961).

It is important to note that while contingencies in the process of becoming labelled as mentally ill have long been recognized (Jarvis, 1885), they were not conceived as having theoretical significance. Rather, they were used to indicate the "methodological" limitation of official institutional data in giving a measure of the "nature" of mental illness in terms of incidence, prevalence, and social correlates. As such, this methodological significance has generated a whole literature concerned with the search for a "true" measure of mental illness—the search for an abstracted non-social measure of a social phenomenon (Dohrenwend and Dohrenwend, 1965; Hare and Wing, 1970; Phillips and Clancy, 1970; Phillips, 1972). What is unique to societal reaction theory is that contingencies are given central theoretical significance rather than peripheral methodological significance in explaining the phenomenon of mental illness.[1]

The question of whether the contingencies are accorded methodological or theoretical significance in essence revolves around our conceptions of the nature of "illness". It really depends on whether or not we conceive of illness as being universal signs and symptoms of deviation that can be interpreted "objectively", irrespective of the circumstances in which they occur. It depends on whether or not we accept the ontology of medicine. However, if illness is defined in socially concrete terms, if it is seen as social deviation—as a social status—then the contingencies have theoretical significance. They are theoretically significant for they are the determinants of why or how people come to be labelled "sick".

From this theoretical perspective, it is the "incidental factors" (incidental, that is, to the ontology of psychiatric medicine) which lead an individual to be labelled mentally ill, rather than the essential attributes, the symptoms of mental illness, stemming from the ontology of psychiatric medicine.[2]

The perspective of the contingencies and of societal reaction theory of mental illness formulated here may be seen as an explanation, a theory if you will, of the utilization of mental health facilities, provided, of course, that such an idea of utilization is seen to encompass the decision-making, and the "incidental factors" that influence the decision-making of professionals as well as lay persons in the construction of mental illness. Utilization should not be seen solely as a result of lay decision-making.

It has been noted that this perspective has not really dealt adequately with these contingent factors, either conceptually or propositionally, largely because of the emphasis on the effects of being labelled rather than on the creation and application of labels (Rushing, 1971; Schur, 1971; D'Arcy, 1976).

However, despite this and other shortcomings,[3] it is possible to develop a taxonomy of these contingencies along the axes of a two-dimensional space. In this connection, Freidson's *the lay-professional construction of illness* dimension is extremely useful. The second useful dimension is some idea of a continuum of articulation from the general through specification and interpretation to negotiation, that operates in both the lay and professional construction of illness.[4]

These two can be represented as follows:

FIGURE 1:
CONTINGENCIES IN BECOMING LABELLED AS MENTALLY ILL

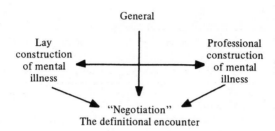

Process of articulation

General

Lay construction of mental illness ←→ Professional construction of mental illness

"Negotiation"
The definitional encounter

The conceptual framework can be more conventionally diagrammed in terms of the following six-fold typology:

Types of social contingencies		
Level of articulation	Construction of illness	
	Lay	Professional
Macro (general)	Social cultural	Institutional
Meso	Social structural	Organizational
Micro (specific)	Everyday interpersonal	Personal professional

The complexity of the various and interacting contingent factors is more appropriately represented by the flow-chart shown in Figure 2.

Further elaboration

As noted earlier, societal reaction theory of mental illness has largely emphasized the effects of being labelled rather than the creation and application of labels. What work that has been done on the generation of deviance outcomes has largely concentrated on deviance outcomes at the individual level and their negotiated character. In addition, there have been a few works concerned with deviance outcomes in terms of creating new deviance categories or new types of deviants. These works have been primarily

FIGURE 2:

INTERACTING CONTINGENCIES IN LABELLING MENTAL ILLNESS

Lay construction ←→ Mediating structures ←→ Professional construction

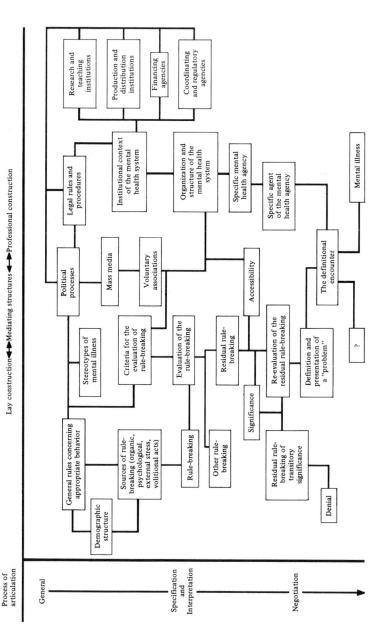

A more detailed presentation of this explicated conceptual framework is presented in D'Arcy, 1974.

concerned with either mass movements of moral entrepreneurship (Erikson, 1964; 1966; Currie, 1968), or executive movements of moral entrepreneurship (Conner, 1972).

Most of the authors in this area have emphasized the creation of "new deviance" but have paid little attention to subsequent decline of such moral categories even though history is full of them. Where there has been a concern for the "elasticity" in the amount of deviance recognized in a society, some rather realistically restrictive conditions for its occurrence have been posited (Conner, 1972).

However, the creation or decline of moral categories, rates of deviance, or types of deviants are not solely a result of the action of a social movement but may also result from much more mundane and less dramatic events.[5] As Currie (1968) points out:

> By playing down the importance of intrinsic differences between deviants and conventional people, and between the social situation of deviants and that of non-deviants, the focus on social response implies much more than the commonplace idea that society defines the kinds of behavior that will be considered odd, disgusting or criminal. It implies that many elements of the behavior system of a given kind of deviance, including such things as the rate of deviances and kinds of people who are identified as a deviant, will be significantly affected by the kind of control system through which the behavior is defined and managed.

One important product of this line of thought is the seeing of the traditional social correlates of mental illness, such as age, sex, marital status, etc., less as causes or consequences of psychiatric disorders—as they have been traditionally viewed in the literature—and more as artifacts of the organization and structure of the mental health system—as artifacts of the system of social control.[6]

The research problem

What we are interested in doing here is demonstrating the effects of changes in a control system upon the rates of deviance and the kinds of persons identified as deviant.

We are concerned with the "manufacture" and "obsolescence" of "mental illness" in the 70 year-plus age group in the Province of Saskatchewan during the period 1946-1970. More specifically, we are interested in demonstrating the effects of such mundane things as the organization and structure of the delivery of health and welfare services, interacting within a unique social and institutional context, both amplifying and dampening the patterns of psychiatric morbidity of the 70 year-plus age group, over a relatively short period of time.

The Province

The Province of Saskatchewan is particularly suitable as a focus for study for two major sets of reasons. The first set of reasons has to do with the extent of changes that have occurred in the provincial mental health system. During the time period in question there has been an extensive reorganization of its mental health services. The mental health system of the province has changed from being what might be termed a "traditional" (asylum-oriented) mental health system to a more "community-oriented" mental health system. There has been the addition of a wider range of facilities and modalities of treatment. There has been a substantial change in the number, types, and training of personnel employed. The mental health services have become decentralized and regionalized (Smith, 1970; 1971; Lipscomb, 1970; Neufeldt, 1972). Secondly, there exist very good statistical records providing detailed information on the social, demographic, and psychiatric attributes of patients of the mental health system for the time period involved.

The fact that substantial changes in the direction of increasing "community orientation" have occurred in the mental health system of Saskatchewan is not as surprising or unusual as it may first appear. During the period in question there has been an extensive reorganization of the province's total health care system, including its mental health services. Indeed, the province has pioneered a large number of innovative programs, especially in the context of the Canadian and North American milieu, in the health area such as: a comprehensive diagnostic and therapeutic service for cancer (1946); publicly financed care and treatment of the mentally ill (1946); a comprehensive, publicly financed hospital insurance program (1947); a comprehensive, publicly financed medical care insurance program (1962); and a publicly financed prescription drug program (1975) to mention but a few of the changes. Much of this innovation, at least initially, was derived from the Sigerist Report (Saskatchewan, 1944).

For the province, this history of innovation in terms of social legislation has not been confined to the health field; such programs as umbrella legislation for co-operatives, publicly financed compulsory auto insurance, rural electrification, provincial ownership of electric, gas, and telephone utilities, and participation in industries, etc. have also been initiated during this time period.

Despite this obviously fertile environment for change, the changes in the Saskatchewan mental health system cannot be explained solely in terms of such tendencies or socio-cultural conditions. The shape of the mental health system is also the result of influential individuals who as a result of their positions of responsibility profoundly altered its direction and shape.

In addition, political considerations and tight economic conditions, provincially coupled with the willingness of the Federal Government, via the National Health Grants, to support specific "community oriented" mental health programs, personnel training, and services, are also factors that have figured prominently in the present development of the mental health services in Saskatchewan.

No doubt, it was the unique and perhaps haphazard coincidence of these socio-cultural, politico-economic and personality sets of variables that led to the present development of the Saskatchewan mental health system. However, all this aside, it is the nature of these changes, irrespective of their ultimate or more immediate origin, and their effects upon the phenomenon of mental illness that is the interest here. It is recognized that all the changes that have occurred have not necessarily been planned for or intended.

Changing patterns of psychiatric morbidity in the province[7]

The change from a traditional asylum-oriented mental health system to a community-oriented mental health system is usually documented in terms of

FIGURE 3:

RATE OF PATIENTS IN MENTAL INSTITUTIONS

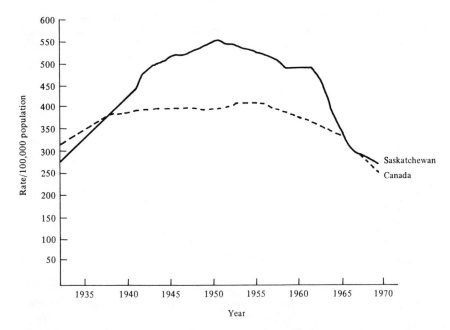

The data reported here are taken or derived from the annual publication of Statistics Canada on the topic of mental health. For ease of presentation they are reported in graphic form. Because of the theoretical orientation of this paper and because the institutions were until recently administered under the same act and had a unified administration, the institutions reported on here and the data reported here cover provincial mental hospitals, psychiatric wings of general hospitals and inpatient institutions for the retarded.

a declining bed capacity or number of patients resident in institutions. As can be seen from the data presented in Figure 3, there has been a significant decline in the number of patients in mental institutions in the province during the last decade or two. A smaller decline in the ratio of beds available has also occurred.

The rise and relatively high rate of patients resident in institutions in Saskatchewan during the 1940s and 1950s, in contrast to the data for Canada, can be partially explained in terms of the psychiatric morbidity patterns of the aged to be discussed presently. It is, however, important to notice the decline in the rate of patients resident in institutions, occurring during the period from 1961 onwards. It is this period that essentially coincides with the speeded-up shift to a community-oriented mental health system. In addition to the decline in patients resident in institutions, one of the more general effects of changing from a traditional to a community-oriented mental health system has been to dramatically increase the number of persons being treated for "mental illness". The substantial shortening of the length of hospital stay that has occurred allows the system to process a greater number of people in spite of a decline in bed capacity. In this sense the shortened length of stay acts as a "technological factor" in improving the productivity of the system. The consequent dramatic increases in first admissions, re-admissions, and discharges that have occurred can be amply seen from the data reported in Figure 4. In addition, concurrent changes in

FIGURE 4:
RATE OF INSTITUTIONAL ADMISSIONS AND DISCHARGES OF PATIENTS

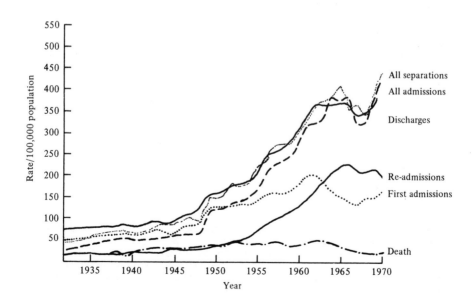

the modality of treatment have also led to a concurrent dramatic increase in the number of patients treated as outpatients, from 1678 in 1953 to 11,067 in 1970.

To some extent, the data reported here suggest that the shift to a community-oriented mental health system has seen a shift to a new plateau

FIGURE 5:

RATE OF INSTITUTIONAL ADMISSIONS AND DISCHARGES OF PATIENTS AGED 70 YEARS OR OVER

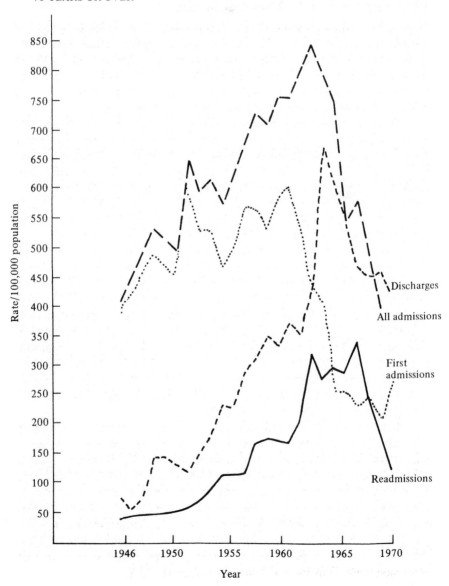

in terms of patient movement indicators, with higher input and output levels.

However, contrary to what one would initially and superficially assume, the same changes in patient movement characteristics have not been mirrored in all segments of the population. The data reported for the mentally ill population as a whole contrasts with the data reported for the older 70 year-plus age group.

Changing patterns in the 70 year-plus age group

In contrast to data presented in the preceding section similar indicators of patient movement for the 70 year-plus age category do not exhibit the general overall increase. Rather, they exhibit an initial elevated level of increase in first admissions, re-admissions, total admissions, death and discharge rates followed by a quite drastic decline in the general level of activity of these input and output measures (see Figure 5).

This rise and decline in the psychiatric morbidity patterns of the aged is in contrast with the more straightforward increase in psychiatric morbidity for the provincial population as a whole. The net result of the changes that have occurred in the delivery of psychiatric services, for the older age category, has been to decrease the level of psychiatric activity in terms of input and output measures. In contrast to the data for the population as a whole, there are proportionately fewer aged persons being treated as in-patients for "mental illness" today than in the previous two decades.

In the late 1940s and 1950s there was a significantly greater proportion of older persons being treated in the Saskatchewan mental health system.

The rise and subsequent decline in the treatment of older persons in psychiatric hospitals in Saskatchewan is dramatically illustrated by the data on deaths in psychiatric institutions. In 1946 the number of deaths in such institutions was 244, in 1963 it was 438 and 108 in 1970. These figures give ratios per 100,000 population of 29, 47, and 12 respectively. Comparable data for Canada yield ratios of 25 in 1946, 23 in 1963, and 14 in 1970. The marked contrast between the experience in Saskatchewan as opposed to the experience in Canada points out to some extent the uniqueness of the Saskatchewan experience in this regard.

However, the most telling data are contained in Figure 6 which deals with data on rates of first admissions for various age categories. What is remarkable about this graph is that it shows for the 70 year-plus category a significant increase in the rates of first admissions from 1946 onwards with a relatively high but erratic plateau from 1952 to 1960 and from 1961 onwards a relatively sharp decline. In 1946 the rate of first admissions per 100,000 population in the 70 year-plus age group was 375, in 1961 it was 607, in 1970 it was 283. This contrasts with similar data reported for other age categories. For the provincial population as a whole, the comparable rates of first admission were 77 in 1946, 198 in 1961 and 213 in 1970.

FIGURE 6:

RATE OF FIRST ADMISSIONS BY AGE GROUP

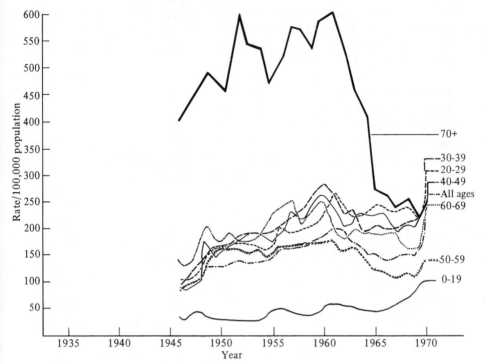

Changing social policy and psychiatric morbidity in the aged

It is not coincidence that the year 1946 marked the introduction in the province of a program guaranteeing free hospitalization for mental illness. The year 1961 marked the introduction of a new Mental Health Act (modelled on the British Act of 1959). What was different about the 1961 Act was that in comparison to its predecessor, admission to a psychiatric inpatient facility was now discretionary on the part of the admitting facility. In addition, the period 1959-1963 was one in which there was a great deal of interest in the care and treatment of the aged. Important changes in the delivery of health and welfare services to the aged occurred in this period.

These pieces of legislation and social policy changes have had, perhaps, a more dramatic impact on psychiatric morbidity (particularly rates of first admission), in terms of the manufacture and obsolescence of madness, because of two specific aspects of the province, namely, the changing of the demographic structure, and the lack of facilities for the care of the aged.

Saskatchewan is a relatively recently settled area of the country. European settlement only became feasible, on a large scale, after the completion of the Canadian Pacific Railroad in the 1880s. The greatest period of settlement occurred during the decade between 1901 and 1911. By 1901, the districts of Saskatchewan and Assiniboia, slightly larger than the future Province of Saskatchewan (which became a province in 1905), had a population of 93,064. By 1911 the province had a population of 492,432. The population at the next census in 1921 was 757,510. The estimated population in 1970 was 941,000.

As a result of this recency of settlement, until the late 1940s Saskatchewan had substantially fewer older age people in its population in comparison with the country as a whole.

Following the period of initial settlement and accompanying boom, the province was severely afflicted by both the worldwide depression and a severe drought during the 1930s and then World War II. The concurrent social changes resulting from the depression, drought, war, and the mechanization of farming changed living patterns throughout the province. From a demographic point of view, these changes resulted in the emigration of some middle age groups out of the province and an increased urbanization of the province's population with its attendant disruption of community life (Richards and Fung, 1969).

The increase in immigration into Canada following the Second World War did not take place in Saskatchewan. Consequently, since the 1940s, Saskatchewan in comparison to the country as a whole has had a rapidly aging population. More generally, the province has a population with a high dependency ratio. In 1921, 1.2 percent of the population of Saskatchewan was 70 years-plus of age, in 1931 — 1.9 percent, in 1941 — 2.9 percent, in 1946 — 3.6 percent, in 1951 — 4.5 percent, in 1961 — 6.2 percent, in 1971 — 6.9 percent. Comparable percentages for Canada are 2.8, 3.3, 4.0, 4.2, 4.6, 4.9, and 5.2 (Statistics Canada, 1973b).

Not surprising, in view of the recency and nature of settlement, and partially aggravating this problem of a rapidly aging population, Saskatchewan had few facilities for the care of the aged. It is only since the early 1960s that the facilities available come anywhere near meeting demand. For example, in 1944 when the provincial Department of Social Welfare was formed, there were six homes for the aged that accommodated approximately 350 persons (Saskatchewan, 1965). Indeed, the 1959 Aged and Long-Term Illness Conference, convened by the provincial government, noted that one of the major problems in the care and treatment of the aged was the lack of provision of adequate housing for single persons and geriatric centre beds. There was also a lack of the provision of facilities for persons needing a minimum of care. The Conference noted the Saskatchewan Hospital Services Plan, which provided for publicly financed hospitalization in general hospital wards, by providing relatively cheap hospital care encouraged the utilization of general hospitals for the care of the aged. This was especially true in rural areas (Saskatchewan, 1959).

It is argued here that the introduction by the provincial government of a program that provided for "free", publicly financed hospitalization for the treatment of illness in 1946 coupled with the phenomenon of a rapidly aging population and the critical lack of alternative facilities for the care of the aged, was responsible for the large increase in psychiatric morbidity that occurred in the 70 year-plus age group during the 1940s and its subsequent maintenance at a high level during the 1950s. This is especially evident in the data on first admission by age group presented in Figure 6. It is important to note in this regard that under the Mental Health Acts and regulations in operation during this period, hospitalization for mental illness could be effected on the basis of two medical certificates, signed by two medical practitioners. More importantly, the medical officers in charge of these facilities did not have any discretion in regard to admission. Those presented with certificates had to be received.

FIGURE 7:
RATE OF FIRST ADMISSIONS IN CANADA VS. SASKATCHEWAN

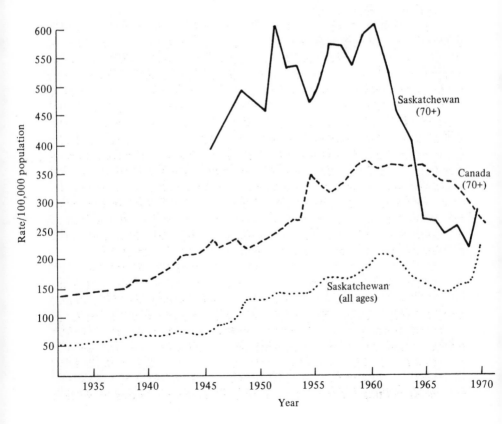

The introduction of this program, coupled with the unique demographic situation and lack of facilities for the care of the aged, resulted in the "manufacture", so to speak, of "madness" in the older age categories during the 1940s and 1950s. While the problem of the aged and psychiatric hospitalization is not unique to Saskatchewan, the magnitude, because of some unique aspects of the province, is. The data presented in Figure 7, which compares the first admission experience of the 70 year-plus age group in Canada with that of Saskatchewan shows to some extent the magnitude and atypicalness of the Saskatchewan experience in the context of Canada.

The tragic consequences of such misplacement of the elderly in mental hospitals has been demonstrated by Kidd (1962) in terms of increasing the rate of mortality. No doubt this phenomenon in part accounts for the particularly high rates of death in Saskatchewan mental institutions during the late 1940s and 1950s.

During the period of the 1940s and 1950s, the problem of the aged in mental hospitals generated numerous comments concerning the appropriateness of treatment and therapy, overcrowdings, etc. It was a general problem, frequently commented upon in annual reports of the provincial Psychiatric Services Branch.

The problem of the care of the aged and treatment of the elderly also generated a good deal of concern in other branches of government. In 1959 the provincial government convened a conference on the Aged and Long-Term Illness. This was a conference of field workers, interested persons, professionals, and experts. A major thrust of the report was a recommendation for greater assistance for the community care of the aged. This included recommendations for the provision of greater housing facilities for the ambulatory and semi-ambulatory aged. As a result of the conference and its recommendations the following year, the provincial government set up an Aged and Long-Term Illness Survey Committee which was commissioned to conduct surveys and reports and make recommendations concerning the care, treatment, employment, etc. of the aged. Again some of the major recommendations of the committee were also concerned with the lack of provision of facilities for the care of the aged, especially in regard to the provision of housing and economic security (Saskatchewan, 1963).

All this activity and concern with the problem of the care of the aged no doubt had its effects on the implementation of social policy. But more importantly, the significant changes occurring in the delivery of health and welfare services during the 1959 to 1962 period had the greatest impact in terms of decreasing the psychiatric morbidity in the older age category. The relevant changes in terms of delivering welfare services were increased old age allowance and increased supplemental allowance, the shift in the basis of allocating monies from a "means test" to a "needs test", increased provincial funding for low cost housing, increased provisions of hostels, nursing homes, and approved homes for the care of the aged, and the development of mechanisms for the payment of services rendered to persons requiring various levels of care. This last change was particularly important in terms of providing intermediate levels of care, consequently allowing public funding for a wider range of sheltered accommodation and nursing home care.

In addition to these changes in the delivery of essentially welfare services, there was a significant change in the delivery of mental health services: the introduction of a new Mental Health Act which attempted to make admission for treatment of psychiatric illness similar to admission for any other illness. The most important aspect of this new act in the context of the present discussion was the making of admission discretionary. The medical officer in charge of the psychiatric institution could now have some discretion in terms of judging the suitability of the patient for admission.

It is argued here that the various concurrent changes in the delivery of health and welfare services had the effect of widening the range of alternatives available, to both lay and professional persons, for the care of the aged. They also closed off or made more difficult the use of some of the more traditional means of coping. These organization and policy changes had the effect of making "obsolescent" the phenomenon of the extremely high rates of psychiatric morbidity in the province's older age population. That decline is especially evident from the period 1961 onwards, in terms of declining rates of first admission (see Figure 6).

The peak in the discharge rates for the 70 year-plus age group seen in Figure 5 also reflects this wider concern with delivery of care to the older age group. This increased rate of discharge is the result of efforts to come to grips with the build-up of older age patients in psychiatric inpatient facilities in the province by discharging them and more appropriately placing them in the community and in nursing homes, etc. (Smith and McKenacher, 1963; Fakhruddin, 1972).

Conclusions

What has been argued here is that the program and policy changes discussed have had a significant impact upon the rates of mental illness recorded in the province and upon the types of persons caught up in the mental health system. In more technical sociological terms, we have demonstrated the effects of changes in a control system upon the rates of deviance and kinds of persons identified as deviant.

Initially, the introduction of a program of free hospitalization for mental illness interacting in the context of a rapidly increasing older age component in the provincial population and the lack of provision of facilities for the care of the aged, had the effect of dramatically increasing the rate of mental illness in this age category. The subsequent generation of large numbers of the aged in mental institutions and the more general problem of the provision of adequate care and facilities for the aged acted back as a "problem" into the social and political milieu of the province. The subsequent responses in terms of changes in the Mental Health Act and in the delivery of psychiatric care, and concomitant changes in the provision of social welfare services, including the provision of a wider range of facilities for the care of the aged, resulted in a drastic decrease in the rate of mental illness in this age category.

In this sense, the particular organization and structure of the system for the delivery of psychiatric care in the province, acting within a social and institutional context, have acted as contingent factors, on one hand contributing (in the 1940s and 1950s) and on the other hand not contributing (in the 1960s) to mental illness outcomes—to the process of becoming mentally ill—in the older age category.

In the context of the data presented here, and keeping in mind the "general systems theory" nature of the guiding theoretical perspective utilized in this thesis, it should be emphasized that the conditions and circumstances that govern the application of the idea of mental illness as an explanation of human behavior are not static, invariable entities but rather dynamic—subject to evaluation, change, and variability—social processes. Pertinent here is Lemert's comment (1967):

> ...there is a limiting or cost aspect of meanings and values, based on physiological, ecological and technological facts...the rise of new moral categories is related to changes in such facts, although the precise nature of these relationships is often elusive.

Notes

1. The points elaborated by Kitsuse and Cicourel (1963) on the use of official statistics are a logical extension of seeing the contingencies as having theoretical rather than methodological significance.

2. Freidson (1970) gives an excellent discussion of the distinction between illness as a social phenomenon as opposed to a medical one and the centrality and importance of this distinction for the sociology of medicine.

3. Other shortcomings are the passive conception of the deviant (Lorber, 1967; Strauss, 1964) and the inclusion by some authors of the functionalist idea of boundary maintenance (Lemert, 1967; Schur, 1971). This idea seems to run counter to Becker's notion (1964) of moral entrepreneurship. The data reported in this paper can also be seen to question this notion.

4. The idea of a continuum of articulation encompasses the three levels of social action of (1) collective rule-making, (2) organizational processing, and (3) interpersonal reactions, in which the processes of social definition contribute to deviance outcomes that Schur (1971) specifies. Strauss et al (1964) provide an excellent example of such a continuum of articulation for the organizational processes in psychiatric institutions whereby abstract organization policy is transformed into actual events.

5. It is of interest here that Cicourcel (1968) attributes changes in the amount of juvenile delinquency recognized in one of the two communities he was studying to be largely a result of "departmental politics" that resulted in changes in organization policies. He writes:

"Organizational policies and their articulation with actual cases, via the background expectancies of officers differentially authorized to deal with juveniles, directly changed the size of the 'law enforcement net' for the recognizing and processing of juveniles viewed as delinquent and determined the size and conception of the 'social problem'."

6. There is an abundant literature showing significant correlations between social phenomena and treated and untreated psychiatric disorders. Numerous problems surround possible interpretations of these correlates.

7. The data reported here are taken or derived from the annual publication of Statistics Canada on the topic of mental health. For ease of presentation they are reported in graphic form. Because of the theoretical orientation of this paper and because the institutions were until recently administered under the same act and had a unified administration, the institutions reported on here and the data reported here covers provincial mental hospitals, psychiatric wings of general hospitals, and inpatient institutions for the retarded.

17

EVALUATION OF THE PUBLIC HEALTH NURSE AS PRIMARY HEALTH-CARE PROVIDER FOR ELDERLY PEOPLE*

Darlene E. Flett
Health and Welfare Canada

John M. Last
Department of Epidemiology
University of Ottawa

and

George W. Lynch
Department of Community Medicine
Mt. Sinai School of Medicine

In 1972, there were seven newly built, subsidized ("rent-to-income") high-rise apartment buildings in Ottawa with a total of 1,500 tenants. Criteria for admission to these buildings included: age, i.e., 60 years and over; ability to live independently; and a point system which considered prior housing adequacy, percentage of rent-to-income, receipt of notice to vacate previous accommodation, length of time on waiting lists, and ability to climb stairs or walk to stores.

In April 1972, the Ottawa-Carleton Regional Area Health Unit assigned one public health nurse to each of two of the buildings. These nurses conducted programs for all tenants from an office in each building. There were approximately 250 tenants per building. Table 1, which is based on an analysis of the nursing records, indicates the types of problems that the nurses encountered; it is a count of reported problems, not the number of individuals with each type of problem. The problems covered a wide range and remained fairly constant during the study period and between the two buildings. No single type of problem predominated.

*This research was supported by National Health Grant #606-21-78, Health and Welfare Canada and by Project R. D. 10, Ontario Ministry of Health. Parts of this essay were presented at the Canadian Public Health Association Meeting, Moncton, New Brunswick, May 1976 and the Canadian Association on Gerontology Education Meeting, Vancouver, British Columbia, November 1976, and at the Seventh International Meeting, International Epidemiological Association, Puerto Rico, September 1977. An earlier version of this essay appeared under the same title as Staff Paper 78-2, Long-Range Health Planning, Health and Welfare Canada (June 1978).

TABLE 1:

PERCENTAGE DISTRIBUTION OF TYPES OF PATIENT PROBLEMS, BY YEAR[1]

Type of Patient Problem	February – March 1973	February – March 1974[2]	Total
	%	%	%
Medical problem[3]	19	18	19
Symptoms or ill-defined conditions[4]	23	24	23
Health utilization problem	20	22	21
Emotional problem	19	25	21
Functional problem[5]	7	4	6
Socio-economic problem	12	8	11
Total	100	101	101
	N = 472	N = 289	N = 761

[1] Data were based on analysis of nursing records.
[2] One nurse was on vacation from March 1st to 14th; therefore, the data represent one and a half months of health happenings in one building.
[3] The "medical problem" category included only those conditions which are mentioned in the *International Classification of Diseases,* Seventh edition. All other medical complaints are included in the "symptoms or ill-defined conditions" category.
[4] For each consultation with the nurse the symptoms of a patient, whether one or many, were only counted once.
[5] The "functional problem" category included situations where tenants were identified by the nursing record to have difficulty in coping with their environment, mobility, performing self-care activities, and in communication.

TABLE 2:

PERCENTAGE DISTRIBUTION OF TYPES OF NURSE ACTIVITIES WITH PATIENTS, FAMILY OR FRIENDS OF PATIENTS, OR OTHER COMMUNITY WORKERS, BY YEAR[1]

Type of Nurse Activity	February – March 1973	February – March 1974[2]	Total
	%	%	%
Assessment of patient	17	16	17
Direct patient care	3	3	3
Health education and promotion with patient, family, friend, etc.	30	23	27
Emotional counselling and support for patient, family, friend, etc.	10	9	10
Socio-economic counselling, support and education for patient, family, friend, etc.	10	7	9
Planning and coordination with other community workers	21	30	24
Administrative functions	9	13	11
Total	100	100	100
	N = 761	N = 544	N = 1,305

[1] Data were based on analysis of nursing records.
[2] One nurse was on vacation from March 1st to 14th; therefore, the data represent one and a half months of nursing consultations for one building.

Table 2 shows the distribution of the type of nursing activities. The method of practice included: regular office hours, with and without appointments; visits to tenants' apartments; telephone conversations; and group sessions. The nurses were also called upon for emergencies. Thus, the tenants soon identified the nurses as their main source of health care. Analysis of the nursing records revealed that the nurses consulted with approximately 25 percent of the tenants per month. Of the tenants who had contact with the nurses, 55 percent had one consultation and 12 percent had five or more consultations. The nurses believed that they had seen almost all of the tenants during the three-year period.

No public health nurses were located in the five remaining buildings which formed the control group, but these tenants did have access to district public health nurses who visited a maximum of one full day per month, primarily on request. The control group also had access to the same range of community services as the "cases", i.e., the tenants in the buildings to which public health nurses had been assigned. The only major difference between the two groups was the availability of full-time public health nurses in the two experimental buildings.

It was expected that the on-site public health nurses would be in a position to identify real and potential problems at an early stage, and by early intervention prevent or retard a decline in health status which could lead to admission to hospital (MacMillan, 1969). The on-site nurses were also expected to act as a link between the tenants and available community health services. The aim of this study was to demonstrate that this preventive approach would result in a better level of health and fewer hospital admissions among the cases as compared to the control group.

Design of the Program

We interviewed tenants[1] in all seven buildings, randomly selecting only one tenant in apartments occupied by a married couple. This produced a study population of 1,307 people. The interviews were conducted in spring and winter "waves" by interviewing one-half of the population in January-February and the remainder in April-May 1973 (i.e., 10 to 15 months after placement of the nurses). We had an 81 percent response rate (1,061 interviews). In each subsequent year, interviews with the tenants were conducted in the same seasonal period. In subsequent analyses, it was shown that none of our measures proved sensitive to seasonal changes and so seasons were omitted from further consideration.

At the time of the first interviews (i.e., in 1973), the mean age of the tenant population was 70 (almost one-half were between 70 and 79); females outnumbered males by five to one; 88 percent lived alone; and 64 percent were widowed. Their median annual income was $1,968 (compared to the Ottawa median income for this age group of $2,105); 70 percent were English-speaking and 27 percent French-speaking.

Data collected in year one were used to provide the basis for individual matching by age (within five-year categories to age 79 and ten-year categories beyond 79), sex, marital status, past occupation, and language. In addition to the usual categories, matching for marital status included the death of a spouse within the past four years to allow for the possible effects of recent bereavement on physical and mental health (Gerber, *et al.*, 1975; Maddison and Viola, 1968; Rees and Lutkin, 1967). Past occupation was matched according to the following broad categories: business and professional; clerical and skilled; semi-skilled and unskilled; and never worked. The matching for language separated the tenants into English-speaking, French-speaking, and bilingual in these two languages. When possible, cases were matched with two or more controls to permit substitution in the event of the loss of primary controls before follow-up interviews. Initially, 402 matched pairs were identified. This was reduced to 384 when 18 controls could not be replaced after the first year of interviewing.

Interviews in years two and three were restricted to individual matched pairs of tenants from the experimental and control buildings. Thus, this research project was a three-year study of individual matched pairs who were followed throughout the study period (Figure 1).[2]

FIGURE 1:
CHRONOLOGY OF STUDY

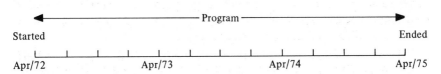

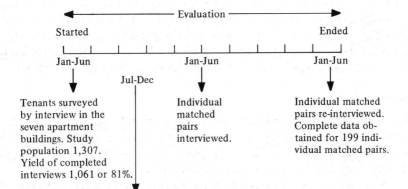

Tenants in buildings with Onsite Public Health Nursing
Program matched with tenants in buildings without this
program using data collected January to June, 1973.
Yield 402 individual matched pairs.

Inevitably, in a three-year study of elderly people, there was some attrition: 25 of the cases died, 28 moved away, and 49 controls were lost. In addition, 74 matched pairs who were still alive but for whom complete data were not available for all three years were omitted from the final analysis. Thus, there were 199 matched pairs for whom complete information was available for the duration of the study.

The initial distributions for these 199 pairs were compared to those for the original 426 users and 635 controls on all of the matching variables and no significant differences were found.

The Survey Instrument

After pretests we used a scale for activities of daily living (ADL) to measure physical health, which was modified and adapted from other scales (Katz *et al.*, 1963; 1970). This scale included questions on self-care, domestic tasks, and mobility. (In the final analysis, we omitted self-care because less than one percent of the respondents reported difficulty with tasks such as bathing, toileting, and dressing.) Our measure of emotional well-being was the Philadelphia Geriatric Center Morale Scale (PGCMS), a 21-item set of statements and questions developed and validated specifically for use with elderly people (Lawton, 1972; also, see Neysmith, this volume). These formed the four measures of health status. Information on use of health services (i.e., doctor visits, hospital stays, and contact with nurses) was obtained by responses to questions adapted from the WHO/ICS/MCU instrument (Kohn and White, 1976:446-526), and verified by search of hospital, medical, and nursing service records.

We also considered factors other than the nursing program that might influence tenants' health status and health-care utilization. Observations were made on: accessibility to a confidante (Moriwaki, 1973) (tenant reporting someone with whom to share personal problems and concerns); availability of kinship support (Townsend, 1963) (tenant reporting at *least* one regular weekly visit with a family member); and the presence of pain/discomfort (Lawton, Ward, and Yaffe, 1967). In addition, the interview included basic social and demographic data. Interviews lasted, on average, 40 minutes.

Results

It is now well established that, where there is individual matching, the statistical analysis must take the matching into account through the use of matched-paired analyses (Pike, Casagrande, and Smith, 1975; Dixon and Massey, 1969:119-21). These analyses were done.

Since initial observations were made 10 to 15 months after placement of the public health nurses, we could only measure changes between initial and subsequent observations while the program was operative. In year one, the cases and controls were comparable on all the measures except morale where the scores of the cases were slightly lower. (In Tables 3 to 5 the positive signs indicate a greater improvement or smaller impairment in cases than in controls.)

Health Status

If morale at the time of initial observation in 1973 is taken as the baseline, cases showed a statistically significant improvement at the end of 1974 when compared to controls; this improvement was further enhanced in the final year (Table 3). In the analyses of mobility and domestic tasks,[3] the trends were toward improvement of cases compared to controls, although the differences were not statistically significant.

TABLE 3:

MEANS AND STANDARD ERRORS (S.E.) OF DIFFERENCES IN HEALTH MEASURES BETWEEN CASES AND CONTROLS

| | Morale | | Mobility | | Domestic Tasks[1] | |
	Year 2 – Year 1	Year 3 – Year 1	Year 2 – Year 1	Year 3 – Year 1	Year 2 – Year 1	Year 3 – Year 1
N	199	199	199	199	171	171
Mean	1.55	1.75	0.08	0.06	0.10	0.02
SE	0.61	0.59	0.11	0.12	0.16	0.12
t	2.54	2.95	0.66	0.51	0.64	0.12
$p<$	0.025	0.005	N.S.	N.S.	N.S.	N.S.

[1]Excludes 18 pairs omitted for lack of information.

Effects of Kin Support, Confidantes, and Pain/Discomfort

We next wanted to assess the effects of the program while *statistically* controlling for some other variables. The first of these was support from kin.

Morale   When both cases and controls had kin support, the improvement in the morale of cases was marked (Table 4). When cases had kin support and controls did not, there was also a significant improvement in the morale of cases over controls; when cases did not have kin support and controls did, the improvement in the morale of cases over controls was still evident (but not statistically significant). Only a few cases and matched controls did not have kin support, and so, no conclusions can be drawn from the slight improvement in morale of cases over controls.

There were similar, though less pronounced, trends in the morale of cases over controls when access to a confidante was considered as the variable on which we statistically controlled.

In the absence of pain/discomfort, there was an increase in the morale of cases compared to controls from Year 1 to Year 2, and a slightly smaller increase from Year 1 to Year 3, but neither increase was statistically significant

TABLE 4:

MEANS AND STANDARD ERRORS (SE) OF DIFFERENCES IN MORALE
SCORES BETWEEN CASES AND CONTROLS

	Both Have Kin Support		Both Have a Confidante		Neither Have Pain/Discomfort	
	Year 2 – Year 1	Year 3 – Year 1	Year 2 – Year 1	Year 3 – Year 1	Year 2 – Year 1	Year 3 – Year 1
N	87	87	116	116	72	72
Mean	2.02	2.27	0.89	1.56	0.36	0.21
SE	0.79	0.76	0.42	0.69	0.65	0.62
t	2.57	3.00	2.12	2.26	0.92	0.34
p<	0.025	0.005	0.05	0.05	N.S.	N.S.

(Table 4). When cases had pain/discomfort and controls did not, there was a significant improvement in the morale of controls over cases in both years; the reverse was evident when the controls had pain/discomfort and the cases did not and this improvement was approximately twice as great. There were few occurrences of the presence of pain/discomfort for both cases and controls, and so in this analysis, no conclusions can be drawn from the improvement in morale of cases over controls.

Mobility   When we compared mobility of cases and controls in the presence of kin support (Table 5), there was a significant improvement in mobility in Year 2 and Year 3 over Year 1. In the other analyses, there were no significant improvements in mobility.

In the absence of pain/discomfort, mobility was significantly improved in Year 2 and Year 3 compared with Year 1 (Table 5). When both cases and controls had pain/discomfort, there was a significant improvement in mobility of cases over controls in both years; no other improvement could be demonstrated from our data.

TABLE 5:

MEANS AND STANDARD ERRORS (SE) OF DIFFERENCES IN MOBILITY
SCORES BETWEEN CASES AND CONTROLS

	Both Have Kin Support		Both Have a Confidante		Neither Have Pain/Discomfort	
	Year 2 – Year 1	Year 3 – Year 1	Year 2 – Year 1	Year 3 – Year 1	Year 2 – Year 1	Year 3 – Year 1
N	87	87	117	117	72	72
Mean	0.40	0.31	−0.11	0.00[1]	0.30	0.31
SE	0.12	0.13	0.15	0.14	0.15	0.15
t	3.34	2.39	−0.76	0.03	2.01	2.05
p<	0.005	0.025	N.S.	N.S.	0.05	0.05

[1]0.00 means less than 0.005.

Competence in domestic tasks   When competence in domestic tasks was measured, our results did not indicate any significant improvement of cases over controls when kin support was considered. In fact, when cases had kin support and controls did not, there was a slight (but non-significant) improvement of controls over cases.

Whether cases or controls had a confidante, there were no significant differences in the ability to accomplish domestic tasks.

When both cases and controls had pain/discomfort, we obtained, from our measure of competence in domestic tasks, a significant improvement of cases as opposed to controls. This improvement was not maintained in Year 3. However, our sample sizes were fairly small. No other significant improvements were obtained from this measurement.

Use of Health Services

More cases than controls visited the doctor in Years 1 and 2, but the pattern was reversed in Year 3 (Figure 2). In all three years, fewer cases than controls were admitted to hospital, and in Years 2 and 3 the difference was statistically significant (Figure 3).

FIGURE 2:
NUMBER OF PAIRS IN WHICH ONLY ONE MEMBER VISITED THE DOCTOR
IN THE LAST TWO-WEEK PERIOD[1]

Cases

Controls

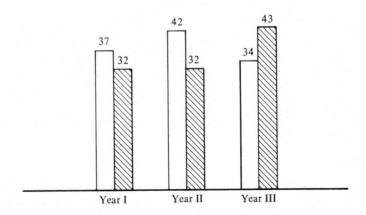

Year I   Year II   Year III

[1] N.S.

FIGURE 3:

NUMBER OF PAIRS IN WHICH ONLY ONE MEMBER WAS ADMITTED TO
HOSPITAL IN THE LAST 12-MONTH PERIOD

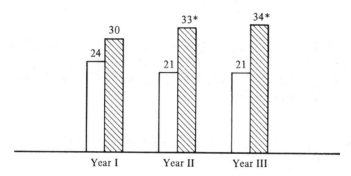

*p< 0.05

In addition, when the total number of admissions to hospital in the last twelve-month period were examined (excluding three or more admissions), there were fewer admissions amongst the cases than controls. This difference was significant at the 5 percent level in Year 3.

When both groups had access to a confidante, fewer cases than controls were admitted to hospital in each succeeding year. However, these differences were not statistically significant. The cases had more admissions in Year 1, but fewer in Year 2 and considerably fewer in Year 3. The same picture was evident when both cases and controls had kin support. In the absence of pain/discomfort, there were no differences between cases and controls in terms of either the number of people admitted to hospitals or the number of admissions to hospitals.

Discussion

The analyses suggested significant improvement in morale during the on-site public health nursing program. When tenants had kin support and were free of pain/discomfort, mobility was also enhanced. However, the program appeared to have had little impact on physical health, i.e., in assisting tenants to become more independent in performing domestic tasks such as shopping, cleaning, and laundry. With the exception of our measure of physical health, these results are consistent with those of Katz *et al* (1972) for the youngest (i.e., between 50 and 64 year of age) and least disabled subgroup of their study population. (This study examined the effects of the public health nurse in the follow-up of chronically ill patients after their discharge from hospital.)

Tenants in our study population obtained accommodation in part on the basis of their ability to live independently, whereas Katz and co-workers studied patients who were discharged from a rehabilitation hospital. Therefore, we would expect our study population to be less disabled than even the youngest and least disabled subgroups of the population of Katz and co-workers. This might partially explain the absence of beneficial effects from the program on our measure of physical function. The absence of a beneficial effect of the public health nurse might also have been because our initial measurements took place 10-15 months after the nurses were placed.[4] In addition, the instrument used in our study only measured gross changes in activities of daily living; a more sensitive instrument would be required to detect minor changes. (Unfortunately, this was not available at the time of the study.)

The effect on activities of daily living might have been more apparent if the nursing program had been directed toward assistance with domestic tasks. However, this is not the most efficient use of nursing personnel, and in Canada is usually the domain of homemaking services. Since as many as one-third of the tenants were unable to perform at least one of these activities unaided, one conclusion of the study is the need for a broad range of home-help services.

The strongest nursing effect was on tenants' morale. This may be due to the placebo effect and a continuing relationship with an interested lay person might have produced the same result. However, the analysis which took into account the presence of a confidante does not support this. For example, when both cases and controls reported a continuing relationship with a "significant" relative or friend, the cases still scored appreciably better on morale.

Perhaps someone with less professional preparation than a public health nurse (for example, a licensed practical nurse) might have had a similar effect on morale. However, the fact that the nurses participated in activities, such as patient assessment and the planning and coordination of patient management with doctors and other health and social agencies, would argue for the continued use of a public health nurse. The positive effects on morale might be accounted for by the reaching out by nurses to contact isolated and withdrawn tenants; the tenants' increased sense of security because the nurses were available and accessible; patient advocacy by the nurses; and, finally, the philosophy of the program which was to promote self-reliance among this elderly population.

Another beneficial nursing effect was the improvement in tenants' mobility. This measure included questions on graded levels of walking, stair climbing, and ability to use private and public transportation. Increased mobility is extremely important for the elderly because it increases their ability to satisfy maintenance needs and indirectly affects health, nutrition, and self-esteem (Carp, 1971; Byerts et al, 1972).

Our analyses also suggested that access to a confidante is an important factor affecting health status of the elderly. We believe that this should be recognized and utilized by health practitioners when assessing the resources of a patient for prognosis and management. Research specifically addressing the role and effect of the confidante within the context of health-care delivery needs further study.

When tenants had at least a weekly visit with a family member, the nursing effect was augmented on all three measures of health status. The professional education of the public health nurse emphasizes the concept of the family and the process of working with the family to achieve better health status for all members. The results of this study suggest that this approach does pay off.

Because of the case-finding function of the Public Health Nursing Program, we expected the cases to have more visits to doctors than the controls in Year 1 and perhaps in Year 2. At the beginning of the program, medical needs of the tenants were identified and as a result they were referred to a doctor for medical treatment. However, once this initial backlog of unmet medical needs was "flushed out", we expected the cases through nursing surveillance to make fewer visits to doctors than the controls. Although the differences in doctor utilization between cases and controls were not significant, the data do support these expectations.

Finally, we expected that, with the on-site Public Health Nursing Program, elderly people might turn less often to the hospital as their source of care and/or that their health might not deteriorate sufficiently to require admission to hospital. The results of the study are in accordance with our expectations.

More studies of this type are required. The research design of further studies should not only include treatment by different types of health workers, but also treatment by interested lay persons. This would help determine whether less qualified health workers could achieve similar beneficial effect on health status and health-care utilization. Further research is required to develop more sensitive and appropriate measures of health outcome for a community-based population.

In summary, the results of this case-control study demonstrated that elderly people, living in high-rise apartment buildings where an on-site Public Health Nursing Program was present, had higher levels of health status and lower rates of hospital admissions than tenants in buildings without such a program. More precisely, tenants exposed to the program achieved higher levels of psychological well-being, walked and used public and private transportation more often, and were admitted to general hospitals less frequently than their counterparts in buildings without the program. Approximately one-third of the tenants in the study, regardless of whether or not a nursing program was operating, needed assistance with domestic tasks, such as shopping for groceries and doing laundry. Tenants who had a confidante were more likely to experience a beneficial effect on health status than those without one.

Notes

1. The interviews were conducted by outside observers, that is, fourteen women were recruited and specifically trained for the task.

2. It would have been preferable to collect baseline data before the program started. Unfortunately, the fiscal arrangements were such that the nursing program had to begin before the interview schedule for the evaluation could be prepared. We therefore had a limited range of options for evaluation methods and chose what seemed to be the best possible under the circumstances.

3. Data concerning competence in domestic ranks will be found in the staff paper from which this report is drawn.

4. In the previously mentioned study, Katz *et al* found that measurable changes resulting from program intervention did not appear until 6 to 12 months after the nursing program was initiated.

ACKNOWLEDGEMENTS

We wish to thank Lois Knowles of the University of Florida for her contributions as nursing consultant, Stephen Walters of Yale University for his statistical guidance at the beginning of the project, and Gerry Hill for his suggestions during the final analysis. We also thank Gilles Mousseau for his programming expertise; Joyce Pearson for her contribution to the development of the interview schedule; and Claire Fair, Roberta Dupuis, and all the interviewers and coders for data collection and coding.

18

THE ELDERLY AT HOME AND IN RETIREMENT HOUSING
A Comparative Study of Health Problems, Functional Difficulties, and Support Service Needs*

Gloria M. Gutman
Department of Psychology
University of British Columbia

The rate of institutionalization of the elderly in Canada is one of the highest among the industrialized countries of the world (Schwenger, this volume). According to the Final Report of the Special Committee of the Senate on Aging (1966), in 1962-63, 7.7 percent of Canadians 65 and over were in institutions such as Homes for Special Care, Mental or TB Hospitals, and General and Allied Special Hospitals. In comparison, Shanas (1974) reports institutionalization rates of about 1 percent in Poland and from 3 to 5 percent in Denmark, Britain, the United States, and Israel.

Flett (1976) gives several reasons for the high rate of institutionalization of our elderly. These include what Schwenger (1974) describes as a general tendency in this country to institutionalize, at excessively high rates, so-called "deviant" groups, whether criminals or invalids, young or old. Additionally, as evidenced by Cape, *et al.* (1977), a lack of sophistication in assessing problems of the aged results all too frequently in misdiagnoses and inappropriate institutionalization. Canada's dearth of home-care services as compared to other countries has also been mentioned frequently as a factor contributing to excessive institutionalization.

Studies in many communities call for an increase in home-delivered services, medical and non-medical (Chene, *et al.*, 1977; Garrett and Hill, 1972; Hannochko, *et al.*, 1974; Kraus, *et al.*, 1976b; Social Planning Council of Hamilton and District, 1965; Social Planning and Review Council of B.C., 1976; West Vancouver Community Council, 1971). But are such diverse services as homemakers, home handymen, meals-on-wheels, home nursing, transportation services, etc., all needed in the same quantity? In order to

*Based on a paper presented at the Annual Meeting of the Canadian Association on Gerontology, Edmonton, October 1978. This project was supported by a LIP grant awarded to the Senior Citizens' Resource Committee of the Comox-Strathcona Regional District.

answer this question we need to know more about the characteristics of the elderly living at home. We need to know, for example, what proportion have serious health problems which interfere with daily functioning; what proportion have problems bathing, dressing, preparing or eating meals, with cleaning or home repairs; what proportion are now receiving assistance with activities of daily living or home maintenance or would use such assistance if it were made more readily available. Most of the information we have now is global—that is, for the category 65 and over without regard for whether the person is living at home or in an institution.

Among those living at home we also need to know more about those living in retirement housing as distinct from those living in non-age-segregated settings. In working with various professional and community groups interested in providing retirement housing one generally begins by talking about the need to provide an environment that is safe and will maximize independence as well as provide stimulation and opportunities for social interaction. One generally outlines changes which take place in various organ systems in the body and in health status. One outlines the various social losses that can occur. The implications of these changes and losses vis-à-vis the built environment are then discussed. For example, there is evidence that with increasing age the sense of hearing becomes less acute (Kimmel, 1974:357-72). One implication of this finding is the need in retirement housing for stronger than average soundproofing between suites so that the person who is hard of hearing and turns up the volume of his TV set will not unduly disturb his neighbours. There is evidence that the prevalence of arthritis increases with age—one recommends installation of lever-type taps in kitchens and bathrooms which are easier for arthritics to manipulate. There is evidence that various kinds of accidents, especially falls, are an important cause of injury and chronic impairment in the elderly—one recommends installation of grab bars near toilets and tubs to prevent falls and to facilitate independent transfer. One points out the need to make doorways wide enough to accommodate a weelchair not only for the benefit of those who move into retirement housing in a wheelchair but also so that the previously ambulatory tenant who suffers a health change need not relocate. Costs being what they are, designers and/or sponsors, while agreeing with the points being made, often ask how many of their prospective tenants will really need these special design features? How many will have serious hearing impairments? How many will have disabling arthritis? How many will suffer from dizziness or otherwise be at risk for falls? How many are likely to need wheelchairs? The implicit question is: Are there sufficient numbers to justify the extra cost presumed to be involved in designing for persons with sensory, motor, or perceptual handicaps? Questions about the need for what may be termed "prosthetic" design features also arise from another consideration. Most designers and sponsors want to provide housing that has a homelike rather than an institutional quality. The fear is that if prosthetic design features are included an institutional atmosphere will prevail.

Other questions that are frequently raised by designers and sponsors are: What motivates a person to move into retirement housing? What facilities and services do seniors need and want provided on-site? How do they feel about "multi-level" accommodation—that is, accommodation in which two or more levels (self-contained, board-residence, personal, inter-mediate, or extended-care) are combined in the same building or on the same site?

In order to obtain answers to these and other questions so as to facilitate planning and provision of additional community-support services and retirement housing units, a study was conducted in B.C. in the spring of 1977, in the Comox-Strathcona Regional District (CSRD). In the study, two groups of seniors were interviewed—a group living at home in non-age-segregated settings and a group living in retirement housing. This chapter describes some of the findings obtained in the CSRD study focusing on similarities and differences between the two groups in (a) socio-demographic characteristics; (b) incidence of health problems and functional disabilities; and (c) in the degree to which they are now receiving assistance with activities of daily living (ADL), home maintenance, etc., or would use such assistance if it were made more readily available. Wherever possible results will be compared with those obtained in other Canadian studies.

Method

The Comox-Strathcona Regional District includes 20,280 square kilometres (7,834 sq. miles) in an irregularly shaped area that encompasses the north central portion of Vancouver Island, the area surrounding Bute Inlet on the mainland, and the islands between. More than half of the total area is on Vancouver Island. There are eight organized communities on the island in which the bulk of the population reside, while the remainder of the population is unevenly distributed throughout the rural areas.

According to a list drawn up from various sources (voter's registrations for federal, provincial, and municipal elections, Legions, old age pensioners' organizations, senior citizens' clubs, etc.) there were 6,659 people believed to be 60 or over living in the Regional District. In the first part of the study, interviews were completed with 811 people systematically selected on an area-proportional basis from among those 60 and over and living at home (Group AH). In the second part of the study interviews were conducted with 90 persons living in retirement housing (Group RH). All subjects were interviewed in their current residence by 12 specially trained interviewers, all female, all residents of the Regional District, and ranging in age from 30 to 50. Interviews lasted from 40 to 120 minutes.

Socio-Demographic Characteristics

Those living in retirement housing (Group RH) were considerably older than those living at home (Group AH). In Group RH, 56 percent were aged 75 or older as compared with 20 percent in this age-range in Group AH. There were more females in Group RH than in Group AH (78 percent *vs.* 48 percent), fewer married persons (20 percent *vs.* 72 percent) and more living alone (79 percent *vs.* 22 percent). Another difference between the two groups was in socio-economic status. Whereas the mean monthly income in Group RH was $325 (s.d. $126.40) in Group AH it was $608 (s.d. $413.98).

Findings regarding the socio-demographic characteristics of tenants in retirement housing are consistent with those obtained by Audain (1973) in the cross-country *Beyond Shelter* study, by Flett (1976) in a study conducted in Ottawa, by Stevenson (1974) in a study conducted in Vancouver and with the 1971 *Aging in Manitoba* study. All agree that retirement housing is populated more by females than by males and more by persons who are single and/or living alone than by married persons, with at least a third of the tenants (Flett, 1976) and more often half or more (Audain, 1973; Stevenson, 1974; Manitoba, 1971) being 75 or over.

Also consistent with other Canadian studies are findings regarding the elderly living at home. For example, in both the *Aging in Manitoba* study and in a study conducted by Kraus, *et al.* (1976a) in the Kingston area, the majority of those living at home were found to be under rather than over 75; sex ratios were approximately equal; and more were married and living with their spouse than single and/or living alone.

Health Problems and Functional Difficulties

The section of the interview concerned with health problems and functional difficulties was prefaced with the question "How would you describe your health at this time? Would you say it's excellent, good, fair, poor, or very poor?" Subjects were then asked what kinds of health problems and physical disabilities they had. This was followed by a checklist of health problems supposedly common in the elderly. Included in the checklist were problems with nervousness, arthritis or rheumatism, varicose veins, heart, diabetes, dizziness, high blood pressure, and kidneys or bladder. For each problem mentioned, subjects were asked whether it was a very serious problem, a fairly serious problem, or not a very serious problem and what things they were unable to do because of it. Subjects were also asked about "functional difficulties": whether and to what extent they had problems seeing even when wearing eyeglasses, hearing even when wearing a hearing aid, with control of bowel or bladder, sleeping, and remembering things. Subjects were also asked about their ambulatory status, whether they could dress themselves completely, take a bath or shower unassisted, prepare their own meals, and eat without assistance.

TABLE 1:

INCIDENCE OF HEALTH PROBLEMS AND FUNCTIONAL DIFFICULTIES BY AGE, CSRD STUDY

	% Group AH			% Group RH		
	Under 75 (N = 641)	75 or Over (N = 165)	All (N = 806)	Under 75 (N = 38)	75 or Over (N = 50)	All (N = 88)
Health Checklist "Any problems with:"						
Nervousness	19.8	20.1	20.1	28.9	48.0	38.9
Arthritis or Rheumatism	48.6	48.6	48.6	57.9	64.0	64.4
Varicose Veins	14.5	15.2	15.2	23.7	36.0	31.1
Heart	14.2	18.2	18.2	23.7	36.0	30.0
Diabetes	5.1	4.9	4.9	5.3	4.0	4.4
Dizziness	11.2	13.9	13.9	18.4	40.0	32.2
High Blood Pressure	17.2	17.9	17.9	36.8	24.0	30.0
Kidneys or Bladder	11.1	12.3	12.3	13.2	38.0	26.7
Functional Difficulties "Any problems with:"						
Seeing (even when wearing glasses)	12.6	30.3	17.1	26.3	36.0	33.3
Hearing (even when wearing hearing aid)	24.2	43.0	29.0	28.9	40.0	36.7
Control of bowel or bladder ("Accidents")	3.4	4.9	3.9	0.0	8.0	4.4
Sleeping	21.2	23.6	22.2	26.3	40.0	37.8
Remembering things	26.4	37.6	29.1	44.7	60.0	52.2

Fewer subjects in Group RH (55.5 percent) than in Group AH (74.7 percent) perceived themselves in good or excellent health. On almost all health checklist items more in Group RH than in Group AH reported having a problem (see Table 1). On four of the five items relating to functional difficulties (seeing even when wearing glasses, hearing even when wearing a hearing aid, sleeping, and remembering things) problems were reported more frequently in Group RH than in Group AH. There were also more in Group RH than in Group AH who reported lack of independence in moving about the house, dressing, bathing, and preparing and eating meals.

Since subjects in Group RH were older than those in Group AH it seemed important to ascertain whether the differences between the two groups were primarily a function of age. Subjects in each group were therefore dichotomized into those under and over 75.

In both the under- and over-75 groups there were fewer in Group RH than in Group AH who rated their health as good or excellent. In the case of

TABLE 2:

COMPARISONS BETWEEN THE ELDERLY LIVING AT HOME IN THE COMOX-STRATHCONA REGIONAL DISTRICT (CSRD) AND THOSE LIVING IN KINGSTON, EDMONTON, AND MANITOBA.

	% of subjects in CSRD study (N = 811)	% of subjects in Kingston study (N = 141)	% of subjects in Edmonton study (N = 672)	% of subjects in Manitoba study (N = 3558)
Health Ratings				
Excellent	22.9	13	—	13.3
Good	51.8	52	—	46.3
Fair	20.7	32	—	27.2
Poor	4.2	3	—	9.4
Health Checklist	"any problems with"	"any problems with"	"any problems with"	"any problems with"
Nervousness	20.1	—	24	13.9
Arthritis or Rheumatism	48.6	—	42	46.3
Varicose Veins	15.2	—	—	—
Heart	18.2	—	23	33.0
Diabetes	4.9	—	5	5.3
Dizziness	13.9	—	23	—
High blood pressure	17.9	—	19	—
Kidneys or bladder	12.3	—	11	8.9
Functional Difficulties	"any problems with"	"any problems with"	"any problems with"	"any problems with"
Seeing (even when wearing glasses)	17.1	—	42*	18.1
Hearing (even when wearing hearing aid)	29.0	—	33*	21.1
Control of bladder or bowel ("accidents")	3.9	—	—	—
Sleeping	22.2	—	24	—
Remembering things	29.1	—	—	—

*=Major difference in wording of question.

TABLE 2: (continued)

COMPARISONS BETWEEN THE ELDERLY LIVING AT HOME IN THE COMOX-STRATHCONA REGIONAL DISTRICT (CSRD) AND THOSE LIVING IN KINGSTON, EDMONTON, AND MANITOBA.

Functional Difficulties	% of subjects in CSRD study (N = 811) "very or fairly serious problem with"	% of subjects in Kingston study (N = 141) "much trouble"	% of subjects in Edmonton study (N = 672)	% of subjects in Manitoba study (N = 3558)
Seeing (even when wearing glasses)	9.4	9	—	—
Hearing (even when wearing hearing aid)	8.9	14	—	—
Control of bladder or bowel ("accidents")	1.7	2	—	—
Sleeping	5.5	14	—	—
Remembering things	4.5	—	—	—
Lack of Independence in Ambulation and ADL				
Climbing stairs	1.1	1.4	—	2.2
Moving about the house	.5	0	—	2.1
Dressing	1.7	1	—	1.9
Bathing	4.9	2.8	—	4.1
Preparing meals	3.1	—	—	
Eating meals	.2	1	—	.5

the health checklist, in the under-75 group there were more in Group RH than in Group AH reporting problems on seven of eight items and in the over-75 group on eight of eight items. In the case of functional difficulties in both the under- and over-75 groups there were more in Group RH than in Group AH reporting problems on four of five items. There were also more in Group RH than in Group AH in both under- and over-75 groups who reported lack of independence on three of the four ADL measures.

A similar trend towards greater disability among those in retirement housing than among those living at home was apparent when the severity of the problem was taken into consideration (i.e., there were more in Group RH than in Group AH in both the under- and over-75 groups reporting problems which they classed as very or fairly serious).

Kraus, *et al.* (1976) conducted a study in the Kingston area in which three groups were interviewed, one of which consisted of 141 persons living independently in the community. Their interview, like ours, included questions relating to difficulties in the areas of seeing, hearing, control of bowel or bladder, and sleeping. Respondents were asked to rate subjects' degree of independence in fourteen activities of daily living, five of which overlapped with ours, *viz.*, climbing stairs, moving about the house from room to room, dressing, bathing, and eating. Respondents were also asked to rate subjects' current health. As shown in Table 2 there were more in the Kingston study than in our study with health ratings in the fair to poor category (35 percent *vs.* 25 percent) and fewer in the excellent category (13 percent *vs.* 23 percent). However, the proportions in the Kingston study reporting "much trouble" were highly similar to the proportions in our study reporting "very or fairly serious problems" in the areas of seeing (9 percent in both studies) and control of bowel or bladder (2 percent in both studies). There was also considerable similarity across the two studies (and the Manitoba study) in the proportion reporting that they could not climb stairs or move about the house alone (0-2 percent) and who lacked independence in dressing (1-2 percent), bathing (3-5 percent), preparing meals (3 percent), and eating meals (0.2-1 percent).

Similarities are also apparent between our findings with the health checklist and those obtained in the *Edmonton Senior Residents Survey* (James, 1964) and in the *Aging in Manitoba* study — the only other Canadian studies discovered to date which inquired about specific disabilities and in which data are reported separately for the elderly living at home.

In the case of the retirement housing group there was only one Canadian study with which much in the way of comparisons could be made and that was the *Aging in Manitoba* (1971) study. The Manitoba data, like our own, indicate that when persons living at home and persons living in retirement housing are asked the same questions there is a trend towards higher incidence of health problems and sensory disabilities among those in retirement housing.

Other Problems

Besides inquiring about health problems and functional difficulties, subjects in the CSRD study were asked whether they had any problems with fixing things around the house, household accidents, giving themselves medication, feeling lonely, getting places in the community, and managing their money.

Two percent in each group reported difficulty giving themselves medication. There were more in AH than in RH who reported difficulty fixing things around the house (19 percent *vs.* 16 percent). Rates were higher in RH than in AH, however, when it came to problems with household accidents (8 percent *vs.* 3 percent), feeling lonely (23 percent *vs.* 14 percent), and getting places (22 percent *vs.* 14 percent). Consistent with the difference between the two groups in mean monthly income, more in RH than in AH reported problems managing their money (9 percent *vs.* 7 percent). As regards financial problems, when questioned further it was found that 9 percent in AH and 4 percent in RH reported difficulty finding enough money to pay all the expenses of their accommodation (e.g., rent, taxes, heat, light, home maintenance costs); 7 percent in each group reported that after paying for their accommodation they had trouble finding enough money for groceries, while 19 percent in AH and 32 percent in RH reported that after paying for their accommodation and groceries they did not have money left over for anything else.

When dichotomized into those under and over 75, on all items except fixing things around the house and in the case of the over-75 group, self medication, there were again more in RH than in AH reporting problems.

Support Services

As Garrett and Hill (1973) and Berry and Cameron (1973) have indicated, a number of support services are available in the Comox-Strathcona Regional District. These include home nursing, physiotherapy, homemaker service, meals-on-wheels, a friendly visitors' service, as well as help with transportation.

In attempting to assess the extent and type of assistance now being received as well as to determine the need for additional support services, subjects in each group were presented with a ten-item checklist. They were asked to indicate which of the ten types of assistance they were now receiving—either formally, from community groups or agencies, or informally, from relatives, neighbours, or friends, also, which they would use if more readily available.

In both Group AH and Group RH the three types of assistance most frequently received were help with home repairs, with cleaning, and with transportation. These same three types of assistance were the ones most frequently mentioned by subjects in Group AH as services they are not now receiving but would use if more readily available. Among those in Group

RH not now receiving assistance, transportation service and help with cleaning also were among the top three services they would use if more readily available. The third was meals-on-wheels.

It is interesting to note that for almost all of the types of assistance listed in the checklist, utilization rates were greater for Group RH than Group AH. The same trend was apparent when subjects in each group were dichotomized into those under and over 75.

To the limited extent that comparisons can be made, utilization rates are comparable with those observed in other Canadian studies. For example, the CSRD data show that 2 percent of those living at home were recipients of meals-on-wheels. Snider (1973) reports a rate of 1 percent for the independent elderly living in Edmonton and Orris (1970) a rate of 3 percent for those living in Saskatoon. This study found that 4 percent of those living at home received visiting nursing service; Snider and Orris each report 5 percent. The only other possible comparisons in the case of those living at home concerned help with laundry and housecleaning. In the CSRD study 5 percent were receiving help with laundry and 9 percent with cleaning; in Manitoba, 10 percent were receiving help with laundry while 5 percent were receiving help with light housework and 14 percent with heavy housework.

Similarity of findings was also apparent in the case of those living in retirement housing. For example, in the CSRD study 6 percent were receiving help with cooking; Flett (1976) reports a rate of 4 percent among tenants in retirement housing in Ottawa. This study showed 22 percent receiving help with cleaning; Flett reports 19 percent. In CSRD 12 percent were receiving help with laundry; rates in the Flett study were 14 percent and in the Manitoba study 12 percent. In CSRD, 12 percent had someone visiting on a regular basis; the rate in the *Beyond Shelter* study (Audain, 1973) was 14 percent.

Discussion

The results of this study suggest that tenants in retirement housing have more health problems and functional disabilities than persons of comparable age living at home in non-age-segregated settings. These findings would seem to refute the arguments of Audain (1974) and others to the effect that tenants in retirement housing are no different than other elderly persons and that as a consequence, they have no need for special design features. Tenants in retirement housing *are* different. For one thing, they tend to be older than those living at home; with increasing age the probability of health and functional problems increases. They also appear to be more frail than persons of comparable age living at home. Granted, many persons living at home (particularly those over 75) could probably benefit from placement of grab bars in bathrooms near toilet and tub or from placing kitchen cupboards at a height appropriate for the average "little old lady" so that she doesn't have to stretch or stand on a chair to get things. The need for such prosthetic design features seems, however, to be greater in retirement housing. As evidence, one might note that in the Group RH, 32 percent report problems with dizziness, placing them at risk for falls; 8 percent described their problem as very or fairly serious. The rate for dizziness among the Group AH was 14 percent; 3.5 percent described their problem as very or fairly serious.

Among those reporting very or fairly serious problems with arthritis, heart, or varicose veins, all of which were more prevalent in Group RH, the things they most commonly reported not being able to do were stand for any length of time or walk any distance.

The Central Mortgage and Housing Corporation publication "Housing the Elderly" recommends that in selecting a site for retirement housing "the importance of easy access to public transportation and downtown amenities should be emphasized as a planning factor" (1972:8). Often, however, in the Comox-Strathcona Regional District and elsewhere, sites are selected mainly on economic grounds. This may be why, in the present study, as in others, transportation services are among those used most by tenants in retirement housing. Poor site location may also be the reason why transportation is among those services for which there is greatest additional need. (In the case of those living at home, transportation services are also needed because many persons are living in homes which met their needs when they were younger and able to drive a car but which are innappropriate for their current locational needs.)

The "standing and walking" problem also has implications for unit design. For example, in "Housing the Elderly", CMHC recommends that knee space be provided under the sink to permit the use of a stool while performing kitchen chores. In a survey conducted in B.C. in 1975, of ten apartment buildings for seniors constructed during the previous twelve months (Gutman, 1975) none were found to have such space. Given that two-thirds of those in retirement housing have problems with arthritis and one-third with their heart or legs this design detail should be given greater consideration.

Designers and sponsors might also give greater consideration to provision of services on-site. As Flett (1976; Flett and Associates, this volume) and others have pointed out, some designers, sponsors, administrators, and health professionals fear that provision of on-site services in retirement housing will generate a hospital atmosphere and foster over-dependency. Sherman, addressing this issue, found no evidence of an erosion of independence at sites providing services. "If anything", Sherman reports, "the service provision enables the residents to enjoy independence by maintaining themselves at optimal levels" (1975:245). Gutman (1978) found improvements in morale compared to pre-move levels in a group of seniors in self-contained suites in a building also offering board-residence and personal care and a number of on-site facilities and services. Tenants also reported "dressing up" and "getting out" more than they had prior to moving in. Controls in a building offering only self-contained suites and no services showed no such changes.

The results of this study also have implications for broader policy issues. In British Columbia, the provincial government has declared a virtual moratorium on the construction of new housing units for seniors. On the assumption that most seniors move into retirement housing primarily for financial reasons they have instituted the Shelter Aid for Elderly Renters Program (SAFER). SAFER provides a rent subsidy so that seniors will not have to pay more than 30 percent of their income for shelter costs. This program has had the effect of reducing, but not eliminating, waiting lists for retirement housing. Perhaps waiting lists still exist because, as evidenced by the data on motivations and pathways into retirement housing (Gutman, 1977) financial concerns are *not*, in fact, the only or most common reasons for moving into such housing. Also, although a majority of those applying for retirement housing come from rental housing (mainly apartments), some also come from single-family dwellings. The SAFER program does not benefit home owners.

If present policy continues, we will soon again be in the position of having a major shortage of retirement housing units. Many of those who would have gone into such units will be remaining at home. Whatever need there is now for home support services will be increased not only because of the additional numbers of seniors staying at home but also because these prospective tenants now staying at home will be older and more frail.

A key question and one to which we should be addressing ourselves, is whether, as a number of administrators contend, retirement housing plays a prophylactic or at least a delaying role *vis-à-vis* psychological and physiological deterioration and dependency.

With regard to the question of quantity of community support services required to keep people at home and out of institutions, the question with which this chapter began, one thing is clear and that is that the answer depends on what type of home one is referring to—a house or apartment in the general community or a suite in retirement housing.

VI

Needs and Services for an Aging Population

Perhaps no paper in this collection is without implications for the problem of providing services to meet the needs of an aging population. However, the papers in this section take needs and services as their focus. Central concerns in this area have been to identify the specific needs of older people, to project the extent or volume of such needs as the population changes in the future, and to assess the costs of providing for them. The papers in this section address all these issues.

To better understand the population projections which are utilized in the papers by Powell and Martin and Denton and Spencer, readers might wish to return to Chapter 2, also by Denton and Spencer, which not only gives detailed population projections, but describes the way they are constructed. Powell and Martin are in agreement with Denton and Spencer that, while the long-range implications of changes in the population structure will require adjustments in our social institutions to provide for the needs of an older population, there is no cause for alarm. The changes will be gradual rather than catastrophic and will be within parameters which have already been experienced by other nations (a point also made by Wigdor, 1978).

Powell and Martin in Chapter 19 focus on the social security system and provision for the economic needs of an aging population, whereas Denton and Spencer deal with the second major need area, the provision of adequate health care. Together, these areas represent the largest economic commitment directed toward the aged and will therefore be the focus of the greatest political activity.

When considering how much is spent on providing even a minimal level of economic and health-care security for older people, a broad historical view leads to a conclusion voiced by Robert Butler, the director of the United States' National Institute on Aging, to the 1977 meetings of the Canadian Association on Gerontology. Contrary to popular misconception, Butler argued, the aged are not more neglected in our highly modernized societies than they have been in earlier eras. If dollars committed to programs for the aged are considered as a proportion of gross national product, probably never in human history has such a large proportion of a nation's wealth been devoted to the care of older people.

Nonetheless, advanced age is a strong predictor of poverty, and this is particularly true for women, and especially widows (see also Matthews,

Chapter 15). In many instances social class, age stratification, and sexual inequalities coalesce to produce a large group for whom the later years cannot possibly be a time of security. The theoretical arguments of Chapters 7 through 9 take on added importance in light of this reality.

The paper by Tilquin and his associates demonstrates that many of the aged are highly medicalized: they are very closely tied into a medical care system, and many of them are quite heavily drugged. This is another instance of sex and age conspiring, for women and the aged are major target groups for the drug industry, and the aging of the female population represents one growing market area for those companies who profit from illness. As the birth rate continues to be low, we might expect an increased focus on the aged as such a market for drugs, and the danger of medicalizing the life cycle and treating aging as a disease is very high.

The Havens paper is one report of the most significant survey of needs and services for the elderly ever conducted in Canada, and perhaps anywhere, the *Aging in Manitoba* study. It makes a number of important contributions to this collection in particular. It is an excellent example of the value of conducting cohort analysis. Its explicit attention to sex differences is important in showing that the "young-old/old-old" distinction is quite arbitrary in itself, and that the customary cutting point for making that distinction, age 75, does not apply equally to men and to women.

Havens shows that psychosocial needs of the Manitobans in this study were quite low, but that physical and mental functioning needs were highly correlated. Comparisons might be made to the Flett, Last, and Lynch article in this book (Chapter 17), which showed positive effects on morale as a result of nursing intervention, in the absence of demonstrated improvements in physical mobility.

Another important point of the Havens article is the distinction between availability of a service and accessibility to it. For a variety of reasons, including transportation problems, limitations of physical mobility, lack of information about the program, and a failure to match the needs to the service in the minds of service providers and potential clientele, the mere physical presence of a service does not automatically ensure that people will be able to access it. The article by Gloria Gutman (Chapter 18) provides some additional data from the Manitoba study and compares that study to others done in Canada.

With over 1,000 respondents, the research reported by Tilquin and colleagues in Chapter 21 promises to have an important impact on our understanding of the relationship of services to needs of the elderly population. Like the Manitoba study, this includes data from both urban and rural dwellers, allowing for comparisons which are all too rare in such studies. In this instance, Tilquin *et al* find no important differences on the basis of their measure of urbanization. This might reflect the close geographical and economic links between the South Shore region and Montreal, because other studies such as in Manitoba (Manitoba Department of Health and Social Development, 1971), and Ontario (Schwenger and Sayers, 1971), which compare highly urbanized with more remote rural areas do find important differences in needs and service structures for the aged.

The four chapters in this section should be viewed in the context of other sections of the book. For example, Gutman, in Chapter 18, reviews the major Canadian studies of needs and services, and the four papers on institutionalization and alternatives, found in the concluding section of the book, address one major service response to the needs of a large segment of the older population. Finally, greater attention might be placed on the theoretical interpretation of findings reported in this section. Social theorists and those who investigate social needs seldom collaborate. The work of the former at times seems somewhat ethereal, of the latter at times overly descriptive and lacking in generalizability.

19

ECONOMIC IMPLICATIONS
OF CANADA'S AGING SOCIETY*

Brian J. Powell and James K. Martin
Policy Research and Strategic Planning Branch
Department of National Health and Welfare

The policy issues related to meeting the needs of the elderly population in Canada today, and needs that will arise in the future with the expected increase in both the number and the proportion of the population who are elderly, have been the cause of some considerable and increasing debate during the last couple of years. However, in terms of economic implications of policy regarding the aged, the discussion has often been marred by confusion and unnecessary alarm.

The primary reason for this appears to have been the tendency to compress conceptually, within short time horizons, the deep structural changes which are taking place in the economy, as well as frequently to exaggerate the behavioural adjustments that individuals make to institutional changes. It is not always understood that economic processes often unfold very slowly; indeed, many of the perceived problems frequently discussed these days may not take place until two decades into the next century. Furthermore, major forces may be unleashed in the future to alter completely any projection which we would make today on the basis of past trends and estimated behavioural impacts.

From the individual's point of view, the economic problem of aging is associated with the ability to choose an appropriate pattern of work/leisure and savings/consumption over one's lifetime (for a detailed discussion of the economic theory see Barro, 1977; Feldstein, 1974; and Lucas, 1972). From a more global perspective, the economic problem of an aging society has two separate aspects: first, the problem of developing and planning social and economic institutions for individuals as they age; and, second, the problem of ensuring that these institutions emerge in society in a fair and equitable manner. From this standpoint, the economic problem is largely concerned with the slice of the GNP pie that is allocated to the older members of society. Both these perspectives must be drawn upon to develop an adequate picture of the economic implications of an aging society.

---

*Any points of view, implicit or explicit, that might be contained in the following pages represent the thoughts of the authors and cannot in any way be attributed to the viewpont, official or unofficial, of the Department of National Health and Welfare.

With the aim of exploring these issues, this paper will include a brief discussion of the changing demographic structure, a review of the present social security system as it affects the aged, and, finally, a description of emerging pressures and problems.

The Demographic Factor

In the long run, demographic factors are likely to have decisive effects. It is crucial therefore that we understand the implications of these factors for the objectives and, equally important, for the timing of public policy. Let us start then by looking at Statistics Canada Projection No. 3, one of those frequently used in current discussions of future policy issues.

This projection, shown in Table 1, indicates that the population aged 65 years and over rises slowly from 8.7 percent of the total in 1976 to almost 12 percent in 2001. Then, it grows dramatically to just over 20 percent by the year 2031. Conversely, in this projection, the population in the age group 0-17 not only declines as a percentage of the population, but actually declines in *absolute numbers*. The population in the prime working-age group, 18-64, first rises, both in the absolute number of people and as a fraction of the total population, and then declines.

TABLE 1:

CANADIAN POPULATION PROJECTIONS BY AGE
(Statistics Canada Projection No. 3) (population in thousands)

Year	Total Population	0-17	%	18-59	%	60-64	%	65+	%
1976	22,993	7,312	31.8	12,774	55.6	905	3.9	2,002	8.7
1981	24,330	6,933	28.5	14,134	58.1	963	4.0	2,310	9.5
1986	25,713	6,833	26.6	15,159	58.9	1,110	4.3	2,615	10.2
1991	26,975	6,966	25.8	15,918	59.0	1,114	4.1	2,980	11.0
1996	27,993	6,993	25.0	16,640	59.4	1,115	4.0	3,248	11.6
2001	28,794	6,805	23.6	17,401	60.4	1,165	4.0	3,425	11.9
2011	30,068	6,411	21.3	17,968	59.8	1,764	5.9	3,924	13.1
2021	30,877	6,378	20.7	17,255	55.9	2,151	7.0	5,093	16.5
2031	30,935	6,162	19.9	16,715	54.0	1,817	5.9	6,240	20.2

This projection implies, therefore, that there will be a major re-allocation of expenditure in society from one age group to another. However, it is equally clear that we have time to plan in a rational fashion given the fact that the major demographic changes will not occur until well into the next century; but it must be noted that such relative shifts may be greatly moderated if, in the remaining 20 years of this century, there are major behavioural changes with respect to fertility, or if immigration is manipulated in order to counter declining population trends. Even if such a shift does occur, and provided that the trend towards earlier retirement is halted, the projected percentage of the retired population in Canada in the years 2001 and 2011 will have only increased to a percentage which currently prevails in many European countries: in 1977, 10 European countries had populations with 13 percent or more aged 65 and over.

Despite the length of time before the dramatic shift among age groups occurs, there is one area on which we should focus attention: the whole retirement income field, including the relationship of elderly persons to the labour market, savings decisions, and the impact of inflation. The current retirement income system clearly has problems: almost 54 percent of the present elderly have incomes so low that they are receiving Guaranteed Income Supplement benefits. As we will see below, the fault appears to lie with employer-sponsored pension plans since they generate only 13 percent of all income flowing to those aged 65 and over while over 50 percent comes from government sources. Because changes to the total retirement income system will take many years to become effective, these problems will have to be addressed in the near future if adequate pensions are to await those who will retire during the next century.

The Institutional Setting

As it has evolved, the Canadian social security system for the aged consists primarily of two major components: institutions for the provision of hospital and medical care and a retirement income system.

The retirement income system can be described as a three-tiered system. The federal Old Age Security, Guaranteed Income Supplement, and Spouse's Allowance programs, together with provincial supplements, form the first tier. The second tier consists of the basic public contributory pension schemes: the Canada and Quebec Pension Plans. These two tiers are intended to ensure basic adequacy in income for the retired. Finally, the third tier, which is concerned with ensuring whatever extra margin of comfort individual Canadians might desire, includes the private pensions, savings, and assets that Canadians accumulate themselves, either through employment-related pension plans or through individual savings and investments.

The first tier provides a flat benefit (in the form of Old Age Security) to everyone over age 65 in Canada who has met certain residence requirements. Guaranteed Income Supplement benefits are paid to low-income old-age pensioners with benefits being reduced one dollar for every two dollars of other family income, in most cases. The Spouse's Allowance is another income-tested program providing benefits to those aged 60 to 64 whose spouses are old age pensioners. Some provinces augment these income-tested payments further. The importance of all income-tested benefits can be seen in the fact that in 1978 about 54 percent of pensioners were receiving GIS benefits.

The second tier consists of the CPP and the QPP, twin earnings-related pension plans which cover virtually everyone in the labour force. The maximum retirement benefit will eventually be about 25 percent of average wages and salaries. These plans do away with the problems resulting from a move from one employer to another; they provide survivor's "pensions"; and all benefits are indexed (for further details see Policy Research and Strategic Planning, 1978a).

The details of the third tier are not well known, so we will briefly outline the features (see also Statistics Canada, 1977c; 1978c). Individuals may enter "contracts" by which they save, and the two most important institutions for doing this are private pensions and life insurance. About 3.9 million Canadian workers (41 percent of the employed labour force) are members of job-related pension plans. Contributions are tax exempt, up to a limit, and the first $1,000 of income received from pensions or retirement annuities are also tax exempt. About one million life insurance policies are purchased each year. Contributions are not tax exempt but benefits are not taxable. Although life insurance may not be explicitly intended to provide retirement income, over 87 percent of widows and widowers are aged 55 and over.

Discretionary individual saving is also encouraged by the tax system. Registered Retirement Savings Plans allow an individual to invest a portion of his earnings for himself or his spouse and later convert it into a retirement annuity. Contributions to RRSPs, which are tax exempt up to a limit, totalled more than 2.1 billion dollars in 1976 alone. Private savings over and above contributions to private pension plans and RRSPs are encouraged by the exemption from taxation of the first 1,000 dollars of dividend and interest income from Canadian sources.

In total, the assets held by pension plans, life insurance companies, and in RRSPs totalled about 50 billion dollars in 1975, as Table 2 shows.

TABLE 2:

DEVELOPMENT OF ASSETS HELD BY FINANCIAL INSTITUTIONS

	Assets of		
	Trusteed Pension Plans[1]	Life Insurance Companies[2]	Cumulative Gross RRSP Contributions
1960	3,583	8,260	51
1965	6,541	11,856	310
1970	11,059	15,673	1,077
1975	21,235	24,097	5,733

NOTE:

[1] Book Value.

[2] On behalf of Canadian policy holders. This figure includes some RRSP contributions.

SOURCE:

(a) Statistics Canada, 1973 and 1977c.

(b) Canadian Life Insurance Association, 1977.

(c) Revenue Canada, 1962, 1967, 1972 and 1977.

The other major component of social security, the health care system, has also come to play an important role in the lives of pensioners. Medical and hospital services are heavily utilized by older people who, for instance, account for 34 percent of patient days in general and allied hospitals. Overall, it is estimated that in 1976 expenditure on their behalf amounted to 3.1 billion dollars, that is more than 1½ percent of the GNP and equal to one-third of the cash income of the aged.

Problems and Issues

The Individual Perspective

During the last 20 years, great strides have been made in providing insurance so that health-care costs will not result in the financial ruin of families. The private and public sectors have together been able to provide less secure protection against reductions in real retirement disposable income.

In terms of the adequacy of the basic public programs, an appropriate yardstick for measuring the effectiveness of the plans is the ratio of pre-retirement income replaced. Table 3 shows that for those retiring at this time, these programs alone (without any private income) can replace a fairly high percentage in some circumstances: for a couple, both pensioners, one

TABLE 3:
PERCENTAGE OF PRE-RETIREMENT DISPOSABLE INCOME REPLACED AT THE LEVEL OF AVERAGE INDUSTRIAL EARNINGS BY OAS/GIS/SA AND CPP/QPP IN THE ABSENCE OF ANY PRIVATE RETIREMENT INCOME, 1977

Marital Status	Gross Earnings 1976 (One Earner)	Disposable Income Before Retirement*	OAS/GIS/SA and CPP/QPP**	Disposable Income After Retirement as a Percentage of Disposable Income Before Retirement
Single Person	$11,858	$9,310	$4,023	43%
Married Couple: One OAS Pensioner Spouse ineligible for OAS or a Spouse's Allowance	11,858	9,864	4,971	50
Married Couple: One OAS Pensioner and One Spouse's Allowance	11,858	9,864	6,205	63
Married Couple: Two OAS Pensioners	11,858	9,864	6,721	68

*Disposable income is gross earnings minus federal and provincial income tax, CPP/QPP contributions, and UI premiums.
**No federal or provincial income tax would be paid on these amounts.
SOURCE: Table 8 in Policy Research and Strategic Planning, 1978a.

of whom had been earning the average wage, the replacement ratio would be almost 70 percent. For those earning less than the average industrial wage, the replacement rate is higher still, reaching over 100 percent for couples with pre-retirement income of 7,000 dollars. However, all families with earnings above the level of average industrial wages and salaries before retirement would find relatively high reductions in post-retirement income if there were total reliance on public programs. In the long run, the mature CPP and QPP in conjunction with OAS should maintain the standard of living for those with low income but not for those with higher incomes. This leads many to say that the pension plan failure is largely an "income continuity problem", which is to say the problem of maintaining a relatively constant income into and throughout retirement, and that this is primarily a middle-class problem.

Of course, the majority of those now aged 65 and over did not retire in just the last couple of years, but rather during a time when the CPP/QPP was not yet generating significant benefits; hence, a low-income problem remains.

In fact, the vast majority of middle-aged Canadians are middle class and are not poor. In 1975, fully 61 percent of elderly, unattached individuals and 22 percent of elderly couples, nearly half of all pensioners, were below the Statistics Canada Revised Income Cut-Off.[1] Most of those in poverty are unattached individuals of whom 75 percent are women. This ill treatment of women by the retirement income system has been well publicized, and the relatively greater increase in GIS benefits to single individuals, as opposed to couples, that occurred on January 1, 1979, was designed to relieve this situation to some degree.

With this initiative, and the improvement in the CPP/QPP benefits as the system matures, the future looks rosier than the past for the public pension plans. However, let us turn to the problem-areas frequently attributed to employer-sponsored pension plans.

Table 4 shows that the employer-sponsored pensions did not account for a high percentage of retirement income: only about 13 percent in contrast to over 50 percent for public programs. Thus, it is not unreasonable to conclude that the source of the income problem of pensioners largely has its roots in the private pension plans.

Although the employer-sponsored pension plan system has been slowly expanding over the last two decades, the participation of workers in these pension plans has increased from 31 percent in 1960 to 41 percent in 1976, critics of the system claim that the rate of growth of coverage is not proceeding fast enough, that coverage increases without improvements in portability and vesting provisions will not suffice, and that the private system either will not or cannot deal with inflation, so that the purchasing power of the aged continually decreases.

TABLE 4:

SOURCES OF INCOME OF THE AGED IN 1975

	Persons Not in a Family Aged 66 or Over		Couples, Both Aged 66 or Over
	Men	Women	
	%	%	%
OAS/GIS	44	54	45
CPP/QPP	4	3	4
Investment Income	20	22	22
Pension Income from Employer Plans	14	10	13
Earnings	13	6	12
Other Income	5	5	4
Total	100	100	100

SOURCE: Special Tabulations from Statistics Canada, Census Family micro data tape for the Survey of Consumer Finances, 1976.

Cross-section evaluations of coverage can be misleading. The number of those in pension plans has increased. However, theoretically, it is possible to have the entire working population in pension plans at any point in time but to have no one qualify for a pension. The reason for this is, of course, the obstacles to pension portability and vesting. Current legislation calls for vesting and locking-in of pensions only after 10 years of employment and providing that the employee is 45 or over.

Society is developing in a manner such that job mobility seems to be increasing, but job mobility may be still less than optimal because vesting and portability arrangements retard potential movers.

Besides the vesting issue, the basic structure of pension plans has deficiencies. Most employees are in defined-benefit plans, with the benefit being a function of the last few years of service. Plans of this kind which, at present, tend to favour those who remain with one particular employer, have often been referred to as part of the "gold watch" syndrome: longer service leads to better benefits. However, in view of the number of surprised elderly workers who end up with small pensions as a result of job moves, a more appropriate phrase might be the "gold watch illusion".

Employees in their mid-working years tend to have limited time-horizons, and pension plans boasting 60 to 70 percent of the last six years' salary tend to encourage short-sightedness. Even in the Public Service Superannuation Plan, where long service is more typical than in the private sector and pension benefits are indexed, there are many difficulties. Even though the plan promises up to 70 percent of the last six years' salary, the average annual pension being paid is in the neighbourhood of 5 to 6 thousand dollars. Thus, the "gold watch illusion" suggests that major revisions to the employer-sponsored pension plans are required.

These shortcomings cause particular difficulties for women. Women tend to work in occupations with high job turn-over and to work for non-unionized, frequently small, employers: thus, women are less often in pension plans and the current portability and vesting restrictions prevent most from building up significant pension entitlement to qualify for benefits.

Many solutions have been suggested, some of which require turning the system on its head. Some examples include forcing the majority of pension plans to become savings accounts that can be moved from one job to another, expanding the breadth and depth of coverage by the CPP, and placing greater reliance on incentives for personal savings (as under RRSPs). Solutions are available and, through social debate, change will occur. But, in view of the fact that changes to the pension system require up to 40 years to have their full impact on retirement income (because only young workers are able to *fully* benefit from a change in a system in which all future liabilities must be accounted for immediately), any delay would worsen the situation for most current employees.

Perhaps most controversial is the issue of the indexing of pension benefits. Although the basic government programs automatically index pensions in pay, very few employers outside of the public sector provide pension benefits which maintain their real value. In general terms, inflation is a problem because it transfers resources from some parties to others. In this context, pensioners are in the unique position that, unlike ordinary owners of capital, they cannot protect themselves by trading their pension entitlements to ensure a reasonable return on their investment. The problem of pension benefit indexing is thus a question of basic equity—pensioners are discriminated against by the current system of pension rules and regulations and the result is frequently a low retirement income. It could be argued that, at the very least, pension regulations should ensure that pensioners are given a fair return for their contributions; that is, pensions should be indexed at least on the basis of appropriate interest rates. We see little reason why pensioners, one of the most vulnerable groups in society, should be artificially put into the situation where their incomes and assets are depleted through the ravages of inflation.

If it is resolved that pension plans should provide benefits indexed to the cost of living, then it may be necessary to develop new financial instruments to reduce the risk to current contributors. One suggestion has been to create indexed bonds guaranteeing a real rate of return—either government or a semi-private institution insured by government—could be the issuer of these bonds. Another suggestion has been the creation of a "stabilization mechanism" to allow pension funds to pool their risk of inflation by paying into a fund when inflation is less than expected and withdrawing, when inflation is greater (see Pesando and Rea, 1977, for a discussion of various mechanisms).

TABLE 5:
PROJECTED EXPENDITURES ON CURRENT PROGRAMS: IMPLICATIONS OF THE CHANGING AGE STRUCTURE (1976 $)

	OAS[1]	GIS[1]	CPP/QPP	CAP	WVA	General Allied Hospital	Other Hospital	Medical	Total	GNP	Total/GNP
1976	3,268	1,016	584	670	637	1,869	422	306	8,722	190,027	4.6%[2]
1981	3,768	1,006	1,769	853	738	2,379	537	389	11,434	231,554	4.9
1986	4,266	978	2,665	1,066	757	2,974	671	487	13,863	275,501	5.0
1991	4,862	957	3,831	1,340	664	3,742	844	613	16,853	318,410	5.3
1996	5,299	992	5,020	1,614	506	4,503	1,016	739	19,687	366,467	5.4
2001	5,590	996	6,783	1,880	340	5,244	1,183	863	22,373	423,086	5.3
2011	6,405	1,031	8,721	2,626	77	7,324	1,652	1,203	29,034	548,176	5.3
2021	8,310	1,209	12,946	4,153	10	11,584	2,613	1,895	42,721	657,192	6.5
2031	10,185	1,341	17,508	6,204	—	17,306	3,904	2,844	59,277	765,044	7.7

NOTE:
[1] It must be emphasized that it is assumed that OAS/GIS payments are not escalated in line with average wages and salaries but only with the CPI. Furthermore no cost reduction in health care is assumed although cheaper methods of chronic care are possible.
[2] The total GNP allocated to the aged is 7.2% including earned income and investment.
SOURCE: Powell and Martin (1978).

Without resolution of these kinds of issues, rational savings plans by individuals are severely impeded.

The National Perspective

As noted in the introduction, the problem from a larger perspective is concerned first with the development and planning of economic institutions that allocate resources to the aged and, second, with ensuring that these institutions emerge in society in a fair and equitable manner. This involves decisions about the proportion of the GNP which is required for tax-financed goods and services for elderly Canadians.

Table 5 shows a projection of the cost implications of the current public pension and health programs up to the year 2031 and shows a significant, but not revolutionary, increase (see also Denton and Spencer, 1977): by the year 2011 the relative allocation of GNP to the elderly will have increased by less than 1 percent and the increase in the following two decades, up to the year 2031, is only about 2½ percent.

Considering that, during those years, the relative expenditures on the young will be decreasing, this increase can hardly be thought alarming. However, if the retirement income system is improved in order to clear up the problems as seen from the individual perspective, then the proportion of GNP going to older people will increase a good deal further. Provided that individuals save more as a result, and provided that such saving is translated into measured investment, the total amount of resources in society will be greater than otherwise would be the case, so that it is "easier" to allocate resources to the aged. In addition, the aged themselves will have direct claims to the resources and will not have to rely on government transfer programs.

Another important contribution to economic growth is a highly productive and growing workforce. Because the working-age group 18-64 will begin to grow less rapidly after 1986 and, in fact, after 2011 will start to decline just at the time that the baby boom begins to retire, another issue from the global perspective is the question of retirement age. Over the last twenty years, the labour participation rate of males over the age of 55 has declined from 58 percent to 47 percent. The decline in participation of males aged 65 and over is positively dramatic, falling from 48 percent to 16 percent (see various Statistics Canada publications on the labour force such as Statistics Canada, 1977a). Thus, it appears necessary to consider ways for increasing retirement flexibility without encouraging early retirement. This becomes particularly important in light of increasing opportunities for retirement that could be created by an improved pension system (see Policy Research and Long Range Planning, 1977, for data relevant to this point). The dramatic fall in labour participation which we have already seen coincides with the continued expansion of public and private pensions, including the lowering of the age of eligibility for public benefits and the rapid increase in provision for both reduced and unreduced early retirement benefits in the employer-sponsored pension plans. A continued decline in participation would add to the incremental cost of improving the retirement income system and so would make it more difficult to introduce those changes which would benefit those most in need. Perhaps the ultimate issue is how work can be made attractive enough so that more people will prefer to not retire.

Conclusion

The main message of this paper is that the most pressing of the economic implications of an aging society is the need to find ways to improve the effectiveness of the retirement income system. These improvements are required regardless of the forecasted demographic shifts, but the eventual retirement of the "baby boom" generation increases the importance of the issue, particularly when one also considers the declining trend in labour force participation. Finally, if the retirement income system is improved by increased savings during working years, and such saving is translated into investment, and greater participation in the labour force of those over 55 is achieved, the probabilities are such that the necessary "slice of the GNP pie" will be there in the future because of increased economic growth.

Notes

1. Someone is deemed to be in poverty if they spend more than 70 percent of their income on necessities. Statistics Canada calculates these poverty lines, which depend upon family size and the region. Data are from Statistics Canada, 1977a.

20

DIFFERENTIATION OF UNMET NEEDS USING ANALYSIS BY AGE/SEX COHORTS*

Betty Havens
Department of Health and
Community Services
Province of Manitoba

Aging in Manitoba, a field survey of the unmet needs of almost 5,000 elderly Manitobans, was based on an area-probability random sample design. This sample was drawn from the heterogeneous population of some 98,000 Manitobans age 65 and over. While the primary analyses were based on geographically defined aggregates, secondary analyses were based on ethnically defined aggregates and on age/sex cohorts. The latter analyses were essential in order to assure those using the results of the study that the geographic aggregates were, in fact, the most appropriate units of analysis relative to the needs of Manitobans age 65 and over.

This study measured the level of need in nine areas: psycho-social; shelter; household maintenance, food, and clothing; ethno-cultural; physical health functioning; mental health functioning; economic; accessibility of resources and availability of resources. The study assessed need in nine areas, each with a scale measuring from little need (independent) to high need (dependent). Methods were chosen to yield a configuration of both the needs and resources of the elderly in a given area as well as to show the percentage of surveyed elderly having need at each level. With the sampling techniques used, these percentages could then be generalized to the total elderly population and to projected population figures for future planning. The need areas and levels of need were identified initially in consultation with elderly and professional persons and subsequently refined following correlational analysis of results from a pilot study undertaken prior to the full survey. A complete description of the larger study may be found in *Aging in Manitoba*, Volume I (Manitoba, 1973).

In this chapter, the findings of the study in the nine need areas are presented by age and sex, for the province as a whole. Need area variations

*This essay is part of the larger, ten-volume study, *Aging in Manitoba*, financed by the Manitoba provincial government with some assistance from the federal government. Cooperation with Enid Thompson, Director, Office of Continuing Care and assistance from Harbins Rehail, MSW student, University of Manitoba, is acknowledged.

are discussed for the province as a whole, as derived from need profiles, while those for the regions are derived from graphs, by need area. The following should be noted:

1. The needs reflect the needs of all the elderly. Whereas it is often the well, active elderly and/or the ill, needy elderly, who are visible, the sampling method used in this study also includes all the elderly who are between these extremes. For example, the findings on economic need do reflect the needs of all elderly, from those who are in extreme poverty through to, and including, those who are extremely affluent.

2. The needs profiled or graphed for the elderly represent unmet need. These are the needs perceived by the elderly persons themselves. They do not represent judgments of absolute need based on external standards nor are they based on professional/clinical judgment.

In addition, the following data on the age-sex distribution of the Manitoba population age 65 and over in 1971 and of the study sample in 1971 provide a background against which to view the similarities and differences in need by age and sex categories. The 1971 Statistics Canada Report shows the age-sex distribution as follows:

| | Statistics Canada 1971 Elderly Manitobans | | | | Study Sample 1971 Elderly | | | |
| | Males | | Females | | Males | | Females | |
Age	No.	%	No.	%	No.	%	No.	%
65 – 69	15,805	16.5	16,570	17.3	655	13.6	642	13.4
70 – 74	11,155	11.7	12,800	13.4	576	12.0	572	11.9
75 – 79	8,330	8.7	10,120	10.6	459	9.6	508	10.6
80 – 84	5,475	5.7	6,685	7.0	303	6.3	432	9.0
85 – 89	2,745	2.9	3,635	3.8	192	4.0	271	5.6
90 – 94	740	.8	1,080	1.1	62	1.3	82	1.7
95 and over	150	.2	268	.3	16	.3	35	.7
Total	44,400	46.5	51,158	53.5	2,663	47.1	2,542	52.9

While the representation of the age/sex cohorts in the study sample is close to that in the population as a whole for the age cohorts 70 to 79, the study sample under-represents both males and females in the age cohort 65 to 69 and over-represents both sexes in the age cohorts 80 to 89. In the total study sample there were slightly more males and slightly fewer females than occurred in the total population.

Further detail relative to the age/sex distribution of the study sample which reflects the variations and similarities across the regions of the province is available from the author, upon request.

Background

As indicated earlier, it was necessary to perform certain analyses which were not the primary objective of the applied research study in order to assure those using the results that geographic aggregates were in fact the most appropriate units of analysis relative to the needs of elderly Manitobans. Consequently, both age/sex cohort analyses (as reported here and in Manitoba, 1975) and ethnic analyses (Havens and Thompson, 1975) were undertaken. This would allow those using the study data to comment that while certain unmet needs increased or decreased generally, throughout the province, with age or varied by sex, that in the particular geographic area (since age and sex varied much as it did in the province as a whole) the unmet needs which varied from other areas or from the province as a whole were not a function of the age or sex distribution. It also tended to guard against such statements as "the older they are, the poorer they are", or "the older they are, the sicker they are". Such statements tend to inhibit service or program planning as if in the face of the inevitable.

However, quite apart from these applied requirements for age/sex cohort analyses, it is also important to treat all data relative to the elderly as potentially useful in the developing body of knowledge on age stratification. Matilda White Riley's book (1972) points out that cohorts vary both chronologically and historically in what they bring to any given cross-sectional analysis, while Clark (1967) points out definitional variability. In this respect it is useful to recall that while the youngest respondents in the 1971 Manitoba Survey were only 12 at the end of the First World War and 33 at the beginning of the Second World War, the oldest respondents were 40 at the turn of the century, 58 at the end of the First World War and 79 at the beginning of the Second World War, having turned 65 in 1925 long before anyone seriously considered pensions for those over 65. Therefore, it is of limited utility to consider those over 65 as "the" elderly, as if they were "the same" i.e., a homogeneous social category or group. In this study those over 65 spanned 46 years, considerably more than the traditional 37.5-year "generation" of demographic analyses.

Relatively early in the studies of aging, researchers began to refer to the "young" elderly and the "old" elderly. The age at which this distinction was made has varied somewhat from study to study and to some extent from one dependent variable to another (see Havighurst, 1968; Martin, 1973; Brody, 1974; Friedman, 1974; Newcomer, 1974; Wilkinson, 1974; Zander, 1974; and Neugarten, 1975). In most instances this concept is used to distinguish the elderly population under 75 years of age from those over age 75. A few studies have distinguished the elderly as being the "young" elderly, the "middle" elderly, and the "old" elderly (see Randall, 1966; Nash, 1970; Schreiber, 1972; and Powers, 1972). To date, no observable consistency has developed in the literature as to the usual age designations for these three sub-categories. Finally, if sex variations exist in the data with either of these age sub-category approaches, these differences have been inadequately documented in the literature. These points will be discussed further relative to this study in the conclusions.

Needs By Age and Sex—Province of Manitoba

The profiles of unmet need for the *female* elderly respondents living in the province were constructed by five-year age cohorts from age 65 to 95 and over. (The complete set of tables is too large to include here, but is available from the author on request, and is included in *Aging in Manitoba,* Volume IX A [Manitoba, 1973]).

These data show that the female elderly respondents in each age cohort have unmet need in each need area and that the mean need, for each age cohort, ranges from scale value 1 to well above scale value 1 across the need areas. In each age cohort, the need for resources to be more *accessible* is the highest mean unmet need, while the need for resources to be more *available* is the lowest mean unmet need. It is crucial, then, to distinguish availability (the existence of a service) from accessibility (the ability to use a service). The range of need, from minimum to maximum, is widest in the economic-need area for the age cohort from 65 to 69, in the shelter-need area for the age cohort 70 to 74, and in the ethno-cultural-need area for the age cohorts from age 75 to 95 and over. This means that the greatest spread in need is in these areas for these age cohorts. With some need-area exceptions, the range of need tends to narrow with the older age cohorts; that is, with the minimums rising on the scale and the maximums lowering on the scale.

In each age cohort, most female elderly respondents have unmet need in each need area at level 1 or level 2. Only a small percentage have unmet need below level 1 or above level 2. In each age cohort, the highest percentages of elderly females have unmet need at level 1 in each need area except in accessibility of resources need area where the highest percentage have need at level 2, and except in the household maintenance, food, and clothing need area where the highest percentage of those age 90 and over have unmet need at level 2.

Further study of those data reveal the following characteristics concerning the ranking of need areas across the age cohorts: *Psycho-social*—This need area ranks as the second or third lowest need area in each age group. *Shelter*—This need area ranks as the second highest need area for females age 65 to 79, as third highest need area for females 80 to 84, and as the fourth or fifth highest need area for females age 85 and over. *Household Maintenance, Food, and Clothing*—This need area ranks as the second lowest need area from age 65 to age 74, as the fourth lowest need area from age 74 to age 84, as the third highest need area from age 85 to age 95 and over. *Ethno-cultural*—This need area ranks fourth lowest for the age cohorts 65 to 69 and 85 to 95 and over and ranks fourth highest from age 70 to 84. *Physical Health Functioning*—Of the nine need areas, this need area ranks fourth or fifth for all age groups. *Mental Health Functioning*—This need area ranks third for age 65 to 75, and second for age 75 to 95 and over. *Economic*—This need area ranks fourth for ages 65 to 69, sixth for ages 70 to

74, seventh for ages 75 to 79, and eighth for ages 80 to 95 and over.

In summary, as age progresses, the need for resources to be more *accessible* remains the highest need and the need for resources to be more *available* remains the lowest. Between these extremes, as age progresses, the ranking of psycho-social need remains about the same as the second or third lowest need; the ranking of shelter need tends to lower at age 85 while remaining among the higher or middle needs; the ranking of household maintenance, food, and clothing need tends to rise from a low need below age 74 to a high need at age 85 and over; the ranking of ethno-cultural need tends to rise from a low middle need before age 70, to a high middle need from age 70 to 84, and then lower to low middle need from age 85 to 95 and over; the ranking of physical health functioning need tends to remain at the middle, even though it rises some with advancing age; the ranking of mental health functioning need tends to rise from a high middle need at age 74, to a high need from age 75 to 95 and over; the ranking of economic need tends to lower from a middle need to age 69, to a low need from age 75 to 95 and over.

The profiles of unmet need for all the *male* elderly respondents living in the province also were constructed by five-year age cohorts from age 65 to age 95 and over.

These data show that the male elderly respondents in each age cohort have unmet need in each need area and that the mean of this unmet need, for each age cohort, ranges from scale value 1 to approaching scale value 2 across the need areas. In each age cohort, the need for resources to be more accessible is the highest mean unmet need, while the need for resources to be more available is the lowest mean unmet need. The range of need, from minimum to maximum, is widest in the economic need area for the age cohorts 65 to 79 and 85 to 95 and over, and in the physical health need area for the age cohort 80 to 84. The characteristics of a general narrowing in the range of need as age progresses, found to exist for the female elderly respondents, does not apply to the male elderly respondents.

From the percentages of mean responses, it can be seen that, in each age cohort, almost all unmet need for elderly males in the province exists at levels 1 or 2. Only small percentages have unmet need below level 1 or above level 2, although 6.3 percent of the elderly males age 95 and over experience unmet economic need at or above level 3. In each age group, the highest percentages of elderly males have unmet need at level 1 in each need area except in the accessibility of resources need areas where the highest percentages have need at level 2 and except for the age-group 95 and over where the highest percentages also have unmet shelter and unmet household maintenance, food, and clothing needs at level 2.

Further investigation of the data reveals the following characteristics concerning the ranking of need areas across the age cohorts: *Psychosocial* — This need area ranks second lowest (eighth) for males age 65 to 84, seventh for males age 85 to 94, and eighth for males age 95 and over. *Shelter* — This need area ranks second highest for males age 65 to 89 and from 95 and over whereas it is fourth highest for males age 90 to 94. *Household Maintenance, Food, and Clothing* — This need area ranks seventh for those age 65 to 79, sixth for those age 80 to 84, fourth for those age 95 and over. *Ethno-cultural* — This need area ranks sixth for those age 65 to 79 and from 89 to 95 and over, and ranks fifth for those age 80 to 84. *Physical Health Functioning* — Whereas this need area ranks fifth for those age 65 to 79 and age 85 to 94, it ranks fourth for those age 80 to 84 and for those age 95 and over. *Mental Health Functioning* — This need area ranks fourth for those age 65 to 79, third for those age 80 to 89 and for those age 95 and over, and second for those age 90 to 94. *Economic* — This need area ranks third at age 65 to 79, seventh at age 80 to 84, eighth at age 85 to 94, and again seventh at age 95 and over.

In summary, as age progresses, the need for resources to be more *accessible* remains the highest need and the need for resources to be *available* remains the lowest need. Between these two extremes, and as age progresses, psycho-social need remains a low need from age 65 to age 95 and over; shelter remains the second or fourth highest need through all age-groups; household maintenance, food, and clothing needs move from a low need from age 65 to 84 to a high or moderately high need after age 85; the ranking of ethno-cultural need remains a moderately low need across the age-groups; physical health functioning ranks as a high-middle need (fourth or fifth) through all age-groups; mental health functioning need progresses from a moderately high need at age 65 to 74, to a second or third highest need at age 75 to 79, to low need at age 80 and over.

In reference to similarities or differences in the ranking of need across the age cohorts for males and females, these are as follows: *Psycho-social* unmet need is generally a low unmet need in respect to other unmet needs for males and females. *Shelter* unmet needs are high or moderately high for elderly males and females of all age-cohorts and are higher for the men than for the women. *Household Maintenance, Food, and Clothing* unmet needs increase with age for both males and females with the greatest increase, in respect to other unmet needs, after age 85. *Ethno-cultural* unmet needs are moderate across the age cohorts for both elderly males and females. *Physical Health Functioning* unmet needs remain moderate, in respect to other unmet needs, for both elderly males and females for all age cohorts. *Mental Health Functioning* unmet needs increase with age, in respect to other unmet needs, for both males and females but are generally higher for females. *Economic* unmet needs generally decrease with age in comparison to other unmet needs, especially for females after age 69 and males after age 79.

Correlation analyses of each scale of need with every other scale of need were also carried out for each age cohort. For both the female and male elderly, it was found that a high positive correlation exists between physical health functioning need and mental health functioning need in each age cohort. The lowest correlation between these two scales was 0.71 in the age-cohort 85 to 89.

The correlations across all other scales of need, both for the male and female elderly respondents, were found to be so low, or, if high, so scattered as to indicate that the need areas are independent of each other except where some special features occur in scattered but specific age cohorts.

Conclusions

From the foregoing, it is possible to add to the empirical evidence for age/sex cohort descriptions of an elderly population. If one wishes to designate only two sub-categories, i.e., the "young" elderly *versus* the "old" elderly, the data reported above would indicate that the appropriate age designation for females is under and over age 85 while the appropriate age designation for males is under and over age 80. In other words, these data raise the serious question of whether or not the more typical age distinction of those under and over age 75 or even age 80 remains the most adequate for studies of aging, especially those relative to the needs of the elderly. This study further raises the other serious question of whether such age distinctions are appropriate when not specifically and simultaneously related to sex distinctions. That is, in the data reported here, no single dichotomizing age designation is appropriate to both male and female respondents.

If, on the other hand, one chooses to designate the elderly as divided into three sub-categories; i.e., the "young" elderly, the "middle" elderly, and the "old" elderly, the evidence from the data reported here indicates that the sex distinction disappears as a useful discriminatory tool. That is, both the male and female respondents may be sub-categorized as "young" from age 65 to 79, and "middle" from age 80 to age 94, and as "old" from age 95.

These findings suggest that the more appropriate sub-categorization of the elderly population may be three categories rather than the dichotomy of "young" *versus* "old" elderly. While these data indicate that in the use of three age sub-categories the sex distinction disappears, these same data, when age dichotomized, serve to emphasize the sex distinction. This contrast calls attention to and warns the researcher that age-category analysis should be expanded to age/sex category analysis in order to be adequate. These data further underline the necessity for serious consideration about the most appropriate ages for delineating age sub-categories. Such sub-categories should be kept under review as the ages may be expected to change quite dramatically over time based on historical perspective. Finally, these conclusions emphasize the importance, from both the standpoint of research and theory construction, of considering age as both an independent and dependent variable (see Bengtson, 1973; Riley, 1972).

21

THE PHYSICAL, EMOTIONAL, AND SOCIAL CONDITION OF AN AGED POPULATION IN QUEBEC*

Charles Tilquin, Claude Sicotte, Thérèse Paquin, Francine Tousignant, Gisèle Gagnon, and Pierre Lambert

In the Spring of 1978 the EROS research team (Equipe de Recherche Opérationnelle en Santé) from the University of Montreal carried out a survey of the population aged 65 years and over in one of Quebec's social/health regions, Montreal's South Shore. This survey was undertaken within the framework of a research project aimed at creating instruments for the evaluation of old people's needs (Tilquin, 1976; Tilquin, *et al.*, 1977a; 1978). Given this objective, the individuals interviewed had to represent all types of needs (physical, psychological, and social) prevalent among a population of old people. This chapter reports some preliminary analyses of data collected from over 1,000 respondents from within and without the institutional social service network, from both rural and urban areas, who were interviewed in either French or English as appropriate.

Methodology

The population of the region was treated as a group of clusters of individuals, each cluster comprising the aged population of a municipality (under Statistics Canada definitions). These clusters were then distributed into thirteen strata according to the degree of urbanization, which is measured by a combination of total population and population density. An additional stratification criterion was whether or not the person was implicated in the long-term care network, and receiving services through that network. To be "within the network" meant to be involved in one of the following programs or institutions: short- and long-term hospital centres, reception centres, home-care centres, and foster family care. Persons not involved were deemed to be "outside the network". Old people outside the network (i.e., living at home and not benefitting from services identified in the long-term care network) and old people who receive service in the network's programs were equally represented in the sampling. We therefore decided to over-represent the population served by the network because we thought that

*This research project was made possible by a grant from Health and Welfare Canada, within the framework of the National Health Research and Development Program, and with the help of the Department of Social Affairs of Quebec. It has been translated from the French by Munirah Amra.

this population was the one showing the greatest variability and the largest number of needs.

Men and women are also equally represented in the sampling, because we wanted to have sufficient data on this population in order to test certain hypotheses; for example, to assess different needs peculiar to male and female populations of the same age group.

Finally, we designed our sampling in order to ensure that different programs in the health and social services network would be proportionally represented in relation to their population. These programs included the short- and long-term hospital centres, reception centres, home-care centres, and foster family care programs already mentioned.

To summarize, we developed an elaborate sampling design, taking each of these stratification principles in sequence, in order to assure the equal representation of populations inside and outside the network, and of the two sexes, the proportional representation of municipality strata and of the network's programs.

As mentioned previously, we wanted to ensure that both sexes were equally represented in the sampling. Our initial concern was also to ensure an equal representation of the population of three age groups defined *a priori* (65-69 years, 70-74 years, and 75 years and over). In practice, this proved to be impossible outside the network because of more frequent refusals to be interviewed from people who were younger, and in the network, where the oldest groups are the most populated. In this way, our sampling clearly over-represents the oldest population. From the viewpoint of our objectives, this unexpected phenomenon is interesting because we feel that *a priori* it is this population that manifests the greatest and most varied needs.

The interview schedules (Tilquin, *et al.*, 1977b, 1977c) included items on the individual's socio-demographic features, physical ability, living habits (nutrition, drinking, smoking, sleep), degree of autonomy in life's daily activities, family and social relationships, social environment, and income. The final section of the form was reserved for the interviewer's remarks on the individual's psychological condition, and was completed immediately after the interview. The average interview at home lasted one hour, and in an institution, forty minutes. The sixteen interviewers, the majority of whom were nurses and social workers, were chosen for their experience in the social/health field.

The interviews and data codification process having just been completed, we are here only in a position to present preliminary results. We will limit ourselves to a parallel between the populations within and outside the network and to a brief analysis of the variable "degree of urbanization" as well as a few considerations on special variables such as medication and income.

TABLE 1:
PERCENTAGE OF THE AGED WITHIN THE SAMPLING NEEDING HELP FOR CERTAIN ACTIVITIES OF DAILY LIVING

| | Outside the Network | | | | | | | Within the Network | | | | | | |
| | Female | | | Male | | | | Female | | | Male | | | |
	65-69	70-74	75 and over	65-69	70-74	75 and over	Total	65-69	70-74	75 and over	65-69	70-74	75 and over	Total
Rising and going to bed	—	—	2.83*	2.94	—	2.70	1.43	24.59	27.03	33.0	22.58	36.23	32.26	29.85
Daily personal hygiene	2.67	—	3.77	4.41	1.03	4.50	2.68	36.07	32.43	44.0	38.71	49.28	44.09	41.18
Walking around inside	4.0	—	2.83	1.47	—	2.70	1.79	27.87	31.08	41.0	27.42	40.58	39.78	35.51
Bath/shower	2.67	3.92	4.72	5.88	2.06	8.11	4.65	59.02	51.35	67.0	53.23	66.67	62.37	60.57
Shopping in summer	20.0	21.57	43.40	10.29	5.15	18.92	20.75	77.05	63.51	76.0	62.90	66.67	69.89	69.72

*The interpretation of each percentage must be understood like this: for example, 2.83 percent of the 75 years old and over females outside the network need help (partial or complete) to rise and to go to bed; 97.17 percent can do it alone.

Physical Aspects of Well-Being

We present, in Table 1, data concerning a series of indices of the ability of old people to carry out various activities associated with day-to-day living. These data correspond to a self-appraisal of their level of physical functioning by people outside the network while, within the network, the data represent the judgement of a care person on the condition of each individual. Of the people interviewed in the network 26.6 percent were not able to reply by themselves, mainly for psychological reasons. We preferred therefore to use data from the care team member's appraisal, which were available for almost all cases, in order to make our comparison on the basis of all the people we met in the two population groups.

The data relative to the activities of daily living allow a specific definition of the lack of autonomy in the two population groups. Lack of autonomy is defined for an old person as the fact of having to rely on the partial or total help of another person. For the purposes of the present analysis we have combined the categories "partial help" and "complete help".

Three observations must be made with respect to these data. First, the percentage of the people who can manage on their own is very high for institutional settings. A more detailed analysis is needed to show the difference between the various types of programs covered by the sampling; but 81.8 percent of the sample population "within the network" come from programs that should have serious cases, i.e. short- or long-term hospital centres or reception centres. It must also be considered that a certain section of the beneficiary population suffers from problems that are mainly psychological but the question remains whether the place where these aged are accommodated corresponds adequately to their condition.

The second remark is a reminder of the reality underlying these figures. One has to remember that our sampling "outside the network" is approximately representative of 92 percent of the aged population while our sampling "within the network" is only representative of the remaining 8 percent who are institutionalized (these figures are approximations in the absence of recent figures). Hence the importance of a phenomenon that appears very weak in the sampling "outside the network" in relation to its importance within the network may be the reverse when it is referred to the actual population.

Finally, these data for daily activities indicate the level of disability for each of the activities independently from each other. This type of approach, however, gives a partial view, and a distorted one, because in many individuals disabilities accumulate. To overcome this problem, we constructed a global indicator based on the number of disabilities accumulated by each individual in the sample. These data are given in Table 2. It is apparent not only that persons within the network accumulate many more disabilities, but also that age differences beyond age 65 are very great. This is a phenomenon noted by Gutman and by Havens in other chapters in this volume.

TABLE 2:

INDICATOR OF THE LEVEL OF PHYSICAL DISABILITIES WITHIN THE SAMPLE POPULATION

	Outside the Network				Within the Network			
	65-69	70-74	75 and over	Total	65-69	70-74	75 and over	Total
No disability*	83.91	85.43	67.29	78.0	25.20	30.07	19.70	24.40
1 disability	11.19	12.06	27.19	17.71	17.07	13.99	13.99	14.81
2 disabilities	1.40	2.51	1.38	1.79	19.51	9.79	15.54	14.81
3 disabilities	1.40	–	1.38	0.89	13.00	12.59	17.10	14.60
4 disabilities	1.40	–	0.92	0.72	6.50	7.69	9.84	8.28
5 disabilities	0.70	–	1.84	0.89	18.70	25.87	23.83	23.10
Total	100%	100%	100%	100%	100%	100%	100%	100%

*A disability or handicap is defined as the need for partial or total help in carrying out an activity of daily life. The indicator is based on the following five activities: rising and going to bed; daily personal hygiene; walking around inside; bath/shower and shopping in summer.

Psychological Aspects of Well-Being

Observations of the psychological health of respondents were made by interviewers immediately following the interviews and were collected from the care staff in the institution for that part of the "within the network" sample not seen by the interviewers for psychological reasons. The judgmental nature of these observations should be borne in mind, although it should also be remembered that interviewers were selected on the basis of their experience in the health-care field. Persons within the network were adjudged to be much less well-oriented than those outside it. Only 33 percent of persons within the network were adjudged well-oriented with intact memory, as contrasted to over three-quarters of those outside the network (the figures varied predictably with age, but sex differences were not great). While only about 1 percent of those outside the network were adjudged "very confused", 17 percent of females and 14 percent of males within the network were adjudged "very confused".

In Table 3, we indicate the percentages of individuals who were adjudged on scales of psychological functioning to have problems related to selected psychological variables. As with the data on physical disabilities given in Table 1, these data refer to judgments that the individual is partially or totally deficient on the given psychological scale.

Finally, with respect to psychological functioning, a global index was constructed from the information above, to describe the accumulation of psychological problems in a manner analogous to the method portrayed in Table 2. These data are given in Table 4. Although psychological problems,

TABLE 3:
PERCENTAGE OF OLD PEOPLE HAVING PROBLEMS WITH RESPECT TO THE FOUR OBSERVED DIMENSIONS: CONCENTRATION; JUDGMENT, UNDERSTANDING AND CONTACT WITH REALITY

| | Outside the Network | | | | | | | Within the Network | | | | | | |
| | Female | | | Male | | | | Female | | | Male | | | |
	65-69	70-74	75 and over	65-69	70-74	75 and over	Total	65-69	70-74	75 and over	65-69	70-74	75 and over	Total
Concentration	5.33*	1.96	10.38	–	2.06	5.40	4.47	45.90	36.49	49.0	35.48	42.03	48.39	43.57
Judgment	4.0	–	5.66	–	–	3.60	2.33	39.34	35.14	40.0	38.70	40.58	38.71	38.78
Understanding	5.33	0.98	6.60	1.47	1.03	7.20	3.94	36.07	31.08	44.0	40.32	36.23	38.71	38.13
Contact with reality	4.0	–	6.60	–	1.03	3.60	2.68	45.90	33.78	50.0	40.32	30.43	44.09	42.05

*The interpretation of each percentage must be understood like this: for example, 5.33 percent of the 65-69 years old females outside the network have been adjudged having problem with concentration; in contrast, 94.67 percent have no problem.

TABLE 4:

INDICATOR OF THE PSYCHOLOGICAL STATE OF THE SAMPLE POPULATION

	Outside the Network				Within the Network			
	65-69	70-74	75 and over	Total	65-69	70-74	75 and over	Total
No problem*	95.80	96.98	90.32	94.10	46.72	53.47	41.45	46.62
1 problem	0.70	2.01	2.77	1.97	10.66	6.94	10.88	9.59
2 problems	1.40	1.01	0.92	1.07	3.28	5.56	4.66	4.58
3 problems	–	–	0.92	0.36	4.10	2.78	5.18	4.14
4 problems	–	–	2.77	1.07	9.02	5.56	9.85	8.28
5 problems	2.10	–	2.30	1.43	26.23	25.69	27.98	26.80
Total	100%	100%	100%	100%	100%	100%	100%	100%

*A problem is defined as a result that is "partially deficient" or "totally deficient" for each of the chosen dimensions. There are five chosen dimensions: Confusion, Concentration, Judgment, Understanding, and Contact with Reality.

at least as indicated by our rather crude measures, do not accumulate to the same extent as the physical problems described earlier, the same pattern does exist when considering age and network distinctions. Older persons, and those within the institutional network, are characterized by a more pronounced accumulation of psychological problems.

Social Aspects of Well-Being

In this report we will consider only some quite explicit measures of social activity which may be assumed to relate to well-being. Because of the necessity of relying on the reports of care-givers for the sample within the institutional network, we restricted a consideration of familial contacts to the immediate family. For those living freely in the community, we found that 44 percent of women and 75 percent of men saw a spouse every day. This difference reflects the availability of spouses and sex differences in widowhood (see chapters by Abu-Laban and by Matthews in this volume). In contrast, only 4.6 percent of women and 11.5 percent of men in the network saw a spouse daily; the great majority (82.9 percent of the women and 69.7 percent of the men) of course having no spouse to see.

Whether or not a child was seen also depended to a great extent on availability. Less than 9 percent of men and women in the community appeared to be lacking a child, and another 9 to 11 percent had children but never saw them. However, about 70 percent saw a child as often as two or three times per week. By contrast, those within the network were much less likely to have a child, or to see one. For 47 percent of women and 41 percent of men, contact with a child was considered a topic either "not applicable" (women: 39.7 percent; men: 35.0 percent) or one where "no information" was available (women: 7.1 percent; men: 6.2 percent). Within the network, 28 percent of women and 22 percent of men see a child as often as two or three times per week, indicating much less than half the contact with a child than is found for the community sample outside the network.

In summary, our data concerning family-status characteristics of persons living in the community and those living within the institutional network are consistent with the findings reported and reviewed elsewhere in this volume (Flett, *et al.*; Gutman and studies cited therein) showing that the ability to remain in the community is greatly enhanced when family members are available. Absence of spouse or children is a high-risk factor leading to intensive contact with the institutional network. This can be readily seen by looking at aggregate figures for the population outside the network: 36.1 percent of these people are never alone in terms of the *physical* presence of another person; 37.4 percent are alone for short periods only. In this way, a total percentage of 73.5 percent can rely on a certain feeling of security and a minimum of social contacts. The number of individuals who are alone for prolonged periods, whether during the day, evening, or night, is 9.1 percent; of these 8.9 percent are alone during the day. Finally 13.6 percent of individuals seen are always totally alone.

Another indicator of social well-being is financial status. We failed to obtain information on the financial situation of 36.2 percent of cases interviewed from the free-living sample outside the network because of refusals. The information represents individual and not family income. Thus, for certain individuals family income would include spouse's income, but we do not here present data in that manner. For the sample within the institutional network, only 30 percent of the sample are in charge of managing their own budget. We therefore obtained information for only one-fifth of this sample. Despite these limitations, which might affect the representativeness of the data, the economic differences associated with contact with the health and social service institutional network are suggestive, as is evident in Table 5. Those managing their own financial affairs are located primarily outside the institutional network. While this is not a wealthy sample of individuals, when it is considered that many family incomes would represent combinations of the different income-level categories for those outside the network (who are more likely to be married), it can be presumed as a prelude to further analysis that a combination of family and economic considerations is of great importance as a variable affecting institutionalization.

TABLE 5:

REPORTED INDIVIDUAL INCOME FOR PERSONS WITHIN AND OUTSIDE THE NETWORK (INCOME ON AN ANNUAL BASIS)

	Population: *"Outside the network"* Percent	*"Within the network"* Percent
Less than $3,000.:	27.6	6.4
$3,000 – 4,000.:	20.7	10.5
$4,000 – 5,000.:	5.0	1.5
$5,000 – 8,000.:	6.4	0.6
$8,000 and more:	3.5	0.6
No information:	36.2	80.2

Medical Services

With respect to medical services, for the population outside the network, 88.5 percent of the people interviewed have a family physician, defined as a physician who knows them and on whom they can call; 10.4 percent consider themselves deprived in this respect; 68.3 percent had been to see a physician during the six months prior to the interview. To the question: "Are you being treated by a physician at the moment for one or several specific conditions?", 45.4 percent of the people consider themselves "not under medical treatment for one or several specific conditions" as against 53.7 percent who consider themselves as "being treated for one or several specific conditions".

The network's population replies to the same question in the following way: "not being treated" — 43.8 percent and "treated" — 45.9 percent. The information was not collected for 10.3 percent of people interviewed. To the question of whether a physician visits them regularly at the present time, 87.3 percent replied in the affirmative and 10.3 percent in the negative.

Data were also gathered with respect to medication. For the population outside the network 24.7 percent of those people interviewed do not take medication while 74. 8 percent do. In the network, the proportions become 10.1 percent for those not taking medication against 89.1 percent who are. People within the network are more likely to be taking tranquillizers and sleeping tablets on medical prescription than are people in the community.

The Urban vs. Rural Population Outside the Network

We also carried out a rapid study of the variable, "degree of urbanization". For the purposes of this study, we considered only the population outside the network and regrouped our thirteen municipality strata to form four groups of municipalities. These groups are defined on the basis of both population size and density, and may be thought of as differentiating the South Shore communities into four groups from small, low-density, to large, high-density. The former community type would have fewer than 2,500 individuals and fewer than 8,000 persons per square mile; whereas the latter could have as many as 120,000 people, living at a density of as much as 20,000 per square mile.

When controlling for community type along this rural-urban dimension, several indicators were observed which may be significant from the viewpoint of future resource planning. We earlier observed that the degree of support from another person, such as a family member, was an important risk factor associated with institutionalization. However, on the basis of the type of regroupment chosen for the municipalities, neither marital status nor living situation (whether one lives alone, with spouse, children, etc.) is related to the degree of urbanization. If these variables are suggestive of social support, then such support appears in no way greater in the city than in the country.

Therefore, pressure for institutionalization for reasons of lack of personal social support should be no greater in one milieu than in the other.

As an exploratory measure, we checked to see whether there was a difference between urban and rural settings for problems that might be encountered in five areas of daily living. In four areas, differences were small and insignificant: ability to rise and get out of bed without assistance; to walk around inside; to bath or shower; and to maintain daily personal hygiene without assistance. These activities occur indoors. However, a fifth activity, shopping in summer, did vary considerably by community type. In the most urban community type, 13 percent of the respondents required assistance with shopping during the summer months. In the most rural setting, 26 percent required such assistance (the figures for the remaining two community types were intermediate at near 20 percent). This situation may be explained by the more difficult accessibility to shops experienced by older people living in a rural setting.

Conclusion

The preliminary information presented in this text results from the initial processing of an imposing data bank. These data should be interpreted with a great deal of care in view of their aggregate nature (the distinction is not always made by age groups, for example) and the characteristics of non-proportionality of our sampling. Our premise in presenting these data was mainly to give an initial glimpse or "snapshot" of an aged population. The information in this "snapshot" will be made available in more detail in the near future.

22

HEALTH-CARE COSTS WHEN THE POPULATION CHANGES*

Frank T. Denton and Byron G. Spencer
Department of Economics
McMaster University

This paper is intended as a contribution to a better understanding of the way in which the costs of health care might be expected to vary in response to demographic influences. At a time when governments have come to assume a large portion of the costs of health care, the changing level of such costs is a matter of considerable interest from the point of view of public planning and policy. Population change may be one of the major elements in the determination of this level. Changes in the size and age composition of the population affect not only the demand for health services but also the productive capacity of the economy and hence the relative burden of health-care costs.

Other elements also enter into the health-care bill, of course. In particular, policy decisions to change the quality of health-care services which are provided could lead to dramatic consequences even if there were no population changes. In this paper, however, we assume that the quality of health care provided in the course of an individual's life remains constant over time, and we investigate the extent to which demographic change alone might be expected to contribute to cost changes.

In order to take into account both the direct and indirect effects of population change on the burden of health-care costs, it is necessary to consider such change in the context of the complete economic-demographic system. Our approach is to make use of a theoretical but numerically specified model of this system. Although the model is theoretical, we have attempted to make it as realistic as possible by drawing heavily on Canadian data, especially with regard to demographic relationships.[1]

---

*This paper is one of a series reporting results obtained from a continuing project involving the study of economic-demographic relationships. We gratefully acknowledge the support of this project at various stages by McMaster University, the Canada Council, and the Ford and Rockefeller foundations. Some extremely helpful advice and suggestions regarding the present paper were received from Hugh D. Walker, Medical Economist, McMaster University Department of Clinical Epidemiology and Biostatistics. We are grateful also for the comments from the editor and two anonymous referees. Finally, we note with appreciation the valuable research assistance provided by Christine Feaver. Reprinted, with permission, from the *Canadian Journal of Economics*, VIII, no. 1 (February, 1975), 34-48.

We start by describing the derivation of a set of age-sex-specific measures of relative health-care costs per capita. These cost profiles are incorporated in the economic-demographic model. The model is employed in computer simulation experiments, which subject it to a variety of demographic stimuli. These take the form of controlled changes in fertility and migration patterns, some of which are roughly based on Canadian demographic experience and others of which are purely artificial. The consequences are observed in terms of the impact they have on the time paths of certain variables in the system. In particular, we observe the time paths of health-care expenditure per capita and of the ratio of health-care expenditure to gross national product as the size and age structure of the population change.

Health-Care Costs: an age-sex profile

The purpose of this section is to describe briefly the derivation of the age-sex-specific per capita health-care costs used in subsequent analysis. The three major components of health care are hospital services, physicians' services, and drugs. Separate measures of cost per capita were derived for each component. These were then combined into an over-all set of measures of relative costs — the over-all age-sex profile, so to speak.

In the case of hospital services, we have used Canadian data for 1969, this being a recent year for which relevant data were available. Statistics Canada classifies hospitals into three types: general and allied special, mental, and tuberculosis.[2] For each type, total expenditure was allocated among twenty age-sex categories (ten age groups for each sex) on the basis of a selected age-sex-specific series.[3] Number of days of stay in hospital was used in the case of both general and allied special hospitals and mental hospitals. For tuberculosis hospitals, a days-of-stay series was not available, and number of patients at year's end was used instead. The three sets of results were then combined into a single set representing total expenditure on hospital services associated with each of the twenty age-sex groups.[4]

The age-sex distribution of expenditure on physicians' services is based on Ontario data for the year 1971, relating to persons insured under the province's health insurance program. More specifically, the data relate to all persons whose health insurance was handled directly by the provincial government, as distinguished from those whose contracts were handled by private insurance companies acting as designated agents for the province.[5]

In the absence of any direct information, it was assumed that expenditure on drugs is distributed by age and sex in the same way as expenditure on physicians' services. This assumption seems reasonable — at least as a rough approximation, which is all that we require.

For each category of health-care costs, the female age-specific per capita series was calculated net of costs associated with pregnancy. In the case of hospital services, this was accomplished for each age group by deducting from the days-of-stay series the number of days associated with pregnancy and related conditions.[6] In the case of physicians' services (and hence drugs), it was assumed that for each age group the proportion of use associated with pregnancy was the same as in the case of hospital services.

The total cost associated with pregnancy was calculated by summing the differences between the female series with and without pregnancy costs included. This total was then divided by the number of births to obtain a factor representing the proportionate relationship between births and those costs associated with pregnancy.[7] Noting that costs for newborn infants are already represented in the age-specific series, this calculation completes the direct link between fertility levels and all related health-care costs. Such a link is an important one for our purpose.

FIGURE 1:

RELATIVE PER CAPITA COSTS OF HEALTH CARE FOR MALES AND FEMALES, BY AGE

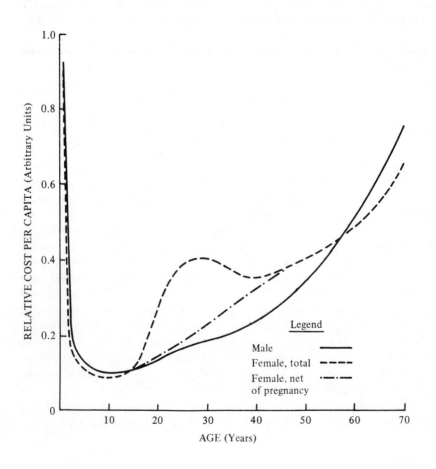

The combination of the series for hospital services, physicians' services, and drugs into one over-all cost series was carried out using weights based on Canadian expenditure data for the three categories in 1969. For convenience, the resulting series was 'standardized' by dividing by total expenditure, so that the series summed to one. The series was then converted into per capita form by dividing the figure for each age-sex group by the group's 1969 midyear population (and the pregnancy-related figure by the total number of births in 1969). Per capita figures for single years of age were derived from the age-group series by graphic interpolation.

The relative per capita health-care coefficients, arrived at in the foregoing way, are plotted in Figure 1. Although there are some differences over particular age intervals, the general patterns are the same for males and females (excluding pregnancy costs): the costs are relatively high for infants, drop sharply during the first few years of life, and then rise, at first gradually and later more sharply. The male coefficients are somewhat lower than the female coefficients, even aside from pregnancy, between the midteens and the late fifties, and somewhat higher thereafter. Among infants, the coefficients are higher for males than for females.

Health-Care Costs in a Complete Model of the Economic-Demographic System

The profile of relative costs of health care is used in conjunction with a complete model of economic and demographic activity. Detailed descriptions of similar models have been provided elsewhere (Denton and Spencer, 1973a), and here we present only a summary.

The model is represented schematically in Figure 2. Those variables that are endogenously determined are represented by rectangles, while parameters or exogenously determined variables in the system are represented by circles. In order to avoid unnecessary complexity, the figure shows only the main features of the model.

In broad outline, the model assumes that population changes influence the economy by altering the level of production but that the population itself is not affected by economic events.[8]

Beginning with the demographic side of the model, female fertility rates are specified exogenously.[9] (All age-related calculations in the model are for single years of age.) The number of births is calculated by applying age-specific fertility rates to the population of women in the childbearing range, which we assume to be from exact age fifteen to exact age fifty. Births are allocated between males and females on the basis of a constant sex ratio.

Death rates are assumed constant for individual age-sex groups and are set equal to those in the official 1960-62 Canadian life tables.

Net immigration is determined by specifying, for each year, the ratio of total immigration to domestic population. The total is then allocated by age

FIGURE 2:
OUTLINE OF THE COMPLETE ECONOMIC-DEMOGRAPHIC MODEL

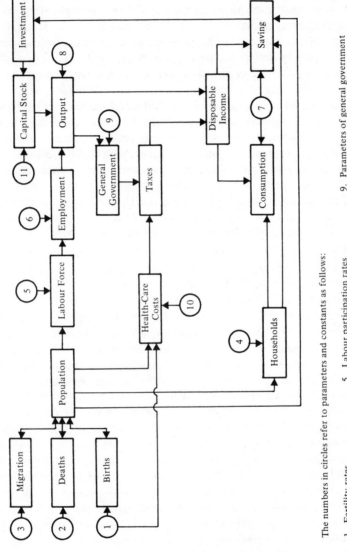

The numbers in circles refer to parameters and constants as follows:

1. Fertility rates
2. Death rates
3. Migration rates
4. Household headship rates

5. Labour participation rates
6. Unemployment rates
7. Parameters of consumption function
8. Parameters of production function

9. Parameters of general government
   expenditure function
10. Parameters of health-care cost function
11. Depreciation rate on capital stock

and sex in accordance with fixed proportions based on the observed average age-sex distribution for immigrants to Canada during the period 1951-66. This distribution reflects the typical concentration in the young adult age groups.

The population at the middle of each year is calculated by applying the death rates to the previous year's population, incorporating births and adding net immigration.[10]

The labour force is calculated by applying age-sex-specific participation rates to the population fourteen years of age and over. These rates are assumed constant. They are set equal to the Canadian rates obtained in 1966.

The model operates always at "full employment," but over-all "full employment" is consistent with unemployment rates which vary by age and sex, in accordance with variations in basic levels of "frictional" unemployment. We use the Canadian unemployment rates of 1966. (The year 1966, it may be noted, was a year of relatively full employment in Canada, with an average unemployment rate of 3.6 per cent.)

The number of households is computed by applying household headship rates to the population, by age and sex. The headship rates, which are held constant, are based on 1961 Canadian census data.

Turning to the economic side of the model, the level of aggregate output is determined by a Cobb-Douglas production function which combines two inputs — capital and labour — and produces a single output. However, the labour input combines workers of different sexes and ages, and hence different productivity characteristics. Thus, the actual number of inputs is quite large. Constant returns to scale are assumed.

The total capital stock is obtained as the sum of depreciated investment in all previous periods. The annual rate of depreciation is assumed constant at 5 per cent.

For present purposes, the government is assumed to make claims of two types on the output of the economy — first, for general government expenditures, and second, to meet the costs of health care. General government expenditures are taken to be a constant fraction of an aggregate income base. To allow for political and other institutional lags, the income base is defined as a weighted average of total output in previous years, the weights declining geometrically with length of time lag.

Aggregate health-care expenditure in the model is established as a fraction of total output in some base period.[11] Having fixed the total level, the absolute levels of per capita expenditures associated with the various age-sex groups and with the total number of births are determined by proportionate adjustment of the relative age-sex-specific health-care co-efficients discussed in the previous section. Any change from the base-period population will then tend to affect the fraction of output which must be directed to meet the costs of health care if the quality of health care is to be maintained. "Quality" is interpreted as the allocation of a given level of real resources per capita to each age-sex-specific group.

Let H stand for total expenditure on health care, h for health-care cost per capita, N for population, p for pregnancy costs per live-born baby, and f for fertility rate (number of live births per woman). Attach subscripts i for sex ($i = 1$ for males, $i = 2$ for females), j for age (j going from age 0 to age 109 in the model), and t for time. The total health-care cost function may then be written as

$$H_t = \sum_{i=1}^{2} \sum_{j=0}^{109} h_{ij} N_{ijt} + p \sum_{j=15}^{49} f_{jt} N_{2jt}$$

The total of taxes collected is set equal to the amount required for general government expenditures plus the amount required for health-care expenditures. Thus, the government's budget is always in balance. For convenience it is assumed that all health-care expenditures are channelled through the government.

Total consumer expenditure is determined with reference to the number of households, the size and age-sex composition of the population (children are given lower consumption weights than adults), and private disposable (after-tax) income. Two components of consumption are distinguished: *committed consumption* is determined by the number of households and the population size and age composition, allowing for slowly changing tastes; *discretionary consumption* is a constant proportion of income remaining after deducting expenditure for committed consumption.[12]

Saving is the difference between disposable income and total consumer expenditure and is therefore also affected by the number of households and the size and age composition of the population. Investment is then obtained by equating it with savings.

As noted above, the model permits migration of population. This implies that inflows or outflows of labour may take place. However, in all other respects the model is closed. In the interest of avoiding some undesirable complexities, no allowance is made for imports or exports.

Simulation Experiments

We turn now to consider some simulation experiments based on the model just described.[13] In each case, we stimulate the model in some particular way and thereby set in motion a series of changes in the population. The results are reported in Tables 1 to 3. Tables 1 and 2 pertain to experiments in which the stimuli take the form of changes in fertility patterns; Table 3 relates to experiments involving changes in immigration.

TABLE 1:

POPULATION SIZE AND THE BURDEN OF HEALTH-CARE COSTS, STARTING FROM
THE 1961 CANADIAN POPULATION, UNDER ALTERNATIVE ASSUMPTIONS ABOUT
THE PATTERN OF FERTILITY

	FP1			FP2		
Time elapsed	N	H/Q	H/N	N	H/Q	H/N
Initial state	100.0	0.060	100.0	100.0	0.060	100.0
Years after shock						
0	101.8	0.060	99.7	101.8	0.060	99.7
5	111.2	0.062	99.3	109.6	0.059	95.3
10	121.9	0.065	100.0	115.0	0.059	96.0
15	134.6	0.067	100.5	121.4	0.060	99.1
20	149.1	0.069	100.0	128.7	0.060	101.2
25	165.1	0.071	99.0	136.3	0.061	101.9
30	182.6	0.071	98.2	143.1	0.061	101.8
35	202.1	0.072	97.7	149.0	0.061	102.4
40	224.4	0.072	97.2	154.7	0.060	103.8
45	249.9	0.071	96.6	160.6	0.060	105.2
50	278.5	0.071	96.0	166.8	0.061	106.3
55	310.4	0.072	95.7	172.7	0.062	107.3
60	346.1	0.072	95.8	178.1	0.063	108.6
65	386.1	0.072	96.1	183.0	0.064	110.0
70	430.7	0.073	96.1	187.7	0.064	110.9
75	480.5	0.073	96.1	192.2	0.064	111.0
80	535.8	0.073	96.0	196.6	0.063	110.6
85	597.4	0.073	96.0	201.1	0.063	110.2
90	666.2	0.073	96.0	205.8	0.063	110.2
95	743.1	0.073	96.1	210.7	0.063	110.5
100	828.8	0.073	96.1	215.8	0.063	110.6
∞	∞	0.073	96.0	∞	0.063	110.5

NOTE: H is annual cost of health-care; Q, annual output; N, population size. N and H/N are indexed at 100.0 in the initial state.

In Table 1, each of the simulation experiments starts with the 1961 actual Canadian population. From that base, two alternative hypothetical patterns of fertility experience are applied to the population. We consider the effects over time of each of these fertility patterns on population size as well as on two measures of cost: the ratio of the costs of health care to the total gross output or income and an index of the per capita costs of health care. (All costs are in real terms; the model abstracts from price changes.)

In the case of fertility pattern 1 (hereafter FP1), we assume that the actual 1961 age-specific fertility rates are maintained for all subsequent periods. The 1961 rates were high by Canadian historical standards, so that their continuation results in a larger proportion of young people in the population than was observed in 1961. As we have already noted, young people — at least after the first year of life — experience relatively low medical costs. But associated with the younger population is a higher dependency ratio (the ratio of those not in the labour force to those in the labour force), which implies that a smaller fraction of the population is responsible for producing the total output of the economy. Thus, output per capita tends to fall at the same time that per capita health-care costs are declining. The net effect, as evident in Table 1, is that while health-care costs per capita drift down to a level about 4 per cent below the initial level, once the system has arrived at a final equilibrium, the fraction of total output allocated to health care increases appreciably — from 6.0 per cent to 7.3 per cent of total output.

The second fertility pattern (FP2) again starts from the 1961 population but assumes that fertility rates follow the course of the actual Canadian rates from 1961 to 1969 and remain constant at the 1969 levels thereafter. It should be noted that the period 1961-69 witnessed a steady decline in fertility rates, and that by 1969 the rates were very low by Canadian standards. Thus FP2 represents a sharp but realistic drop in the rates to a low level that is sustained indefinitely.

In the early years of the FP2 simulation, the assumed pattern of fertility results in a population which grows rather quickly and a dependency ratio which rises. However, the proportion of older people remains roughly constant. In consequence, the fraction of total output allocated to health care is temporarily reduced and the per capita costs decline. By two decades after the shock, though, the lower fertility rates come to have a major effect on the age distribution of the population. The dependency ratio continues to fall while the proportion of older people rises. The over-all effect is to increase somewhat the fraction of output going to health care and to increase by more than 10 per cent the per capita costs of health care.

We turn now to Table 2. Here our initial state is not an actual population but one which is stationary — a population the total size and age distribution of which remain constant over time. The use of a stationary population is a particularly convenient analytical device for our purposes since the impact of experimental stimuli is not obscured by the peculiar dynamic character-istics of any actual population that might be chosen. In consequence, we can see more clearly the results associated specifically with the change in fertility pattern or other stimulus under consideration. We report two sets of fertility simulation results based on an initial stationary population. The particular population that we have used is the one implied by the 1960-62 official Canadian life tables.

FP3 involves a sudden 50 per cent increase in all age-specific fertility rates. The full increase is assumed to occur in the first period of the shock, after which the new level is maintained. The higher fertility rates result in a steady transition to a younger population, one with a higher dependency ratio. While the reduction in the average age tends to reduce the costs of health care, and hence the fraction of total output claimed, the higher dependency ratio means that there is a relative decrease in the size of the

TABLE 2:

POPULATION SIZE AND THE BURDEN OF HEALTH-CARE COSTS, STARTING FROM A STATIONARY POPULATION, UNDER ALTERNATIVE ASSUMPTIONS ABOUT THE PATTERN OF FERTILITY

Time elapsed	FP3			FP4		
	N	H/Q	H/N	N	H/Q	H/N
Initial state	100.0	0.060	100.0	100.0	0.060	100.0
Years after shock						
0	100.7	0.062	103.4	100.1	0.060	100.3
5	104.1	0.064	101.7	101.4	0.062	101.7
10	107.5	0.064	99.4	104.4	0.064	101.5
15	110.9	0.065	97.2	107.8	0.064	99.2
20	114.4	0.065	95.8	111.2	0.064	96.8
25	119.4	0.066	95.6	113.6	0.063	94.3
30	126.1	0.066	94.5	115.2	0.062	93.3
35	133.9	0.066	92.3	117.4	0.061	93.9
40	142.1	0.066	90.1	120.3	0.060	93.9
45	151.0	0.065	88.7	123.2	0.059	93.2
50	161.3	0.065	88.2	125.7	0.058	92.6
55	173.5	0.065	87.7	127.7	0.058	92.8
60	187.2	0.064	86.9	129.7	0.057	93.7
65	201.8	0.064	86.1	131.9	0.058	94.9
70	217.4	0.065	86.0	134.0	0.058	95.9
75	234.5	0.065	86.4	135.7	0.059	97.0
80	253.3	0.066	86.7	136.8	0.060	98.3
85	273.6	0.066	86.6	137.4	0.061	99.5
90	295.3	0.066	86.4	137.7	0.062	100.3
95	318.4	0.066	86.3	137.8	0.061	100.4
100	343.4	0.066	86.4	137.7	0.061	100.0
∞	∞	0.066	86.5	137.7	0.060	100.0

NOTE: See note to Table 1.

labour force. It turns out that the net effect of these offsetting tendencies is to increase the fraction of output claimed to meet the costs of health care by about 10 per cent. At the same time, per capita health-care costs fall by about 13.5 per cent, compared with their initial level, although there is a temporary increase in the early years associated with the sharp rise in fertility and the concomitant pregnancy costs.

FP4 assumes a uniform annual increase in fertility rates, taking them to a level 50 per cent above their initial level over a period of 10 years. Once achieved, the new levels are maintained for 10 years. The rates then subside, taking a further 10 years to return to their initial levels. The consequence of this temporary increase is to raise both the cost-output ratio and the per capita costs of health care. Both of these measures then experience a series of damped cycles, reflecting the echo effects on the population of the temporary change in fertility rates. Eventually the age composition of the population (though not its size) returns to its initial state, as do the two cost variables shown in the table.

TABLE 3:

POPULATION SIZE AND THE BURDEN OF HEALTH-CARE COSTS, STARTING FROM A STATIONARY POPULATION, UNDER ALTERNATIVE ASSUMPTIONS ABOUT THE PATTERN OF MIGRATION

	MP1			*MP1*		
Time elapsed	*N*	*H/Q*	*H/N*	*N*	*H/Q*	*H/N*
Initial state	100.0	0.060	100.0	100.0	0.060	100.0
Years after shock						
0	101.0	0.060	99.6	101.0	0.060	99.6
5	106.6	0.060	98.3	106.6	0.060	98.3
10	113.1	0.060	96.9	112.0	0.060	97.2
15	120.4	0.060	95.4	113.0	0.060	96.9
20	128.4	0.059	94.3	113.6	0.059	97.1
25	137.3	0.059	93.5	114.2	0.059	97.7
30	147.1	0.059	93.1	114.9	0.059	98.4
35	157.9	0.059	92.8	115.5	0.060	99.0
40	169.6	0.059	92.7	116.0	0.060	99.4
45	182.3	0.060	92.8	116.2	0.061	99.8
50	195.9	0.060	92.9	116.2	0.061	100.3
55	210.4	0.061	93.1	116.2	0.061	100.6
60	226.0	0.061	93.2	116.1	0.061	100.5
65	242.6	0.061	93.2	116.0	0.060	100.2
70	260.5	0.061	93.1	115.9	0.060	99.9
75	279.6	0.061	93.1	115.8	0.060	99.9
80	300.2	0.061	93.1	115.8	0.060	100.0
85	322.3	0.061	93.1	115.9	0.060	100.1
90	346.1	0.061	93.1	115.9	0.060	100.1
95	371.6	0.061	93.1	115.9	0.060	100.0
100	398.9	0.061	93.1	115.8	0.060	99.9
∞	∞	0.061	93.1	115.9	0.060	100.0

NOTE: See note to Table 1.

The implicit assumption that no migration occurs is relaxed in the results reported in Table 3. Here again we assume, initially, a stationary population to which we apply, in turn, two patterns of migration experience.

In the first migration pattern (MP1), it is assumed, starting suddenly at some arbitrary time, that in each year a level of net immigration occurs equal to 1 per cent of the domestic population. The age and sex distributions of the migrants, both here and in the other migration experiment, are based on the distributions for immigrants to Canada over the period 1951-66; as is typical of migrants generally, the age distribution is relatively concentrated in the younger adult age groups.

As a result of the input of migrants into the population, the average age falls and the dependency ratio rises. While the long-run effects are less pronounced than those discussed in connection with the 50 per cent rise in fertility (FP3), they are of a similar nature and occur for the same reasons. The short-run impact, however, is rather different and reflects the fact that migrants are distributed among different ages, whereas new births are not.

We note, for example, that unlike the response to a sharp rise in the fertility rate, the per capita costs of health care do not rise temporarily in response to the sudden migration inflow, but instead decline steadily.

In MP2, we assume a sharp increase in the level of net immigration, allowing it to rise in one period from 0 to 1 per cent of the population per annum. The rate is maintained at that higher level for 10 years, after which it falls back to 0. The result is a succession of damped cycles in both the cost-output ratio and per capita costs. About 15 years after the shock, we find the maximum discrepancy — of about 3 per cent — from the initial equilibrium per capita health-care costs. As time passes and the echo effects of the temporary migration influx disappear, both variables return to initial levels.

Concluding Remarks

In this paper we have attempted to provide some quantitative evidence relating to the effects of population change on the cost of health care when the quality of the health care is maintained. By using a model of the complete economic-demographic system we are able to take into account not only the extent to which health-care costs adjust in response to changes in the size and age distribution of the population, but also the impact these changes have on the productive capacity of the economy, and hence on the relative burden of such costs.

We have provided two measures of the burden of health care — cost as a fraction of total output, and cost per capita. By considering each of these measures in a variety of simulation experiments relating to changes in fertility and migration, we are able to indicate the extent to which demographic factors alone might account for historic changes in the costs of providing health-care services. For example, our analysis suggests that population changes can be expected to have a substantial impact on the cost of health care in the longer term. However, it seems clear that large increases in the cost of health care that occur within a decade or so are not likely to be primarily the result of population changes but rather to reflect changes in the quality of services provided. Our analysis suggests also that changes in fertility rates are likely to be of much greater quantitative importance than changes in migration rates.

Notes

1 We think that the results obtained by the use of the model have general relevance to countries with developed economies and health-care systems. For a discussion of demographic effects on the costs of health care in the context of a developing country, see Corsa and Oakley (1971).

2 The publication which provides expenditure data by type of hospital is Statistics Canada (1972b).

3 The age-sex-specific hospital expenditures are based on Statistics Canada (1970, 1972a, 1972c). The choice of ten age groups was dictated by the available data.

4 The allocation of health-care costs by age and sex based on patient-days may overstate somewhat the costs associated with elderly people, inasmuch as they tend to stay longer but to require less expensive treatment per day stayed. Unfortunately, however, there seems to be no better way currently available to establish a series of costs by age group.

5 We are grateful to Dr. Hugh D. Walker for making these unpublished data available to us.

6 The category relating to pregnancy is described as 'Complications of pregnancy, childbirth, and puerperium.' This title notwithstanding, the largest subcategory is 'Delivery without mention of complication.'

7 Not all pregnancies result in live births, of course. For our purpose, we assumed that the ratio of total pregnancies to total live births is constant.

8 For an analysis in which we allow for possible feedback relationships, see Denton and Spencer (1972, 1973c).

9 For convenience, we approximate the schedule of age-specific fertility rates by a Gompertz function. This function has been used by various authors; in particular, see Murphy and Nagnur (1972) and Denton and Spencer (1973b, 1974a) for applications to Canadian data. The use of the Gompertz function avoids the necessity of specifying all of the individual age-specific rates and makes it possible to change the shape of the schedule by simply varying one or more of the function's three parameters. The use of the function in this way is discussed in Denton and Spencer (1974a).

10 Births are adjusted for mortality. However, no adjustment is made to immigration, it being assumed that deaths to migrants are negligible in the year in which they migrate.

11 An indication of the magnitudes of total health-care expenditure, by type of expenditure, is provided in Anderson and Hall (1969).

12 For detailed derivation and discussion of the consumption function incorporated into the model, see Denton and Spencer (1974b).

13 The results of additional simulation experiments are reported in an earlier version of this paper available on request to the authors (McMaster University Department of Economics Working Paper 73-26).

VII

Institutionalization
and Alternatives

In this section I have brought together some papers which allow us to raise the important question, what kind of society have we which relies on extensive institutionalization as a means of providing for the needs of an aging population? Much of the general literature on the institutionalized aged fails to question the assumptions upon which a policy of institutionalization would rest. None of these papers make that error.

In Canada as a whole, and, in particular, in such provinces as Ontario, Manitoba, and Alberta, there is little question that we institutionalize too many of the elderly. Recognition of this fact of over-institutionalization is leading to the growth of alternative programs, especially home-care programs, in several provinces. Even more than 8 or 9 percent of those over age 65 will spend some time in a nursing home or other institutional setting before they die, for various U.S. studies show that while only 4 or 5 percent of the U.S. population aged 65 and over are institutionalized at any one time, about one-fourth of older people actually die in such institutions (most others dying in hospitals, and very few dying at home) (Ingram and Barry, 1977; Kastenbaum and Candy, 1973; Lesnoff-Caravaglia, 1978-79; Marshall, forthcoming, ch. 6; Palmore, 1976; Wershow, 1976). Over the course of their dying, many older people move back and forth between nursing homes, hospitals, and their own homes for variable periods of time (Glaser and Strauss, 1968).

While not included in this book, there have been some excellent studies of the meaning and experience of being an institutionalized person in the Canadian context. Judy Posner has discussed the problematics of securing entry into rehabilitation programs within one setting (Posner, 1974); and Neena Chappell has reported on awareness of death and its implications, and on the everyday worlds of senile patients, from another institution (Chappell, 1975, 1978).

Alternative service-delivery mechanisms, such as home-care programs, are generally under medical control, even though there is usually no need for high-level or high-technology intervention (see Flett, Last and Lynch, ch. 17). Thus, in Ontario to take one example, entry into the very limited home-care program which aims at helping elderly persons with acute or chronic illnesses to be able to remain at home is determined by a physician (Ontario Council of Health, 1978). This is one of many instances of medicalization of later life.

245

Schwenger and Gross, in Chapter 23, call for a reduction of institutional care paralleled with growth of alternative services, of which the foster home situation described by Neysmith in Chapter 26 would be one example. But Neysmith reports that almost two-thirds of possible foster home candidates in her study preferred to remain in their present accommodations. Lawton's ecological model of aging, which Neysmith uses, suggests that their ability to do so rests not entirely with themselves, but in the broader environments in which they live as well.

When the broader context is considered, Myles argues in his paper on institutionalizing the elderly (Chapter 24), the negative implications of institutionalization may be less severe than is sometimes suggested. He argues that, for a small segment of the population, institutionalization provides a positive welfare function, i.e., contributes to the well-being of the residents. Penning and Chappell, in Chapter 25, take issue with Myles' social-welfare model, calling attention to the diversity of types of institutional setting. Schwenger and Gross argue that there is still a need for some institutionalization for a small segment of the elderly.

It seems imperative to devote more attention to increasing the fit between the individual and the broader environment, whether institutional or not. With this said, however, two points might be emphasized: first, all too often the stance taken by gerontological scientists and practitioners had been to fit the individual to the environment (the "adjustment ethic" of gerontology) rather than to fit the environment to the needs of the individual (Marshall and Tindale, 1978-79); secondly, without attempting to glorify the past, we should not forget that there have been and are still many societies in which institutionalizing any elderly would be almost unthinkable.

The relationship between perceived health and self-reported well-being is strongly documented in the articles by Neysmith and by Penning and Chappell. Readers may also wish to place these results alongside those of Gutman, Flett, Last and Lynch and Tilquin and associates, in other chapters.

The analysis by Sheila Neysmith of possible candidates for foster care gives some perspective on the phenomenon of institutionalization of the aged. Institutionalization is in a sense an expulsion process which removes people from full participation in the society (see Mathiesen, 1974). Removal of some participants has a function of creating a boundary which in turn has definitional effects in creating what we might take to be *normal* society. By focusing on people right on that boundary, Neysmith clarifies the meaning of being in as opposed to being out of the society.

Myles goes so far, in his paper, as to maintain that the status of the elderly in institutions merely symbolizes their low status in advanced capitalist societies. While Myles sees institutions for the aged (although he differentiates between "good" and "bad" ones) as generally positive adaptations *within* advanced capitalist society, he is an advocate for neither that form of societal organization nor that specific adaptation. His recommendation is to focus on the larger issues at the societal level, which provide a contemporary rationality to institutionalizing such a large segment of our population.

23

INSTITUTIONAL CARE AND INSTITUTIONALIZATION OF THE ELDERLY IN CANADA*

Cope W. Schwenger
Department of Health Administration
University of Toronto

and

M. John Gross
Extendicare Limited
Toronto

> Old peoples' homes, nursing homes, and hospitalization should be considered only if absolutely necessary. There is a great deal more preaching of this principle in Canada than actual practice.

This statement was made by the Special Committee of the Senate on Aging (1966:108). Little has happened since that time which would permit us to amend their observation. The Senate committee came to its conclusion more than a dozen years ago based on information submitted to it by the Department of National Health and Welfare (Special Committee, 1964). The Department estimated, from admittedly incomplete data, that on any given day in 1962-63, 7.7 percent of Canadians 65 years and over were residing in institutions (Table 1) (Special Committee, 1966:106). This rate varied among the provinces and ranged from a low of 3.9 percent in Newfoundland to a high of 9.3 percent in Alberta. Moreover, among Canadians who had reached or exceeded the age of 75, it appeared that as many as 15 percent of them might be found in institutions at any given time (Special Committee, 1966:107).

These rates compared unfavourably with the records of other countries. One international study by Shanas, Townsend, *et al.* (1968:78) indicated that in 1961-62 the average daily proportion of persons 65 and over in institutions was only 4.5 percent in Great Britain and 4.6 percent in the U.S. The lack of available home-care services in Canada has been one of the reasons frequently given for the high level of institutional utilization among our older population (Schwenger and Sayers, 1971; Markus, 1974). As noted by

---

*Prepared for this volume. Material for this chapter was collected in conjunction with a study which the authors are conducting for the Ontario Economic Council.

TABLE 1:

INSTITUTIONAL CARE OF AGED PERSONS IN CANADA, 1962-63

	Estimated Beds Used by Persons 65 and Over*	
	Number of Beds	Bed Rate (% Population 65+)
Newfoundland	1,073	3.9
Prince Edward Island	771	7.0
Nova Scotia	2,931	4.6
New Brunswick	3,260	6.9
Quebec	23,006	7.3
Ontario	43,883	8.5
Manitoba	6,864	8.1
Saskatchewan	6,261	7.3
Alberta	8,843	9.3
British Columbia	12,443	7.4
Yukon	78	19.5
Northwestern Territories	20	4.0
Canada	109,423	7.7

SOURCE: *Final Report of the Special Committee of the Senate on Aging* (1966:106).

*Includes General and Allied Special Hospitals, Mental Hospitals, Tuberculosis Sanitoria, and Homes for Special Care.

many observers, this could not be supported by the Shanas study. Despite the nearly identical rates of institutional care among the aged in the U.S. and Great Britain, American home-care services were as underdeveloped as those in Canada, while in Britain they were much more widespread and comprehensive.

Recent Canadian Experience

More recent assessments of institutional use by the elderly have been made for the province of Ontario (Schwenger and Palin, 1974; Schwenger, 1974) and for Canada as a whole (Gross, 1978; Schwenger, in progress). Our most up-to-date Canadian compilation is based on utilization data for the year 1976 supplied to us by Statistics Canada. Excluded are all institutional facilities in the Yukon and the Northwest Territories and special care facilities in Quebec. Table 2 reveals the rates of institutional use among aged Canadians in that year. This table shows that on any given day in 1976, approximately 8.4 percent of the population 65 and over was in some kind of institution. Viewing the provinces, Alberta still holds first place with a rate of 9.4 percent. (This figure excludes the more than 4,000 residents in Alberta's "lodges", which have been described as at least semi-institutional.) Next is Manitoba (9.1 percent) which has taken over second spot from Ontario (8.9 percent). Saskatchewan follows closely behind (8.7 percent).

How do these rates compare with more recent figures from the United States and Great Britain? The answer is given in Table 3. Definitions of

TABLE 2:
NUMBER AND PERCENT OF AGED PERSONS IN VARIOUS TYPES OF INSTITUTIONS AT ANY GIVEN TIME, CANADA AND THE PROVINCES, 1976

Provinces	Population 65 Years and Over	Hospitals[a]		Special Care Facilities[c]		Mental Health Facilities[d]		All Types[i]	
		Persons[b]	% Pop.	Persons	% Pop.	Persons	% Pop.	Persons	% Pop.
Newfoundland	36,535	504[e]	1.4	1,495	4.1	30	0.1	2,029	5.6
Prince Edward Island	13,245	199[e]	1.5	842	6.4	8	0.1	1,049	7.9
Nova Scotia	80,730	1,258	1.6	4,228	5.2	208	0.3	5,694	7.1
New Brunswick	61,080	1,185[e]	1.9	3,107	5.1	206	0.3	4,498	7.4
Quebec[f]	481,360	11,455	2.4	—	—	3,181	0.7	—	—
Ontario	738,290	16,309	2.2	48,158	6.5	1,517	0.2	65,984	8.9
Manitoba	106,560	2,318	2.2	6,892	6.5	458	0.4	9,668	9.1
Saskatchewan	102,175	2,263	2.2	6,476	6.3	188	0.2	8,927	8.7
Alberta	137,925	4,675	3.4	7,297	5.3	983	0.7	12,955	9.4
British Columbia	242,055	5,150	2.1	10,304	4.2	1,353	0.6	16,807	6.9
Canada	2,000,585	45,316	2.3[g]	—	5.8[h]	8,132	0.4[g]	—	8.4[h]

SOURCES: Gross, 1978; Schwenger, in process.

[a] "Hospitals" include all General and Allied Special Hospitals in the reporting provinces. Data were supplied by the Hospital Morbidity Section, Health Division, Statistics Canada.

[b] "Persons" are calculated as 1/366 of all days used by separated hospital patients.

[c] Age classified year-end census counts on reporting facilities were supplied by the Special Care Facilities Section, Health Division, Statistics Canada. From this sample, estimates for the complete universe of facilities were made based on inventory data furnished by the same section.

[d] Preliminary age-classified year-end census counts for all mental health facilities were provided by the Mental Health Section, Health Division, Statistics Canada.

[e] Persons in "Hospitals" on any given day in 1976 are estimated from 1975 utilization data in the case of Newfoundland, Prince Edward Island, and New Brunswick. This estimate was made on the basis of the percentage change in the elderly population of these provinces between 1975 and 1976.

[f] No data are available on Quebec special care facilities.

[g] National rates for "Hospitals" and "Mental Health Facilities" are based on the Canadian population 65+ exclusive of the Yukon and the Northwest Territories.

[h] National rates for "Special Care Facilities" and "All Types" are based on the Canadian population 65+ exclusive of Quebec, the Yukon, and the Northwest Territories.

[i] Percentages in this table may not add to "All Types" total due to rounding of numbers.

TABLE 3:

PERCENTAGE OF PERSONS 65 AND OVER IN VARIOUS TYPES OF INSTITUTIONS
AT ANY GIVEN TIME CANADA, ENGLAND AND WALES AND THE U.S., 1970-77

Type of Care	Canada[1] (1976)	England and Wales (1970-71)	U.S. (1973-77)
Hospital Care	2.3	1.8	1.0
Nursing Home-Residential Care	5.8	2.4	5.0
Psychiatric Care	0.4	0.9	0.3
All Types of Institutional Care	8.4	5.1	6.3

SOURCES: Gross, 1978; Schwenger, in progress; Grimley Evans, 1977; National Center for Health Statistics, 1977; 1978; Ball, 1977.

[1]Percentages do not add up to "All Types of Institutional Care" due to rounding of numbers.

"institution" are inconsistent among the three countries. Consequently, the comparisons made in Table 3 are necessarily tentative. It appears, however, that with the exception of institutional psychiatric care, Canada's rates continue to be greater in every way than those of the U.S. and England and Wales.

TABLE 4:

PERCENTAGE OF PERSONS 65+ IN INSTITUTIONAL CARE ON ANY ONE DAY, CANADA, GREAT BRITAIN AND THE U.S., 1961-63 and 1970-77

Canada	Great Britain	United States
1962-63	1961-62	1961-62
7.7	4.6	4.7
	(England and Wales)	
1976	1970-71	1973-77
8.4	5.1	6.3

SOURCES: Gross, 1978; Schwenger, in progress; Special Committee, 1966; Shanas, *et al.,* 1968; Grimley Evans, 1977; National Center for Health Statistics, 1977; 1978; Ball, 1977.

Table 4 makes a longitudinal comparison among the three countries. Although caution is again advised because of differences in geography, definitions, methodology, and, particularly, time intervals, it is interesting to note that Canada experienced an absolute increase in institutional utilization of 0.7 percent as compared with 0.5 percent in Great Britain (England and Wales) and 1.6 percent in the United States. Stating this a different way, there was a proportionate increase of only 9 percent for Canada as compared with 11 percent for Great Britain and a remarkable 34 percent for the U.S. This probably reflects the rapid and minimally controlled expansion of nursing-home care in the United States following the introduction of Medicare and Medicaid.

Institutionalization versus Institutional Care

All institutional rates thus far discussed refer to proportions of the elderly on any one day. Nothing has been said about how long they have been there or how many have become "institutionalized". It was estimated by the Special Committee of the Senate on Aging that about 80 percent of the 109,423 beds used by the elderly in 1962-63 were occupied by persons whose length of stay was longer than two months (Special Committee, 1966:32). At that rate, some 6.2 percent of elderly Canadians were institutionalized on a long-term basis. Compared with the findings of the Shanas study mentioned earlier, total long-stay proportions in Great Britain were 3.6 percent and in the U.S. 3.7 percent (Shanas, *et al.*, 1967).

It is not possible from the above data from Statistics Canada to separate short- from long-stay cases in Canada in 1976. We have, however, made this assessment for the province of Ontario (Gross, 1978; Schwenger, in progress). If we accept the conventional definition of "long-stay" care as care which is given over a continuous period equalling or exceeding one month (Commission on Chronic Illness, 1956:5) and if we assume that experience in the rest of Canada is similar to Ontario's, it is estimated that about 1 percent of aged Canadians were in short-stay care in 1976, and almost 7.5 percent in long-term care, or a rate of institutionalization which remains excessive by international standards.

Why Canada's High Rate?

Part of the reason for Canada's climbing rate of institutional usage by the elderly can be ascribed to an aging of the already aged population (Auerbach and Gerber, 1976). That is, not only do we have proportionately more persons above 65 than in the past but the relative numbers of the very old (85+) and the middle-old (75-84) have increased at an even greater rate. These middle and very old groups require more institutional and health-care services (Schwenger, 1977). In Ontario, for example, over one-third of the population 85 years and over were in some kind of institutional setting on any given day in 1976. Looking to the future, this is the group which is also expanding at a far faster rate than the remainder of the Ontario population (Denton and Spencer, this volume).

Aside from the demographic factor, Canada's institutional rate among the aged must be placed within the context of the general tendency in this country to institutionalize our "deviant" citizens, be they criminals or invalids, young or old. Factors such as geography and climate are also important. It is not surprising that older people will remain longer in institutions in regions where there are vast distances to be travelled and few amenities at home. Isolation is compounded by adverse climate. Hospitality is extended to patients or residents, especially older ones, who tend to stay longer in institutions when the weather is colder. These factors are evidenced by different north/south utilization rates, for example, in Ontario (Schwenger and Palin, 1974).

Another important influence is population mobility. More neighbourly concern is inevitable where families have lived in close proximity for long periods. Community care in Great Britain may well have been more successful for this reason while the much more frequent movement occurring in many Canadian neighbourhoods has not been particularly conducive to community support and caring. Since daughters and daughters-in-law have traditionally borne most of the responsibility of looking after aged parents, changing sex roles and the need for additional family income have affected the ability to keep the elderly in the community as women increasingly seek work outside the home. It has been recommended that we should compete with this trend by paying relatives in order to supply the necessary family support to keep older persons out of institutions. Declining fertility rates in Canada will also tend to raise levels of institutional use — with fewer sons and particularly daughters, future elderly populations will have even less filial support to help them stay at home. Alternative roles for women have also decreased the availability of both commercial home support services, such as maids and cleaning ladies, and have provided competition for crucial publicly financed programs, such as visiting homemakers.

The Effect of Insured Health Services

Without question, one of the strongest influences on institutional care in Canada has been the bias of our health insurance scheme. In this country, home-care services were not insured simultaneously with hospital and institutional care as was done in Great Britain under the National Health Service. As a result, Canadians have been forced to seek institutional solutions to the health-care problems of the aged. The public, the elderly, and their families have been persuaded that hospital is the best and frequently the first resort for the sick and dying elderly. No doubt, this thinking has been fostered by health professionals who are more comfortable and more highly rewarded when practicing in the hospital. On the one hand, we have asked older people to pay for community-care services while we have made it easy and cheap for them to go into hospitals. The incentive has been almost irresistable.

Our record with the frail but otherwise well older populations has been no better. Instead of relying on community alternatives, we have too readily provided an abundance of homes for the aged and nursing home beds. Paradoxically, it was Britain's historic advantage to have been too poor to afford expensive institutional facilities. As an alternative, less costly home-care services and sheltered housing were provided for the frail elderly. Many Western European countries have developed a considerable range and supply of home-care services for the old. Because we chose not to supply them from the beginning, community services are minimal and continue to be sacrificed in Canada to meet enormous institutional budgets.

Great Britain and the U.S. provide Canadian health-care planners with two extreme examples. Britain may well be accused of putting too much pressure on the individual, the family, and the community in holding the line on institutional care of the elderly; it appears somewhat under-institutionalized. The United States, in comparison, had, until recently, the worst of both worlds — far too few institutional beds on the one hand plus a dearth of community services on the other. In the past decade there has been a great upsurge in the number and proportion of aged Americans in nursing homes with accompanying difficulties in maintaining quality and standards.

Canada went along the combined path of excessive institutional and medical care, the two most expensive parts of the system. Now that these two have consumed so much money it is extremely difficult to find resources for institutional alternatives, particularly in a time of economic restraint. It should also be kept in mind that the hospital is the workshop of the physician, who may feel uncomfortable or unwilling to work in other settings. Of course, resistance is also coming from hospital administrators and those responsible for homes for the aged and nursing homes who have a vested interest not only in filling existing beds but in increasing the supply.

Governments are now finding it extremely difficult to develop an optimally balanced system in an over-institutionalized setting.

Future Trends

Because of the forecasted growth of the aged Canadian population, the federal and provincial governments are very concerned about the future cost of institutional care (Health and Welfare Canada, 1975; Manitoba Department of Health and Social Development, 1975; Health and Welfare Canada, 1976b; Ontario Council on Health, 1978). It has been determined that in Ontario, for instance, the elderly will consume over 50 percent of *all* health-care resources shortly after the turn of the century, if present rates of utilization continue. A great part of this will be due to the increase in institutional costs (Gross, 1978; Schwenger, in progress). In response to such prospects, all levels of government are attempting to reduce the trend towards expensive institutional care. In Ontario, for example, there has been a decrease in the elderly utilization of psychiatric and residential care facilities. This seems to indicate that the government's initiatives are having an effect (Gross, 1978; Schwenger, in progress).

However, merely curbing the supply of institutional services is not the complete answer. First of all a simple reduction of beds will not ensure that persons use institutional services appropriately. Second, there is some limit below which bed supplies should not be allowed to drop if we are to meet genuine needs. Exclusive preoccupation with reduced institutional supply may put the health-care system in an increasingly precarious position. What is needed in addition is the development of many more "alternative" or "complementary" services to supplement the institutional care of our elderly citizens.

The dual approach — the reduction of institutional care and the promotion of alternative services — is embodied in policy statements of both provincial and federal governments. Unfortunately, the pursuit of this objective has too frequently been one-sided. In Ontario, for example, the government has embarked on a bold campaign to lower bed-to-population levels. At the same time, those community programs which would serve the chronic and disabling conditions of the elderly are only sporadically funded and loosely organized.

In fairness to governments, their apprehensions about expanding alternative services should be explained. There is still little hard evidence that community care programs will save money by keeping the elderly and others out of institutions. The fear is that this will merely become an "add-on" policy. However, this argument makes less and less sense as governments implement "subtract-from" measures in the institutional sector. It should be possible to save on future capital expenditures if suitable alternatives are introduced simultaneously as bed-to-population ratios are permitted to drop. A great deal more use must be made in Canada of such alternative programs as periodic admissions, vacation care, day hospitals, day care, foster care, hostels, and home care. A much higher proportion of institutional savings should be directed into these services and facilities.

Other economizing approaches must also be tried. Our system of care could become more efficient with more appropriate assessment and placement of persons needing institutional care. Also crucial is the improved coordination of housing, income maintenance, recreation, education, and social and health care. These services are intimately interrelated and program efforts should be either integrated or at least better coordinated at federal, provincial, regional, and local levels. Gerontology by its nature is an interdisciplinary matter, not only with regard to education and research, but particularly at the service delivery level.

Cautionary Notes

Relocation of the elderly has been shown to be potentially dangerous to health and life. This applies to movement to and from institutions as well as within facilities themselves. The risk is particularly great for the aged who are male, very old, living alone, or in poor physical or mental health (Kasl, 1972). Consequently, it would be a mistake to relocate very old persons who have been institutionalized for long periods of time merely in the interest of a more efficient health-care system. It would seem wiser, and certainly more humane, to leave these persons where they are and be content with a more gradual shift in the system as we concentrate on the appropriate placement of prospective institutional admissions. The lure of the community may be a siren call for persons who have become dependent on institutional facilities. The older person may be much worse off, even more "institutionalized" in a certain sense, if bedfast or housebound and with few available home-care services.

The home is cherished by most older people. It becomes a part of their identity, a place where things are familiar and in which they try to maintain autonomy and control. There is no doubt that older Canadians want to remain at home as long as possible. Nevertheless, the slogan, "Keep the old folks at home", can be a cruel and onerous message to some elderly persons and their relatives. There is a point beyond which it is no longer fair to older people, their families, or to the community to sustain the psychological, social, or financial costs of home care. There comes a time when institutions are quite appropriate in the life of a residual proportion of elderly Canadians, particularly at very advanced ages. At this stage institutional placement should be encouraged.

Canada has one of the highest rates of institutional care and institutionalization of its aged of any country in the world. There is no reason why this record must continue if we reduce institutional access and simultaneously foster an increasing variety of non-institutional alternatives. Better planning, management, and coordination of facilities is also crucial. On the other hand over-zealousness must not lead us to deny care to those elderly persons who need it. The balance we should strive for might be described in the re-wording of an old Canadian aphorism: "Institutionalization if necessary, but not necessarily institutionalization."

24

INSTITUTIONALIZING THE ELDERLY
A Critical Assessment of the
Sociology of Total Institutions*

John F. Myles
Department of Sociology
Carleton University

Since the appearance of *Asylums* (Goffman, 1961), sociological discussion of such diverse organizations as hospitals, prisons, and homes for the mentally and physically disabled has been dominated by Goffman's model of the "total institution". Though Goffman's own research was conducted primarily in a specific set of institutions (mental hospitals) within a specific historical period, his object was to construct a general theory of the total institution (Goffman, 1961: xiii). Despite the ostensible diversity of such organizations with respect to their goals, technologies, and clientele, the effort to apply the theory to all institutions has rarely been systematically criticized either with respect to its theoretical assumptions or with respect to its capacity to explain empirical findings. Elsewhere (Myles, 1978a; 1978b; and forthcoming), I have presented the results of an empirical analysis of the institutionalized and noninstitutionalized elderly of the Province of Manitoba which, I have suggested, raise doubts about the usefulness of Goffman's model for understanding and evaluating the institutionalization of the elderly. The Manitoba data indicated that institutionalization reduces the negative consequences of physical disability and thereby increases overall levels of life satisfaction. Inmates were found to have higher levels of social interaction and, in general, to derive greater satisfaction from their social relationships. Finally, institutionalization was found to provide significant relief, both objective and subjective, from the conditions of poverty which characterize the noninstitutionalized elderly. The purpose of the present paper is to supplement this empirical critique of Goffman's analysis with a theoretical critique. In order to do so, however, it is first necessary to identify the key analytical assumptions upon which his "sociology of total institutions" has been constructed.

The Sociology of Total Institutions: The Spectre of Bureaucracy

In order to locate the underlying assumptions about social reality adopted by a particular author, it is useful to identify the manner in which that author

---

*Prepared for this volume.

establishes the linkages between what Mills (1959:8) refers to as "personal troubles of milieu", on the one hand, and "public issues of social structure", on the other. For many, the major threat to modern man has been the spectre of bureaucracy, the omnipresent official — commissar or social worker — who usurps control over every aspect of modern life. Warnings against the potential threat posed by the "dictatorship of the official" have come from such diverse sources as Orwell's *1984* and Burnham's *Managerial Revolution*. Perhaps the major representative of this position is Max Weber who exclaimed (quoted by Giddens, 1971:236):

> ...the great question then is...what can we set against this mechanization to preserve a certain section of humanity from this fragmentation of the soul, this complete ascendancy of the bureaucratic ideal of life.

It is precisely within such a perspective that the attempt of Goffman to identify the effects of total institutions on the "structure of the self" (Goffman, 1961:xiii) can be located. Gouldner (1970:382) has pointed out that for Goffman the total institution is indicative of the situation of modern man overpowered by "the crushing impact of organization". Bureaucracy is not merely the symptom of some more fundamental underlying pathology; rather, it is the disease which leads, in Goffman's terms, to a sense of "personal inefficacy", "failure", "self-pity", and a tendency towards "situational withdrawal"; in effect, alienation from oneself and from society.

Within the bureaucratic paradigm, the starting point of analysis, the prime mover in the chain of social causation, as it were, is power. As Manning (1976:15) notes, *Asylums* is predicated on the assumption of the "centrality of power and authority as a feature of social life". As for Weber, it is the "dictatorship of the official" and its consequences which are of primary concern to Goffman and those who have followed in this tradition (e.g., Freidson, 1970). In the context of total institutions, then, the focus is on the *de facto* domination of clients by the organizational staff. The producer-consumer relationship becomes bureaucratized in the sense that the client becomes subject to the formal authority of agency officials. As Goffman points out (1961:10), this is an abnormal situation compared to that of most individuals in the larger society where bureaucratic authority tends to be confined to the sphere of production while consumption activities take place within the relatively autonomous domain of the private household. It is this bureaucratization of consumption, the disruption of the individual's "personal economy of action" (Goffman, 1961:38), which provides the structural basis to account for the "private troubles" of the inmate. This disruption takes the form of a "stripping process" in which any other status or role is subordinated to the specific inmate role peculiar to the institution; a new "identity kit" is provided and the individual enters the inmate career. This, in effect, constitutes the "management technique" by which agency officials exercise their control over clients. The combination of the inmates' subordinate status and identification with the deviant condition implied in the inmate role ("prisoner", "patient", etc.) creates "a milieu of personal failure in which one's fall from grace is continuously pressed home" (Goffman, 1961:61).

Based on Goffman's powerful analysis, the bureaucratic thesis emerged during the sixties as the dominant paradigm informing analyses of such diverse organizations as prisons, hospitals, and homes for the aged and disabled. Despite the diversity among such organizations, it was (and continues to be) construed as a *general* theory which could be fruitfully employed in all organizations meeting Goffman's definition of the "total institution" (see Goffman, 1961:xiii). Writing specifically of institutions for the aged, for example, Brody (1973:433) states:

> The institution actively participates in reducing the resident to a total lack of power....Admission is accompanied by a series of procedures that transfer the individual's power over his own life to the personnel of the institution.

Brody then proceeds to list the results of this situation (1973:433), namely the "iatrogenic diseases of institutional life: dependency; depersonalization; low self-esteem; lack of occupation or fruitful use of time...".

The bureaucratic thesis views these devastating consequences as being the result of two separate but interrelated aspects of the total institution: (a) the bureaucratic relationship itself; and (b) the disruption, which results from this relationship, of the individual's "personal economy of action". By "the bureaucratic relationship itself" I refer to the assumed loss of individual autonomy which accompanies institutionalization as a result of the formal subordination of the client to the authority of the agency staff. It is assumed that this loss of autonomy is experienced as a form of degradation resulting in a sense of personal failure. The disruption of the individual's "personal economy of action" refers to the fact that individuals are constrained by the institutional regime to allocate their time, energy, and resources in a manner which is different than that which they would ordinarily choose were they not so constrained, and/or they must consume goods and services of a combination and type which they would not normally choose for themselves. Here we are referring to such things as the constraints imposed by the institutional timetable on the individual's daily routine; the type and quality of food, clothing, and shelter consumed; the kinds of leisure activities permitted; and so forth. These constraints arise from the bureaucratic tendency towards the standardization of "raw materials" on the one hand and the routinizing of the procedures for handling "raw materials" on the other (see Perrow, 1967). Goffman captures these two tendencies with his description of the "stripping process" and creation of the "inmate role". He assumes that because of these constraints, individual patterns of consumption, use of time, etc., are so out of keeping with the inmate's own preferences and values that a high level of dissatisfaction and deprivation is induced. In short, the implicit analogue for all total institutions is the prison or concentration camp.

In the critique which follows, I do not intend to question the fact that inmates of institutions for the elderly are subordinate to the agency staff or that there is an institutional regime which imposes restrictions on inmates. Moreover, as I have argued elsewhere (Myles, 1978b), it is my view that the well-being of inmates of institutions for the elderly would be significantly enhanced were the authority relations in the institution reversed, i.e., if the staff were subject to authority of clients and the institutional regime determined through a decision-making process controlled by clients. What I shall suggest here is that for the typical elderly individual who becomes institutionalized the lack of autonomy characteristic of institutionalional life does not constitute a profound discontinuity from his or her noninstitutionalized condition and that, despite the constraints on consumption and use of time, the actual level and pattern of consumption and use of time will, in general, be more congruent with his or her preferences than would be the case were the client not institutionalized. Accordingly, theorization of the institutional life of the elderly must begin with a theorization of its alternative — the noninstitutional life of the elderly, a group who are relatively poor, and often widowed and/or suffering from some degree of physical disability.[1] Institutions for the elderly must be seen and understood in the context of the larger social formation which creates such organizations and of which they are a part.

Institutionalizing the Elderly: The Societal Context

In contrast to those who have identified "bureaucracy" as the principle nemesis of modern man, an alternative tradition locates the ultimate source of "private troubles" in the contemporary period in the development and extension of the market and in particular the formation of a labour market which transforms human labour into a commodity. Such a view is found within the Marxist tradition but also characterizes a theorist such as Polanyi (1944:73) who writes:

> To allow the market mechanism to be sole director of the fate of human beings...would result in the demolition of society. For the alleged commodity "labor power" cannot be shoved about, used indiscriminately, or even left unused, without affecting also the human individual who happens to be the bearer of this peculiar commodity. In disposing of a man's labor power the system would, incidentally, dispose of the physical, psychological, and moral entity "man" attached to that tag.

Among the major casualties of the fully developed labour market were the aged. As Lubove (1968:114-15), paraphrasing Rubinow, writes with respect to the situation in early twentieth-century America:

> ...the capacity of the aged for self-support was being undermined. Changes in economic organization and family structure had relegated them to a marginal status in the modern industrial society. The key to the plight of the aged, Rubinow explained, was the increasing dependence of the "majority of mankind...upon a wage-contract for their means of existence." The wage-system led to economic superannuation in advance of "physiologic old age." It made no difference if the aged worker remained "fit for productive activity"; he experienced an abrupt and total economic disability if he fell "below the minimum level of productivity set by the employer." Modern industrial techniques, including scientific management, hastened economic superannuation by using up "human energy at greater speed within a short time."

The subsequent development of industrial capitalism did nothing to relieve the source of this condition and, indeed, exacerbated it. Barred from selling their labour power and owning little productive capital, the relationship of the elderly to the means of production becomes a very simple one — they are excluded. The elderly have come to make up a major portion of the new postindustrial proletariat (O'Connor, 1970), dependent on the state for their survival. This condition of dependency means that the elderly, like children, have little influence over the terms of their participation in the larger society — whether at the level of the nation state, the local community, or the family.

The condition of the aged in advanced capitalist societies is perhaps best described by the Weberian concept of a negatively privileged status group (Neuwirth, 1969). The concept was employed by Weber to describe those groups who, on the basis of some distinguishing characteristic such as race, age, or sex, are excluded from access to economic and political opportunities and denied social esteem. As Neuwirth (1969:152) notes:

> Two additional consequences follow from the vulnerability implicit in negatively privileged status. The denial of economic and political opportunities prevents these individuals from influencing the terms of their participation in the larger society. Moreover, representatives of the dominant communities will regulate those affairs and interests of the negatively privileged which, if left uncontrolled, might affect the interests and relative positions of the dominant communities within the larger society.

By characterizing the elderly in this way, are we not also perhaps creating a caricature of the elderly? We have been warned many times against treating the elderly as though they were a single homogeneous group. Certainly the above passage does not describe many of the elderly during their initial retirement years when their incomes may still be relatively high, their health good, and they continue to be actively involved in community and social affairs. If, however, we view this situation as the outcome of a process which occurs gradually over the post-retirement period, then it would appear to describe the process of aging for most individuals rather well, a sort of "career trajectory" of ever-increasing dependency. Entry to a nursing home or home for the aged is simply the end of this process. Accordingly, the subordinate status of clients in institutions for the aged does not represent a radical disjuncture with the past but simply the next step in the evolution of the "aging career".

The bureaucratic thesis assumes that the individual's experience when entering an institution is one of radical disjuncture, as would be the case, for example, in most instances of imprisonment. It is crucial for this thesis that inmates not only *lack* autonomy but, in addition, experience this lack as a significant *loss*. Goffman (1961:66-67) points this out when he notes that the inmate culture is to be understood as a function of the "low position of inmates relative to their stature on the outside...". If this assumption falls, then with it falls the entire rationale for focusing on the bureaucratic relationship as constituting the core experience of institutional life. The bureaucratic thesis assumes that the "total institution" is an aberrant social structure in an otherwise healthy society, that it is the *cause* of the subordinate status of its clients. If, however, the social relations of domination and subordination which characterize institutional life simply reflect the typical social relations of the client group in the larger society, we must adopt a quite different view of these particular organizations. In order to establish what this view might be, it is necessary to situate these organizations within their broader social and historical context, just as we have done for the elderly themselves.

Institutions for the Aged and the Welfare State

Polanyi (1944:76) describes the modern period in western societies as being characterized by a double movement: the extension of market organization into all spheres of life on the one hand and the establishment of a network of measures and policies (the "welfare state") to check the action of the market relative to labour on the other. The one represented the principle of economic liberalism and *laissez-faire*; the other represented the principle of social protection "...aiming at the conservation of man" from the ravages of the marketplace (Polanyi, 1944:132). Among the major consequences of this protectionist countermovement was the establishment of a variety of social-welfare measures for the aged — including the expansion of institutional care — designed to protect the aging individual from the consequences of losing or being deprived of his only commodity — his labour power.

Expressed in purely monetary terms the welfare functions of institutional care are quite evident. In Manitoba, for example, transfer payments to the institutionalized elderly are on the average more than twice as large as those provided to the noninstitutionalized elderly. Even in the United States, with its curious welfare traditions, approximately two out of every three dollars in nursing home revenue comes from public funds (U.S. Senate Committee on Aging, 1974:25). Given the limited incomes which characterize the elderly population and, in particular, the oldest of this group who are disproportionately represented in the institution, the majority would be unable to afford institutional care were it not for the direct or indirect intervention of the state. In addition to bureaucratizing consumption (Goffman's starting point), institutionalization usually provides the individual with a higher level of consumption of goods and services than would normally be available through the normal functioning of the marketplace. In effect, institutional care for the elderly is also institutional welfare for the elderly.

It does not necessarily follow, of course, that inmates are better off as a result. Since these resources are under the control of the agency staff, it is quite possible that they are allocated in a manner that leaves the situation of clients unchanged or indeed worse than before. For example, the total value of the goods and services consumed by prisoners may well be higher than that which they would otherwise consume outside the prison. We do not usually consider incarceration as enhancing the welfare of prisoners, however, since a substantial portion of these resources are used to constrain their freedom of action, something which for most individuals constitutes a disutility. To use Goffman's terminology, the disruption of the individual's "personal economy of action" is such that institutional life is experienced as a form of deprivation. Is this also likely to be the case in the contemporary institution for the aged? To assume that such is the case is to assume that in advanced capitalist societies the functions of welfare policy in general, and institutional welfare for the aged in particular, have gone unchanged since the nineteenth century.

As both Polanyi (1944) and Bendix (1956) have noted, the primary function of welfare policy in nineteenth-century Britain and North America was to mobilize an unwilling population to enter the nascent industrial labour force. All outdoor relief was abolished or greatly restricted and institutional welfare established in the form of poorhouses and houses of industry according to the doctrine of "less eligibility". The conditions of life in the institution were to be made deliberately undesirable ("less eligible") in order to induce an unwilling labour force "to offer themselves to any employer on any terms" (Piven and Cloward, 1971:34). Writing on the situation in nineteenth-century America, Rothman (1971:195) notes:

> The influential Quincy report was filled with unqualified testimony of the power of the institution to terrorize the poor and thereby keep them off the relief rolls....Or as Duxbury's officials counselled, make the poorhouse unpleasant enough and the needy will go to great lengths to avoid public support.

By effectively abolishing all outdoor relief and restricting welfare to the poorhouse, the government made labour a commodity whose price could be set by the self-regulating market.

Initially, it was intended that the sick, the aged, and the mentally deficient would be cared for in separate institutions specifically designed for this purpose. However, in Canada (Splane, 1965) as in Britain (Bendix, 1956) and the United States (Rothman, 1971), paupers of all types were crowded together under the same roof. These included orphans, the aged, vagrants, and, not infrequently, the criminal and the insane. In effect, all those who were not directly engaged in production, or could not be supported by those who were, were submitted to the less than pleasant regime of the poorhouse. Such was the fate of the indigent elderly which resulted from a welfare policy based on a principle of deterrence. However, while this doctrine continued to have a significant influence on the development of welfare policy, it was not long before it became clear that such a policy was inadequate to deal with the problems generated by an industrialized market economy.

As Polanyi (1944:130-50) has shown, the life span of the pure self-regulating market was a short one, and by the late nineteenth century the state was already taking a variety of measures to mitigate the consequences of such an economic system. It was soon apparent that welfare expenditures were necessary not only to maintain discipline in the labour force, but also for the maintenance of social harmony and to mute potential civil disorder. Bismarck was among the first to recognize such a need with his invention of compulsory old-age insurance. As Heclo (1974:291) notes with respect to the introduction of old-age assistance in Britain and Sweden, these programs "were seen as a palliative technique to prevent social unrest and diminish the appeal of socialism".

This shift of emphasis from deterrence to relief was already apparent in the institutional sector of late nineteenth-century Canada where institutions were increasingly seen as "houses of refuge" for the destitute elderly and the sick. The inspector of institutions for the Province of Ontario wrote in 1884 (cited by Splane, 1965:96-97):

> As regards these Refuges, there is really nothing much to be said...
> except that in a quiet way they relieve a great deal of distress and afford
> places where many of the aged and infirm can pass away the last years
> of their lives in comparative peace and comfort.

As Splane (1965:97) comments, there was little indication of a desire to
operate such institutions in the spirit of "less eligibility" by this point in time.

The shift from deterrence to relief was no doubt a significant one from
the point of view of those elderly individuals who actually entered the
various "houses of refuge". It is clear, however, that until the post-Second
World War era such institutions were designed to harbour only the most
destitute segments of the aging population and were hardly considered
appropriate for the aging members of an emerging middle-class society.
These institutions continued to be viewed as "homes for the poor" rather
than as "homes for the aged" or "nursing homes". Social welfare in general
continued to be viewed as "charity" for the destitute rather than as a "right"
of citizenship (Herman, 1971).

It was precisely such a shift which occurred after the Second World
War, facilitated in large measure by the "medicalization" of the institution.
Poverty as such was to be handled once again by "outdoor relief", i.e., old-
age pensions and assistance programs. Institutions increasingly assumed the
function of caring for the medically indigent, a category covering almost the
entire spectrum of the aging population once the diseases of old age begin to
take their toll. In its most recent form, then, institutional welfare has
changed from being primarily a form of poor-relief for the most marginal
sectors of the elderly population to something more akin to "social insurance"
against the risks of sickness and disability which are likely to strike all
sectors of the aging population including the aging members and parents of
the new middle class. In the contemporary period, institutional care for the
elderly has become another part of the bureaucratic organization of the
middle-class life cycle. Despite its affluence, the new middle class is usually
ill-equipped to care for aging family members; whether this be in terms of
financial and housing resources or the capacity and time to provide the
elderly with the personal care and medical services they require. As a result,
the responsibility of caring for the aged has shifted from the family to the
state. How might we expect the modern welfare state to exercise this
responsibility?

First, it is important to recognize that the problems of advanced
industrial capitalism are not those of nascent industrial capitalism. Whereas
nineteenth-century social-welfare policy was designed to drive workers into
the labour force, twentieth-century welfare policy for the aged has been

more often designed to induce older workers to leave the labour force. Expanded social security for the aged has been used as a key strategy to reduce unemployment rates during periods of economic decline by encouraging older workers to leave the work force and by legitimating obligatory retirement policies (Kreps, 1976:279). As involuntary retirement became a normal part of the middle-class life cycle, the level of inducements had to be raised accordingly to include not only a minimally acceptable level of income in retirement but also the promise of access to personal and medical care when required. O'Connor (1973) has argued that such welfare provisions for the elderly have become indispensable for the continued functioning of capitalist economies. He writes (1973:138):

> ...the primary purpose of the system is to create a sense of economic security within the ranks of employed workers...and thereby raise morale and reenforce discipline. This contributes to harmonious management-labour relations which are indispensable to capital accumulation and the growth of production.

Systematic failure by the state to ensure an adequate level of care for the institutionalized elderly would clearly be counterproductive in this respect. Furthermore, while the aged themselves may lack the capacity to influence the provision of public goods and services, the same cannot be said of their middle-aged (and usually middle-class) offspring who tend to have a high degree of emotional involvement in the fate of their institutionalized parents (Brody, 1970:290, 294-96). Where institutional care for the elderly has failed to meet minimal standards of acceptability in the eyes of the larger community, it has become the object of intensive public scrutiny and widespread demands for reform. This would appear to be the case generally in the United States (see, for example, U.S. Senate Committee on Aging, 1974). In sum, in view of the broader social functions of welfare policy for the aged in advanced capitalist societies, it is to be expected that the quality of institutional care provided to the elderly will increasingly conform to the expectations and demands of the new middle class who, after all, have a reasonable chance of experiencing this fate themselves.

One caveat to the preceeding discussion is in order. Our analysis is based on the assumption that the provision of institutional care is determined primarily by policies emanating from the modern welfare state. In situations where institutional care is shaped primarily according to the market criterion of profits and/or where the regulatory power of government is weak, we might reasonably assume considerable client abuse and exploitation. Where the private sector tends to dominate the provision of goods and services to the elderly, a separate conflict tends to arise between producer and consumer, namely, that arising from the profit motive. For example, although the state is the major source of finance for institutional care in the United States, its involvement tends to be indirect as a result of the practice of simply "purchasing services" from private, profit-seeking entrepreneurs. As Mendelson (1974) has shown, subsequent regulation of these entrepreneurs tends to be weak. The problem is not the absence of regulations but the failure of government to enforce them. The abuses characteristic of the U.S. nursing home industry, however, are less likely to be found in those countries, including Canada, where a tradition of effective state intervention in the economy has tended to be stronger (Baum, 1977:67). Note, moreover, that this sort of conflict between producer and consumer is not one which arises from Goffman's model; that is, it is not inherent in the bureaucratic structure of the total institution as such but rather arises from the market and regulatory structure in which these institutions are embedded.

Implications for Policy

The practical results of the bureaucratic thesis as applied to institutional care for the elderly are significant, for if the model is correct then the welfare of the aged can be enhanced simply by closing down such institutions. Within this perspective it is not meaningful to talk of "good" nursing homes or "bad" nursing homes; it is not "quality of care" which is at issue but rather the nature of institutional life as such. This is a point which has not been missed by government administrators pressed to make budget cuts. The search for alternatives to institutional care has been primarily motivated by a desire to save money (Baum, 1977:72), and the myth of the "total institution" has frequently provided a legitimating cover for this exercise.[2] Among the consequences of this critique, therefore, is the implication that we should turn our attention away from blanket condemnations of the total institution and direct our energies to the much more difficult task of eliminating abuses which exist and improving the quality of care made available to the institutionalized elderly.

Equally important, from the point of view adopted here, is that we learn not to confuse the symptoms with the disease. The problems of the institutionalized elderly cannot be separated from the problems of aging in contemporary society more generally. The subordinate status of inmates in institutions for the elderly does not reflect a radical disjuncture from the "normal" situation of the elderly in the advanced capitalist nations. The social relations in such organizations simply reflect and reinforce those which prevail in the larger society. Accordingly, we should not delude ourselves by believing that the problems of the institutionalized elderly can be resolved simply at the level of the institution itself. Both analysis and praxis with respect to the elderly must begin at the societal level where such problems originate.

Notes

1. The issue here is methodological as well as theoretical. Determination of an effect, e.g., of institutionalization, requires a standard of comparison. A careful reading of Goffman's analysis suggests that the implicit standard of comparison being employed is the situation of the normal, middle-class, middle-aged individual in the larger society rather than the mentally disabled who are not institutionalized. Goffman (1961:x) himself acknowledges this as a potential source of bias in his analysis.

2. In personal conversation, an American psychiatrist indicated that among the major proponents of Goffman's thesis were the government bureaucrats charged with the closure of numerous American mental institutions during the sixties. Following the model to its logical conclusion, many of the mentally disabled were simply turned into the community without alternative forms of assistance. Not surprisingly, follow-up studies found many of these individuals in the skid row hotels and run-down cores of the large central cities. Ironically, those who were more fortunate found their way into nursing homes and institutions for the elderly.

25

A REFORMULATION OF BASIC ASSUMPTIONS ABOUT INSTITUTIONS FOR THE ELDERLY*

Margaret J. Penning
Department of Sociology
University of Manitoba

and

Neena L. Chappell
Department of Social and Preventive Medicine
University of Manitoba

As interest in gerontology grows among social scientists, a particular focus on the effects on institutionalization has been evident. Most of this literature compares institutional with community living for the elderly, while fewer studies compare institutional facilities. However, both types of studies tend to share the assumption that one major underlying dimension characterizes the institutional environment. This assumption of homogeneity is explicit, for example, in both the bureaucratic and social-welfare models. The former argues that the most influential element of such socio-cultural environments for those within them is the bureaucratic structure. The latter argues that the social-welfare or relief functions of such environments are of primary importance for those living within their confines.

Using the bureaucratic and social-welfare models, this essay provides a critique of the assumption of unidimensionality found within such approaches. It is argued that the complexity and variations among institutional settings for the elderly necessitate a multidimensional approach to adequately reflect the nature of their experience. In view of the current trend away from costly acute-care facilities and the search for alternative forms of living environments for the aged, an assessment of the adequacy of current approaches to institutionalization assumes primary importance so that comparative evaluations of alternative types of programs can be made.

*This is part of a larger work reported in M.J. Penning, *Institutionalization of the Elderly: An Assessment of Competing Perspectives*, unpublished M.A. thesis, University of Manitoba, 1978. This research was supported in part by a National Health Research Scholar award (6607-1137-48) to the junior author. The data for analyses were provided by the Manitoba Department of Health and Social Development, *Aging in Manitoba*, 1971.

An empirical test of these approaches is reported through an investigation of perceptions of well-being among a sample of elderly residents living in diverse institutional settings. The results are then discussed in terms of the greater applicability of a multidimensional approach. The implications of the findings suggest the potential for less costly home-care programs for the elderly and the need for continued research in this area.

The Bureaucratic and Social-Welfare Models of Institutionalization

The bureaucratic model, derived largely from Goffman's concept of total institutions (1961), argues that the process of bureaucratization leads to withdrawal, self-mortification, and sick-role identification. In this way, institutions are said to adversely affect the inmate's perceived well-being. The specific characteristics which are ultimately responsible for these consequences are (1961:6): the fact that all aspects of life are conducted in the same place under the same single authority; that all phases of the resident's daily activities are carried out in the immediate company of others, all of whom receive similar treatment; that all aspects of daily life are tightly scheduled and imposed from above through a system of explicit formal rulings and administered by a body of officials; and that the contents of such activities are regarded as rationally planned, supposedly designed to fulfil the goals of the particular institution. In other words, the primary fact of total institutions, according to this view, is the bureaucratic organization of a facility designed to administer to the needs of many people at one time.

To Goffman, the result of this bureaucratically organized system lies within the alterations it requires in the inmates' personal identities. These alterations begin to occur largely upon entrance to the institution where new inmates face gross changes in their moral careers, careers which are defined by "the progressive changes that occur in the beliefs that [they have] concerning [themselves] and significant others" (Goffman, 1960:454). Inmates are immediately confronted by a standardized system of defacement, a stripping process which will now characterize their careers. Increased affronts to the maintenance of one's personal identity through enforced routinization of activity, deference requirements, and verbal and other profanations, tend to result in the inmate's adopting the definition of self proffered by the particular institution.

The possibility of both inter-institutional variation and variation within the same institution is acknowledged within this perspective (1969:5, 21) but is assigned secondary significance. The main focus is upon the uniformities of the institutional experience for the inmates (1969:123). The bureaucratic model postulates that the institutional environment differs qualitatively from that of the community and that this difference is due to the bureaucratic nature of the former. Institutions for the elderly may vary. But this variation is seen to occur along the one dimension. (For other writings presenting a similar view see Gustafson, 1972; Freidson, 1970; Garfinkel, 1973.)

The social-welfare perspective similarly posits one underlying characteristic of the institutional experience. Contrary to the bureaucratic model, however, it postulates a different dimension and argues for a positive effect on the residents' identity and morale. This theory formalizes the traditional thinking behind the establishment of institutions for the aged, reiterating a belief in the medical, social, and economic benefits to be derived from these facilities. Only recently, and notably through the work of Myles (1977; 1978a; forthcoming), has this perspective been utilized as a theoretical framework to guide social science investigation (this framework is elaborated in Myles, this volume).

Myles notes that the position of the elderly within modern society is one characterized by gradual pauperization, increased illness with age, and social isolation due to reduced opportunities for social participation. Furthermore, he asserts that it is precisely these three conditions which the institution is both designed and equipped to deal with, thus concluding that the experience of institutionalization is beneficial rather than detrimental to the well-being of the elderly. He supports his argument with studies showing the most important correlates of life satisfaction and morale among the elderly to be, either directly or indirectly, poverty, illness, and social isolation. In other words, the key fact of institutionalization is the provision of relief.

Differing from the bureaucratic perspective, the social-welfare model argues that the same dimension is operative for both the institutionalized and community elderly. Illness, poverty, and social isolation are considered the primary factors within either environment, but it is argued that their impact is decreased within the institutional environment designed specifically for their relief. Therefore, although both of these theories characterize the institution in terms of a single defining characteristic, they clearly differ in terms of which dimension they assign paramount importance as well as their evaluation of institutions as "good" or "bad" for the residents. Neither theory argues for the relative importance of a number of dimensions for resident consequences within alternative institutional settings. This failure to take such variations into account and the consequent isolation of "institutionalization" as the solitary independent or explanatory variable necessarily assumes inter-institutional homogeneity.

It can be argued, however, that this assumption of similarity is particularly hazardous when studying institutions designed for the elderly. Facilities for the aged, for example, vary widely in terms of the populations which they are designed to serve. Contrary to Myles' (1977:27) assertion that all such settings are mechanisms for the relief of poverty, illness, and social isolation, others (such as Kahana, 1971; Tobin and Lieberman, 1976) suggest the service orientations of the various types of settings are more specific.

Whereas personal-care homes are designed to serve the mentally and physically capable who require security due to a variety of economic and/or social problems, nursing homes and chronic-disease hospitals have been designed to meet the needs of the physically ill aged requiring long-term, routine nursing care. Psychiatric hospitals, on the other hand, serve (at least in part) the mentally ill or "senile" aged. The levels of care provided by institutions for the elderly in Canada also vary (Myles, 1977:55 from *Statistics Canada*, unpublished data).

In addition, institutional settings for the elderly can be differentiated in terms of sponsorship and ownership. Whereas prisons and mental hospitals are largely governmentally sponsored, personal-care and nursing homes are more likely to be administrated by religious, fraternal, and legion organizations as well as by private individuals and larger business interests. Canadian statistics indicate that 45 percent of the institutionalized elderly in the country were in proprietary institutions in 1973. The remainder of the homes were sponsored by religious and governmental organizations (Statistics Canada, 1973).

A brief look at the past research identifies a host of different dimensions potentially useful when studying institutions (Scott, 1955; Coe, 1965; Bennett and Nahemow, 1968; Marshall, 1975; Wolk and Telleen, 1976). One of the most notable early attempts to integrate numerous dimensions was by Kleemeier (1961), who isolated three dimensions which he argued ultimately defined the lifestyle of elderly institutional residents: age segregation — non-segregation; the institutional — non-institutional dimension (imposition of rules, regulations, and sanctions); and the congregate — non-congregate dimension (such as group size, closeness of individuals, and a degree of privacy).

Based on a review of the literature and an attempt to refine Kleemeier's formulations, Pincus (1968) argued that a multidimensional approach would allow a greater degree of flexibility in exploring the interaction between characteristics of the residents and of the institution. He proposed four dimensions of the setting considered most relevant to a study of the aged institutionalized: the public — private dimension; the structured — unstructured dimension; the resource-sparse — resource-rich dimension; and the isolated — integrated dimension.

In sum, the basic tenets of two perspectives which attempt to account for the experience of institutionalization of the elderly within an unidimensional framework have been outlined. It was argued that the refusal by these perspectives to recognize inter-institutional heterogeneity prevents these attempts from accounting for possible differences among institutions caring for the elderly and the possibility that a number of factors are important to well-being. Available literature indicates that a more comprehensive approach may be warranted. The remainder of this essay deals with an empirical assessment of these competing perspectives.

Data and Methodology

The present study is based on a secondary analysis of the Aging in Manitoba study, conducted by the Manitoba Department of Health and Social Development in 1971 (Manitoba, 1973; see Havens, this volume). An area probability sample of 4,805 elderly persons (aged 65 and over) was obtained and interviewed. Respondents included 3,433 community residents and 911 institutional residents.[1] An asessment of the representativeness of the study sample when compared with both Manitoba and Canada has been reported elsewhere (Penning, 1978:93-102). In general the sample appears to approximate the populations of elderly in Manitoba and Canada in 1971. It is highly representative when sex, formal education, income, occupation, and marital status are compared. Slight age differences appeared, probably due to the inclusion of a relatively large proportion of the institutionalized elderly. (It should be noted that these data were collected prior to the implementation of universal home care in Manitoba.)

Because the present study has been limited to the identification of sources of variation among institutional environments, the current analyses were restricted to those living within institutions at the time of data collection. This restricted sample consisted of 911 elderly residents living in housing units (376 or 41 percent), hostels (191 or 21 percent), nursing homes (302 or 33 percent), and mental and extended-care hospitals (42 or 5 percent).

Perceived well-being was chosen as the dependent variable on the assumption that individuals themselves are the only proper judges of their own well-being (Neugarten, et al., 1961:134). It was operationalized using the Life Satisfaction Index 'A' (LSIA), labelled here as perceived well-being, rather than life satisfaction or morale, to reflect recent findings indicating that such concepts may properly be considered more general, summary constructs (Larson, 1978; see Adams, 1969 and Larson, 1978 for a discussion of the LSIA as a measuring instrument).

Numerous independent variables were chosen from the original data bank, to incorporate both the major underlying dimensions identified by the bureaucratic and social-welfare models, and potentially important dimensions for exploring the multidimensional model. Bureaucratization was operationalized using level of care within the facility and size of residence (similar items have been used by others, Bennett and Nahemow, 1965; Coe, 1965). Reflecting the observation that institutions offering a more intensive level of personal care should also reflect a higher degree of formal organization, residence types were ranked from low to high: housing units, hostels, nursing homes, and mental and extended-care hospitals. Using the total number of residents as an indicator of size, facilities were ranked from small to large.

Within the social-welfare model, the provision of relief was specified as the major underlying dimension. Because increasing levels of care can be interpreted as reflecting increasing amounts of relief provided, the level-of-care variable can also serve in assessing this perspective. Other variables reflected the type of relief. The following question measured perceived health: "For your age would you say that, in general, your health is excellent, good, fair, or poor?" Perceived economic well-being was operationalized for both the present and the future: "How do you think your income and assets currently (will) satisfy your needs (in future)?" The objective counterparts of the illness and economic relief variables were included. Two indicators, one measuring chronic health problems and the other measuring assistance with functional tasks, were used to represent objective health status.[2] Average monthly income was used as an indicator of actual economic well-being.

The Social Life Space Index adapted from Cumming and Henry (1961) measured social participation through the total frequency of interactions engaged in by the individual. Frequencies of interaction with others in the household, with friends, neighbours, and relatives, with people seen for specific purposes (such as storekeepers), and individuals seen in the course of work (for those employed) were included. The individual items have also been utilized to enable an examination of the relative importance of the various types of interactions for perceptions of well-being. Additional measures of social isolation included the presence or absence of children, grandchildren, brothers, sisters, and other relatives, as well as items on the respondent's marital status and proximity of nearest relatives.

The other variables included for an assessment of a multidimensional approach were: availability of privacy within the residence, opportunities for freedom of decision making and behaviour, the integration of the setting into the larger community, the availability of resources allowing for participation and interaction, the major service orientation of the residence, as well as age, sex, nationality, occupation, education, and length of residence.

To recapitulate, the purpose of the current analysis was to test the adequacy of unidimensional theories in accounting for the impact of institutionalization on elderly residents. Two unidimensional approaches were therefore chosen and their primary underlying dimensions operationalized. To further assess the adequacy of a multidimensional approach, numerous other variables derived from past research were included. Multiple regression analysis was chosen as the statistical technique which would allow such an assessment while incorporating numerous independent variables (Blau and Duncan, 1967; Cohen and Cohen, 1975; Kerlinger and Pedhazur, 1973).[3]

Correlates of Well-Being: A Reinterpretation to Replace Past Assumptions

The results are generally consistent with past research. Perceived health emerged as the most important predictor of perceptions of well-being (see Table 1), accounting for 7.9 percent of the variance ($p < .001$). The relationship between perceived health and perceived well-being indicated that the more positive the perceptions of health status, the more positive the overall evaluations of well-being (Myles, 1977a; Palmore and Luikart, 1972). The importance of perceptions of health among the elderly appears understandable in view of the decline of physical capacities which tends to accompany growing older. (The present research confirms earlier findings revealing that the individual's own evaluation of health is of greater importance to well-being than actual level of health or disability).[4]

The appearance of perceived future economic well-being as an important predictor of perceptions of well-being is also consistent with past research (Larson, 1978; Myles, 1977a). The more secure one feels about one's future (or current) financial situation, the higher one's evaluation of well-being. Perceived economic well-being appears to be of greater importance to general assessments of well-being than does the objective measure. In fact, income displayed very modest correlations with both perceived economic security (r = .06) and with perceived well-being (r = .11).

Also of importance to perceptions of well-being is the degree of autonomy involved in choosing the residence. Those who were more directly

TABLE 1:

REGRESSION COEFFICIENTS: PERCEPTIONS OF WELL-BEING

Independent Variables**	Standardized Betas	F*	P
Perceived Health	0.21	47.52	0.001
Frequency of Contact with Closest Friends	0.19	36.91	0.001
Nationality – Polish, Russian Ukrainian	−0.16	27.21	0.001
Degree of Autonomy in Choice of Residence	0.14	18.51	0.001
Perceived Future Economic Well-Being***	0.11	12.68	0.001
Frequency of Contact with Closest Relatives	0.11	12.25	0.001

*D.F. = 1 and 863

Overall F = 36.78; D.F. = 6 and 863; P = 0.001

R^2 = 0.20

The following were deleted because their standardized coefficients were less than 0.10 in the original analysis: age, sex, health, education, current and past occupation, income, marital status, length of residence, frequencies of contact with others in household, neighbours, specific people, and co-workers, the availability of social supports, the availability of privacy and freedom, the availability of resources, and integration into the community, service orientation, level of care provided, and size of the residence.

**Examination of interaction effects using analysis of variance revealed no significant interaction between the predictor variables.

***Perceived future and perceived current economic well-being correlated 0.71 revealing multicollinearity. Each emerges as an important predictor.

involved in choosing the residence were more satisfied than those who were either less involved or totally uninvolved. Just as choosing the place of residence appears to reflect individual autonomy or independence in decision making, perceptions of health status and economic self-sufficiency may be indicative of the extent to which the elderly individual is free from constraints (physical and economic) which impose limits on behaviour (Maxwell, *et al.*, 1972; Palmore and Luikart, 1972; Smith and Lipman, 1972; Wolk and Telleen, 1976).

Much of the literature on the correlates of perceptions of well-being among the elderly has found social participation to be highly related (Bley, *et al.*, 1972; Lemon, *et al.*, 1972; Palmore and Luikart, 1972; Tobin and Neugarten, 1961). Within the current analyses, the Social Life Space index was unrelated. However, two of the items, frequency of contact with closest friends and frequency of contact with closest relatives, emerged as significantly related. The fact that contact with staff, voluntary workers, and other organizational groups and activities were not significant suggests the greater importance of informal social interaction.

Finally, there is considerable debate in social gerontology over the importance of the various demographic variables as indicators of perceived well-being. While associations have been reported with sex, age, health, education, occupation, and income (Larson, 1978; Palmore and Luikart, 1972; Riley and Foner, 1968), these data fail to provide evidence of their importance. A single demographic variable — nationality — was an important predictor among these institutionalized elderly. It appears that being Polish, Russian, or Ukrainian is indicative of relatively low levels of well-being. This may be the result of a number of factors. Being of Polish, Russian, or Ukrainian descent was associated with residence in a high level of care facility ($r = .10$) and having a low level of education ($r = -.33$). Furthermore, 66 percent ($N = 60$) of this ethnic minority were still using the language of their country of national origin and they were more likely to have been interviewed in this language than were respondents of other nationalities (37 versus 15 percent). Finally, Havens and Thompson (1975) report that Polish, Russian, and Ukrainian (along with Asia/Oceanic) groups ranked unmet ethno-cultural needs as second or third highest compared with other groups who ranked them as seventh or eighth. In other words, the emergence of nationality appears to reflect the distinctiveness of certain groups as ethnic subcultures (encompassing friends, family, services and/or facilities in their own language, religion, or similar heritage).

These findings suggest that perceptions of well-being among the institutionalized elderly are contingent on a number of factors, not on a single underlying dimension. Specifically, personal independence (evidenced in the emergence of perceived health, perceived economic well-being, and autonomy in choosing the residence), informal social relationships, and nationality appear as the best predictors of this subjective variable. In addition, these factors together explain only 20 percent of the variance in the dependent variable, suggesting that other factors not included here may also be important to the well-being of the elderly, and further supporting the critique of a unidimensional approach.

These data also suggest a refutation of the bureaucratic and social-welfare models. Turning first to the bureaucratic model, neither measure of bureaucratization (level of care or size of residence) emerged as significant within this analysis. A simple cross-tabulation shows a weak, non-significant relationship of level of care with perceived well-being ($r = -.06$), although the direction is consistent with Goffman's tenets. Similarly, residence size did not emerge as an important predictor. Although there was a tendency for respondents living in the larger institutions to display lower evaluations of personal well-being than respondents within smaller institutions ($r = -.10$) this was, once again, not significant. Support is therefore not established for the view that increasing bureaucratization within institutions is directly responsible for lowered evaluations of well-being.

However, it might be argued that perceived health as an important predictor of well-being is indicative of an indirect effect of bureaucratization causing adoption of the patient or sick role. To ensure that differences in perceived health are not reflecting actual differences in health status within each of the level of care categories, it is necessary to look at the relationship between self-assessed health and levels of care, controlling for objective health. Such an analysis reveals no association between perceived health and level of care when controlling for either chronic illness, or assistance with functional tasks (not shown here).

In other words, although objective health is related to perceived health and perceived health is related to well-being, variation in bureaucratization (as measured by increased levels of care) has little or no role in altering this relationship. (Similarly, size of institution was unrelated to perceived health, $r = .02$). This finding contradicts the expectation that residents of institutions characterized by increasing bureaucratization will be more likely to define themselves as ill and consequently to adopt the sick role.

The finding that social participation (specifically contact with friends and with relatives) is related to well-being might also be interpreted as an indirect effect of bureaucratization if it can be shown that social participation decreases as levels of care increase, thus generating withdrawal as the totality of the institutional environment increases. A negative correlation ($r = -.13$) between level of care and frequency of contact with close friends and relatives ($r = -.19$) suggests that increasing levels of care are accompanied to some extent by decreasing amounts of contact. This is so despite the fact that increased levels of care are not indicative of decreased objective health status, a factor which may have otherwise served to explain reduced frequency of contact. In this instance, therefore, it can be argued that institutions indirectly detract from perceptions of well-being. The size of the institution, however, did not affect the level of social participation.

The social-welfare model, on the other hand, postulated the provision of relief as the major determinant of perceived well-being. Assuming that a greater measure of relief is evident in institutions offering higher levels of care, the results refute this claim. Contrary to the social-welfare model, there appeared to be a tendency for increased levels of care to be accompanied by decreased levels of perceived well-being.

Examination of the relationships between perceptions of well-being and social participation, perceptions of health, and economic well-being, also fail to support the social-welfare perspective. Although each emerged as an important predictor, none was found to increase with the level of care provided when other variables were controlled. Conversely, there was a tendency for perceptions of health and frequency of contact with friends and relatives to decrease with increased level of care, or increased provision of relief.

The results of the analysis did indicate that perceptions of health, perceptions of economic security, and contact with friends and relatives are all important to the institutionalized elderly person's perceived well-being. One may object, therefore, that although these "relief" functions are unrelated to level of care, they are nevertheless related to perceived well-being. We suggest a different interpretation: these variables are indicative of the importance of personal autonomy and independence. Perceptions of poor health have been related to identification with the sick role and adoption of dependence on others (Freidson, 1970; Illich, 1976; National Health and Welfare, 1978); economic resources are, of course, necessary for freedom from constraints in our society (Porter, 1965). It is suggested here that this notion of autonomy or independence is of more importance than that of relief since the latter can serve to diminish opportunities for independence (for example, within custodial-care settings).

If neither the bureaucratic nor the social welfare models adequately explain the experience of institutionalization for the elderly, is there an alternative approach? In the final section of this essay, the applicability of a multidimensional approach is elaborated.

Conclusions

The results clearly demonstrate the operation of more than one main factor within institutions (eg., independence, social participation, and nationality). Perceptions of well-being among the institutionalized do not appear to be conditioned by a single defining characteristic of the institutional environment. Neither bureaucratic organization nor the provision of relief are sufficient in explaining the experience of institutionalization for the elderly.

Indeed, in the present analysis, they are unimportant. Aside from autonomy in choice of residence, neither was support forthcoming for those environmental factors identified by Kleemeier (1961) and Pincus (1968).

These data do support a multidimensional approach, emphasizing those factors which enable the elderly to maintain independence, and informal social interaction. These factors suggest not only the inadequacy of current approaches but also the potential fallacy in distinguishing the institutional environment as inherently different from the rest of society. Forces operating within institutional environments cannot be divorced from the wider societal context. Those variables relevant to the quality of life for all societal members emerged as important sources of variation within these facilities.

While this comparability between institutional and community living obviously requires empirical testing, the implication of this interpretation is clear. It suggests that institutions for the elderly are not inherently "good" or "bad" in themselves. However, environments which do not maintain autonomy and social interaction for their residents will not provide accommodation satisfactory for well-being. A custodial and caring approach which develops dependence rather that independence will not achieve this goal either (National Health and Welfare, 1978). Recent studies of "successful" communities of the aged (see, for example, the case studies reported in Audain, 1973; Hochschild, 1973b) support this claim. However, to the extent that institutions provide an environment which will maintain or enhance a high quality of life, these data suggest they can be "good".

This interpretation is relevant within the current atmosphere of economic restraint and the growing awareness of increasing health costs in Canada (Lalonde, 1974). These findings present no rationale to maintain the elderly in costly institutional facilities if their quality of life can be maintained by less costly means. While additional research is required, if health and economic levels, as well as social participation, can be maintained at less expense (such as the provision of home-care services and day hospitals), major detriment to the elderly would be unanticipated. Comparisons with the community elderly and also with those receiving alternate forms of community service are needed to test these implications.

Finally, since perceptions of adequate health and economic status in addition to informal social interaction are of primary importance for these elderly, future research should investigate factors affecting these variables. These, of course, are factors of primary importance to all members of our society and while the aged often times require special services to meet their needs, this research suggests they may not be as distinctively different from the rest of us as is commonly assumed.

Notes

1. 461 respondents were excluded, primarily because proxies were utilized when necessitated by physical and/or mental incapacitation. Many of the variables included in the current analyses were attitudinal and proxies did not answer such questions on behalf of the respondent. A comparison of those interviewed by proxies and other respondents on selected characteristics has been reported elsewhere (Penning, 1978:160-163).

2. The following 14 problems were summed as the measure of chronic illness: heart and circulation, stroke, arthritis and rheumatism, palsy, eye trouble, ear trouble, dental problems, chest problems, stomach trouble, kidney trouble, diabetes, foot trouble, nerve trouble, skin problems.

Aid with the following functional tasks measured functional 'disability': going up and down stairs, getting about the house, going out of doors in good weather, going out of doors in any weather, getting in and out of bed, washing or bathing and grooming, dressing and putting on shoes, cutting toenails, feeding/eating, taking medication or treatment, nursing care, watching television, listening to the radio, reading or writing, using the telephone.

Both of these measures were used in Myles' (1977a) test of the social welfare theory. However, the interpretation of the second measure which he labelled functional disability, more accurately measures assistance currently received rather than actual incapacity. In other words, a person with less incapacity could nevertheless receive more assistance.

3. The use of multiple regression analysis with ordinal data is far from a resolved issue in the social sciences. See for example Kim (1975) and Borhnstadt and Carter (1971) for a discussion. However, when nonparametric correlation coefficients were compared with the pearson correlation matrix, significant differences were not evident.

4. For well-being and chronic illness, $r = .15$. For well-being and functional disability, $r = .17$. For perceived health and chronic illness, $r = .36$. For perceived health and functional disability, $r = .15$.

26

MARGINALITY AND MORALE*

Sheila M. Neysmith
Faculty of Social Work
University of Toronto

The relationship between living situations and sense of well-being among elderly persons will be examined in this essay. It is postulated that the influence of current environment on well-being can only be understood when viewed within the context of past events experienced by any group of individuals.

Factors Affecting Well-Being

Many conclusions about the negative effects of institutionalization on the elderly have been based on studies of residents whose physical and social well-being have been found to be lower than that of their community counterparts (Lieberman, 1969). Since most of the aforementioned research was cross-sectional in nature, it is difficult to tease out the effects of institutionalization from factors which may have precipitated the decision to enter an institution. In a recent longitudinal study, Tobin and Lieberman (1976) assessed a group of elderly persons before, during, and after they entered homes for the aged. Their work demonstrated that the greatest psychological damage occurred after the *decision* had been made to seek institutional care.

Perceived functional capacity has been found to correlate with measures of well-being (Larson, 1978), but the nature of the relationship is uncertain. It is most consistent at lower socioeconomic levels, but objective measures of health seldom correlate with either functional capacity or well-being scores. For instance, not all persons who live in protective settings have low morale (Adams, 1971; Edwards and Klemmach, 1973; Larson, 1978). It seems logical to conclude then, that an individual's sense of well-being results from the interaction of several factors. One would expect these would include personal competence, availability and use of social supports, economic resources, and present living arrangements.

Personal sense of well-being was utilized as an outcome measure in a study by the author of candidates for a foster-home program (Neysmith,

*The author was a faculty member of the School of Social Work, McGill University, Montreal, Quebec, at the time this study was undertaken. Jewish Family Services Social Service Centre, Montreal, Quebec, was the sponsor. Financial support was received from Grant #291 Ministère des Affaires Sociales, Gouvernement du Québec.

1978). The 170 respondents (103 female; 67 male) had been selected by social workers as potential users of this service because their functioning had deteriorated to the point where they were thought to require some kind of protective setting.[1] Thus, at least in the eyes of the referring social workers, these persons were seen as marginally functioning older people.

Sample Description

The respondents were at the extreme end of the age spectrum (70 percent were over 75 years), and their present incomes were low (65 percent were receiving the Old Age Security Supplement). Futhermore, since most of the household heads had been in semi-skilled trades or service during their working years, they had a history of low income. Over 70 percent of the women were widowed compared to 40 percent of the men. All were Jewish, and two-thirds immigrated to Canada before 1930. Most understood and spoke English, although many had difficulty reading it.

The respondents lived in various types of accommodations. The majority lived in their own apartments or homes (56 percent), or in hotel apartments which provided some services (21 percent). While most had resided in the area for many years, less than a third were at their present address five years previous to the study; although 30 percent lived alone at the time of the interview, only 15 percent had done so before their most recent move; similarly, 14 percent currently lived with spouse, compared to 40 percent earlier. These figures suggest that many respondents had undergone important, recent changes in lifestyle.

When people were asked if they wished to remain in their present accommodations, 62 percent replied in the affirmative. Both positive and negative reasons were probed. Most people could provide specific reasons for their choice. In addition, if contemplating any changes in their living situation, privacy[2] (especially an individual toilet) and the availability of home help would be key factors in their decision.

The average foster-home candidate had at least one child living in the city who was seen several times a month. Usually the adult child came to visit the respondent, seldom vice versa; telephone contact was more frequent. Overall involvement was estimated as moderate. Only half the respondents had even sporadic contact with a friend or other meaningful non-familial persons.

Perceived health, as measured by a functional capacity scale, indicated some deterioration, but all were mobile and able to care for most of their daily needs.[3] The social workers' perceptions of functional ability in both communication and self-maintenance categories corresponded very closely to the respondents' self perceptions (communication ability: $t=1.15$; $p=.245$; self-maintenance: $t=1.65$, $p=.102$).

Finally, morale among the group as a whole was extremely low. The highest possible score on the morale scale used to measure psychological well-being is 22.[4] The mean score for this group was 8.5 and the distribution was negatively skewed with 40 percent scoring lower than 5. Unlike previous studies (Larson, 1978) functional capacity did not correlate with morale ($r=-.049$, $p=.29$), neither did income. In addition, when these two variables, along with quantity and quality of family contacts, were regressed on morale scores, less than 5 percent of total variance was explained ($R^2 = .0421$). This is lower than in many studies (Larson, 1978).

Morale seemed much more related to attitude toward current living arrangements. Those who wished to remain in their present set-up, and gave positive reasons for their choice, were significantly higher in morale than those who were dissatisfied with their accommodations ($t = 2.62$, $p = .006$). Amongst the latter group, there was no significant difference in morale between those who wanted to move and those who felt they would remain where they were for lack of feasible alternatives. However, the latter group scored significantly lower on functional capacity than both those who were contented with their arrangements ($t = 2.85$, $p = .005$), and those who stated that they wanted to move ($t = 3.23$, $p = .002$).

Implications

If one accepts that a personal sense of well-being is a crucial ingredient in quality of life, then such uniform low morale in any group should be examined.

One of the qualifying factors in this study is that the sample represented a limited social strata. Consequently, there was little variation in SES. Studies indicate that health status may have a differential impact across income levels — being less crucial at higher income levels (Larson, 1978). Therefore, it may be that in this low-income group impaired functional capacity, as limited as it was, affected morale levels. This would be especially so in a community where home-care services are limited.

Dowd and Bengtson (1978) have suggested that regular contact with friends may be a characteristic of North Americans. Since the respondents in this study were foreign born, and a large percentage were female, the paucity of non-familial links may be culturally normative. However, even where family members were seen regularly, morale remained low. What we seem to be defining is a group of individuals with diminished health who both presently and in their past have had limited resources.

Lawton's (1973) ecological model of aging can provide a framework for examining current morale. In brief, the model postulates several environmental components which together interact with an individual's level of competence to affect adaptation to any situation. The ecosystem is seen as consisting of five components: (1) the individual, which includes perceptual and cognitive skills, and life experience; (2) the interpersonal environment, which consists of significant others, for example, family, friends, community persons; (3) the supra-personal environment, which refers to the modal characteristics of spatially clustered persons around the individual; (4) the social environment, which consists of social structures, norms, and institutions which characterize the milieu; (5) the physical environment, which comprises the non-personal, non-social residue of physical features. All are potential behavioural influences (Lawton, 1970).

The foregoing model provided the conceptual basis for choosing variables in this study. It helps to explain higher morale in individuals living in congregate facilities, especially the hotel apartments. (See Table 1). Since the respondents or their families paid for this type of accommodation, they were probably better off financially than most others in the sample. In these apartments certain services were available which could be demanded as a right. Most had private living quarters which assured privacy. Social contact was promoted through central eating facilities, daily maid service, and telephone contact by someone in the administration if a resident did not appear for several meals.

TABLE 1:
DISTRIBUTION OF RESPONDENTS AMONG VARIOUS TYPES OF ACCOMMODATION

Category	%	N
Apartment/House	52.3	94
Senior Citizen Apartment	4.7	8
Apartment Hotel	20.7	35
Roomer	3.5	6
Peer Apartment[a]	2.3	4
Foster Home[b]	7.7	13
Nursing Home	5.8	10

[a] A non-supervised group living arrangement.
[b] A home manager lived in the house

The lowest level of morale was amongst a group of some 30 individuals who were over some 75 years of age, of low income, widowed, mildly impaired and, for lack of alternatives, living alone in an apartment. Their contacts were few. This isolated group was perhaps the most precarious. They appeared mildly disengaged or discouraged about their ability to manipulate their present environment or control future events. These are to be compared to others with similar demographic profiles living in the community whose functional health was no better, but who seemed to be able to sustain themselves. It is important that future research examine this group both to determine what support networks they utilize and how these could be strengthened or supplemented to facilitate independent living. As Beattie (1970) pointed out almost a decade ago, the need for new conceptual frameworks in designing supportive environments is pressing.

Morale — The Present and Future as History

Well-being for the elderly, like all age groups, can be seen as a reflection of present status modified by personal history. High morale reflects some feeling of control over our lives; its decline is associated with losses which occur in an increasingly hostile environment. In stressful life situations social supports buffer or protect individuals from the pathological effects of these phenomena. Schooler (1969) found that the direction of the relationship between social relations and morale changed under different environmental conditions. He concluded that "the social processes of aging may be seen to go on because of, or in spite of, but hardly irrespective of the qualitative aspects of the environment." From a different perspective, Kahn (1978) has suggested that each person can be seen as moving through the life cycle meshed within a set of "significant others" to whom that person is related by the giving and receiving of social support. These he calls one's "convoy" of social support. Building on his work, one could hypothesize that as a person ages the composition of these buffers changes and may not be as effective. What is more, the make-up of the "convoy" may be very different depending on the age cohort and segment of society in which the individual has lived and worked (see Tindale and Marshall, this volume).

In conclusion, it can be argued that morale may be a measure of current psychological well-being, but more importantly, it is certainly a reflection of the accumulated effects of a lifetime of adapting to social, economic, and political pressures. These forces have worked longer on elderly people, the present environment is hostile for this quasi-status age group, and their personal resources are less. The result, not surprisingly, is a decreased perception of well-being.

Notes

1. For a thorough discussion of the goals of a protective service, see Ferguson (1978).

2. This is not to be confused with a wish for isolation. Four basic states of privacy, along with related functions, have been postulated: solitude, intimacy, anonymity, and reserve (Pastalan, 1970:89).

3. This instrument was obtained from the *Referral Form*, Assessment and Placement Service, Hamilton District Health Council, Hamilton, Ontario, p. A-3. The scale has two sections. Part A measures communication ability. A perfect score is 25; the mean score for this group was 21.9. Part B measures self-maintenance. A perfect score is 70; mean score for this group was 59.1. Many self-report measures of functional ability have been developed. For a review of some of these see Gibbon and Stevens (1977:23-26).

4. The *Philadelphia Geriatric Center Morale Scale* was utilized (Lawton, 1975). This particular measure was chosen because it was developed for use with the old-old. Also, it had been validated on a group of individuals with similar ethnic origins, who were living in semi-supervised settings. Details on the scale and its validation can be found in Lawton (1972).

BIBLIOGRAPHY

Adams, Bert N.
  1968a   Kinship in an Urban Setting. Chicago: Markham.
  1968b   "The middle-class adult and his widowed or still-married mother." Social
          Problems 16: 51-59.
Adams, David L.
  1969   "Analysis of a life satisfaction index." Journal of Gerontology 24(4): 470-4.
  1971   "Correlates of satisfaction among the elderly." The Gerontologist 11 (4, part 2):
          64-68.
Aitken, John
  1975   "Guilt is the enemy; grief the friend: surviving the death of a spouse." Weekend
          Magazine 25 (no. 3, January 18): 1-5.
Anderson, Michael
  1977   "The impact on family relationships of the elderly of changes since Victorian times
          in governmental income-maintenance provision." Pp. 36-59 in E. Shanas and
          M.D.Sussman (eds.), Family, Bureaucracy, and the Elderly. Durham, North
          Carolina: Duke University Press.
Anderson, Ronald, and John T. Hall
  1969   "Hospital utilization and cost trends in Canada and the United States." Medical
          Care 7 (6, Supplement): 4-22.
Andreopoulos, Spyros (ed.)
  1975   National Health Insurance: Can We Learn from Canada? Toronto: John Wiley.
Arensberg. C.M., and S.T. Kimball
  1940   Family and Community in Ireland. Cambridge, Mass.: Harvard University Press.
Arling, Greg
  1976   "The elderly widow and her family, neighbours, and friends." Journal of Marriage
          and the Family 38 (November): 757-68.
Atchley, Robert C.
  1971   "Retirement and leisure participation: continuity of crisis?" The Gerontologist
          1: 13-17.
  1972   The Social Forces in Later Life. Belmont, Calif: Wadsworth.
  1975   "Dimensions of widowhood in later life." The Gerontologist 5 (2): 176-78.
  1977   The Social Forces In Later Life. Second Edition. Belmont, Calif: Wadsworth.
Audain, M.J.
  1973   Beyond Shelter—A Study of NHA Financed Housing for the Elderly. Ottawa:
          Canadian Council on Social Development.
  1974   "Rethinking housing for the elderly." Paper presented at Canadian Council on
          Social Development Workshop on Housing for the Elderly in Winnipeg.
Auerbach, L., and A. Gerber
  1976   Implications of the Changing Age Structure of the Canadian Population
          (Perceptions 2). Ottawa: Science Council of Canada.
Bahr, Howard M., and T. Caplow
  1974   Old Men Drunk and Sober. New York: New York University Press.
Bairstow, D.
  1973   Demographic and Economic Aspects of Housing Canada's Elderly. Ottawa:
          Central Mortgage and Housing Corporation.

288

Ball, R.
    1977   "United States policy toward the elderly." In A.N. Exton-Smith and J. Grimley
             Evans (eds.), Current Issues in the United Kingdom in the Care of the Elderly.
             New York: Grune and Stratton.
Barber, C.L.
    1972   Welfare Policy in Manitoba. Winnipeg: Report to the Planning and Priorities
             Committee of the Province of Manitoba.
Barrett, Carol J.
    1978   "Sex differences in the experience of widowhood." Paper presented at the
             American Psychological Association Annual Meeting in Toronto.
Barro, Robert
    1977   "Social security and private saving—evidence from the U.S. time series."
             Mimeograph. University of Rochester.
Barron, Milton L.
    1953   "Minority group characteristics of the aged in American society." Journal of
             Gerontology 8: 477-82.
Baum, Daniel J.
    1974   The Final Plateau: The Betrayal of our Older Citizens. Toronto: Burns and
             MacEachern.
    1977   Warehouses for Death: The Nursing Home Industry. Don Mills: Burns and
             MacEachern.
Bayne, J.R.D.
    1978   "Health and care needs of an aging population." Paper prepared for the National
             Symposium on Aging in Ottawa.
Beale, Calvin L.
    1976   "A further look at nonmetropolitan population growth since 1970." American
             Journal of Agricultural Economics 58 (5): 953-58.
Beattie, Walter M., Jr.
    1970   "The design of supportive environments for the life-span." The Gerontologist 10
             (3): 190-93.
Becker, Howard S.
    1964   Outsiders. Glencoe Ill.: The Free Press.
Becker, Howard S., Blanche Geer, Everett C. Hughes and Anselm Strauss
    1961   Boys in White. Chicago: University of Chicago Press.
Becker, Howard S., and Anselm Strauss
    1956   "Careers, personality and adult socialization." American Journal of Sociology 62:
             253-63.
Begin, Monique
    1978   "Federal social policies on aging." Address by the federal Minister of Health and
             Welfare to the Canadian Association on Gerontology in Edmonton.
Bendix, R.
    1956   Work and Authority in Industry. New York: Harper and Row.
Bengtson, Vern L.
    1973   The Social Psychology of Aging. Indianapolis: Bobbs-Merrill.
Bengtson, Vern L., and Neal E. Cutler
    1976   "Generations and intergenerational relations: perspectives on age groups and
             social change." Pp. 130-59 in Robert H. Binstock, Ethel Shanas and Associates
             (eds.), Handbook of Aging and the Social Sciences. New York: Van Nostrand
             Reinhold.
Bennett, Ruth G.
    1963   "The meaning of institutional life." The Gerontologist 3(3): 117-25.
    1970   "Social context—a neglected variable in research on aging." Aging and Human
             Development 1: 97-116.

Bennett, Ruth G., and Lucille Nahemow
  1965   "Institutional totality and criteria of social adjustment in residences for the aged."
          Journal of Social Issues 21 (October): 44-76.
Berardo, Felix M.
  1967   Social Adaptation to Widowhood Among a Rural-Urban Aged Population.
          Washington Agricultural Experimental Station Bulletin 689 (December).
  1970   "Survivorship and social isolation: the case of the aged widower." The Family
          Coordinator 19 (1): 11-25.
Bernard, Jessie
  1972   The Future of Marriage. New York: World.
Berry, E., and M.L. Cameron
  1973   "A study of needs of senior citizens in the Comox Valley." Health Unit Summer
          Student Program.
Blalock, Hubert M.
  1967   Towards a Theory of Minority-Group Relations. New York: John Wiley.
Blau, P.M., and O.D. Duncan
  1967   The American Occupational Structure. New York: John Wiley.
Blau, Zena S.
  1961   "Structural constraints on friendships in old age." American Sociological Review
          26: 429-39
  1973   Old Age in a Changing Society. New York: New Viewpoints.
Blauner, Robert
  1969   "Internal colonialism and ghetto revolt." Social Problems 16: 393-408.
Bley, N.B., et al
  1972   "Characteristics of aged participants and non-participants in age-segregated
          leisure programs." The Gerontologist 12: 368-70.
Blood, Robert O., Jr. and Donald M. Wolfe
  1960   Husbands and Wives. Glencoe, Ill.: The Free Press.
Blumer, Herbert
  1969   Symbolic Interaction. Englewood Cliffs, N.J.: Prentice-Hall.
Bock, E. Wilbur
  1972   "Aging and suicide: the significance of marital, kinship and alternative relations."
          The Family Coordinator 21: 71-79.
Borhnstadt, G.W., and T.M. Carter
  1971   "Robustness in agression analysis." Sociological Methodology 3: 118-46.
Breen, Leonard Z.
  1960   "The aging individual." In Clark Tibbits (ed.), Handbook of Social Gerontology.
          Chicago: University of Chicago Press.
Brim, Orville, Jr.
  1976   "Major contributions to theories of the male mid-life crisis." The Counseling
          Psychologist 6 (1): 2-9.
Brody, Elaine M.
  1970   "Congregate care facilities and mental health of the elderly." Aging and Human
          Development 4: 279-320.
  1973   "A million Procrustean beds." The Gerontologist (Winter): 430-35.
Brody, Elaine M., and Stanley J. Brody
  1974   "Decade of decision for the elderly." Social Work 9 (5): 546.
Broverman, Inge K., et al
  1972   "Sex-role stereotypes: a current appraisal." Journal of Social Issues 28: 59-78.
Bryden, K.
  1974   Old Age Pensions and Policy-Making in Canada. Montreal: McGill-Queen's
          University Press.

Burch, Ernest
   1975   Eskimo Kinsmen: Changing Family Relationships in Northwest Alaska. New
           York: West Publishing Company (American Ethnological Society Monograph
           No. 59).
Byerts, T., et al
   1972   "Transportation." The Gerontologist 12 (2—summer): 11-16.
Cain, Leonard D., Jr.
   1964   "Life course and social structure." Pp. 272-309 in Robert E.L. Farris (ed.),
           Handbook of Modern Sociology. Chicago: Rand, McNally.
   1967   "The AMA and the gerontologists: uses and abuses of 'a profile of the aging:
           I.S.A.'" Pp. 78-114 in G. Sjoberg (ed.), Ethics, Politics and Social Research.
           Cambridge, Massachusetts: Schenkman.
Caine, Lynn
   1974   Widow. New York: Wm. Morrow.
Canada, Government of
   1970   Income Security and Social Services: Government of Canada Working Paper on
           the Constitution. Ottawa: Queen's Printer.
   1971   "Labour force and individual income." Census 3 (pt. 1): 2-1, 2.2.
   1973   The Canada Yearbook, 1973. Ottawa: Information Canada.
Canadian Council on Social Development
   1973   Beyond Shelter. Ottawa: The Canadian Council on Social Development.
   1973   Social Security for Canada: A Report of the Task Force on Social Security.
           Ottawa.
Canadian Life Insurance Association
   1977   Canadian Life Insurance Facts
Canadian Radio-Television Commission
   1974   Reaching the Retired. Ottawa: Information Canada.
Cape, Elizabeth
   1978   "Going downhill: responses to terminality among the institutionalized aged ill."
           Paper presented at 7th scientific and educational meeting, Canadian Association
           on Gerontology in Edmonton.
Cape, R.D.T., et al
   1977   "Square pegs in round holes: a study of residents in long-term institutions in
           London, Ontario." Canadian Medical Association Journal 117: 1284-87.
Capital Region Planning Board of B.C.
   1969   Retirement in the Capital Region of B.C. Victoria.
Carp, Frances M.
   1971   "Walking as a means of transportation for retired people." The Gerontologist 11
           (2, pt. 1): 104-11.
Central Mortgage and Housing Corporation
   1972   Housing the Elderly. Ottawa.
Chappell, Neena L.
   1975   "Awareness of death in the disengagement theory: a conceptualization and an
           empirical investigation." Omega 6 (4): 325-43.
   1978   "Senility: problems in communication." Pp. 65-86 in Jack Haas and William
           Shaffir (eds.), Shaping Identity in Canadian Society. Scarborough: Prentice-Hall
           of Canada.
Cheek, N., and W. Birch
   1976   The Social Organization of Leisure In Human Society. New York: Harper and
           Row.

Chen, Mervin Y.T.
1974   The Influence of Social Structure, Technology, and Background Factors on
        Supervisory Style in Industry. Unpublished doctoral dissertation. McMaster
        University.
Chene, B., A. Davis, G. Greene and P. Trott
1977   A Survey of the Needs of the Senior Citizens in the Parkdale Community.
Chodorow, Nancy
1971   "Being and doing: a cross-cultural examination of the socialization of males and
        females." Pp. 173-97 in Vivienne Gornick and Barbarak Moran (eds.), Woman in
        Sexist Society. New York: Basic Books.
Cicourcel, A.V.
1968   The Social Organization of Juvenile Justice. New York: John Wiley.
Ciffin, S., and J. Martin
1977   Retirement in Canada. Volume I: When and Why People Retire. Staff Working
        Paper 7704. Ottawa: Policy Research and Long Range Planning, Health and
        Welfare Canada.
Clark, J., and N. Collishaw
1975   "Canada's older population." Staff paper. Ottawa: Long Range Health Planning,
        National Health and Welfare.
Clark, Margaret
1967   "The anthropology of aging: a new area for studies of culture and personality."
        The Gerontologist 7 (1): 55-64.
Clark, Margaret, and Barbara Anderson
1967   Culture and Aging. Springfield, Ill.: Charles C. Thomas.
Coburn, David, Carl D'Arcy, Peter K.M. New and George M. Torrance
1980   Health and Canadian Society: Sociological Perspectives. Toronto: Fitzhenry and
        Whiteside.
Coe, R.M.
1965   "Self-conception and institutionalization." Pp. 225-243 in A.W. Rose and
        R.W. Peterson (eds.), Older People and Their Social World. Philadelphia:
        F.A. Davis.
Cohen, J.. and R. Cohen
1975   Applied Multiple Regression Correlation Analysis for the Behavioral Sciences.
        New York: John Wiley.
Collins, Kevin
1978   Women and Pensions. Ottawa: The Canadian Council on Social Development.
Collins, Randall
1975   Conflict Sociology: Toward an Explanatory Science. New York: Academic Press.
Commission on Chronic Illness
1966   Care of the Long-Term Patient. Vol. 2 of Chronic Illness in The United States.
        Cambridge, Mass.: Harvard University Press.
Connor, Walter D.
1972   "The manufacture of deviance: the case of the Soviet purge, 1936-38." American
        Sociological Review 37: 403-13.
Copp. T.
1974   The Anatomy of Poverty: The Condition of the Working Class in Montreal.
        Toronto: McClelland and Stewart.
Corsa, Leslie, Jr., and Deborah Oakley
1971   "Consequences of population growth for health services in less developed
        countries—an initial appraisal." Pp. 368-402 in Rapid Population Growth.
        Prepared by a Study Committee of the Foreign Secretary, National Academy of
        Sciences. Baltimore and London.

292

Counts, David
1977   "The good death in Kaliai: preparation for death in western New Britain." Omega
        7 (no. 4): 367-72.
Crouch, B.M.
1972   "Age and institutional support: perceptions of older Mexican Americans." Journal
        of Gerontology 27: 524-29.
Crozier, M.
1971   The World of the Office Worker. Chicago: University of Chicago Press.
Cumming, E., and W.E. Henry
1961   Growing Old. New York: Basic Books.
Currie, E.P.
1968   "Crimes without criminals: witchcraft and its control in Renaissance Europe."
        Law & Society 3: 7.
Curtin, Sharon
1972   Nobody Ever Died of Old Age. Boston: Little, Brown.
Davis, Ann E.
1969   "Women as a minority group in higher education." American Sociologist 4: 95-99.
D'Arcy, Carl
1974   "Social contingencies and mental illness: explicating a conceptual framework."
        Mimeographed. Saskatoon: Psychiatric Research Unit, University Hospital.
1976   "The contingencies and mental illness in societal reaction theory: a critique.
        Canadian Review of Sociology and Anthropology 13 (1): 43-54.
Dawe, A.
1970   "The two sociologies." British Journal of Sociology 21: 207-18.
Dean, John P., Robert L. Eichhorn and Lois R. Dean
1967   "Establishing field relations." Pp. 281-83 in John T. Doby (ed.), An Introduction to
        Social Research. Second edition. New York: Appleton-Century-Crofts.
de Beauvoir, Simone
1953   The Second Sex. New York: Alfred Knopf
1961   The Second Sex. New York: Bantam
1972   Old Age. London: Weidenfeld and Nicholson.
De Carlo, T.J.
1974   "Recreation participation patterns and successful aging." Journal of Gerontology
        29: 416-22.
De Jong, Gordon F., and Ralph R. Sell
1977   "Population redistribution, migration, and residential preferences." Annals of the
        American Academy of Political and Social Sciences 429 (January): 130-44.
Denton, Frank T.
1970   The Growth of Manpower in Canada. Ottawa: Statistics Canada.
Denton, Frank T., and Sylvia Ostry
1967   Historical Estimates of the Canadian Labour Force. Ottawa: Statistics Canada.
Denton, Frank T., and Byron G. Spencer
1972   Economic-Demographic Interactions and Long Swings: Some Experimental
        Results. McMaster University Department of Economics, Working Paper No.
        72-15.
1973a   "A simulation analysis of the effects of population change on a neoclassical
        economy." Journal of Political Economy 81: 356-75.
1973b   On the Use of the Gompertz Function in the Analysis and Projection of Fertility
        Trends. McMaster University Department of Economics. Working Paper No.
        73-02.
1973c   Fertility, Income, and the Labour Force Participation of Married Women.
        McMaster University Department of Economics. Working paper No. 73-05.

1974a   "Demographic consequences of changing cohort fertility patterns: an investigation using the Gompertz function." Population Studies 28: 309-18.

1974b   Household and Population Effects on Aggregate Consumption. McMaster University Department of Economics. Working Paper No. 74-08.

1975   Population and the Economy. Toronto: D.C. Heath Ltd.

1977   "Some economic and demographic implications of future population change." McMaster University Department of Economics. Working Paper No. 77-14.

1979   "Some economic and demographic implications of future population change." Journal of Canadian Studies 14 (no. 1): 81-93.

Dixon, W.J., and F.J. Massey

1969   Introduction to Statistical Analysis. Third Edition. New York: McGraw Hill.

Dohrenwend, B.P., and B.S. Dohrenwend

1965   "The problem of validity in field studies of psychological disorder." Journal of Abnormal Psychology 70: 52-69.

Dowd, James J., and V.L. Bengtson

1978   "Aging in minority populations: a study of the double jeopardy hypothesis." Journal of Gerontology 33 (3): 427-36.

Dubin, R., et al

1965   Leadership and Productivity. San Francisco: Chandler.

Dulude, Louise

1978   Women and Aging: A Report on the Rest of our Lives. Ottawa: Advisory Council on the Status of Women.

Dumazedier, J.

1974   Sociology of Leisure. Amsterdam: Elsevier.

Edwards, John N., and D.L. Klemmach

1973   "Correlates of life satisfaction: a re-examination." Journal of Gerontology 28 (4): 497-502.

Eichler, Margrit

1973   "Women as personal dependents." Pp. 36-55 in Marylee Stephenson (ed.), Women in Canada. Toronto: New Press.

Environics Research Group

1972   State of the Art: Research on the Elderly, 1964-1972. Ottawa: Central Mortgage and Housing Corporation.

Epstein, Cynthia Fuchs

1973   "Black and female: the double whammy." Psychology Today 7 (3): 57-61,89.

Erikson, E.

1959   Identity and the Life Cycle. Psychological Issues 1: 1. Monograph 1.

Erikson, K.T.

1957   "Patient role & social uncertainty—a dilemma of the mentally ill." Psychiatry 20: 263-74.

Estes, C.L., and Howard E. Freeman

1976   "Strategies of design and research for intervention." Pp. 536-60 in Robert H. Binstock, Ethel Shanas and Associates (eds.), Handbook of Aging and the Social Sciences. New York: Van Nostrand Reinhold.

Etzioni, A.

1961   A Comparative Analysis of Complex Organizations. New York: Free Press.

Evans, Jocelyn

1971   Living with a Man Who Is Dying: A Personal Memoir. New York: Taplinger.

Fakhruddin, A.K.M., et al

1972   "A five year outcome of discharged chronic psychiatric patients." Canadian Psychiatric Association Journal 17: 433-35.

Feidler, F.E.
   1967   A Theory of Leadership Effectiveness. New York: McGraw-Hill.
Feldstein, Martin
   1974   "Social security, induced retirement and aggregate capital accumulation." Journal
          of Political Economy 82 (5): 905-26.
Ferguson, Elizabeth J.
   1978   Protecting the Vulnerable Adult. Ann Arbor, Michigan: The Institute of
          Gerontology, Wayne State University.
Fernberger, Samuel W.
   1948   "Persistence of stereotypes concerning sex differences." Journal of Abnormal and
          Social Psychology 43: 97-101.
Fischer, David Hackett
   1977   Growing Old in America. Oxford: University Press.
Fleishman, E.A., E.F. Harris and H.E. Burtt
   1955   Leadership and Supervision in Industry. Ohio State Business Education Research
          Monograph.
Flett, Darlene
   1976   "Health status of elderly people in public housing." Research project submitted to
          School of Health Administration, University of Ottawa, in partial fulfillment of
          requirements for a Master's degree in Health Administration.
Foner, Anne
   1974   "Age stratification and age conflict in political life." American Sociological
          Review 39 (April): 187-96.
   1975   "Age in society: structure and change." Pp. 13-34 in Anne Foner (ed.), Age in
          Society. Beverly Hills: Sage.
   1978a "Age stratification and the changing family." American Journal of Sociology 83,
          supplement.
   1978b "Age stratification and the changing family." Pp. 340-65 in John Demos and
          Sara Spence Boocock (eds.), Turning Points: Historical and Sociological Essays
          on the Family. Chicago: University of Chicago Press.
Foner, Anne, and David Kertzer
   1978   "Transitions over the life course: lessons from age-set societies." American
          Journal of Sociology 83 (5): 1081-1104.
Foote, Nelson
   1960   "The old generation and the new." Pp. 1-24 in E. Ginzberg (ed.), The Nation's
          Children. Volume 3: Problems and Prospects. New York: Columbia University
          Press.
Francher, J. Scott
   1973   "It's the Pepsi generation: accelerated aging and the television commercial."
          International Journal of Aging and Human Development 4 (3): 245-55.
Francis, E.K.
   1951   "Minority groups—a revision of concepts." British Journal of Sociology 2: 219-29,
          254.
Freidson, E.
   1970   Profession of Medicine. New York: Dodd Mead.
Freuchen, Peter
   1961   Peter Freuchen's Book of the Eskimos. Cleveland: World.
Friedman, R.M., and S.S. Tobin
   1974   "Home maintenance of the future impaired elderly." Paper delivered at
          Gerontological Society 27th Annual Scientific Meeting.

Galbraith, J.K.
1964   The Scotch. Toronto: McClelland and Stewart.
Garfinkel, H.
1973   "Conditions of successful degradation ceremonies." Pp. 89-94 in E.W. Rubington
        and M.S. Weinberg (eds.), Deviance: The Interactionist Perspective. New York:
        Macmillan.
Garrett, Gerald R., and Howard M. Bahr
1976   "The family background of skid row women." Signs: Journal of Women in Culture
        and Society 2 (2): 369-81.
Garrett, L., and M. Hill
1973   Community Care for Seniors Study. Vancouver: Social Planning and Review
        Council of B.C.
Gerber, I., R. Rusalim, N. Hannon, D. Battin and A. Arkin
1975   "Anticipatory grief and aged widows and widowers." Journal of Gerontology
        30: 225-29.
Gerson, Lowell W., and James K. Skipper
1972   "A conceptual model for the study of the health action process." Canadian
        Journal of Public Health 63: 477-85.
Gibbon, M., and E. Stevens
1977   "Nurse influence on the quality of life of elderly patients with chronic illness."
        Mimeo. Hamilton, Ont.: Victorian Order of Nurses.
Giddens, A.
1971   Capitalism and Modern Social Theory. Cambridge: Cambridge University Press.
Glaser, Barney G., and Anselm L. Strauss
1968   Time for Dying. Chicago: Aldine.
1971   Status Passage. Chicago: Aldine, Atherton.
Goffman, Erving
1961   Asylums. Garden City, N.Y.: Doubleday Anchor.
1963   Stigma. Englewood Cliffs, N.J.: Prentice-Hall.
1969   The Presentation of Self in Everyday Life. Garden City, N.Y.: Doubleday Anchor.
Goldfarb, Charles
1969   "Patients nobody wants: skid row alcoholics." Diseases of the Nervous System 31
        (4): 247-81.
Goode, W.J.
1963   World Revolution in Family Patterns. Glencoe, Ill.: Free Press.
Gordon, C., C. Gaitz and J. Scott.
1973   "Value priorities and leisure activities among middle-aged and older anglos."
        Diseases of the Nervous System 34: 13-26.
Gordon, Milton M.
1964   Assimilation in American Life. New York: Oxford University Press.
Gouldner, Alvin
1970   The Coming Crisis of Western Sociology. New York: Avon.
Granatstein, J.I., and Peter Stevens (eds.)
1972   Forum: Canadian Life and Letters, 1920-70. Toronto: University of Toronto Press.
Granovetter, Mark S.
1973   "The strength of weak ties." American Journal of Sociology 78 (6): 1360-80.
Grayson, L.M., and Michael Bliss (eds.)
1971   The Wretched of Canada. Toronto: University of Toronto Press.
Grimley Evans, J., and A.N. Exton-Smith (eds.)
1977   Current Issues in the United Kingdom in Care of the Elderly. New York: Grune
        and Stratton.

Gross, M.J.
    1978   Present and Future Costs of Health Services to the Aged in Ontario. Masters
              Thesis, Department of Community Health, University of Toronto.
Gubrium, Jaber F.
    1973   The Myth of the Golden Years: A Socio-Environmental Theory of Aging.
              Springfield: Charles C. Thomas.
Gubser, Nicholas J.
    1965   The Nunamiut Eskimo: Hunters of Caribou. New Haven: Yale University Press.
Guemple, Lee
    1969   Human Resource Management: The Dilemma of the Aging Eskimo. Sociological
              Symposium 2: 59-74.
Gustafson, E.
    1972   "Dying: the career of the nursing home patient." Journal of Health and Social
              Behavior 13: 222-35.
Gutman, Gloria M.
    1975   Extent of implementation of recommendations contained in "Housing the Elderly"
              in ten recently completed projects in British Columbia. Ottawa: Central Mortgage
              and Housing Corporation and U.B.C. Centre for Continuing Education.
    1977   "Motivations and pathways into multi-level versus traditional retirement housing."
              Paper presented at Annual Meeting of Canadian Psychology Association in
              Vancouver.
    1978   "Issues and findings relating to multi-level accommodation for seniors." Journal of
              Gerontology 33, 592-600.
Haas-Hawkings, Gwen
    1978   "Intimacy as a moderating influence on the stress of loneliness in widowhood."
              Essence 2 (4): 249-58.
Hacker, Helen Mayer
    1951   "Women as a minority group." Social Forces 30: 60-69.
    1974   "Women as a minority group: twenty years later." Pp. 124-34 in Florence
              Denmark (ed.), Who Discriminates against Women? Beverly Hills: Sage.
Hall, Richard
    1977   Organizations: Structure and Process. Second edition. Englewood Cliffs:
              Prentice-Hall.
Hannochko, F., et al
    1974   Operation New Roof — A Study of the Housing of Senior Citizens in Edmonton: A
              New Horizons Project.
Hare, E.H., and J.K. Wing (eds.)
    1970   Psychiatric Epidemiology. London: Oxford University Press for the Nuffield
              Provincial Hospital Trust.
Hareven, Tamara K.
    1977   "Family time and industrial time: family and work in a planned corporation town,
              1900-1924." Pp. 187-207 in T.K. Hareven (ed.), Family and Kin in Urban
              Communities, 1700-1930. New York: New View Points.
Harris, Louis, et al
    1976   The Myth and Reality of Aging in America. Washington, D.C.: National Council
              of the Aging.
Harvey, Carol D., and Howard M. Bahr
    1974   "Widowhood, morale, and affiliation." Journal of Marriage and the Family 36
              (February): 97-106.
Havens, Betty
    1977   "Social planning implications of needs assessment." Paper presented at the
              World Conference on Aging: A Challenge to Science and Social Policy in Vichy,
              France.

Havens, Betty, and E. Thompson
  1975   Research results: ethnic variations in needs of the elderly." Paper presented at the
          Canadian Association on Gerontology meetings in Toronto.
Havighurst, Robert J.
  1972   "Life-style and leisure patterns: their evolution through the life-cycle." Pp. 35-48 in
          Leisure In The Third Age. Paris: International Center For Social Gerontology.
  1973   "Social roles, work, leisure and education." Pp. 598-618 in C. Eisdorfer and
          M.P. Lawton (eds.), The Psychology of Adult Development and Aging.
          Washington, D.C.: American Psychological Association.
Havighurst, Robert J., and A. De Vries
  1969   "Life-styles and free time activities of retired men." Human Development 12: 34-54.
Havighurst, R.J., B.L. Neugarten and S.S. Tobin
  1968   "Disengagement and patterns of aging." Pp. 161-77 in Bernice L. Neugarten (ed.),
          Middle Age and Aging. Chicago: University of Chicago Press.
Hawkes, E.W.
  1916   The Labrador Eskimo. Canada Department of Mines, Geological Survey Memoir
          91. Anthropological Series No. 14. Ottawa: Government Printing Bureau.
Hays, H.R.
  1966   The Dangerous Sex. New York: Pocket Books.
Health and Welfare Canada
  1975   Hospitals and the Elderly—Present and Future Trends. Long Range Planning
          Branch. Ottawa.
  1976a   Basic Facts on Public Retirement Income Programs. Ottawa: Queen's Printer.
  1976b   Health Services for the Elderly. Final Report of a Working Group of the Federal-
          Provincial Advisory Committe on Community Health.
Heclo, H.
  1974   Modern Social Politics in Britain and Sweden. From Relief to Income
          Maintenance. New Haven: Yale University Press.
Hendricks, Jon, and C. Davis Hendricks
  1977   Aging in Mass Society: Myths and Realities. Cambridge, Mass.: Winthrop.
Henretta, John C., Richard T. Campbell and Gloria Gardocki
  1977   "Survey research in aging: an evaluation of the Harris survey." The Gerontologist
          17 (2): 160-67.
Herman, K.
  1971   "The emerging welfare state: changing perspectives in Canadian welfare policies
          and programs, 1867-1960." Pp. 131-41 in D.I. Davies and K. Herman (eds.), Social
          Space. Canadian Perspectives. Toronto: New Press.
Hewitt, J.
  1976   Self and Society. Boston: Allyn and Bacon.
Hobart, C.W.
  1975   "Active sports participation among the young, the middle-aged and the elderly."
          International Review of Sport Sociology 10 (3-4): 27-40.
Hochschild, Arlie Russell
  1973a   "A review of sex role research." American Journal of Sociology 78: 1011-29.
  1973b   The Unexpected Community. Englewood Cliffs. N.J.: Prentice-Hall.
  1975   "Disengagement theory: a critique and proposal." American Sociological Review
          40 (5): 553-69.
Hoffman, Adeline M. (ed.)
  1970   The Daily Needs and Interests of Older People. Springfield, Ill.: Charles C.
          Thomas.
Holmes, T.H., and R.J. Rahe.
  1967   "The social readjustment rating scale." Journal of Psychosomatic Research
          11: 213-18.

298

Horn, Michiel (ed.)
    1972   The Dirty Thirties. Toronto: Copp Clark.
Horney, Karen
    1972   "The dread of woman." In Nona Glazer-Malbin and Helen Youngelsen-Waehrer
            (eds.), Woman and the Man-Made World. Chicago: Rand MacNally.
Hughes, Everett C.
    1937   "Institutional office and the person." American Journal of Sociology 43
            (November): 404-13.
    1971   The Sociological Eye: Selected Papers. Chicago: Aldine, Atherton.
Illich, Ivan
    1976   Limits to Medicine, Medical Nemesis: The Expropriation of Health. London:
            Marion Boyers.
Ingram, Donald K., and John R. Barry
    1977   "National statistics on deaths in nursing homes: interpretations and implications."
            The Gerontologist 17 (4): 303-08.
Institute of Gerontology
    1974   No Longer Young — The Older Woman in America: Work Group Reports. Ann
            Arbor: Institute of Gerontology, University of Michigan — Wayne State University.
    1975   No Longer Young — The Older Woman in America: Proceedings of the 26th
            Annual Conference on Aging. Ann Arbor: Institute of Gerontology, University of
            Michigan-Wayne State University.
James, R.L.
    1964   Edmonton Senior Residents' Survey Report. Edmonton Welfare Council.
Jarvis, E.
    1855   Insanity and Idiocy in Massachusetts: Report to the Commission on Lunacy.
            Reprinted with a critical introduction by G.N. Grob. Cambridge: Harvard
            University Press, 1971.
Jarvis, George K.
    1972   "Canadian old people as a deviant minority." Pp. 605-27 in Craig L. Boydell, Carl
            F. Grindstaff and Paul C. Whitehead (eds.), Deviant Behavior and Societal
            Reactions. Toronto: Holt, Rinehart and Winston.
Jenness, Diamond
    1922   The Life of the Copper Eskimos. Report of the Canadian Arctic Islands. Ottawa:
            Government Printing Bureau.
Johnson, Gregory, and J. Lawrence Kamara
    1977-78 "Growing up and growing old: the politics of age exclusion." International Journal
            of Aging and Human Develpoment 8 (2): 99-110.
Johnson, Leo A.
    1977   Poverty in Wealth. Revised edition. Toronto: New Hogtown Press.
Kahana, E.
    1971   "Emerging issues in institutional services for the aging." The Gerontologist 2 (1):
            51-58.
Kahn, Robert L.
    1978   "Aging and social support." Paper presented at the Annual Meeting of the
            American Association for the Advancement of Science in Washington, D.C.
Kahn, Robert L., and Daniel Katz
    1953   "Leadership practices in relationship to productivity and morale." Pp. 612-28 in
            D. Cartwright and A. Zander (eds.), Group Dynamics: Research and Theory.
            Evanston, Ill.: Row, Peterson.
Kalbach, Warren W., and Wayne W. McVey, Jr.
    1976   "The Canadian family: a demographic profile." Pp. 94-108 in Lyle E. Larson, The
            Canadian Family in Comparative Perspective. Scarborough, Ontario: Prentice-
            Hall.

Kalish, Richard A.
  1975   Late Adulthood. Monterey, California: Brooks/Cole.
Kasl, S.V.
  1972   "Physical and mental health effects of involuntary relocations and institutionaliza-
          tion on the elderly—a review." American Journal of Public Health. 62 (3): 377-84.
Kastenbaum, Robert S., and S. Candy
  1973   "The four percent fallacy: a methodological and empirical critique of extended
          care facility program statistics." Aging and Human Development 4 (1): 15-21.
Katz, Daniel, N. Maccoby, G. Gurin and L.G. Floor
  1951   Productivity, Supervision and Morale among Railroad Workers. Franklin DeKlein.
Katz, D., N. Maccoby and N.C. Morse
  1950   Productivity, Supervision, and Morale in an Office Situation. Detroit: Darel Press.
Katz, S., T.D. Downs, H.R. Cash and R.C. Grotz
  1970   "Progress in development of the index of ADL." Gerontologist 10 (1, Part 1):
          20-30.
Katz, S., A. Ford, T. Downs, M. Adams and D. Rusby
  1972   Effect of Continued Care: A Study of Chronic Illness in the Home. Washington
          D.C.: U.S. Department of Health Education and Welfare, National Centre for
          Health Services Research and Development.
Katz, S., A.B. Ford, R.W. Moskiwitz, B.A. Jackson and M.W. Jaffe
  1963   "Studies of illness in the aged, the index of ADL: a standardized measure of
          biological and psychosocial function." Journal of the American Medical
          Association 185: 914-19.
Kerlinger, F.W., and E.J. Pedhazur
  1973   Multiple Regression and Behavioral Research. New York: Holt, Rinehart, and
          Winston.
Kidd, C.B.
  1962   "Misplacement of the elderly in hospital: a study of patients admitted to geriatric
          and mental hospitals." British Medical Journal 2: 1491.
Kim, J.
  1975   "Multivariate analysis of ordinal variables." American Journal of Sociology, 81 (2):
          261-98.
Kimmel, D.C
  1974   Adulthood and Aging. New York: John Wiley.
Kinloch, Graham C.
  1974   The Dynamics of Race Relations. New York: McGraw-Hill.
Kirkpatrick, Clifford
  1955   The Family. New York: Ronald.
Kitsuse, J., and A. Cicourcel
  1963   "A note on the use of official statistics." Social Problems 11: 131-39.
Kleemeier, Robert W.
  1961   "The use and meaning of time in special settings: retirement communities, homes
          for the aged, hospitals and other group settings." Pp. 273-308 in Kleemeier (ed.),
          Aging and Leisure. New York: Oxford University Press.
  1963   "Attitudes toward special settings for the aged." Pp. 101-21 in R.H. Williams,
          C. Tibbitts and W. Donahue (eds.), Processes of Aging, Volume I. New York:
          Atherton Press.
Kohl, Seena B.
  1976   Working Together: Women and Family in Southwestern Saskatchewan. Toronto:
          Holt, Rinehart and Winston.
Kohn, R., and K.L. White
  1976   Health Care: An International Study. New York: Oxford University Press.

300

Koyl, L.F.
   1977   "The aging Canadian." Pp. 57-79 in Blossom T. Wigdor (ed.), Canadian
           Gerontological Collection I. Calgary: The Canadian Association on Gerontology.
Kraus, A.S., R.A. Spasoff, E.J. Beattie, D.E.W. Holden, J.S. Lawson, M. Rodenburg and
G.M. Woodcock
   1976a "Elderly applicants to long-term care institutions I: their characteristics, health
           problems and state of mind." Journal of the American Geriatrics Society 24 (3):
           117-25.
   1976b Elderly applicants to long-term care institutions II: the application process—
           placement and care needs. Journal of the American Geriatrics Society 24: 165-72.
Kreps, Juanita M.
   1976   "The economy and the aged." Pp. 272-85 in Robert H. Binstock, Ethel Shanas and
           associates (eds.), Handbook of Aging and the Social Sciences. New York: Van
           Nostrand Reinhold.
Laing, R.D., and A. Esterson
   1964   Sanity, Madness and the Family. London: Tavistock.
Lalonde, Marc
   1975   A New Perspective on the Health of Canadians. A Working Document. Ottawa:
           Information Canada.
Larson, Reed
   1978   "Thirty years of research on the subjective well-being of older Americans."
           Journal of Gerontology 33 (1): 109-25.
Laslett, Peter
   1971   The World We Have Lost. London: University Paperbacks.
   1977   Family Life and Illicit Love in Earlier Generations. Cambridge: Cambridge
           University Press.
Lawton, M. Powell
   1970   "Ecology and aging." Pp. 619-74 in L.A. Pastalan and D.H. Carson (eds.), Spatial
           Behavior of Older People. Ann Arbor, Michigan: University of Michigan Press.
   1972   "The Dimensions of morale." Pp. 144-65 in D. Kent, R. Kastenbaum and S.
           Sherwood (eds.), Research Planning and Action for the Elderly. New York:
           Behavioral Publications.
   1975   "The Philadelphia Geriatric Center Morale Scale: a revision." Journal of
           Gerontology 30 (1): 85-89.
   1978   "Leisure activities for the aged." The Annals 438: 71-80.
Lawton, M.P., and L. Nahemow
   1973   "Ecology and the aging process." Pp. 619-74 in C. Eisdorfer and M.P. Lawton
           (eds.) The Psychology of Adult Development and Aging. Washington, D.C.:
           American Psychological Association.
Lawton, M.P., M. Ward and S. Yaffe
   1967   "Indices of health in an aging population." Journal of Gerontology 22: 334-43.
Leake, C.D.
   1962   "Social status and aging." Geriatrics 17: 785.
Leavitt, Harold
   1964   Managerial Psychology. Chicago: University of Chicago Press.
LeClair, M.
   1975   "The Canadian health care system." Pp. 11-93 in S. Andreopoulos (ed.), National
           Health Insurance: Can We Learn from Canada? Toronto: John Wiley.
Lee, P.R.
   1975   "Foreward." Pp. xvii-xxii in S. Andreopoulos (ed.) National Health Insurance: Can
           We Learn from Canada? Toronto: John Wiley.

Lemert, Edwin M.
1951   Social Pathology. New York: McGraw-Hill.
Lemert, Edwin M. (ed.)
1967   Human Deviance, Social Problems, and Social Control. Englewood Cliffs, New
        Jersey: Prentice-Hall.
Lemon, B.W., Vern L. Bengtson and J.A. Peterson
1972   "An exploration of the activity theory of aging: activity types and life satisfaction
        among in-movers to a retirement community." Journal of Gerontology 27: 511-23.
Lesnoff-Caravaglia, Gari
1978-9 "The five per cent fallacy." International Journal of Aging and Human
        Development 9 (2): 187-92.
Lieberman, M.
1969   "Institutionalization of the aged: effects on behaviour." Journal of Gerontology
        24: 330-40.
Levinson, Daniel J., Charlotte N. Darrow, Edward B. Klein, Maria H. Levinson and
Braxton McKee
1978   The Seasons of a Man's Life. New York: Alfred A. Knopf.
Lieberson, Stanley
1970   "Stratification and ethnic groups." Sociological Inquiry 40: 172-81.
Likert, R.
1961   New Patterns of Management. New York: McGraw-Hill.
Lipscomb, C.F.
1970   "The Yorkton psychiatric centre: a five year review." American Journal of
        Psychiatry 127: 232.
Lofland, John
1968   "The youth ghetto." Journal of Higher Education 39 (3): 121-43.
Long Range Planning, Welfare
1973   Early Retirement: a Preliminary Analysis. Ottawa: Govt. of Canada. Publication
        SWP-7302.
Lopata, Helena Z.
1970   "The social involvement of American widows." Pp. 40-56 in Ethel Shanas (ed.),
        Aging in Contemporary Society. Beverly Hills: Sage.
1973a   Widowhood in an American City. Cambridge, Massachusetts: Schenkman.
1973b   "Self-identity in marriage and widowhood." The Sociological Quarterly
        14 (Summer): 407-18.
1973c   "Loneliness: forms and components." Pp. 102-15 in Robert S. Weiss (ed.),
        Loneliness: The Experience of Social Isolation. Cambridge: MIT Press: 102-15.
1973d   "Living through widowhood." Psychology Today 1 (July): 87-92.
1977   "The meaning of friendship in widowhood." Pp. 93-105 in Lillian Troll, Joan
        Israel, and Kenneth Israel (eds.), Looking Ahead: A Woman's Guide to the
        Problems and Joys of Growing Older. Englewood Cliffs, N.J.: Prentice-Hall.
1978   "Contributions of extended families to the support systems of metropolitan area
        widows: limitations of the modified kin network." Journal of Marriage and the
        Family 40 (May): 355-64.
1979   Women as Widows: Support Systems. New York: Elsevier.
Lorber, Judith
1967   "Deviance as performance." Social Problems 14: 302-10.
Love, Ann Burnside
1974   "Surviving widowhood." Ms. Magazine 3 (4): 86-91, 110.
Low, A.P.
1906   Report on the Dominion Government Expedition to Hudson Bay and the Arctic
        Islands. Ottawa: Government Printing Bureau.

Lowenthal, Marjorie Fiske, and Clayton Haven
1976   "Interaction and adaptation: intimacy as a critical variable." Pp. 94-110 in Robert
        C. Atchley and Mildred M. Seltzer (eds.), The Sociology of Aging: Selected
        Readings. Belmont, California: Wadsworth. Originally published in American
        Sociological Review 33 (1968): 20-30.

Lubove, Roy
1968   The Struggle for Social Security — 1900-1935. Cambridge: Harvard University
        Press.

Lucas, Robert E., Jr.
1972   "Expectations and the neutrality of money." Journal of Economic Theory 4
        (April): 103-24.

Lynd, R.S., and H.M. Lynd
1956   Middletown: A Study of Modern American Culture. New York: Harcourt Brace
        and World.

MacMillan, D.
1969   "Features of senile breakdown." Geriatrics (March) 109-18.

Maddison, David, and Agnes Viola
1968   "The health of widows in the year following bereavement." Journal of Psychoso-
        matic Research 12: 297-306.

Maddox, George L., and James Wiley
1976   "Scope, concepts and methods in the study of aging." Pp. 3-34 in Robert H.
        Binstock, Ethel Shanas and associates (eds.), Handbook of Aging and the Social
        Sciences. New York: Van Nostrand Reinhold.

Manitoba, Government of
1973   Aging in Manitoba—Volume One. Winnipeg: Department of Health and Social
        Development.
1975   Aging in Manitoba: Needs and Resources, 1971. Winnipeg: Department of Health
        and Social Development.

Manning, P.
1976   "The decline of civility: Goffman's sociology." Canadian Review of Sociology and
        Anthropology 13: 13-25.

Marcus, Lotte
1978   "The situation of the elderly and their families: problems and solutions." Report
        prepared for the National Symposium on Aging in Ottawa.

Markus, Nathan
1974   "Home care for the aged." On Growing Old 12 (1): 1-8.

Marshall, Victor W.
1974a   "The last strand: remnants of engagement in the later years." Omega 5 (1): 25-35.
1974b   "The life review as a social process." Paper presented at the 27th Annual
        Scientific Meeting of the Gerontological Society in Portland, Oregon.
1975a   "Socialization for impending death in a retirement village." American Journal of
        Sociology 80 (5): 1124-44.
1975b   "Age and awareness of finitude in developmental gerontology." Omega 6 (2):
        113-29.
1975c   "Organizational features of terminal status passage in residential facilities for the
        aged." Urban Life: a Journal of Analytic Ethnography 4 (4): 349-68.
1979   "Age irrelevance or generational conflict: contrasting images of the future." In
        Couchiching Institute on Public Affairs, The Young-Old...A New North
        American Phenomenon. Toronto: Proceedings of the 30th Annual Winter
        Conference, Couchiching Institute on Public Affairs.
forth- Last Chapters: a Sociology of Aging and Dying. Monterey, California:
coming Brooks/Cole.

Marshall, Victor W., and Joseph A. Tindale
  1978-79 "Notes for a radical gerontology." International Journal of Aging and Human
      Development 9 (2): 163-75.
Martin, William C.
  1973   "Activity and disengagement: life satisfaction of in-movers into a retirement
      community." Gerontologist 13 (2): 224-27.
Marx, Karl
  1890   Capital. Volume I. Moscow: Progress.
Mathiesen, Thomas
  1974   The Politics of Abolition. Oslo: Martin Robertson.
Maxwell, R.J., J.E. Bader, and W.H. Watson
  1972   "Territory and self in a geriatric setting." The Gerontologist 12: 413-17.
McKain, Walter C.
  1972   "A new look at older marriages." The Family Coordinator 21: 61-69.
McKee, John P., and Alex C. Sherriffs
  1956   "The differential evaluation of males and females." Journal of Personality 25:
      356-71.
McPherson, B., and N. Guppy
  1979   "Pre-retirement life-style and the degree of planning for retirement." Journal of
      Gerontology 34 (2): 254-63.
Meissner, Martin
  1969   Technology and the Worker: Technical Demands and Social Processes in
      Industry. San Francisco: Chandler.
Mendelson, Mary A.
  1974   Tender Loving Greed. New York: Vintage Books.
Merton, Robert K., George Reader, and Patricia L. Kendall (eds.)
  1957   The Student Physician. Cambridge: Harvard University Press.
Miller, Debert C., and William H. Form
  1964   Industrial Sociology: The Sociology of Work Organizations. Second edition. New
      York: Harper and Row.
Miller, Stephen J.
  1965   "The social dilemma of the aging leisure participant." Pp. 77-92 in A. Rose and
      W. Peterson (eds.), Older People and Their Social World. Philadelphia:
      F.A. Davis.
Mills, C. Wright
  1959   The Sociological Imagination. New York: Oxford University Press.
Milton, B.G.
  1975   Social Status and Leisure Time Activities: National Survey Findings For Adult
      Canadians. Monograph 3, Canadian Sociology and Anthropology Association
      Monograph Series, Montreal.
Modell, J., and T.K. Hareven
  1973   "Urbanization and the malleable household: an examination of boarding and
      lodging in American families." Journal of Marriage and the Family. 1973: 467-78.
Montgomery, L.M.
  1968   Anne of Green Gables. Toronto: McGraw-Hill Ryerson.
Moore, Robert J., and James H. Newton
  1977   "Attitudes of the life threatened hospitalized elderly." Essence 1 (3): 129-38.
Moore, W.E.
  1966   "Aging and the social system." Pp. 23-41 in John C. McKinney and Frank T.
      DeVyver (eds.), Aging and Social Policy. New York: Appleton-Century-Crofts.
Moriwaki, S.Y.
  1973   "Self-disclosure, significant others and psychological well-being in old age."
      Journal of Health and Social Behavior 14: 226-32.

304

Murphy, Edmund M., and Dhruva N. Nagnur
　　1972　"A Gompertz fit that fits: applications to Canadian fertility patterns." Demography
　　　　　9: 35-50.
Myles, John F.
　　1977a　Institutionalizing the Elderly: An Empirical Assessment of the Sociology of Total
　　　　　Institutions. Unpublished Ph.D. dissertation, University of Wisconsin, Madison.
　　1977b　"Institutionalization and sick role identification among the elderly." Paper
　　　　　presented at the meetings of the Canadian Sociology and Anthropology
　　　　　Association, Fredericton, N.B.
　　1977c　"Institutionalization and disengagement among the elderly." Paper presented at
　　　　　the meetings of the Canadian Sociology and Anthropology Association,
　　　　　Fredericton, N.B.
　　1978a　"Institutionalization and sick role identification among the elderly." American
　　　　　Sociological Review 43: 508-21.
　　1978b　"The bureaucratization of consumption: institutional welfare for the aged." Paper
　　　　　presented at the 9th World Congress of Sociology, Upsalla, Sweden.
　　forth-　"Institutionalization and disengagement among the elderly." Canadian Review of
　　coming Sociology and Anthropology.
Myrdal, Gunnar
　　1944　An American Dilemma. 2 vols. New York: Harper and Row.
Nash, B.E.
　　1970　"New dimensions in the care of the aging." Hospital Progress 51 (12): 69-72.
National Center for Health Statistics
　　1977　Utilization of Short Stay Hospitals: Annual Summary of the U.S., 1975.
　　　　　Washington, Department of Health, Education and Welfare.
　　1978　"A comparison of nursing home residents and discharges from the 1977 National
　　　　　Nursing Home Survey." U.S. AdvanceData 29: 1-8.
National Health and Welfare
　　1970　Legislation, Organization and Administration of Rehabilitation Services for the
　　　　　Disabled in Canada. Health Care Series, No. 27. Ottawa: Queen's Printer.
　　1973　Working Paper on Social Security in Canada. Second edition. Ottawa: Queen's
　　　　　Printer.
　　1974　Progress Report of the Working Party on Income Maintenance. Ottawa:
　　　　　Information Canada.
Nealey, S.M., and M.R. Blood
　　1966　Leadership Performance of Nursing Supervisors and Two Organizational Levels.
　　　　　Urbana, Ill.: Group Effectiveness Research Laboratory, University of Illinois.
　　　　　Mimeo. Cited by F.E. Feidler, A Theory of Leadership Effectiveness, New York:
　　　　　McGraw-Hill, 1967.
Neufeld, A.H.
　　1972　The Developing Community Health Centre: A Study of Referral and Treatment
　　　　　Patterns Before and After the Opening of a Modern "Total Care" Psychiatric
　　　　　Facility. Mimeo. Marcotte Research Centre, Saskatoon.
Neugarten, Bernice L.
　　1970　"Dynamics of transition of middle age to old age." Journal of Geriatric Psychiatry
　　　　　4 (1): 71-87.
　　1973　"Patterns of aging, past, present, and future." Social Service Review 47 (4) 571-80.
　　1974　"Age groups in American society and the rise of the young-old." Annals
　　　　　of the American Academy of Political and Social Science 415 (September):
　　　　　187-98.
　　1975　"The future and the young old." The Gerontologist 15: 4-9.
　　1979　"The young-old...a new North American phenomenon." Keynote address, 30th
　　　　　Annual Winter Conference, Couchiching Institute on Public Affairs, Toronto.

Neugarten, Bernice L., and N. Datan
1973   "Sociological perspectives on the life cycle." Pp. 53-69 in P. Baltes and
        K.W. Schaie (eds.), Life-Span Developmental Psychology: Personality and
        Socialization. New York: Academic Press.
Neugarten, Bernice L., R.J. Havighurst and S.S. Tobin
1961   "The measurement of life satisfaction." Journal of Gerontology 16 (2): 134-43.
Neugarten, Bernice L., J. Moore and J. Lowe
1965   "Age norms, age constraints, and adult socialization." American Journal of
        Sociology 70 (6): 710-17.
Neugarten, Bernice L., and Karol K. Weinstein.
1964   "The changing American grandparent." Journal of Marriage and the Family 26:
        199-204.
Neuwirth, G.
1969   "A Weberian outline of a theory of community: its application to the 'dark
        ghetto'." British Journal of Sociology 20: 148-63.
Newcomer, R., L. Gelwicks and S. Newcomer
1974   "An analysis of the potential market feasibility of semi-dependent housing for the
        elderly in 21 states: evidence in support of broadening subsidy programs."
        Address delivered at the Gerontological Society 27th Annual Scientific Meeting.
Newman, William M.
1973   American Pluralism: A Study of Minority Groups and Social Theory. New York:
        Harper and Row.
Neysmith, Sheila M.
1978   "A look at potential candidates for a foster home programme for the elderly."
        Paper presented to the Canadian Association on Gerontology in Edmonton,
        Alberta.
Norland, J.
1974   The Age-Sex Structure of Canada's Population. Ottawa: Statistics Canada.
O'Connor, James
1970   "Some contradictions of advanced US capitalism." Social Theory and Practice
        1: 1-11.
1973   The Fiscal Crisis of the State. New York: St. Martin's.
Ontario Council on Health
1978   Health Care for the Aged 1978. Toronto: Ontario Council on Health.
Orbach, Harold L.
1978   "Mandatory retirement and the development of adequate retirement provisions
        for older persons." Paper presented at the 7th Scientific and Educational Meeting,
        Canadian Association on Gerontology in Edmonton, Alberta.
Orris, M.S.
1970   Factors Which Contribute to the Social and Economic Independence of People
        Over 60. Saskatoon: The Joint Advisory Committee on Aging.
Ossowski, Stanislaw
1963   Class Structure in the Social Consciousness. London: Routledge and Kegan Paul.
Palmore, Erdman
1969   "Sociological aspects of aging." Pp. 33-69 in Ewald W. Busse and Eric Pfeiffer
        (eds.), Behavior and Adaptation in Late Life. Boston: Little, Brown.
1976   "Total chance of institutionalization among the aged." The Gerontologist 16
        (6): 504-07.
Palmore, Erdman, and C. Luikart
1972   "Health and social factors related to life satisfaction." Journal of Health and Social
        Behavior 13 (1): 68-80.
Parker, S.
1976   The Sociology of Leisure. London: George Allen and Unwin.

306

Parsons, Talcott
  1951   The Social System. Glencoe, Ill.: Free Press.
Pastalan, Leon A.
  1970   "Privacy as an expression of human territoriality." In L.A. Pastalan and D.H.
          Carson (eds.), Spatial Behavior of Older People. Ann Arbor, Michigan:
          University of Michigan Press.
Penning, M.J.
  1978   Institutionalization of the Elderly: An Assessment of Competing Perspectives.
          Unpublished M.A. thesis, University of Manitoba.
Peppers, L.
  1976   "Patterns of leisure and adjustment to retirement." The Gerontologist 16: 441-46.
Perrow, C.
  1967   "A framework for the comparative analysis of organizations." American
          Sociological Review 35: 503-15.
Pesando, J., and S. Rea
  1977   Public and Private Pensions in Canada: An Economic Analysis. Toronto: Ontario
          Economic Council.
Pfeiffer, Eric, and G.C. Davis
  1971   "The use of leisure-time in middle life." The Gerontologist 11 (3, pt. 1): 187-95.
Phillips, Derek L.
  1972   "Data collection as a social process: its implications for free 'prevalence' studies
          of mental illness." Pp. 453-72 in E. Freidson and J. Lorber (eds.), Medical Men and
          Their Work. Chicago: Aldine and Atherton.
Phillips, Derek L., and Kevin J. Clancy
  1970   "Response biases in field studies of mental illness." American Sociological Review
          35: 503-15.
Pike, M.C., J. Casagrande and P.G. Smith
  1975   "Statistical analysis of individually matched case-control studies in epidemiology:
          factor under study a discrete variable taking multiple values. British Journal of
          Preventive and Social Medicine 29: 196-201.
Pincus, A.
  1968   "The definition and measurement of the institutional environment in homes for
          the aged." The Gerontologist 8 (3): 207-10.
Pincus, A., and V. Wood
  1970   "Methodological issues in measuring the environment in institutions for the aged
          and its impact on residents." Aging and Human Development 1: 117-26.
Pirenne, Henri
  1932   "Guild-Europe." Pp. 208-14 in Encyclopedia of Social Sciences. Volume VII.
Piven, F.F., and R.A. Cloward
  1971   Regulating the Poor: The Functions of Public Welfare. New York: Random
          House.
Poe, H.A., and I.A. Berg
  1952   "Psychological test performance of steel industry production supervisors." Journal
          of Applied Psychology 36: 234-37.
Polanyi, K.
  1944   The Great Transformation: The Political and Economic Origins of Our Time.
          Boston: Beacon Press.
Policy Research and Long Range Planning
  1977   Retirement in Canada: Summary Report. Social Security Research Report
          Number 3. Ottawa: Department of National Health and Welfare.
  1978   The Changing Dependence of Women: Roles, Beliefs and Inequality. Social
          Security Research Report Number 5. Ottawa: Department of National Health and
          Welfare.

Policy Research and Strategic Planning
    1978a   Basic Facts on Public Retirement Income Programs. Ottawa: Department of National Health and Welfare.
    1978b   The Incomes of Elderly Canadians in 1975. Mimeographed working paper.
Porter, John
    1965   The Vertical Mosaic. Toronto: University of Toronto Press.
Posner, Judith
    1974   "Notes on the negative implications of being competent in a home for the aged." International Journal of Aging and Human Development 5 (4): 357-64.
    1976   "Death as a courtesy stigma." Essence 1 (1): 39-50.
Powell, B., and J. Martin
    1978   "Economic implications of an aging society in Canada." Paper presented at the National Symposium on Aging in Ottawa.
Powers, Edward A., and G.L. Bultena
    1972   "Characteristics of deceased dropouts in longitudinal research." Journal of Gerontology 27 (4): 530-35.
Psychology Today
    1973   "Body image research." Psychology Today 7 (6).
Randall, Ollie A.
    1966   "Aging in a modern society." Pp. 37-50 in Proceedings, The Canadian Conference on Aging. Toronto: Canadian Conference on Aging.
Rasmussen, Kurt
    1908   People of the Polar North. London: Kegan Paul, Trench, Trubner.
Rees, D.W., and S.C. Lutkin
    1967   "Mortality of bereavement." British Medical Journal 4: 13-16.
Revenue Canada
    1962   1962 Taxation Statistics. Ottawa.
    1967   1967 Taxation Statistics. Ottawa.
    1972   1972 Taxation Statistics. Ottawa.
    1977   1977 Taxation Statistics. Ottawa.
Richards, J.G., and K.I. Fung
    1969   Atlas of Saskatchewan. Saskatoon: University of Saskatchewan.
Riley, Matilda W.
    1971   "Social gerontology and the age stratification of society." The Gerontologist 11 (1, pt. 1): pp. 79-87.
    1976   "Age strata in social systems." Pp. 189-217 in Robert Binstock, Ethel Shanas, and associates (eds.), Handbook of Aging and the Social Sciences. New York: Van Nostrand Reinhold.
Riley, Matilda W., and Anne Foner
    1968   Aging and Society. Volume 1: An Inventory of Research Findings. New York: Russell Sage Foundation.
Riley, Matilda W., John W. Riley, Jr. and Marilyn E. Johnson
    1969   Aging and Society. Volume 2: Aging and the Professions. New York: Russell Sage Foundation.
Riley, Matilda W., Anee Foner, B. Hess and M. Toby (eds.)
    1969   "Socialization for the middle and later years." Pp. 951-82 in D.R. Goslin (ed.), Handbook of Socialization Theory and Research. Chicago: Rand, McNally.
Riley, Matilda W., Marilyn E. Johnson and Anne Foner
    1972   Aging and Society. Volume 3: A Sociology of Age Stratification. New York: Russell Sage Foundation..
Roberts, K.
    1970   Leisure. London: Longmans.

308

Robins, L.E.
  1969   "Social correlates of psychiatric disorders: can we tell the causes from the consequences?" Journal of Health and Social Behavior 10 (2): 95-104.
Roethlisberger, F.J., and Wm. J. Dickson
  1939   Management and the Worker. Cambridge, Mass.: Harvard University Press.
Rollins, Boyd C., and Harold Feldman
  1970   "Marital satisfaction over the family life cycle." Journal of Marriage and the Family 32: 20-28.
Rooney, James F.
  1976   "Friendship and disaffiliation among the skid row population." Journal of Gerontology 31 (1): 82-88.
Rose, Arnold M.
  1962   "The subculture of the aging: a topic for sociological research." The Gerontologist 2: 123-27.
  1965   "The subculture of aging: a framework for research in social gerontology." Pp. 3-16 in A.M. Rose and W.A. Peterson (eds.), Older People and Their Social World. Philadelphia: F.A. Davis.
Rosen, G.
  1968   Madness and Society: Chapters in the Historical Sociology of Mental Illness. London: Routledge and Kegan Paul.
Rosenberg, George S.
  1970   The Worker Grows Old. San Francisco: Jossey-Bass.
Rosenhan, D.L.
  1973   "On being sane in insane places." Science 179 (4070): 250-58.
Rosow, Irving
  1967   Social Integration of the Aged. New York: Free Press.
  1974   Socialization to Old Age. Berkeley, California: University of California Press.
Ross, David P.
  1975   Canadian Fact Book on Poverty. Ottawa: Canadian Council on Social Development.
Rothman, D.J.
  1971   The Discovery of the Asylum: Social Order and Disorder in the New Republic. Boston: Little, Brown.
Rowe, G., and R. Pong.
  1978   "Interprovincial migration of the elderly." Paper presented at the Canadian Gerontology Meetings in Edmonton.
Rushing, W.A.
  1971   "Individual resources, societal reaction and commitment." American Journal of Sociology 77: 511-26.
Sagarin, Edward (ed.)
  1971   The Other Minorities. Waltham, Mass.: Xerox College Publishing.
Saskatchewan, Government of
  1944   Saskatchewan Health Services Survey Commission Report (Sigerist Report). Regina: King's Printer.
  1959   Report of the Conference on the Aged and Long-Term Illness. Regina.
  1963   Aged and Long-Term Illness Survey Committee Report. Volume I: Report and Recommendations. Regina: Queen's Printer.
  1965   Department of Welfare Summary. Mimeo. Regina: Queen's Printer.
Scheff, T.J.
  1966   Being Mentally Ill: A Sociological Theory. Chicago: Aldine.
Schermerhorn, R.A.
  1970   Comparative Ethnic Relations. New York: Random House.

Schooler, Kermit S.
1969   "The relationship between social interaction and morale of the elderly as a function of environmental characteristics." The Gerontologist 9: 25-29.
Schreiber, Marvin M.
1972   The aged of the 70's—perspectives." Pp. 2-25 in Lola Wilson (ed.), Report, Training Institute for Directors of Senior Centres. Ottawa: Canadian Council on Social Development.
Schulz, James H., and associates
1974   Providing Adequate Retirement Income. Hanover, New Hampshire: Brandeis University Press.
Schur, E.M.
1971   Labelling Deviant Behavior. New York: Harper and Row.
Schwenger, Cope W.
1974   "Keep the old folks at home." Canadian Journal of Public Health 65: 417.
1977   "Health care for aging Canadians." Canadian Welfare 52 (6): 9-12.
in   Health Care for the Aged in Ontario. Research Report to the Ontario Economic
progress Council.
Schwenger, Cope W. and G.K. Palin
1974   Community Health Services in Grey and Bruce Counties: Problems of an Aging Population. Study commissioned by the Ontario Ministry of Health.
Schwenger, Cope W., and L.A. Sayers
1971   "A Canadian survey by public health nurses of the health and living conditions of the aged." American Journal of Public Health 61 (June): 1189-95.
Scott, F.G.
1955   "Factors in the personal adjustment of institutionalized and non-institutionalized aged." American Sociological Review 20 (5): 538-46.
Shanas, Ethel
1967   "Family help patterns and social class in three countries." Journal of Marriage and the Family 29 (2): 257-66.
1974   "Health status of older people: cross-national implications." American Journal of Public Health 64: 261-64.
Shanas, Ethel, Peter Townsend, Dorothy Wedderburn, Henning Friis, Poul Milhøj and Jan Stehouwer
1968   Older People in Three Industrial Societies. New York: Atherton Press.
Shapiro, E., with N. Roos
1978   "The geriatric 'bed blocker': a critique of the problem and the proposed solutions." Paper presented at the Canadian Association on Gerontology meetings in Edmonton, Alberta.
Sheppard, Harold L.
1970   Toward an Industrial Gerontology. Cambridge, Mass.: Schenkman.
Sherman, S.R.
1975   "Provision of on-site services in retirement housing." International Journal of Aging and Human Development 6: 229-47.
Shibutani, Tamotsu, and K.M. Kwan
1965   Ethnic Stratification. New York: Macmillan.
Silverman, Phyllis
1968   "The widow-to-widow programs: an experiment in preventive intervention." Mental Hygiene 53: 333-39.
Simmons, Leo W.
1945   The Role of the Aged in Primitive Society. London: Oxford University Press.
Smith, C.M.
1970   "Mental health developments in Saskatchewan: a decade of change." Canadian Mental Health 17: 15.
1971   "Crises and aftermath: community psychiatry in Saskatchewan, 1963-69." Canadian Psychiatric Association Journal 16: 65.
Smith, C.M., and D.G. McKenacher
1963   "Geriatric aspects of a psychiatric home care programme." Journal of the American Geriatrics Society 11: 339.

Smith, K.J., and A. Lipman
1972   "Constraint and life satisfaction." Journal of Gerontology 27 (1): 77-82.
Snider, E.L.
1973   Summary Report: Medical Problems and the Use of Medical Services among Senior Citizens in Alberta: A Pilot Project. Medical Services Research Foundation of Alberta.
Social Planning and Review Council of British Columbia
1976   Health Needs of the Independent Elderly: A Report from Four Communities.
Social Planning Council of Hamilton and District
1965   Senior Citizens' Survey.
Sontag, Susan
1972   "The double standard of aging." Saturday Review 55 (39): 29-38.
Special Committee of the Senate on Aging
1964   Proceedings. Volume 24: Testimony of Dr. Joseph W. Willard, Deputy Minister of Welfare, December 10. Ottawa: Queen's Printer.
1966   Final Report. Ottawa: Queen's Printer.
Spencer, (Sir) Baldwin, and Frances J. Gillen
1966   The Arunta. Oosterhout, Netherlands: Anthropological Publications.
Spencer, Robert F.
1959   The North Alaskan Eskimo. Washington: Smithsonian Institute. Bureau of American Ethnology, Bulletin 171.
Splane, R.B.
1965   Social Welfare in Ontario, 1791-1883: A Study of Public Welfare Administration. Toronto: University of Toronto Press.
Spradley, James P.
1970   You Owe Yourself a Drunk. Boston: Little, Brown.
Statistics Canada
1962   Pension Plans: Non-Financial Statistics, 1960. Ottawa: Queen's Printer.
1970   Tuberculosis Statistics. Volume I: Tuberculosis Morbidity and Mortality. 1969 catalogue no. 82-206. Ottawa: Queen's Printer.
1971   Bulletin 92-715.
1972a   Hospital Morbidity. 1969 catalogue no. 82-206. Ottawa: Queen's Printer.
1972b   Hospital Statistics. Vol. VI: Hospital Expenditures. 1969 catalogue no. 83-215. Ottawa: Queen's Printer.
1972c   Mental Health Statistics. Vol. I: Institutional Admissions and Separations. 1970 catalogue no. 83-204. Ottawa: Queen's Printer.
1973a   1971 Census of Canada: Income of Individuals by Age, Sex, Marital Status and Period of Immigration. Catalogue 94-760.
1973b   Population 1921-1971: Revised Annual Estimates. Ottawa: Information Canada.
1973c   Trusteed Pension Plans: Financial Statistics, 1971. Ottawa: Queen's Printer.
1974a   Perspective Canada. Ottawa: Information Canada.
1974b   Population Projections for Canada and the Provinces, 1972-2001. Series A, Series C, Series E, Series F. Ottawa: Queen's Printer.
1975   1971 Census of Canada: Population: Marital Status by Age Groups. Catalogue no. 92-730.
1976a   Culture Statistics, Recreational Activities, 1976. Ottawa Catalogue no. 87-501.
1976b   Population Growth in Canada. Volume 5, Pt. 1. 1971 Census Profile Studies, catalogue no. 99-701.
1977a   Income Distribution by Size in Canada, 1975. Catalogue no. 13-207.
1977b   The Labour Force, December 1976.
1977c   Labour Force Participation of Persons Aged 25-64 and 65-and-over, by Sex. Catalogue no. CS11-508.
1977d   1971 Census of Canada, Profile Studies: The Family in Canada. Catalogue no. 99-725.
1977e   Trusteed Pension Plans: Financial Statistics, 1975.
1977f   Perspective Canada II.

1978a   1971 Census of Canada, Profile Studies: Marital Status and Nuptiality in Canada. Catalogue no. 99-704.
1978b   1976 Census of Canada: Marital Status. Catalogue no. 92-824.
1978c   Pension Plans in Canada, 1976. Catalogue no. 74-401.

Stearns, Peter N.
1972   "Working class women in Britain, 1890-1914." Pp. 100-120 in Martha Vicinus (ed.), Suffer and Be Still: Women in the Victorian Age. Bloomington: University of Indiana Press.

Stefánsson, Wilhjalmur
1914   "The Stefánsson-Anderson arctic expedition of the American Museum." Anthropological Papers of the American Museum of Natural History. Volume 14, Part 1.

Stevenson, B.W.A.
1974   Social Functioning of the Aged as It Relates to the Utilization of Health and Medical Services. Unpublished master's thesis. Department of Health Care and Epidemiology, University of British Columbia.

Stoll, Clarice Stasz
1974   Female and Male. Dubuque, Iowa: Wm. C. Brown.

Stone, Leroy O.
1977   "Employment opportunity and the achievement of adequate income for the baby boom generation." In Blossom T. Wigdor (ed.), Canadian Gerontological Collection. Volume 1. Calgary: Canadian Association on Gerontology.

Stone, L., and S. Fletcher
1978   A Profile of Canada's Older Population. Ottawa: background document prepared for the Economic Council of Canada.

Strauss, Anselm L., et al
1964   Psychiatric Ideologies and Institutions. Glencoe, Ill.: Free Press.

Strauss, A., L. Schatzman, D. Ehrlich, R. Bucher and M. Sabshin
1963   "The hospital and its negotiated order." Pp. 147-69 in Eliot Freidson (ed.), The Hospital in Modern Society. London: Collier-Macmillan.

Strauss, George
1968   "The changing role of the working supervisor." Pp. 232-42 in R. Dubin (ed.), Human Relations in Administration. Third edition. Englewood Cliffs: Prentice-Hall.

Streib, Gordon F.
1965   "Are the aged a minority group?" Pp. 311-28 in Alvin W. Gouldner and S.M. Miller (eds.), Applied Sociology. New York: Free Press.
1976   "Social stratification and aging." Pp. 160-85 in Robert H. Binstock and Ethel Shanas (eds.), Handbook of Aging and the Social Sciences. New York: Van Nostrand Reinhold.

Streib, Gordon F., and Clement J. Schneider
1971   Retirement in American Society. Ithaca, New York: Cornell University Press.

Sudnow, David
1967   Passing On: The Social Organization of Dying. Englewood Cliffs, N.J.: Prentice-Hall.

Sussman, Marvin B.
1976   "The family life of old people." Pp. 218-43 in Robert H. Binstock and Ethel Shanas (eds.), Handbook of Aging and the Social Sciences. New York: Van Nostrand Reinhold.

Synge, Jane
1976   "Immigrant communities—British and continental European—in early 20th century Hamilton, Canada." Oral History 4 (2): 38-52.

Szasz, Thomas S.
1961   The Myth of Mental Illness. New York: Hoeber-Harper.
1970   The Manufacture of Madness. New York: Harper & Row.

Taylor, K.W.
  1978   "Old age and the social wage: theories on the development of pensions." Paper
          presented at the Canadian Sociology and Anthropology Association meetings in
          London, Ontario.
Taylor, Malcolm G.
  1978   Health Insurance and Canadian Public Policy. Montreal: McGill-Queen's
          University Press.
Third Career Research Society
  1976   Retirement in Alberta. Edmonton.
Thomas, Keith
  1976   "Age and authority in early modern England." Proceedings of the British
          Academy 42: 206-48.
Thompson, Wayne E., and G.F. Streib
  1958   "Situational determinants: health and economic deprivation in retirement."
          Journal of Social Issues 14: 18-34.
Tilquin, C.
  1976   "Modeling a health services system." Medical Care 14: 222.
Tilquin, C., et al
  1978   "An information system for administration and planning of long term care for the
          aged." The Annals of the World Association for Medical Informatics.
Tilquin, C., R. Pineault, C. Sicotte et L.-M. Audette
  1977a   "Administration d'un réseau de services socio-sanitaires pour les personnes âgées."
          Administration hospitalière et sociale 23 (4): 26.
Tilquin, C., C. Sicotte, F. Hirbour et R. Pineault
  1977b   Functional Evaluation Form of People Living at Home. EROS - Département
          d'Administration de la Santé, Université de Montréal.
  1977c   Functional Evaluation Form of People Living in Institutions. EROS - Département
          d'Administration de la Santé, Université de Montréal.
Tindale, Joseph A.
  1974   Old and Poor: Old Men on Skid Row. Unpublished masters thesis. Hamilton,
          Ontario: McMaster University.
  1977   "The management of self among old men on skid row." Essence 2 (1): 49-58.
Tobin, Sheldon S.
  1975   "Social and health services for the future aged." The Gerontologist 15 (1, Pt. 2):
          32-37.
Tobin, Sheldon S., and Morton Lieberman
  1976   Last Home For The Aged: Critical Implications of Institutionalization. San
          Francisco: Jossey-Bass.
Tobin, Sheldon S., and Bernice Neugarten.
  1961   "Life satisfaction and social interaction in aging." Journal of Gerontology 16:344-
          46.
Toronto Star
  1978   "Here's how young teachers can get jobs." Toronto Star (May 6): C2.
Townsend, Peter
  1963   The Family Life of Old People. Harmondsworth, Middlesex: Penguin Books.
Treas, Judith
  1975   "Aging and the family." Pp. 92-108 in Diana S. Woodruff and James E. Birren
          (eds.), Aging: Scientific Perspectives and Social Issues. New York: Van Nostrand.
Troll, Lillian E.
  1971   "The family of later life: a decade review." Journal of Marriage and the Family,
          33:263-90.

Troll, Lillian E., Sheila J. Miller and Robert C. Atchley
1979   Families in Later Life. California: Wadsworth.
Tucker, C. Jack
1976   "Changing patterns of migration between metropolitan and nonmetropolitan areas in the United States: recent evidence." Demography 13 (4): 435-43.
Tuckman, Jacob, and Martha Lavell
1957   "Self classification as old or not old." Geriatrics 12: 666-71.
Tunstall, Jeremy
1966   Old and Alone. London: Routledge and Kegan Paul.
Turner, Ralph H.
1962   "Role-taking: process versus conformity." Pp. 20-40 in A. Rose (ed.), Human Behavior and Social Processes. Boston: Houghton Mifflin.
Uhlenberg, Peter R.
1969   "A study of cohort life cycles: cohorts of native-born Massachusetts women, 1830-1920." Population Studies 23: 407-20.
Unger, Rhoda K., Beth J. Raymond and Stephen M. Levine
1974   "Are women a 'minority' group? Sometimes!" Pp. 73-83 in Florence Denmark (ed.), Who Discriminates Against Women? Beverly Hills: Sage.
United Nations
1973   The Determinants and Consequences of Population Trends. Volume I. New York.
United States Senate Committee on Aging
1974   Nursing Home Care in the United States: Failure in Public Policy. Washington, D.C.: U.S. Government Printing Office.
Urqhart, M.C., and K.A.H. Buckley (eds.)
1971   Historical Statistics of Canada. Toronto: Macmillan.
Vachon, Mary L.S.
1976   "Grief and bereavement following the death of a spouse." Canadian Psychiatric Association Journal 21 (1): 35-44.
van den Berghe, Pierre
1967   Race and Racism. New York: John Wiley.
Vining, D.R. Jr., and A. Strauss
1977   "A demonstration that the current deconcentration of population in the United States is a clean break with the past." Environment and Planning A 9: 751-58.
Walker, Kenneth N., Arlene MacBride and Mary L.S. Vachon
1977   "Social support networks and the crisis of bereavement." Social Science and Medicine 11: 35-41.
Wallace, Samuel J.
1965   Skid Row. New York: Harper & Row.
Wardwell, John M.
1977   "Equilibrium and change in nonmetropolitan growth." Rural Sociology 42 (2): 156-79.
Weiss, Robert S.
1973   "The fund of sociability." In Helena Znaniecki Lopata (ed.), Marriages and Families. New York: Van Nostrand.
Wells, Robert V.
1973   "Demographic change and the life cycle of American families." Pp. 85-94 in Theodore K. Rabb (ed.), The Family in History. New York: Harper & Row.
Wershow, Harold J.
1976   "The four percent fallacy: some further evidence and policy implications." The Gerontologist 16 (no. 1, Pt. 1): 52-55.
West Vancouver Community Council
1971   Report on the Concerns and Needs of Senior Citizens in West Vancouver.

314

Whyte, William F.
 1943   Street Corner Society. Second edition. Chicago: University of Chicago Press.
Wigdor, Blossom T.
 1978   "Implications of the demographic changes in the Canadian population over the
         next 25 years." Paper prepared for the National Symposium on Aging in Ottawa.
Wilkinson, Anne
 1974   "An analysis of the process of change prior to institutionalization." Paper
         presented at the 27th Annual Scientific Meeting, Gerontological Society,
         Portland, Oregon.
Wirth, Louis
 1945   "The problem of minority groups." Pp. 347-72 in Ralph Linton (ed.), The Science
         of Man in the World Crisis. New York: Columbia University Press.
Wiseman, Jacqueline P.
 1970   Stations of the Lost. Englewood Cliffs, N.J.: Prentice-Hall.
Wolk, S., and S. Telleen
 1976   "Psychological and social correlates of life satisfaction as a function of residential
         constraint." Journal of Gerontology 31 (1): 89-98.
Woodward, J.
 1965   Industrial Organization: Theory and Practice. London: Oxford University Press.
Wrong, D.
 1961   "The oversocialized conception of man in modern sociology." American
         Sociological Review 26: 183-93.
Wylie, Betty Jane
 1977   Beginnings: A Book for Widows. Toronto: McClelland and Stewart.
Yeates, M.
 1978   "The future urban requirements of Canada's elderly." Plan Canada 18 (2): 88-104.
Zander, Mary, and Polly Normann
 1974   "Retirement from the long-term volunteer role: a disengagement process." Paper
         presented at the 27th Annual Scientific Meeting, Gerontological Society,
         Portland, Oregon.
Zay, Nicolas
 1978   "Old age and aging in Canada's ethnic population." Paper prepared for the
         National Symposium on Aging in Ottawa.
Zborowski, Mark
 1962   "Aging and recreation." Journal of Gerontology 17: 302-09.
Zola, Irving K.
 1962   "Feelings about age among older people." Journal of Gerontology 17: 65-68.